A Nation of Nations

A
NATION
of
NATIONS

By
LOUIS ADAMIC

HARPER & BROTHERS PUBLISHERS
New York and London

CONTENTS

ILLUSTRATIONS

(These photographs will be found in a group following page 214)

Spanish American: Muskrat trapper in Louisiana
Spanish American: Migratory farm worker in Texas
Swedish American: Manager of a dairy farm in Minnesota
Hispano Schoolboy: In New Mexico
Hispano Americans: The Lopez home at Trampas, New Mexico
German Americans: Farm family in Lincoln County, Nebraska
American Families from Holland and from Russia
Classroom
Home Study
Diversity of Religion: Protestant, Catholic, Jewish
Polish American: Tobacco farmer of Enfield, Connecticut
Polish American: Industrial worker of Hadley, Massachusetts
Negro Americans: Mother and children
From Greece: Grandfather and his American-born granddaughter
Norwegian American: Edward Groe went into war work in 1941
Norwegian American: John Granrud, superintendent of the Springfield,
     Massachusetts, school system
Yugoslav American: Steelworker in Gary, Indiana
Irish American: Bartender, serving British sailors in a Third Avenue,
     New York, bar
Irish Americans: Martin J. Farrell, mason, and Michael Gallagher,
     machinist
Born in Germany: General Walter Krueger, commander of the U. S.
     Army liberating the Philippines 1944-1945
His Father, a Jewish Rabbi, came from Poland: Major General Maurice
     Rose
Yugoslav American: Captain George S. Wuchinich of the Office of
     Strategic Services
Italian American: Marine Gunnery Sergeant John Basilone of Raritan,
     New Jersey
Father and Son: Brigadier General Benjamin O. Davis, the first Amer-
     ican Negro general, and Colonel Benjamin O. B. Davis of the Air
     Corps

This publication was made possible in part by funds granted during 1939-41 by the Carnegie Corporation of New York. That Corporation is not, however, the author, owner, publisher or proprietor of this publication, and is not to be understood as approving by virtue of its grant any of the statements made or views expressed herein.

I owe special thanks to Don Hanson, publisher, and Mabel Souvaine, editor of *Woman's Day*, for allowing me to use the material (some 50,000 words) which appeared in their magazine during 1944-45, and for making me write those articles for them—but for that *A Nation of Nations* might not have been completed before 1946 or '47.

L. A.

. . . Here [in these States] at last is something in the doings of man that corresponds with the broadcast doings of day and night. Here is not merely a nation but a teeming nation of nations. . . .

—WALT WHITMAN,
Preface to 1855 Edition
of *Leaves of Grass*

To
MERRITT H. PERKINS

Dear Merritt:

I dedicate *A Nation of Nations* to you first because your interest in the "project" of which it is a part has meant a great deal to me during the past half-dozen years, and second because you are a New Englander whose Puritan ancestors came to America in the seventeenth century and helped to shape the beginnings of the civilization and culture of the Colonies which became the first thirteen United States. And with your permission I dedicate it through you to other Americans of Anglo-Saxon stock, whether the story of their background in the New World begins with Jamestown or Plymouth Rock, with the Protestants of the Massachusetts Bay Colony or the Catholics who settled in Maryland, with Roger Williams in Rhode Island or Thomas Hooker in Connecticut or William Penn in Pennsylvania. I offer it also, if I may, to those who—unlike you—occasionally remark, "Why don't you go back where you came from?"

Remember our long talk when we first met in 1938? Somehow it took us no time at all to get acquainted. Soon you were telling me about the diaries and letters recently come into your possession after lying for a century or more in a trunk in the attic of your family home in western Massachusetts. They gave a vivid picture of life in a New England town before the Revolution, and I liked the warmth and excitement with which that picture filled you.

I asked if you had heard of the "America letters" written by Scandinavian, Dutch, Polish and other immigrants to relatives in their old countries. You said you had not, and I described them. You were interested, which was all I needed. Presently I went on to say that the whole of American history could stand rethinking, rewriting . . . that the Negroes' American tradition of fighting for liberty dates from 1526; that a handful of Polish, German and Armenian workers at Jamestown, Virginia, in 1619 staged one of the first rebellions in the New World; that John Peter Zenger, a German printer in the 1730s whom the

1

governor of New York jailed for publishing attacks on his regime, fathered the American ideal of freedom of the press; that Philip Mazzei, the Italian friend and neighbor of Thomas Jefferson, influenced the Revolution of 1776; that the Irish were the backbone of the political-military movement that won American Independence—

Just then I was coming upon many neglected bits of Americana and I guess I was trying them out on you. I had an idea that I might write some such book as this, for which I needed not only facts buried in obscure prints and manuscripts but also contact with contemporary Americans of as many backgrounds as possible. I was traveling over the country checking up on my feelings and notions, and you and I chanced to meet in Denver.

You mentioned your family papers again. And I told you of a recent experience in your New England when, walking through the elm-shaded cemetery of a lovely old town, reading the names and dates and epitaphs on the stones leaning this way and that, I had suddenly felt a wonderful sensation of intimacy with early Anglo-Saxon America. I was unable to analyze the feeling verbally. It wasn't necessary. Your face lighted up.

You got me to talk about the people I had been meeting, and I told you of the two days I had spent at a farmhouse north of Bemidji in Minnesota listening to an old immigrant from Norway. He had known O. E. Rölvaag, the author of *Giants in the Earth*, and as he spoke about him his own being seemed to shine. His English had an accent but the meaning of his words came clear. In and around and through what he said I got a feeling of the churning inside of America.

He told me of an "Americanization" campaign in that part of Minnesota around 1905. A poster appeared on walls in little towns and on tree-trunks by the roadsides. It was a picture of an elegant Uncle Sam and an outlandish yokel. In a loop coming out of Uncle Sam's handsome mouth was the word Yes, the loop from the yokel's wide-open mouth read Ya, and across the top in big letters was the admonition: "Don't say 'Ya'—say 'Yes'!"

"That placard," said the old man, "it was as though pasted on a wall in our home and I couldn't pull it down. My oldest boy ran away. The children could not forgive their mother and me that we were 'foreigners.' They would not let us say anything in Norwegian to them—anything intimate. They held us away. It was years before that placard wore off enough for the runaway to come back."—

You nodded slowly—a shadow on your face—as you did when I told you about a Negro friend of mine in Washington whose words and personality, encompassing a big part of the American Story, had repeatedly impressed me, but with whom I could not lunch anywhere outside the Negro section of the National Capital except at the Union Depot.

We talked of other things—a bit about ourselves, getting the range of each other's experience and interests. Given to understatement, you spoke quietly, slowly; from me words sometimes tumble out too fast for precise articulation or meaning. You were born in Massachusetts during the Great Blizzard in 1888; I was born eleven years later at a place that became part of Yugoslavia. You had moved to the Rockies as a young man; I came to the United States at fifteen. You were a businessman with a deep, natural interest in the humanities, in painting and writing, in manners and good taste. You were, I judged, a man of quick perception; outwardly calm, inwardly perturbed about some things in the United States. Focused on the Anglo-Saxon-Protestant phase of America, you were wide-open to other phases as well.

I don't know what was in the back of your mind as we talked; in mine was: "We're both Americans." This had been my unspoken thought many times in the previous months. It had been there while the old Norwegian immigrant was telling me of his life in Minnesota. You and he were as different superficially as two men could well be, yet you had much in common. And you and I had things in common, different as we were.

You were asking me to amplify my remark that our history could stand rethinking and revision.

I wasn't any too clear. There was an enormous mass of American history, I said, that had been "suppressed" (the word wasn't quite what I meant), that did not appear in the standard books; what did appear was fallacious in its emphases. And the trouble was not just with the books; the fallacy diffused throughout our national life and thought. It was like a fog rolling about, spreading everywhere in the American atmosphere, and without a palpable center. The nearest thing I could see to a center was history as written and taught. For to most people, history textbooks are authoritative, the information disseminated by the written word and by teachers is relatively final.

You recalled that Emerson had been dissatisfied with written American history, branding it "a shallow village tale." Malthus had described history as "a chronicle of the upper classes," somebody else had said it was "a tired old man with a long beard." I had a friend, a Missourian, who, agreeing with Henry Ford that "history is bunk," maintained that it was not intelligent to traffic with the past. He was impatient with my question: "But does that make for any sort of continuous communal intelligence?" and with my reminder that Ford in his Greenfield Village had started what was nothing if not a historical museum.

You and I wondered why so many Americans, highly educated or not, took no interest in the history of their country; why some actually had a resistance to it. Were many people untouched by it because it was about somebody else, leaving them out completely? Were they bored with it, feeling somehow that as a record of what really happened it was very inadequate?

But we were not primarily concerned with books, rather with the effect that the information—and the lack of information—in the books had upon American currents of thought, feeling and behavior.

For a long time, I went on, this country had been the scene of a psychological civil war. Once upon a time that had had at least the practical good result of furthering pioneering. When groups faced antagonism, they were likely to pull up stakes and move on, breaking new ground, founding new colonies, opening up new territories. But now the physical frontier had disappeared, distances had shortened, communications spread. Nowadays our psychological civil war was in most respects part of the psychological civil war raging the world over, moving toward a new climax in another military war. (Franklin Roosevelt had delivered his "quarantine" speech at Chicago. Munich was happening.) But it was possible to think of it as an American phenomenon. There were several overlapping fronts: the privileged *versus* the underprivileged, isolationism *versus* internationalism, Catholic *versus* Protestant, Gentile *versus* Jew, White *versus* Negro, the old-stock Americans *versus* the "foreigners," and the "foreigners" one against the other.

I was driving over the continent—some twelve thousand miles that summer and autumn; all that was required of me was my driver's license and money for gasoline and oil, and I was moving about with a physical freedom unimaginable in the Old World. At the same time, however, I saw that this vast and free land was crisscrossed with cultural walls sheltering snipers, bearing ill-considered posters, casting shadows, keeping men from the light, preventing the full flowering of life.

Some of these walls, I thought, might be weakened and eventually tumbled and some of the fronts in our psychological civil war might be eliminated by giving the history books new emphases, by putting into them facts hitherto ignored. Not that I thought accurate history books constituted the whole remedy, or that I knew how accurate, inclusive history books might be brought about—the historians were as much in the fog as other people.

How to get at this "shallow village tale" fog dominating our cultural atmosphere? How did fundamental changes take place in a culture? Where was one to begin? We tossed these questions at each other without expecting answers.

What was desired ultimately, you and I thought, was a reorientation of the American state of mind, or rather states of mind, merging them on some levels without suppressing their special qualities and contents; a revaluation of facts in the American Story so that Immigration might cease to be a footnote on page 317 and become a main subject in the text, so that each group in our population would be seen as a necessary and integral thread and would receive its proper stress in books, in revised attitudes and relationships. But which would come first— rewritten history or a change in the cultural atmosphere? Probably a bit of one and then a bit of the other, each acting upon and reacting to the other, so that widening circles of revision and reorientation would alter both the history books and the American atmosphere. And this could not be brought about from the outside. The American people themselves would have to tear down the walls, dissipate the fog. Many were at it already in the course of their daily living. . . .

This is as far as we got in 1938.

The psychological civil war still goes on. That during 1939-1945 it seldom spilled over into active violence was largely due to F.D.R.'s political wizardry in postponing, smoothing, compromising, adjusting issues between opposing groups. But the psychological civil war was not transformed by his leadership or by the military war into national unity except in appearance and for the duration. On some fronts a kind of armistice was effected. The issues went underground, there to seethe and gain in force like a teakettle with a plugged spout. They are almost certain to break out with increased pressure now the military war is over. One hears: "Wait—we'll fix them," meaning the groups disliked (feared) by those making the remark. Indeed in many departments of our national life, including sections of the Army and Navy, "they" are being "fixed" or put or kept "in their place" during the war. The groups in the most vulnerable positions are trying to forestall what they see is coming by forcing anti-discrimination laws through legislatures. Such laws are probably steps in the right direction, but their observance depends on the weight and spread of intelligent public opinion behind them.

At the same time there is more getting-together among Americans than ever before, more acceptance of people on the basis of their personal qualities regardless of background. This is especially true of the men in the services. There is nothing like being together in a foxhole, a bomber or a submarine.

A good many Americans know that a perplexing, infinitely complicated future is rushing upon us. A few here and there feel that if the issues of the psychological civil war are not weakened or supplanted, if they break out again with fresh vigor, by themselves or in connection with our domestic economic troubles and our foreign policy, they will hamstring our ability to cope with the future. I am one of those who feel this way.

On the other hand, I see more and more clearly that the American Story as it actually happened has within it a tremendous unifying and constructive power. It is an immense story—larger than the sum of its parts, and a good deal larger than most of us realize—so large that the share any element in the population has had in its making does not cast a shadow over the work of any other element—so large that when one sees it, many elements in the psychological civil war become appalling absurdities.

Now in 1945 my ideas shape up as follows.

There are two ways of looking at our history.

One is this: that the United States is an Anglo-Saxon country with a White-Protestant-Anglo-Saxon civilization struggling to preserve itself against infiltration and adulteration by other civilizations brought here by Negroes and hordes of "foreigners."

The second is this: that the pattern of the United States is not essentially Anglo-Saxon although her language is English. Nor is the pattern Anglo-Saxon with a motley addition of darns and patches. The pattern of America is all of a piece; it is a blend of cultures from many lands, woven of threads from many corners of the world. Diversity itself is the pattern, is the stuff and color of the fabric. Or to put it in another way: The United States is a new civilization, owing a great deal to the Anglo-Saxon strain, owing much to the other elements in its heritage and growth, owing much to the unique qualities and strong impetuses which stem from this continent, from the sweep of its land between two oceans, the mixture and interplay of its peoples, the plenitude of its resources, and the skills which we all of us have brought here or developed here in the past three centuries.

The first view prevails in American thinking. We have absorbed the idea, the picture, from the atmosphere; in school, in church, in politics and business; over the radio, in the movies, in books, magazines and newspapers; from each other. It is taken for granted. It is the conceptual core of our uneasy, unformed culture. It furnishes the imaginary American norm, whose hold is strong on the minds of many people, preventing them from seeing that the actual American norm is not only not exclusively Anglo-Saxon, but that it is not yet formed, that it is still in process.

With few exceptions our historians, essayists, novelists, short-story writers, and our editors—geared to the prevailing view, constituting a kind of unconscious working committee to maintain it—minimize or ignore as incidental or irrelevant all but the tough and great Anglo-Saxon thread, and thus—in most cases unwittingly—encourage the psychological civil war. In 1945 the Writers' War Board (proving itself an exception) issued a report concerning popular writing, of which Columbia University's Bureau of Applied Social Research had made a study. The report declared that "constant repetition . . . was exaggerating and perpetuating the false and mischievous notion that ours is a White, Protestant Anglo-Saxon country in which all other racial stocks and religious faiths are of lesser dignity."

The Bureau analyzed 185 short stories published in 1937 and 1943 in eight magazines whose circulation totals about twenty million. "Of 889 identifiable characters 90.8 percent were Anglo-Saxon, whereas only 9.2 percent . . . were drawn from all other population stocks in the United States. Only sixteen Negroes and ten Jews were counted. And where the authors brought in menials, racketeers, thieves, gamblers, shady night club proprietors, crooked prize fight managers, such non-sympathetic characters were seldom Anglo-Saxon.

"To quote the Bureau: 'The overwhelming attention is given to the Anglo-Saxons. The stage and the spotlight belong to them.' They were habitually pictured as the salt of the earth. Their superiority, wealth, and prestige were usually taken for granted, whereas in a few instances where a non-Anglo-Saxon character was represented as rich or important the author offered an elaborate explanation. . . . Again quoting the Bureau: 'The behavior of these fictional characters could easily be used to "prove" that the Negroes are lazy, the Jews wily, the Irish superstitious and the Italians criminal.' "

Advertising copy during 1937-1943 showed "the general acceptance of the whole White-Protestant-Anglo-Saxon myth." Novels, the stage, the movies (including news reels), comic cartoons and the radio are somewhat more pioneering and less prejudiced, though they still have a long way to go.

The important point here is that most of this is done unconsciously. Writers, whether of history or fiction, editors, artists and producers do not intentionally sidestep the truth any more than do the rest of us.

They simply inhale the fallacious cultural atmosphere—and exhale it back again.

The writers and commentators, teachers, preachers and publicists in the United States are in a sense like the European cartographers whose maps were perfectly all right until somebody discovered the world was round, not flat. Then the maps had to be thrown away and new ones made. The new ones gradually discarded the misconceptions and errors of the old, kept what was still true, and rearranged the whole in the light of the new perspective. The cartographers began to draw the world round, and by and by they gave us the globe we can twirl with a forefinger.

Even before scientists said the world was round and navigators set out to prove it, all sorts of people had begun to wonder, to suspect it was not flat. But it took quite a while for the idea of its roundness, struggling against uncertainty and fear of the new, to get into practically everybody's head. When it did, the general current of thinking and feeling changed immeasurably. It led to the discovery of the New World, to the great Atlantic Migration. It gave new thrills, new vistas to human life. Observed facts which had not jibed with the old idea fell into place in the reorientation. Acceptance of this new way of seeing profoundly affected life, released its dammed-up energies, gave it new impetus.

Perhaps we in the United States are today in somewhat the same state of being, of thinking and feeling, that existed before the world's roundness altered the flat, cramped horizons of men's minds. Millions of Americans, all sorts of them, sense the inadequacy of the first way of looking at America. It does not explain enough, take in enough. I have no doubt that we are reaching toward something new, reaching forward, hanging back, struggling betwixt and between, but slowly changing.

With over one-third of our population first-, second- and third-generation non-Anglo-Saxon Americans, with about a tenth of it Negroes, many an old-line American feels a certain despair when he surveys the present and ponders the future. To him the Negroes migrating at will and the "hordes of foreigners" with such names as Krzycki and Ramaganti and Katz seem to threaten rack and ruin to the nature of the country as he conceives it to be. This feeling is not restricted to the fascistic demagogue; it appears in many people who are kindly, sensible and intelligent in other directions, but who still cling to the White-Protestant-Anglo-Saxon-country concept as the fact and the ideal.

On the other hand, the immigrant and his children and grandchildren find their continuity cut off not only from the land of his origin and their descent, but from their heritage here, bequeathed them through the share their forebears—people of their special background—had in building America. Like the Negroes who too have a rich American heritage which few of them know, the so-called new-immigrant groups have little means of learning what their forebears did here; at best they do not learn it as part of the American Story.

Generations have grown up unable to visualize, to know about, to feel attachment to or kinship with the beginnings or growth of their country, unable or hesitant or virtually forbidden to share fully in its life. The American Story as written in standard books, as it pervades our ideas, does not touch any vital chord in many people of Negro, French, Irish, Norwegian, Polish, Russian or Oriental descent, in many people whose names are Schmidt and Ziegler, Basilone and De Capite, Huot and du Vigneaud, McCleary and O'Sheel, Rosenberg and Sulzberger, Havlichek and Markovich, Varnos and Bakjian, Ling-hoy and Kikuchi. Comparatively few succeed in linking themselves to the whole great current of the American experience. To many their name, color or cast of countenance is a prison wall because other Americans, living in the atmosphere of the first view, make it so.

Nothing could be more unfortunate.

The coming of peoples to this continent, voluntary or in chains, is at the very center of our historical process. It is a main constituent of America. A gigantic potential strength, overwhelmingly complex, tremendously alive, it remains "the Immigrant Problem" or "the Negro Problem" only so long as our historical process is considered primarily an Anglo-Saxon process. The potentiality of production, construction, creation will be released only after it is fully realized that what sociologists now call "the Immigrant Problem" and "the Negro Problem" belongs more to the country than to the particular groups which now suffer under it. Widen the view, widen the perception of historical facts about the different elements, and many of the so-called problems which now mark them off will disappear through having merged into a single situation—less problematical than promising.

To say as some politician does every once in a while "Immigrants all —Americans all" is merely gesturing. It changes nothing. We go right on feeling "We—and the immigrants" . . . "We—and the Negroes" . . . "We—and they." By "they" the Negroes mean the Whites, the immigrants and some of their American-born children mean "the Americans," the Gentiles the Jews, the Catholics the Protestants, and vice versa. And the various "we's" crawl into themselves to fret and fear, some to plot and act against their "they's."

More and more of us are beginning to wonder at this, to worry about it. Some of it is dangerous.

More and more of us are perceiving that something fundamental is wrong with our stock of historical facts and ideas. Increasingly we sense the distortions, the omissions, the departure from reality, the chasm between what we think America is and what it actually is. Many Americans, with a growing suspicion that the White-Protestant-Anglo-Saxon-country idea is not adequate, is not true, are on the brink of discovering and adopting the other view.

We are seizing on parts of the puzzle, coming up with fascinating details. Of the hit plays on Broadway in the first half of 1945, five touched on the question of what is America: *Anna Lucasta*, *A Bell for Adano*, *The Late George Apley*, *I Remember Mama* and *Life with Father*. The radio and recorded versions of "Ballad for Americans" stirred many people, as have other occasional radio programs and some of the more imaginative "I Am An American Day" celebrations.

Some details we are so used to that we overlook their significance. Take our place names: Dundee, Schuylkill Haven, Prairie du Chien, Warsaw, Los Angeles, Dublin, Wichita, Lyndhurst, Scandia, Berlin, Traunik, Athens. Our food: roast beef, smörgåsbord, gefüllte fish, pasta, corn, potatoes, consommé, borscht, knedliki, goulash, strudel, wienies, hamburger. People: Lincoln, Roosevelt, Toscanini, Steinmetz, Brandeis, Chavez, Tesla, Kaiser, Benét, Paul Robeson, Ingrid Bergman, Maurice Rose. Where did many of our objects, customs, forms come from? To most of us the Christmas tree is as "purely American" (i.e., Anglo-Saxon slightly modified) as the Thanksgiving turkey, yet the Christmas tree is a German contribution to our way of life and the turkey came from the Indians.

When one mentions facts like these, some people say, "Really?" or "You don't say!" or "Propaganda!" They are interesting (like Ripley's "Believe It or Not" cartoons) or irritating as the case may be, but not so deeply that they effect a change. Most of them slide off the crust of the habitual attitude like water off a duck's back. For in themselves, out of context, like a bit of color out of a spectrum, a theme out of a symphony, they have only a specific, local, thin, flat meaning.

The crust, however, is not invulnerable either within or without. The prevalent view omits so many things around us that most people have a sense of frustration, of dissatisfaction, which in the end—as the crisis about us mounts—will impel us to take a fresh look, to let ourselves see whatever pattern is actually formed by the sum-total of the facts.

To help this process along, the facts have to be available. One purpose of this book is to make some of them easily available. I do not think it is the straw that will break the back of the first view of American history. One does what one can; one makes a beginning. There are many other beginnings at the same time in the same general direction.

In my opinion and in that of a good many others, the facts about America add up to the second view. But the statement *Diversity itself is the pattern of America* will remain a rather chilly formula until we become aware of the abundant details which give it life, until we know more about the experiences and qualities, hopes and achievements of the many kinds of people who have made America. Not until wave after wave of these facts sweeps over us, startles us, rouses our interest, will the second view, or something very like it, ring in the American atmosphere, the American consciousness.

Then the American Story will no longer be shadowy, no longer dominated by a huge image cast upon a screen with trick lighting arranged to fall fully upon one figure alone among the participants on the stage. The lighting will fall impartially upon all the actors, who will assume the proportions they have in our history. The audience will feel their identity with the actors in the past and with each other in the present, drawn together, knit together by a common stake in America.

Then all over the country, from the Atlantic to the Pacific, from the Canadian to the Mexican border, Swedish Americans, Russian, German, Italian, Irish, Negro, French, Spanish, Oriental, Czech and double-check Americans will feel the same warmth and pride in their old, yellowing letters and documents which you felt in yours. They will feel themselves at home in the history of America.

Now the dominating shadow dwarfs the substance, tricking us into misbeliefs. Sometimes the misbeliefs are so grotesque that in rebutting them we approach the reality.

The Negro newspaper *Chicago Defender* said on April 4, 1942, that the New York editorial writers "who refer to the United States as 'We Anglo-Saxons' should see some of the Anglo-Saxons at Forty-seventh and South Parkway."

The January 22, 1945, issue of *Time*, in reviewing Professor Ralph Barton Perry's book *Puritanism and Democracy*, said: "The essential faith of America came into being in the cold, clear-headed, spacious world of Puritan New England." This produced a protest from George Guion Williams of Rice Institute in Houston:

"Can you really believe that? I myself have always believed that Washington, Jefferson, Patrick Henry and James Monroe (Virginians all) had some small part in establishing 'the essential faith of America.' And the Jamaica-born Alexander Hamilton of New York, the illiterate pirate Andrew Jackson of Tennessee, the ribald Abraham Lincoln of

Kentucky and Illinois, the uncouth Walt Whitman of Brooklyn—did
these have no part in the work? . . .

"And are you aware that self-government by means of popularly
chosen representatives had its beginnings in Virginia under Governor
Yeardley in 1619, nearly two years before the Pilgrims landed at Plymouth and eleven years before the Puritans arrived?

"The essential faith of America? There are a dozen essential faiths.
From New England may have come our faith in good morals; but New
York gave us our tolerance, Pennsylvania our faith in justice, the South
our proud independence, the Middle West our practical realism, the
Far West our belief in the impossible. Spice all this with a flavor of
cynicism and humanitarianism from the Jews, sex and sophistication
from the French and sentimentality and love of comfort from the old-
fashioned Germans, and you have a rough outline of essential Americanism. It is a lot bigger—"

It is indeed. There is "essential faith of America" also in the labor of
the Irish and Chinese railroad builders, the mixed-strain Paul Bunyan
work gangs in the North Woods, the Cornish and Montenegrin copper
miners of Keewenaw and Butte, the Finnish iron miners of Ishpeming,
the men of many immigrant stocks who have shoveled the ore of the
Messabi Range into the boats on Lake Superior, the Slavic and Lithuanian steel workers of Pittsburgh and Gary, the Jewish and Italian
garment people of Manhattan, the Russian and Italian sandhogs under
the Hudson River, the Scandinavian and German farm-pioneers in the
Middle West, the dark cotton pickers of the South—

Whatever the particular "essential faith" to which each of us adheres,
most of us know the United States is great, though we do not always
know why. To me, its fundamental meaning, the deepest well-spring of
its greatness, consists of two elements: the idea it brought into government—that all men are created equal and have a voice in how they are
governed—and the variegated texture of its makeup.

To my mind, the combination of the democratic-government idea and
the diversity of peoples has created a situation in human society that,
in spite of depletion by war, in spite of many lapses and lags in our
perceptions, is bounding and seething with strength and vitality. It is a
new situation; the civilization evolving from it is a young civilization,
not yet formed, still in process, still being generated and shaped by the
interflow among its multiple streams.

As a matter of fact the interflow takes place daily, has taken place
since the very beginning. Nothing could have prevented it, no fallacy,
no preconceived idea. Propelled by world forces, which are rivers of
impulses, hopes, urges, ideas in millions and millions of people, such an

interplay was in line with the major direction in which the world has been moving—from the clan through the tribe, through the nation and race toward denationalization, Americanism (democracy), internationalism, humanity. The most any contradictory belief could do was to hamper its movement, check the freedom of its interchange, slow it down temporarily, poison a stream here and there.

The interplay, the diversity, is America; all that lacks is to transplant the fact from obscurity into the American imagination. The rest will pretty much take care of itself, for the readjustment in thinking and feeling will reach into very nearly every phase of American activity.

The reoriented cultural atmosphere of the United States will mean new, freer, broader ways of seeing and reacting, new and freer relationships. It will mean new integrations irrespective of background, integrations which let people remain themselves. It will bring into full view and play the healthy simultaneous tension and fusion of stubborn creative differences. It will enable us to cope more successfully with the future here and abroad.

Yours,
Louis

Milford, New Jersey
August 15, 1945

Dear Louis:

It is natural that I should feel a sense of pride in your dedication of A Nation of Nations to me and through me to others of my background. But as I read again the pages of your prefatory letter and think of your other writings in the project of which this is a part, I am conscious, too, of a sense of humility—I am conscious of the justness in your protest at the popular misconception of our story as a people.

May I quote to you one sentence from your letter: "The United States is a new civilization, owing a great deal to the Anglo-Saxon strain, owing much to the other elements in its heritage and growth, owing much to the unique qualities and strong impetuses which stem from this continent, from the sweep of its land between two oceans, the mixture and interplay of its peoples, the plenitude of its resources and the skills which we all of us have brought here or developed here in the past three centuries." I subscribe to your suggestion for a rewriting of our history on a foundation of this premise.

Mine is a Puritan ancestry, as you say, all of it dating back in this country to the period before 1670; and in this ancestry may be found the farmers, country merchants, innkeepers, ministers and members of the "general court" who are to be found in every family which lived for generations in the New England of Colonial times. I shall not attempt here to measure the contribution of these and later generations to the building of the early America but I do remember that those who in their old age were known to me as a boy were deep-rooted in the land— with something in their traditions that is reminiscent of the churchyard yew in an older England. May I refer, rather, to the family letters which you mention, some of which I have now read again to recall their story.

One or two of these letters picture something of the closing days of the Revolution; another mentions an ancestor who kept an inn on an old coach road between Boston and New York at which Washington stopped on a journey through New England in the fall of 1789; and when the President had reached Hartford he wrote to the innkeeper that he was "very much pleased with the modest and innocent looks of your two daughters, Patty and Polly. I do for these reasons send each of these girls a piece of chintz."

In another letter, written in the spring of 1812, a minister, writing to his "honoured father" to tell him that his little family has come safely through a hard winter, observes in a casual way: "We are like to have war, it seems—& the taxes about which there was so much complaint in Adams' reign." In still another, dated a few years later, a naval officer, writing to his young nephew, describes his voyage into South American waters on a United States man-of-war.

One letter written in February of 1828 is the reply of a woman signing herself "Deborah" who lived in a little village in western Massachusetts to her sister near Hartford. ". . . The day I received your kind letter," it reads, "was the day I was called to follow my dear and affectionate son Dexter to the grave and my feelings were such and my health so poor that I could not answer it.

"After my health returned I thought I should visit you in the fall, and this winter I have had the day fixed to set out but now I give up all hopes of seeing you this winter as the snow is all gone off and it is not likely there will be sleighing to set out on so long a journey. Therefore I resort to writing to converse with you."

The paragraph that follows is no longer legible in its entirety, but it is a statement of the religious faith that helped her son to endure his sickness with fortitude and helped her to accept the loss. Then:

"Horace is in Boston at the assembly, this is the second year he has been in. Omar's family are well. Merrill's wife is very poorly; they have five children, the oldest 6 years last May." (This child was my maternal grandmother.) "Chapin was down in Decm'r. He is doing very well and enjoys himself much better than he used to.

"We have taken out our apples and about half are rotten.

"This town is all in confusion—The opposite party has quarreled away our minister and now we are destitute. . . ."

This yellowed letter, the postage payment endorsed in ink with the address on its outer fold, reveals the simple piety and abiding faith of those people who, a century ago, lived in the smaller towns and villages and on the farms of New England; and it suggests a way of life that had not wholly passed when I first knew some of those same towns and villages and farms—a life that was concerned much with elemental things, with birth and death and faith, with seed time and harvest and the recurrent change of seasons, with distance and the slow movement of time—a way of life marked with a certain reticence in expressing the joys and sorrows and natural intimacies of home and family.

This is the life that I first knew—a life reserved in its social contacts but keenly alive with human sympathy. A way of life which, had it been more articulate, would have been better understood and would better have understood itself. I like to think of the service done to these people of a passing generation by Sarah Orne Jewett in her stories of the fishing villages of Maine. Seated at her mahogany writing desk, with the lights from two silver candlesticks flickering on the figured wallpaper and on a quotation from Flaubert that she kept always before her: "Écrire la vie ordinaire comme on écrit l'histoire," I think she really sought to write history in her lives of common people. She hoped that her *Deephaven* might "help people to look at 'commonplace' lives from the inside instead of the outside, to see that there is so deep and true a sentiment and loyalty and tenderness and courtesy and patience where at first sight there is only roughness and coarseness and something to be ridiculed."

People from other lands had come into our valley at the time of my boyhood—the Poles already taking over some of the farms, and men of French descent, particularly, coming down from Canada to find places in the mills and factories. My more distinct recollection is of two Swedish families whose children were with me in school, and of a Christmas eve at the home of one. It was a winter of much snow, a perfect northland setting, and "old country" customs spiced the holiday fun. There was gay color in the embroidered vests and freshly laundered aprons, striped in bright green and red and yellow, with an edging of black; figures and designs graced many of the cakes and cookies, but the color was not wholly visual. There was the hour of the story-teller whose tales were set in an atmosphere of folklore and tradition. I think my liking for the white birch may reflect an impression one story made on me that evening. There was an overtone of sadness in a few of the legends, and some years later I was reminded of one when I read in the

Atlantic the story of "When Hannah Var Eight Yar Old," the story of the little Swedish girl who cared for the body of her dead mother in the closing weeks of a long winter and took her mother's place in caring for the younger children, because she "var eight yar old."

I have already told you the story of Tony and Aunt Susan—of Tony, the young Italian lad, and his violin with which he brought new happiness into the life of one in whom there lived the New England of an earlier day; and of the light which burned in her window after he died in World War I.

You have remembered a walk through an elm-shaded cemetery in an old New England town in which the stones, ancient for this land, carry in their epitaphs and inscriptions something of the churchyard traditions of an older generation. I am thinking today of another cemetery, a few miles west of Denver, near an early mining camp which once was known as "the richest square mile on earth." The ground slopes upwards toward the rising front range of the Rockies and is almost treeless. Cold winds sweep across the area through much of the year; and many of the gravestones are very small. Often the larger ones reflect the ending of a life before thirty-five years had been lived; and often those same stones bear a name, two dates and the simple inscription: "Born in Cornwall." A few years ago our Colorado State Historical Society, in tribute to these Cornish people, undertook a project to preserve the story and the memory of those hard-rock miners who contributed so much to the development of this section of the west—a generous, spirited, witty, imaginative and superstitious people whose strange dress and gay musical folk ways did much to color the life in the early camps. On Saturday nights the deep harmonies of "Trafalgar's Boy" were blended in many a saloon; and on Sundays the Methodist choir swelled with rich Cornish voices. They were an industrious people, quickly accepted as an integral part of the society into which they came and ethnic conflicts were rare until the later coming of the Irish miners and the Tyrolese.

I have written this letter partly as a note of appreciation to you and partly to recall a few of the incidents of experience and observation— bits of understanding—which support my accord with you that our history as a people should be written as that of a new civilization. Let it be written in recognition of the worth of the man, whoever he may be, to the end that all may learn "to look at 'commonplace' lives from the inside instead of the outside, to see that there is so deep and true a sentiment and loyalty and tenderness and courtesy and patience where at first sight there is only roughness and coarseness and something to be ridiculed."

I now recall that day in October 1944 when Mildred and I stopped at Milford for a visit with you and Stella. There was the afternoon of good talk, with the "surprise muffins" for tea, and then, towards evening, the drive through the beautiful countryside of western New Jersey and the eastern edge of Pennsylvania to catch the train at Easton. An autumn haze was settling over the Delaware when we reached the station, and across the river the buildings of the city took on in this light the blended shape of an Old World town. Something in the picture suggested to me then the thought that America is really a fusion of the old and the new, although fog and haze do not always leave the picture clear; but the rush and noise of the arriving train checked my audible expression of that thought.

As ever,
Merritt

Denver
August 27, 1945

The lists of outstanding people which appear in most of the chapters are not meant to be complete —only suggestive.

To reduce footnotes to a minimum, references are collected in the back of the book, with suggestions for further reading.

I: AMERICANS FROM ITALY

WHEN he started out he didn't know where he was going, when he got there he didn't know where he was, and when he got back he didn't know where he had been."

This attempt to compress Christopher Columbus into a nutshell may be found in books of quotations, which credit it to "An Unknown Author." True enough as far as it goes, it is a little too pat, too clever.

There is no doubt that even though the New World was discovered before him (by Leif Erikson in the year 1000) and even though it would have been rediscovered eventually, Columbus—generally believed to have been a Genoese—is *the* Discoverer. As such he is the first consequential figure in American history. His Discovery took. "Every ship that comes to America," wrote Emerson in 1850, "got its chart from Columbus."

One can speculate on whether Columbus, urged by his uncertain and frightened crew, might or might not have turned back but a day's sailing from San Salvador had he not chanced to see some pieces of wood carved by the hand of man bobbing on the waves by his ship's side. But the adventure of 1492 was no mere accident. It was the massive result of a strong imagination and instinct within this very obstinate pathfinder backed by Marranos, converted Jews who were high in the counsels of the Spanish Court, and intent on thrusting aside the limitations of his time and place.

It has often been argued that by rights the new continent should have been called Columbia instead of America for the later comer, the Florentine traveler Amerigo Vespucci. According to the most recent book about him—*Amerigo Vespucci, Pilot Major* by Frederick J. Pohl (1944)—the vivid descriptions of the New World attributed to him were forgeries based on a letter he had written to his friend and patron Lorenzo Francesco di Pier de' Medici. However, the German cosmographer Martin Waldseemueller did not know this when for the first time he applied the term "America" (the feminine form of Amerigo or Americus) to the Western Hemisphere. But perhaps the error was not very serious. Columbus never knew that what he had discovered was not the eastern shore of Asia, as his brother Bartholomew's map published in 1503 showed, but a new continent. That it was the latter,

Vespucci—another unique Italian—determined in 1502; and the name
"America" is all right on that basis. It takes nothing away from Columbus.

But if it was a mistake and an injustice, America has tried to make
amends. Columbus' statue stands in hundreds of cities, many of which
are named for him, as are the District of Columbia, the Knights of
Columbus, Columbia University, Columbus Circle in New York City,
and the Republic of Colombia. He is indirectly celebrated in the songs
"Hail, Columbia" and "Columbia, the Gem of the Ocean." American
library shelves bulge with books about him. And pictures of him and his
flagship the *Santa Maria* decorate many American homes, especially
those of the approximately six million people who came, or whose forebears came, from Italy.

Other early Italian explorers touched America: Giovanni Da Verran-
sano, who preceded Henry Hudson to the Hudson River; the brothers
Tonti—Enrico and Alfonso, assistants of LaSalle; the brothers Caboto—
Giovanni and Sebastiano (John and Sebastian Cabot), Venetian navi-
gators who in the service of King Henry VII of England discovered
Nova Scotia; and Constantino Beltrami, who found the sources of the
Mississippi. But Columbus overshadows them. Modern American his-
tory begins with him. So does the Italian chapter thereof.

On February 14, 1493, returning from her first westward journey, the
Santa Maria was buffeted by a fierce storm. Fearing the ship would go
down, Columbus wrote out as full an account of the voyage as he could,
wrapped the parchment in waterproof cloth, jammed it into a stout iron-
bound barrel, and threw it into the churning, roaring ocean. "If I
thought there was one chance in a million of finding it," the famous
collector of rare books and manuscripts Dr. A. S. W. Rosenbach once
said, "I would take my power boat and cruise in the neighborhood of
the Azores forever."

I myself would like to find another lost manuscript by another Italian.
It was written in 1774 by Philip Mazzei (Matt-sá-ĕ), whose story, almost
unknown, is an integral part of the chronicle of the United States' beginnings as a Republic.

Born in 1730 near Florence, Tuscany, Mazzei studied and for a time
practiced medicine. Then in his mid-twenties he went to London, where
for seventeen years he lived by importing wine and olive oil. At first he
liked England very much because, as he put it, a lord could be hanged
there. He was by nature a democrat, a passionate believer in the rights
of man.

Business occasionally took him to Italy, where in 1765 he ran into the tail end of the Inquisition. Charged with bringing in forbidden books dealing with dangerous—democratic—ideas, he was saved from banishment by the intercession of his many powerful friends; and he spent the next year helping to organize an anti-Inquisition campaign. Shortly afterwards the Tribunal of the Inquisition was abolished in his native Tuscany.

In 1767 the Grand Duke of Tuscany asked Mazzei to get him a couple of Franklin stoves. Benjamin Franklin, the stove's inventor, was then in London representing the Pennsylvania Colony. The Italian looked him up and they became friends.

Some visiting Virginians to whom Franklin introduced Mazzei talked him into organizing a company to promote the culture of silkworms, olives and wine grapes in Virginia. By then certain political aspects of life in England had begun to jar on him; so in 1773, after a trip to Italy for men and materials, Mazzei led his horticultural outfit to America.

The project got off to a good start. Thomas Jefferson, with whom Mazzei formed a devoted, lifelong friendship, bought shares in the company and placed extensive acreage at his disposal for experimentation. The farm, a few miles from Charlottesville, adjoining Monticello, was called "Colle" (the Hill). But it wasn't long before Mazzei, meeting other foremost men of the day like George Washington, Peyton Randolph, George Mason, James Madison and Patrick Henry, was giving more time and energy to the political aims of the approaching American Revolution than to silkworms, olives and grapes.

At that time, 1773-1775, the remarkable men who were to become the Founding Fathers of the United States of America had no intention of breaking with Britain. Indeed, as late as July 6, 1775, the "Declaration of the Causes and Necessity of Taking up Arms," drafted by a committee including Franklin and Jefferson, announced to "our friends and fellow-subjects in any part of the Empire" that the aim was "not to dissolve the union which has so long and so happily subsisted between us, and which we sincerely wish to see restored. . . . We have not raised armies with ambitious designs of separating from Great Britain, and establishing independent states." As Professor Charles Edward Merriam has pointed out with particular clarity in his book *American Political Theories*, the leaders during the years immediately preceding the Revolution felt no sharp antagonism to the basic British system in the Colonies; both John and Samuel Adams, for example, had only praise for the British system and for many of its institutions.

Mazzei felt differently. Having been a victim of the Inquisition, he had some very definite ideas about religious freedom. His general experience in Europe had matured his naturally liberal political views.

He had no blood ties with England to retard his perception of the issues, and his disillusionment with the British form of government, as he had observed it in practice, went deep. He had been in London when the ruling class clamped down on John Wilkes, the audacious agitator and reformer, and his popular movement.

When he reached America, Philip Mazzei believed more strongly than ever in the equality of men and peoples; he was all-out for democracy, which he did not believe Americans could attain while under British domination. And with his quick Italian temperament, he got impatient at times with his American friends who were slow to see that a break with the Motherland was essential. "Jefferson," he later commented in his Memoirs, "was greatly surprised at this," but the squire of Monticello eagerly listened to his Italian friend, who was politically about two years ahead of him.

Sometime early in 1774 the two agreed that Mazzei would state his views in a series of articles to be written in Italian and translated by Jefferson into English. Mazzei scholars are certain that the articles, signed "Furioso," appeared in John Pinckney's Virginia Gazette during 1774-1775, although no copies containing them are extant. And it is the manuscript of these articles that I would like to find, for in them the Italian who became an American patriot wrote some of the words that his translator, Jefferson, subsequently incorporated in the Declaration of Independence.

Fortunately Mazzei's Memoirs—available since 1942 in English translation by Professor Howard R. Marraro of Columbia University—contain some extracts of these pieces which apparently were written in a highly polemical style, and in which the author identified himself with America:

"To attain our goal it is necessary, my dear fellow citizens, to discuss the natural rights of man and the foundations of a free government. . . . All men are by nature equally free and independent. This equality is essential to the establishment of a liberal government. Every individual must be equal to every other in his natural rights. The division of society into ranks has always been and will always continue to be a serious obstacle to the attainment of this end. . . . I repeat that a truly republican form of government cannot exist except where all men— from the very rich to the very poor—are perfectly equal in their natural rights. Fortunately, we are now free on this continent. . . . Now when certain privileges are exercised by a portion of the inhabitants and denied to others, it is vain to hope for the establishment of a liberal and permanent government, unless the favored citizens are willing to relinquish their privileges and stand on a footing of perfect equality with the rest of the inhabitants. Discrimination inevitably arouses envy and ill-feeling. . . . Therefore, liberty will always be insecure and finally doomed to collapse. . . . Democracy, I mean representative democracy, which embraces all individuals in one simple body, without any distinction whatsoever, is certainly the only form of government under which a true and enduring liberty may be enjoyed. Unfortunately for mankind, this form of government has never existed. The sacred name of democracy has been abused by tumultuous governments built on false and unstable principles. . . ."

Almost from the moment he arrived, Mazzei felt at home in America, "spiritually naturalized." Perceiving immense possibilities in an independent country with a society based on human rights, he stressed the necessity of a separation from Britain at every opportunity—in endless discussions with Jefferson, in frequent conversation with other influential men who used to come as much as a hundred and fifty miles to see him, and at non-official gatherings to which members of the Virginia Assembly invited him.

It is unknown if Thomas Paine was influenced by Mazzei; but Mazzei certainly helped to clear the track for Paine's revolutionary views so that when his famous pamphlet "Common Sense" appeared in January 1776 it did not drive such essentially conservative leaders as the Adamses, Madison, Mason, Franklin and Washington into opposition to what now looks like the will of history. Instead, as Washington said, it "worked a powerful change in the minds of many men." The importance of Mazzei's influence upon Jefferson, through whose mind, working with those of the other Founding Fathers, the American revolutionary aims were finally distilled, is almost beyond exaggeration.

When the Revolution began, Mazzei and some of Mazzei's Italian employees joined the Independence Company of Albemarle County as private soldiers and marched to the coast to fight the British. By the time they got there the British had left. But in thanking the volunteers, Patrick Henry made a special reference to Mazzei and his Italians.

Some of the Italians subsequently re-enlisted in American armies, and in 1777 Mazzei was about to raise a volunteer force of his own when Jefferson, Henry and a few others persuaded him to go to Europe as an agent of the state of Virginia. This, as it turned out, was a mistake. Mazzei became the center of a long controversy between Virginia and the brand-new U.S.A., the latter maintaining that relations between individual states and foreign countries must be conducted through the Federal government.

The controversy dragged on for years, leaving Mazzei pretty well out in the cold. He returned to Virginia. Meantime his agricultural project had been destroyed; he had rented the farm to General Riedesel, whose horses had in a few days trampled the results of four years' experimentation. Also his personal life was very unhappy.

Finally in 1784 Mazzei thought it best to return to Europe permanently. Sad but not bitter, he wrote to Madison: "I am leaving but my heart remains. America is my Jupiter, Virginia my Venus."

A few years later, all but starving in Paris, he wrote a book on the United States in reply to attacks by French writers on what Mazzei called "my adopted country." To the end of his life, he corresponded regularly with his friends in America, particularly with Jefferson.

After Mazzei's death in 1816, Jefferson hoped someone would write a biography of his late friend, but nobody did—not till 1933, and then the book (*Philip Mazzei, Friend of Jefferson: His Life and Letters* by R. C. Garlick Jr.) received very little notice. Mazzei's own *Memoirs* did not appear in Italy until 1845, nearly thirty years after his death. By now, many papers containing details of his contributions to American political thought have been irretrievably lost. And so his story is at best sketchy.

It is, as I say, largely unknown—even among Italian Americans. If they and other Americans were aware of Mazzei's part in the formation of the United States, many would probably hasten to hang his picture beside that of Columbus. Although he had no official position in the creation of the United States of America, he might very well be called an assistant Founding Father. His contemporaries recognized his contribution. When in 1774 he was elected to a local office in Virginia, he was called "after Mr. Jefferson the best leader in the country." In a letter Jefferson referred to Mazzei's "early and zealous cooperation in the establishment of our Independence."

Philip Mazzei was not the only Italian to render the United States a signal service in the Revolutionary period. There was at least one other—Giuseppe Maria Francesco Vigo, a native of Mondovi, Piedmont, a soldier of fortune and fur trader who had entered the service of Spain in the New World and who, in his job as confidential agent to Governor de Leyle of St. Louis, traveled over the whole of the Mississippi watershed and remained on good terms with the French settlers and the Indians in that territory. Spain was then nominal owner of the area west of the Mississippi.

One cold day in January 1779 Vigo came by chance upon hard-pressed Colonel George Rogers Clark of the Revolutionary Army, who thought him a "Spanish gentleman." Clark's task was to clear the British from the "Northwest Territory" (now Michigan, Illinois,

Indiana, Wisconsin and Minnesota), particularly to destroy their garrison at Vincennes; but his resources were next to nothing. His Virginia currency was not recognized by the French inhabitants. Vigo—reflecting Spain's traditional distaste for Britain—put at his disposal men and money, equipment and information. This led to the British surrender, bringing the vast region under United States' control; making possible the subsequent Louisiana Purchase, the opening of the West, and the establishment of the United States as a Pacific power.

After the Revolution, Vigo settled on a farm near Vincennes, married the daughter of Colonel Clark's quartermaster, and became an American citizen. He tried to get the government to repay what he had given Clark, but the Federal Administration rejected his claim on the grounds that Clark had then been acting for Virginia, not the United States.

Like Mazzei, Vigo died in poverty. "When an old man he sold his family silver to buy food," says Stella M. Drumm in the brief sketch in the *Dictionary of American Biography*. "Nearly one hundred years passed before the federal Supreme Court ordered his claims paid, and his heirs received about fifty thousand dollars."

And again like Mazzei, Vigo is mentioned in few American history books. But in 1839, when the rush to the West was under way, Congressman John Law of Vincennes declared in the House of Representatives that except for Vigo the future of the United States might have been profoundly different, certainly more difficult.

In Revolutionary times there were in America only a few hundred Italians. Several were street musicians in the larger cities, precursors of the later organ grinders with their monkeys. Others introduced opera to New York; one started the Marine Band. There were several sculptors who hawked their statuettes on Boston and New York street corners, and were sometimes employed to decorate homes.

Between the Revolution and the Civil War not many Italians came over. In 1820, the first year the United States kept immigration statistics, all of thirty people entered from Italy; sixty-two the following year. In 1833 the figure rose to 1,699; then it declined until 1854, when it bounced back to 1,263.

A large proportion of those who arrived during the early decades of the nineteenth century, when Italy was in turmoil, were educated men —political exiles, leaders of causes still to be won, would-be leaders of uprisings, people of the *Risorgimento*: scholars, painters, adventurous businessmen, idealistic missionaries. Among them were: Philip Traetta, composer and music teacher in Boston, New York and Philadelphia, a

friend of Presidents Madison and Monroe; Constantino Brumidi, who
painted the well-known frescoes in the National Capitol, finishing the
job when he was past seventy; Luigi Palma di Cesnola, soldier, archeologist and secretary and director of New York's Metropolitan Museum
of Art, generally credited with putting the museum on a solid foundation; Benedict Sestini, priest, mathematician, astronomer, architect and
founder and editor of the *Messenger of the Sacred Heart*, long the most
widely circulated Catholic publication in the world; Eduardo Ferrero,
a major-general in the Union Army who distinguished himself in the
battles of Smith Mountain and Antietam; and Antonio Meucci, the
inventor whom the New York *World* on the occasion of his death in
1889 called "one of the most important figures in the scientific world
of the time." His work ran almost parallel to that of Alexander Graham
Bell.

The missionaries were Catholic fathers, a few of whom scattered
through the West as early as the 1830s. In the ensuing decade a handful,
under the orders of Bishop Rosati of St. Louis, and intent on converting the Indians, penetrated into what now are the states of Idaho,
Oregon and Washington. The last of these priests, Father Joseph
Cataldo, died in 1928 in Spokane at the age of ninety-two, after helping
that city grow from a tiny trading post to a municipality of over 100,000.

In 1880 Italian immigration exceeded 12,000; the vast America-ward
movement from Italy was getting under way. Before long ten, twelve,
even fifteen thousand Italians were passing through Ellis Island in a
single day.

The reasons for this migration were economic. The eroded farms on
Italy's crowded slopes yielded less and less, modern industry had not
yet begun, and fewer and fewer Italians were willing to stagnate in
poverty. In the United States economic conditions were almost the
reverse. The great Industrial Revolution, hooked to a consciousness of
immense natural wealth, was in full swing, calling for a lot of new
manpower in a hurry. Railroads and highways had to be laid, and traction systems and pipe lines; reservoirs, viaducts and bridges had to be
built, power and telegraph and telephone lines strung; tunnels had to be
burrowed through the western mountains, and subways under the sidewalks of New York; excavations for new buildings had to be dug, and
the buildings built; more coal was needed; great quantities of stone
and slate had to be quarried.

This new America, caught in a frenzy of expansion, was able to use
all the Italians who poured in from 1880 on—more than 4,700,000 of
them; 3,600,000 in the forty years since 1905. The majority came from

the south of Italy, from sunny Sicily, the Abruzzi, Calabria, Apulia and Campania where a thousand years of unremitting toil had conditioned them to the hardest, dullest kind of work.

Helping to make modern America, the majority were the ditch-diggers, the hod-carriers, the mortar-mixers, the humblest kind of laborers, exploited by American employers who paid them as little as possible, and by their own *padroni* or *agenti* who arranged for their employment and took part of their small wages. But among the workers were also thousands of skilled men with the best Old World traditions in their trades: masons, bricklayers, quarrymen, stonecutters. When it came to working with stone theirs were the deftest hands in America.

The immigrants—mostly men at first—found themselves isolated and in many communities condemned. In 1888 a New York paper editorialized about Italian and Irish immigrants: "The flood gates are open. The bars are down. . . . The sewer is unchoked. Europe is vomiting. In other words, the scum of immigration is viscerating upon our shores. The horde of 9.60 steerage slime is being syphoned upon us from continental mud tanks." But I doubt if many Italian ditch-diggers and sandhogs came across this piece, or ever heard of it. Toiling twelve hours a day, sometimes for less than one dollar, they originated little philosophic sayings like "The poor in America are the rich in Italy," which was almost true.

For decades the human traffic between Italy and the United States flowed in both directions at a tremendous rate. Perhaps half the immigrants went back to the old country within a few years. Many peasants found it unpleasant and unnatural to live in crowded ill-smelling tenements. Some left in disgust after they had been victimized by native-American and Italian sharks, or in protest against anti-foreign prejudice, against being called Wops and Dagoes.

The other half sent for their wives or girls, settling down in the slums—"on the other side of the tracks" or "over behind the gas tanks"—and creating numerous Little Italys and Woptowns, Dago Hills and Macaroni Hollows. In spite of her defects America was so much better than Italy that there was no comparison. Many who had returned to Italy realized this and hastened back to the United States.

Here was the New World; it wasn't Paradise, it wasn't easy, but one could get ahead. And many Italians did; among them too many who preyed on their countrymen. A few were out-and-out sharpers who had come planning to mulct the immigrants. Thousands of others were honest men with a little education who did well as steamship-ticket and foreign-money-order agents, as saloonkeepers and undertakers, as small tradesmen. Thousands of *agenti* became sand and gravel contractors; they had to be on the sharp side to compete with Irish contractors whose knowledge of English and participation in municipal politics gave them the jump when it came to getting desirable construction contracts.

It was the Irish who first popularized "Dago" and "Wop." Irish contractors hired Italian laborers through the *agenti*, but kept them under Irish bosses. It was an iron-bound rule not to give an "Eye-taylian" a break, not to make him even a straw-boss. In consequence there was much antagonism between Italians and the Irish.

It wasn't very pleasant. But you could say this for America: here you could slug it out with your competitors, or you could outwit them if you had the wits. Sometimes you could take a deep breath and plunge ahead in a big way. By and by in nearly every sizable American city there were several millionaires or near-millionaires whose fathers, or who themselves, had started out as Italian immigrant laborers or *agenti* or petty job contractors back around the turn of the century.

Other Italians have gone into other businesses. In Greater New York alone there are over ten thousand Italian grocery stores, thousands of Italian barber and flower shops and shoe-shine stands. All over the country are hundreds of importers of Italian olive oil, wines and prepared foods, and thousands of restaurateurs specializing in Italian dishes.

Only about ten per cent of the total group went on the land. All kinds of Italian farm-colonization schemes sprang up back in the 1890s and later, but several were downright swindles conducted by Italian and non-Italian American crooks. Exposure of these swindles undermined some of the honest schemes. But others succeeded. The Italian vineyards in California are famous. Less well known but also long established are the Italian vineyards in the Hudson River Valley and the Finger Lakes district of New York. In Georgia, Alabama and Louisiana, Italian immigrants and their native-American descendants have done well with cotton, rice, strawberries and sugar cane. And since the 1920s many Italians have gone from Little Italys in cities like New York, Philadelphia, Boston and Bridgeport to near-by farm-lands, where they have started excellent truck gardens.

An interesting Italian farming community is Tontitown in Arkansas, named for Enrico Tonti, the explorer. It dates back to the late 1890s, when a group of immigrants led by a priest decided to escape the evils of urban life. But the prejudice against Italians and Catholics, as against most "foreigners," was very sharp in Arkansas then, and the settlers encountered a good deal of ill will. When they opened a school, a group of local youths burned it. Later when their church was threatened, the priest met the mob with a gun. The people stuck it out; now they have a fairly successful town surrounded by good farms.

According to the census, in 1940 the United States had 1,623,600 immigrants from Italy—our largest foreign-born group. Approximately five-eighths were naturalized; leaving some 650,000 aliens registered with the Department of Justice. But, like the naturalized citizens, most of the aliens are parents and even grandparents of American-born citizens, which brings the grand total of the "Italian" element to about six million.

Their largest organization is the Order of the Sons of Italy in America (Ordine Figli d'Italia in America) a fraternal-insurance society with over 250,000 members, nearly one thousand branches with national headquarters in New York, and about a dozen publications, some in English. Three mutual-aid federations, Order of the Sons and Daughters of Italy in America (Pittsburgh), American Sons of Italy (New York) and Independent Order of the Sons of Italy (Pittsburgh), originated in secession movements from the Order of the Sons of Italy. Then there are Sons of Columbus in America (Pittsburgh) and the Columbian Federation of Italian American Societies (Pueblo, Colorado), both strongly anti-Fascist long before Pearl Harbor. The latter organization publishes a militantly anti-Fascist newspaper L'Unione.

Hundreds of Italian-language newspapers and magazines have been started; over a hundred remain. Some of the largest—New York's Il Progresso Italo-America (daily, 65,000 circulation) published by the gravel contractor and Tammany Hall politician Generoso Pope who once accepted a decoration from Mussolini; La Stella di Pittsburgh (weekly, 17,000), Chicago's L'Italia (weekly, 10,000), Boston's La Gazetta del Massachusetts (weekly, 10,000), Cleveland's L'Araldo (weekly, 12,000), Philadelphia's Il Popolo Italiano (daily, 16,000) and Detroit's La Voce del Popolo (weekly, 12,000)—leaned toward pro-Fascism before the United States entered the war. In part this was due to a lack of perspective on world forces and America's relation to them. Since Pearl Harbor the Italian-language press has supported the prevailing policies of the Washington government.

Except for a few small groups in the larger cities which have their own Protestant churches, the Italians are Roman Catholics. They have thousands of priests; but although they form perhaps one-fifth of the Roman Catholic total in the United States, there have been very few Italian American bishops. The hierarchy consists preponderantly of Irish and German Americans.

America has long welcomed such extraordinary men and women as the late great tenor Enrico Caruso, as conductors Arturo Toscanini and Cleofante Campanini and the coloratura Galli-Curci whose genius originated and developed abroad but who became part of American life and may be regarded as Italy's special gift to the United States. And out of the vast number of plain folk who comprise the bulk of the Italian group, many individuals have risen to become "names."

Fiorello H. La Guardia, son of an immigrant bandmaster in the United States Army, comes to mind instantly. An anti-politician, the three-term mayor of New York City is an extraordinary figure in American politics—a public servant in the best meaning of the term; a brilliant, honest, progressive administrator who when he makes a mistake is apt to make "a beaut," as he himself puts it; a dramatic, very "Italian," sometimes amusing personality, almost eccentrically independent and unconventional; at his best in his weekly radio reports to the people of the greatest city in the world. But the "Little Flower" is likely to be good in a variety of situations. As mayor, under Section 6 of the New York City Charter, he was also a magistrate and he occasionally presided in police court. One wintry day during the Depression a trembling old man charged with stealing a loaf of bread stood before him. He extenuated his act on the ground that his family was starving. "I've got to punish you," said La Guardia. "The law requires me to do that. I sentence you to a fine of $10," reaching into his pocket. "Here is $10 to pay your fine. Now I remit the fine," tossing the ten into his wide-rimmed hat, "and furthermore I hereby fine every person in this room fifty cents apiece, except the prisoner, for living in a town where a man has to steal in order to eat." The old man walked out of the police court with $47.50—according to one reporter, "with the light of Heaven in his eyes."

Other notable names are Judges Ferdinand Pecora, Antonio Capotosto, Luigi Valente, Salvatore A. Cotillo and John J. Freschi; Congressman Vito Marcantonio; Edward Corsi, former commissioner of immigration; Charles Poletti, ex-lieutenant-governor of New York, later an Allied military governor in Italy; Angelo Rossi, long mayor of San Francisco; Leo B. Santangelo, mayor of Middletown, Connecticut; Charles J. Margiotti, one-time attorney-general of Pennsylvania; Peter V. Cacchione, New York councilman.

Also Giuseppe Mario Bellanca, airplane designer; Gino Arturo Ratti, Angelo Patri, Antonio Marinoni, Vittorio Racca and Leonard Covello, educators; Antonio Maramarco, California "vineyard King"; Giuseppe Faccioli (whose father fought under Garibaldi), Samuel S. Torrisi and Philip Torchio, electrical engineers; Joshua D'Esposito, civil engineer; the bankers Giannini; William Francis Verdi, Giuseppe Mario Pellettieri, Richard Paganelli, André Crotti, Gaston Carlucci and Vincent Anthony Lapenta, surgeons.

Also Fortune Gallo, impresario; Remo Bufano, puppeteer; Rudolph Valentino; Alberto Salvi, harpist; Pietro A. Yon and Giuseppe Aldo Bandegger, composers; Frank Capra, movie director; Ferrucio Vitale, landscape architect; Ettore Cadorin, Paul Abbate, Xavier Barile, Ercole Cartotto, Leo Lentelli, Giovanni Castano, Salvatore Pinto, Victor Salvatore, Beniamino Bufano, Pompeo Coppini, Matteo Sandona, Joseph Coletti, Nicola D'Ascenzo, Anthony de Francisci, Luigi Lucioni, Carlo Ciampaglia, Onorio Ruotolo, Oronzio Maldarelli, Attilio and Furio Piccirilli, Salvatore Cartaino Scarpitta, Louis Guglielmi and Patsy Santo, painters and sculptors.

Also Al Capone, Philip Musica (alias Dr. F. Donald Coster) and Lucky Luciano, of less enviable reputations.

Also Enrico Fermi, Noble Prize physicist, who contributed to the realization of the Atomic Bomb in 1945; Edward Chiera, Oriental-ist; Constantine Panunzio, sociologist; G. Bonfante, Dino Bigongiari, Giuseppe Prozzolini, Gabriella Bosano, Rudolph Altrocchi, G. Fucilla, Michele De Filippis and Howard R. Marraro, professors of Italian; E. O. Fenzi, horticulturist; Gaetano Salvemini and George La Piana of Harvard and G. A. Borgese of the University of Chicago, leading experts on the future of Italy; Lisa Sergio, radio commentator.

Also Michael Rafetto, who enacts the popular "Paul Barbour" in Carlton Morse's radio serial "One Man's Family"; Jimmy Savo and Jimmy Durante, comedians; and Frank ("The Voice") Sinatra, who in 1944 emerged also as an effective enemy of racial prejudice.*

Also John Ciardi, poet; Michael De Capite, John Fante, George

---

* "I'm not the kind of guy who does a lot of brain work about why and how I happen to get into something," said Sinatra to a New York newspaper reporter (*PM*, June 10, 1945). "I get an idea—maybe I get sore at something. And when I get sore enough, I do something about it. . . . In show business you get all kinds of people. I've got all kinds of friends, good friends, Negroes, Catholics, Jews. They're nice fellows. We get along great. . . . When some tramp keeps bringing up a person's color, or his religion, it gets me sore. It gets me sore and then I'm *through* with him.

"This prejudice—it's nothing new to me. In Hoboken, when I was a kid, I lived in a plenty tough neighborhood. When somebody called me a 'dirty little Dago,' there was only one thing to do—break his head. When I got older, I realized you shouldn't do it that way. I realized you've got to do it through education. Educa-tion is the right way—with a few exceptions." In the fall of 1944, at a Southern army camp where he and other musicians and actors were entertaining the soldiers, Sinatra didn't like the refusal of a lunchroom counterman to take the order of a Negro member of the troupe. "I didn't like that," he said later. "I watched that guy awhile, then I asked him, 'How come?' When he said 'We don't serve niggers,' I lost my temper. I reached over that counter and smashed him one on the nose."

Panetta, Pietro di Donato, Jerre Magione, Guido D'Agostino, Nicola V. Curinga and Frances Winwar (Francesca Vinciguerra), writers who have begun to put the dramatic Italian chapter of the American Story into books and magazines.

Also Joe di Maggio, the greatest Yankee of 'em all, whose mother became a naturalized American citizen in 1945.

Monsignor L. G. Ligutti of Des Moines leads a movement addressing itself to Midwestern farmers, based on the idea, as he expressed it, that "the profit motive is not the highest or most essential element" in agriculture, that the farm should be the scene of a specially desirable way of life. Ralph Borsodi, economist and one-time industrial consultant, discovered soon after World War I that urban civilization in the United States was sick and the best thing to do was to get out of it and on the land; he has been preaching that idea in *Flight from the City* and other books, in magazine articles and lectures, ever since. "I do not believe that the farmer should be a businessman," he says. "Farm homes are not for the purpose of making money but for a better scheme of living and greater security."

Following construction jobs, Italians shifted around a lot in the United States; now they are unevenly scattered across the country. Well over a million and a half are in Pennsylvania, New Jersey, Massachusetts and Connecticut. All the bigger cities in these states have one or more good-sized Little Italys. Italians are numerically strong also in California, where besides farming they have gone into fishing, the retail and wholesale wine trade, restaurant-keeping, politics and banking.

By hard work and frugal living many Italian laborers have succeeded in sending their American-born sons and daughters to college. In 1941 about ten per cent of the entering class in Columbia College had Italian names.

The largest concentration of Italians and Italian Americans is in Greater New York, which contains about one-fifth of them—1,300,000; a good many more than the population of Rome.

Most of this vast element within Greater New York has lived for a long time in about a dozen Little Italys—shabby, crowded, extremely lively neighborhoods, full of various smells, mostly pleasant. Many of the older men are still laborers, by now used to their position in America. They are still Wops when they venture outside their neighborhood; even so, New York is their city too. They have helped pave its streets, lay its sidewalks, build its bridges, tunnels, elevateds, subways and skyscrapers. Others work in shops and factories and offices. They form a large part of the Amalgamated Clothing Workers and the International Ladies' Garment Workers' unions.

Most of them, poor and humble, engaged in thankless basic and indispensable functions, draw much satisfaction from knowing that Fiorello LaGuardia was mayor, that the late Mother Cabrini is America's one and only Roman Catholic saint; that the city has numerous monuments (to Columbus on Columbus Circle, to Dante at 64th Street, to Verransano at the Battery, to Garibaldi on Washington Square, to Verdi in Central Park) all paid for by Italian immigrants; that in the classified business directory they can count two thousand physicians and as many lawyers with Italian names—their sons and grandsons.

Every now and then the spotlight of publicity turns on some Italian-immigrant worker. In the 1920s there were Nicola Sacco and Bartolomeo Vanzetti whose trial in Massachusetts commanded international interest and roused terrifically strong feelings, dominated by a deep sense of injustice, all over the United States. At the end of the long trial, when both had been sentenced to death, Vanzetti made his eloquent statement: "Now we are not a failure. . . . Never in our full life could we do such work for tolerance, for joostice, for man's understanding of man as now we do by an accident. Our words—our lives—our pains—nothing! The taking of our lives—lives of a good shoemaker and a poor fish-peddler—all! That last moment belongs to us—that agony is our triumph." Now Sacco and Vanzetti are historical figures continuously growing in stature. An extremely successful play in the early 1940s, The Male Animal by James Thurber and Elliott Nugent, was constructed around Vanzetti's little courtroom speech.

Early in 1939 the Italian vice consul at Grand Rapids, Michigan, informed Frank Rusoti, a paper mill worker in the near-by town of Vicksburg, that his father had bequeathed him considerable property on the condition that he renounce his American citizenship and return to the old country. "That I will not do," replied Rusoti, who had fought as an American soldier in France in 1918. "I would rather be a paper mill worker in Vicksburg than the king of Italy."

Mario Izzo came to America in 1932 and settled in Aliquippa, Pennsylvania, to earn his living for a few years at odd jobs. In 1938 the jobs gave out and he had to go on relief. Izzo insisted on working for his weekly $3.60. Every day for six hours the little old man swept the streets of Aliquippa. "You give me money to live," he told the surprised relief officials, "I keep this town clean like a table. I want to be honest with this country that has been good to me." Early in 1939 he fell ill; one cold day as he sat near the stove his clothing caught on

fire and he burned to death. He was buried in potter's field. Then
suddenly Aliquippa and a large part of Pennsylvania realized that Izzo's
philosophy had made him a symbol of a long-recognized American
virtue. The General Assembly of the state passed a resolution honoring him. Money was collected to rebury him and put a stone on his
grave. Seven hundred people attended the services. On the stone were
struck his own words: "My bread, it tastes sweet, and I feel like a man
because I work. The way of life, is it not work?"

Like most of the other new-immigrant elements, the majority in
the Italian group, naturalized and alien, have a tender feeling for
the old country. This feeling is part of human nature; it is blended
from the need for a sense of continuity, from being held at arm's length
in the new country, from homesickness, from remembering vividly the
good things in their background and forgetting the bad. Some of it is
automatically transmitted by Italian parents to their American-born
children.

The immigrant's feeling for the old country is little understood
by most Americans. Many resent it or even condemn it. Few educators,
public officials and other persons of influence who are not themselves
of recent-immigrant stock realize that their disapproval helps to drive
some of the immigrants into the arms of the agents and propagandists
of the government momentarily in power in the old country.

In 1940, when the United States began to be engulfed in the world
crisis, this looked like a serious matter in the case of Italian immigrants.
They had been subjected to long and intensive propaganda directed
from Mussolini's Italy, propaganda which responsible American leadership had done nothing to counteract. Many Italian Americans and alien
Italians in this country became pro-Fascist. But, as we got into the
war, their pro-Fascism turned out to be superficial.

In March 1945 an eighty-two-year old man, Frank Maresca, died in
Jersey City, New Jersey. He had come to America at twelve in 1875.
For nearly fifty years he operated a fruit and vegetable store. He had
thirteen sons and three daughters. Eleven of the boys served in the
United States Army—three in World War I, eight in World War II.
One was killed in France during the Argonne offensive in 1918, one
was wounded on Guam in 1944.

In World War I some two hundred thousand Italian Americans,
mostly immigrants, were in the United States armed forces. Their
number in World War II is about 550,000, the majority of them

second-generation sons and daughters. Thousands were killed or wounded. Hundreds were decorated for valor, for acts beyond the call of duty.

Captain Don Gentile of Lima, Ohio, was an early "ace of aces" in the Army Air Force.

Early in 1945 the parents of Staff Sergeant Edward Chappetta of The Bronx, New York, received a letter from his company commander: "I very simply and humbly tell you that in the Battle of Saipan, where heroism was the rule rather than the exception, your son stood out like a beacon. He lived and fought and died a magnificent soldier . . ." and was posthumously awarded the nation's second highest military honor, the Distinguished Service Cross.

Early in February 1945 the name of Lieutenant Colonel Henry A. Mucci, of Bridgeport, Connecticut, and Denver, Colorado, commanding officer of the 6th Ranger Battalion serving in the Philippines, flashed in the headlines. His commando unit had stormed ashore on Dinagat Island in the Gulf of Leyte three days before the main invasion force arrived. Late in January it was specially picked by General Walter Krueger to liberate the starving, emaciated American and other Allied soldiers and civilians held in a Japanese prison stockade in the interior of Luzon, twenty-five miles from the nearest American line. Under Colonel Mucci's leadership and aided by Filipino guerrillas, the Rangers liberated 513 men, killing 532 of the enemy in the process; whereupon Associated Press correspondent Fred Hampson radioed from Luzon: "Put Lieutenant Colonel Henry Mucci's 6th Rangers with Rogers' Rangers. Put 'em with Allen's Green Mountain Boys. After what happened last night that is where they belong." Colonel Mucci's father, an immigrant from Italy, was a horse dealer in Bridgeport before his death in the early 1920s when Henry was a young boy, the seventh of eight children. His mother, a native of New York, raised the family.

Sergeant John Basilone of Raritan, New Jersey, was the first enlisted marine to win the Congressional Medal of Honor. It was awarded for heroism in the October 24-25, 1942, battle of Lunga on Guadalcanal in which he killed thirty-eight Japanese trying futilely to knock out his machine-gun emplacement. The citation said that Sergeant Basilone contributed "in a large measure to the virtual annihilation of a Japanese regiment" by battling his way through the enemy lines to get ammunition for his isolated machine-gunners. After Guadalcanal the twenty-five-year-old sergeant came home for a visit and spoke at War Bond rallies. But he didn't like to be "a museum piece." He wanted to be in on the recapture of Manila, where he had served before the

war. He was killed while leading his platoon in the opening assault on
the beach of Iwo Jima.

Soldiers of Italian descent were especially valuable in the Italian
campaign. In spite of the lack of clarity in the United States' official
policy through 1943-1945, it was their unique role to carry back to
Italy the passionate belief in equality, in the rights of man, which
Philip Mazzei shared with Thomas Jefferson and the Founding Fathers.

Frank E. Toscani of New York City is a case in point. Before the
war he was a third-grade civil service clerk in the Department of
Sanitation. In 1936 he joined the New York National Guard as a
private. By 1941, when his outfit was activated, he had risen to the
rank of captain. Later, promoted to major, he was attached to the staff
of General George Patton and served with the invasion force in Sicily.
As a member of the Allied Military Government, he was placed in
charge of the town of Licata, and in this capacity he became the
prototype of Major Joppolo in John Hersey's novel A Bell for Adano
(1944).

One day as temporary head of the town of Adano, which is full of
Fascist and also pre-Fascist hangovers, Major Joppolo finds it necessary
to talk to the local officials, one of whom had abused his position by
going to the head of a bread line in which other people had stood
for hours.

"I want you to be my friends," he says. "As my friends, I will consider
it my duty to tell you everything I think, for we do not want Adano to
be a town of mystery and suspicion.

"Adano has been a Fascist town. That is natural, because the country
was Fascist, therefore the town was also. But now that the Americans
have come, we are going to run the town as a democracy.

"Perhaps you do not know what democracy is. I will tell you.

"Democracy is this: democracy is that the men of the government
are no longer the masters of the people. They are the servants of the
people. . . . Who pays the men in the government? The people do,
for they pay the taxes out of which you are paid.

"Therefore you are now the servants of the people of Adano. I too
am their servant. When I go to buy my bread, I shall take my place
at the end of the line, and I will wait my turn. You too must behave
now as servants, not as masters. You must behave as the servants of
the man without shoes just as much as of the baron. . . .

"Remember: you are servants . . . of the people of Adano. And
watch: this thing will make you happier than you have ever been in
your lives."

II: AMERICANS FROM SPAIN AND MEXICO

TWENTY-ONE years after Columbus' First Voyage—in the early spring of 1513—Juan Ponce de León touched the southern coast of Florida, perhaps near where Miami is now. He thought he had discovered another island. It was named La Florida (Flo-rée-da) either for its floral profusion or for the season of its discovery, Pascua Florida —Eastertime.

Past his prime at fifty-three, Ponce de León sought the "Fountain of Youth" which according to Indian lore was somewhere on the "island." But as it turned out, Florida was the death of him. In 1521, his interest in rejuvenation and longevity heightened by eight years, he tried to seize and colonize it. He landed with two hundred men somewhere near Charlotte Harbor or possibly in Tampa Bay, to be confronted by a large force of angry Indians. An arrow struck him and he died of the wound.

Eventually, in spite of Indian hostility, the Spaniards founded settlements in Florida—notably St. Augustine in 1565, forty-two years before the English started Jamestown. They occupied the peninsula until 1763, when it came under the British flag.

St. Augustine is the oldest still-extant community in the United States established by European colonizers. Its founder, Menéndez de Avilés, an Asturian nobleman in the Spanish Navy, had come to Florida with royal orders to expel by whatever means any "settlers who are corsairs, or any other nation not subject to Us." Official Spain supported the Counter-Reformation and Menéndez de Avilés' specific mission was to remove the French Protestants from their recently settled Fort Caroline (near present-day Jacksonville). He carried it out very thoroughly. Attacking with an overwhelming force, he slaughtered hundreds of the "heretic interlopers," reporting the action to his king as "necessary for the service of God Our Lord and of Your Majesty."

Prior to this, in 1539, the fate-driven Hernando de Soto had landed in Florida and thence led his bold horsemen into the regions now called Georgia, the Carolinas, Tennessee and Alabama, fighting the Indians all the way, to discover the Mississippi in 1541—and to die that same year and be buried in the Father of Waters.

The whole Spanish Adventure in the New World was intensely Spanish—romantic in impetus and conception; daring, violent and grandiose in execution, furiously energetic and wonderfully organized in big moves, often indifferent and insensitive to details. It was marked by civilized steps and civilizing influences, also by the cruelty which usually accompanies conquest.

Salvador de Madariaga in *Cortés, Conqueror of Mexico* (1941) characterizes the conquistadores as "gentlemen-adventurers . . . hurling themselves, their persons, fortunes, lives at the unknown continent . . . vigorous centaurs of the Discovery-conquest . . . fearless of native's arrow, nature's inhospitable and cruel ways and their own Christian rivals . . . moved by an unexpressed, inarticulate ambition, born of the mere existence of unknown though known-of lands, of the tensions between the untapped vitality within and the unlimited scope without, a tension which acted on all, for it was in the air, yet which energized everyone in proportion to the quality of his own metal."

Some literature exists in Spanish concerning a man named Gaspar Pérez de Villagrá—probably a typical conquistador operating in Mexico and New Mexico around the year 1600. He is described as "a faithful vassal of the king [who] did not spare himself but contributed money and risked his life. Frequently," when already in his forties, "in a single year he traveled more than fifteen hundred leagues." He "fought heroically . . . was indefatigable; hunger, thirst, long journeys, countless dangers, downpours, scorching heat, and cold snows he experienced with resignation."

The earliest Spaniards were not primarily colonizers, as were the more deliberate, pragmatic, methodical Anglo-Saxons up north many years later. Some were like teen-aged boys out on a tear. They sought and endured hardships for hardship's sake. Apt to scorn any scheme that looked easy, they were adventurers in the name of adventure, for the hell of it, and for the glory of God.

But from its beginning a palpable constructive streak ran through the Adventure. Many of those taking part wanted to establish homes in the New World and brought over domestic animals, numerous kinds of vegetable and flower seeds and fruit pits; also, as historian Herbert Priestly has emphasized, "the arts of courtesy and ceremony . . . which have a spirit and technique all their own."

Some expedition leaders and sub-leaders and some of the priests and friars who came with them were closely representative of Spain at that time (and to some extent since)—"a whale stranded on the coast of Europe," Edmund Burke called her—a country of passion and religion, of drama and color, of high cultural values and also of the Inquisition, of immense vigor and pride, of untamed primitive impulses in its blood, which was a cocktail of numerous ingredients: Iberian, Celtic, Phoenician, Greek, Carthaginian, Roman, German, Arab and Moor. Some of the Spaniards were offenders against the law sentenced to exile in the New World, there to expiate, to redeem themselves. Many ended disastrously. The priests and friars almost sought martyrdom. Coming over one after another, saints and sinners intermingling in their crusades, they individually and collectively personified their homeland. Their careers expressed Spain's sixteenth-century position in history which her great English admirer Havelock Ellis, in his beautifully perceptive book *The Soul of Spain* written four hundred years later, saw as "the summit of worldly power" from which she was about "to plunge into an abyss."

It was at her summit, just before she plunged, that Spain—through Columbus in the 1490s, then apart from him during the sixteenth and seventeenth centuries—took the first steps to add America to the world. Spain led, England followed.

Not until 1577-1580 did the English sea dog Francis Drake make his momentous voyage to the Western Hemisphere, sailing around a major part of it, in the Pacific as far north as California (or even British Columbia, as some writers have it), mainly to plunder Spanish galleons, which were something beautiful to see. He returned with an enormous loot and the exciting report of more to be had where that came from. This yanked Elizabethan England into action. It gave rise to the idea of a "New England" in America.

To backtrack a bit: In 1528, six years after Ponce de León's failure, the Pánfilo de Narváez expedition came to Florida. It failed too, but out of the fiasco unrolled the strongest and longest thread of the Spanish story in the United States.

Some eight years before, at Veracruz, acting under Diego de Velázques, governor of Cuba, Narváez had fought a major military engagement with the successful and independent conqueror of Mexico, Hermán Cortés, whom the jealous Velázques wanted destroyed. Narváez lost an eye and the battle. Now, to erase that blemish on his record, he left Spain with six hundred soldiers, friars and servants, including some African slaves, and the assignment to conquer the Florida Indians and settle the "island." But he got there with fewer than four hundred, the rest having deserted at Santo Domingo, where his ships had put in for supplies.

It is believed he landed near the present site of Pensacola. The royal proclamation adding Florida to the Spanish Crown was read with due ceremony. And that was about all. The Indians were hostile. It was

autumn; the winds blowing fiercely from the Gulf endangered the
anchored ships.

Disagreement over the next move split the expedition and its factions
went their different ways.

By the end of 1528 Narváez and nearly all his men had perished in
storms at sea, in fights with the Indians and among themselves, and
of hunger, exposure and disease. The few known survivors were enslaved by Indians along the northern Gulf coast.

Only one man of standing in the expedition survived: its treasurer,
Alvar Núñez Cabeza de Vaca. He escaped from his captors; then, after
nearly a decade of knocking around, he and three companions—one
named Estevan, probably a Negro, possibly a Moor, a former slave of
another of the party—began the long trek to Mexico over an inland
route previously known only to Indians. Years later Cabeza de Vaca
wrote an account of the odyssey. Apparently he was the first white man
to see the buffalo. The trip took them through endless and rugged
stretches of Texas and northern Mexico. On the way they heard Indians
tell of fabulous golden cities to the north.

In Mexico, Cabeza de Vaca repeated the Indians' tales. They spread
like wildfire. The Spaniards in Mexico were jealous of Pizarro, who in
his conquest of Peru had acquired fabulous quantities of gold and silver.
Perhaps the country to the north had riches that would make Pizarro's
pile look like a pebble beside a boulder.

As soon as possible, in 1539, a scouting party was dispatched in
charge of Friar Marcos de Niza, who took Estevan along as guide.
Pushing ahead of the friar, the Negro (or Moor) presently sent back
word of great cities he saw with his own eyes. He had seen the ancient
Indian pueblos on the mesas, the reddish mud walls shining like distant
gold in the sunlight. While reconnoitering, he was killed by the Indians.

Friar Marcos followed in Estevan's wake till he too, from the top of
a high mesa on a hot afternoon, saw large aggregations of gleaming
edifices—whole cities. He hastened back to Mexico to report what he
had seen.

Fierce competition raged over who would lead the expedition to
capture the "Seven Cities of Cíbola." Francisco Vásquez de Coronado
was chosen. By then the conquest of what is now Mexico was almost
completed; so about two hundred of the best horsemen, mostly noblemen, accompanied Coronado, together with seventy-odd Spanish foot
soldiers and a retinue of about a thousand Indian allies and servants.
The outfit took along herds of cattle and a thousand horses.

No army ever set out with higher expectations, no army was ever more disappointed. The "Seven Cities of Cíbola" of the Indians' tales turned out to be Zuñi and other pueblos huddled up against mountainsides or along streams in the valleys—villages which atmospheric conditions and distance had transfigured and enhanced before the eyes of Estevan and Friar Marcos.

Coronado and some of his captains, however, thought they might as well look around a bit more; and by 1542, amid frequent bloody encounters with nomadic Indians, small detachments had advanced long distances west and east and north, discovering the Grand Canyon, the Colorado River, the Red River, the Arkansas, the Cimarron, the Salt, the Gila. The leader himself got well into present-day Kansas, where the tall grass of the limitless plains teemed with buffalo. Without realizing it, he almost beat De Soto to the Mississippi. He and his officers achieved one of the greatest inland explorations in history, but such were their objectives that they returned to Mexico believing they were failures.

Behind them they left scores of escaped horses which bred wild, eventually producing the mustang (mesteño: "strayed, wild").

Two Franciscan padres remained to do missionary work among the Indians. Both were soon killed. More padres came in 1581; then for a time the Spanish story in the country northward along the Rio Grande spins mostly around priests bent on ministering to the few settlers and on converting the "savages" to Christianity, and around small expeditions of soldiers and Mexican Indians sent to see what had happened to them.

Both priests and soldiers added to the slowly growing fund of knowledge about the northern territory, and toward the end of the sixteenth century it was well established in the minds of the ruling group in Mexico.

What was known of the region—as yet undefined on any map, but more and more referred to as "New Mexico"—evidently made its deepest impression on Juan de Oñate, a native Mexican grandee, a mining tycoon in his fifties with a touch of imagination and a lot of initiative and daring. He fought long and hard for the royal contract authorizing him to conquer and colonize New Mexico. Finally in the late 1590s, at his own expense, he organized some four hundred men, women and children, mostly "pure Spaniards" like himself, and led them into the upper reaches of the Rio Grande Valley.

It was a grueling journey over mountains and streams, through canyons and valleys. The women and children rode in the eighty-three supply wagons. There were two hundred soldiers, eight Franciscan padres and four lay brothers. The vaqueros drove seven thousand cattle, sheep and spare horses, grazing them enroute. These animals were important. The Spanish horse bred with the wild mustang, to produce the hardy western horse of later times.

In 1599, about thirty miles north of today's Santa Fe, the Oñate expedition founded San Gabriel, the first capital of New Mexico. It was a failure. In 1610 a new capital was established at Santa Fe.

Oñate, governor of the province, was an energetic and ambitious explorer. He ranged toward the Gulf and over the plains of Kansas, scattering his forces and calling for more, which the Viceroy in Mexico City sent him grudgingly or not at all. Within a few years Juan de Oñate was through as a colonizer. He returned to Mexico.

In the next seven or eight decades, however, several hundred other settlers, soldiers, missionaries and servants (few women) moved up from Mexico. Some dispersed ineffectively over the adjacent territories, which were "Spanish" only because Coronado or some other explorer or a padre had once visited them. But the majority of newcomers— ordinary men—remained in New Mexico.

By now Spain had been plunging downward for many decades; the English had destroyed her fleet; her empire was disintegrating. A mood of frustration began to envelop the Spanish people, both in the homeland and in the New World. But the original momentum of the Adventure carried it on for several more decades.

Between 1610 and 1640, the Spaniards, using Indians to do the work, built several missions up and down the valley. Some of these were large edifices whose ruins today are tourist attractions. The missions were probably destroyed by the Indians during their full-scale revolt in 1680, which drove the Spaniards to what are now Ciudad Juárez and El Paso, and cut off colonization until Diego de Vargas reconquered the upper Rio Grande country in 1692.

The settlers returned to their former communities; in the next four years De Vargas put down more Indian uprisings; the settlements then appeared permanent and more and more people straggled up from the south. Mostly men, they took Indian women for their wives.

This brought them close to people already adjusted to the physical environment. From the Indian they learned irrigation and harvesting; in turn, they gave the Spanish language to some of the tribes living in villages. It was this intimate contact with the Indians which enabled the Spaniards to send roots into the tough earth of New Mexico.

By 1720 New Mexico's Spanish population—much of it part-Indian— numbered twenty-two thousand; in the next century it increased to nearly one hundred thousand; and gradually during the following hundred years there was created the over-all New Mexican atmosphere that Willa Cather re-created (somewhat idealized perhaps) in the unusual novel *Death Comes for the Archbishop* (1925).

The Spanish colonization of California, Texas and Arizona did not begin for well over a century after the founding of the New Mexico settlements. San Antonio, dating from 1718, was the first permanent community in Texas. But the government of New Spain had little consistent interest in Texas; the province got under way only after Mexico gained its independence in 1821. Then Mexican settlers began to pour over the Rio Grande, and the "gringo" adventurers to drift in from the East. ("Gringo"—perhaps from the word *griego*, Greek, the height of linguistic strangeness and incomprehension—was used in Spain to designate all foreigners.)

Little Spanish colonization took place in Arizona. The first community, Tubac (still extant) was founded in 1720 or thereabouts; Tucson a few years later. By 1732 Arizona had a number of widely separated haciendas—large, self-contained ranches whose owners had absolute power over the *peones* or peasants who worked for them. There was some mining in Arizona, also in Texas and New Mexico.

Strangely enough, California was the last to attract colonizers and colonists. San Diego was founded in 1769. San Francisco, settled in 1776, was called Yerba Buena (good herb) for a mint that grew in the sand dunes. Monterrey, Santa Barbara, El Pueblo de la Reina de los Angeles de la Porciúncula and a dozen other communities came along in quick succession, each with a Roman Catholic mission built by Indian labor under Spanish direction, notably that of the now-legendary Fray Junípero Serra.

Spanish *pobladores* arrived and settled in what is now Colorado around 1770. Some were part-Indian.

These various colonizations were not integrated under a single plan or policy, but were independent—isolated by distances and other geographic conditions. There were horizonless stretches of eye-searing, sun-baked desert, towering mountain ranges, sharp alternations between arid heat and intense cold, sudden cloudbursts flooding arroyos and canyons. The transportation difficulties from, say, Mexico to California or from Texas across Arizona to California were enormous. Anyone who has not driven in an automobile through the Southwest can scarcely imagine the privation and fearsome severity of a long journey over that expanse when it was without roads, railroads and towns.

Simultaneously—in the second half of the eighteenth century—

there was a sudden Spanish development in New Orleans and north-ward west of the Mississippi, in the vast French territory of Louisiana. Entirely separate from what was going on in what we now call the Southwest, it was part of European politics, of the struggle for the control of North America.

Under the Treaty of Paris concluded in 1763 between England and France, England acquired all the territories east of the Mississippi. The year before, by a secret treaty, the French king, Louis XV, had given the Isle of Orleans and all Louisiana west of the Mississippi to his cousin, Charles III of Spain, but he neglected to inform his governor at New Orleans of this trifle until 1764. The Treaty of Paris confirmed the transfer. By and by, to the distress of the New Orleans French, a Spanish governor arrived and took over. He was Almonaster y Rojas, who turned out to be the best administrator New Orleans had ever had. He spent freely of his private money to create a shopping center, to restore a hospital, to build a cathedral.

New Orleans was then a town of three thousand of whom one-third were slaves. The free population was mostly French; none-the-less the Spaniards made a considerable impression upon Louisiana. Some of it is still discernible—in cuisine, in the names of places and plants. The Baton Rouge and New Orleans telephone directories contain a large number of Spanish names. A Spanish-immigrant friend of mine who traveled in Louisiana in 1941 tells me that he found tiny rural com-munities where Spanish is still spoken; in the larger towns he came upon people named Gonzales, Gomez and Dominguez who don't realize their names are Spanish. In the swamplands, many of the muskrat trappers are descendants of the eighteenth-century Spanish settlers.

In New Orleans in 1791 a man named Antonio Méndez started the first sugar refinery in America, presumably continuing to operate it successfully after the French returned to control and later when they sold Louisiana to the United States.

Early in the nineteenth century the English-speaking people of the United States were moving westward in ever increasing numbers. Some reached Texas; others plunged into other parts of the Southwest. The Spanish (or more accurately the Mexicans) called them gringos—later "Americanos" and still later "Anglos." But they were by no means all Anglo-Saxon Americans. Many were Irish, German, Swiss, Scotch immigrants; Catholics, Protestants and Jews.

At first the United States government had next to no interest in its peoples' infiltration through the Southwest. They were simply moving on their own. Theirs was the same impulse that had taken their forebears across the Allegheny Mountains. And on the whole they were not unwelcome to the Mexican people of the Southwest, for some of the newcomers had merchandise which the settlers needed. The Mexican officials were not averse to buying goods from the Anglo wagon trains to avoid paying the duties exacted by the Mexican government. Anglo and Hispano wagons met on the Cimarron with increasing frequency. The wagons went on into Santa Fe.

The huge Spanish empire in the New World was falling apart. Mexico had won its independence. And gradually the United States government became interested in the whole southwestern development. One thing led to another and stirred up widespread border troubles. Texas revolted from Mexico and became a republic in 1836; it was annexed to the United States in 1845. At that time Texas took in parts of present-day Oklahoma, Kansas, New Mexico, Colorado and Wyoming.

The big tussle for territory between Mexico and the United States culminated in the Mexican War (1846-1848) which added California, Nevada, Utah and Arizona, and more of New Mexico, Colorado and Wyoming to the United States. The part of Colorado east of the Rockies was acquired by the Louisiana Purchase in 1803. In 1853 the Gadsden Purchase added territory to southern Arizona and New Mexico.

The Spanish and part-Spanish population in these regions totaled about a hundred and fifty thousand. Their civilization was something as follows, particularly in New Mexico, which had by far the largest number.

The majority lived in small farming communities with a fairly uniform pattern. "The settlers first laid out a *plaza,* or square, from which four principal streets led outward," write Allan Harper and his co-authors in *Man and Resources in the Middle Rio Grande Valley* (1943). "Building lots, called *solares,* were distributed to the settlers. Around the village would be scattered the *suertes,* or agricultural plots. . . . Beyond the agricultural fields was the *ejido,* or town common, used for grazing stock, for recreational purposes, and as a source of fuel and building materials. Smaller community pastures along the river were known as *dehesas* (meadows)." Nearly every family also had its *huerta* (orchard).

At sowing and harvest time neighbors did much of the work together. They raised "corn, wheat, beans, squash and some cotton" and several kinds of fruit: apricots, peaches and plums which were sun-dried for winter. They kept bees; honey was much used instead of sugar. Women spun and wove from cotton and the fleece of their sheep.

Adobe houses were built around patios. Families ran large and followed the patriarchal pattern. There was a great deal of family and communal responsibility. Taxes, paid in kind, were levied on what was produced; none on the land.

Here and there existed a mild form of peonage under *patrones*, most of whom claimed to be "pure Spanish." They were government officials, military officers and specially favored settlers who had obtained individual (as distinct from communal) land grants, and formed a limited rather benevolent economic aristocracy.

In general, farming was not to make money; it was a way of life—and as such it has been idealized by many writers, including Willa Cather and Mary Austin. It was not commercial farming chiefly because it could not have been, especially in New Mexico. For one thing, there was no ready market; for another, the narrow valleys and simple irrigation systems were not conducive to large production. Nature was not generous in New Mexico. There were droughts and floods, sometimes unfriendly Indians; pestilences often ravaged the population of this or that valley. The Spaniards had qualities that enabled them to stick it out, but the main factor in the survival of those who stayed was, as already indicated, their close and early connection—through intermarriage—with the friendly Indian tribes living in pueblos to whose agricultural techniques the Spaniards added their own native ability.

The village was usually within riding distance of a town, where the church, shops, whatever sort of government office there might be, and the houses of the more or less élite were built around the plaza. Towns were less business than cultural centers. There were the skilled craftsmen: shoemakers and saddlers, silversmiths, carpenters, toolmakers. The emphasis was on quality.

Education was largely limited to drilling in religious tenets under priests. Most of the people were illiterate.

Few in the village aspired to riches. There were stretches of land which no one bothered to claim. Grants rested on Old Spanish and Mexican laws; often they "overlapped," but there was no "friction" over who owned what, since "use and occupancy rather than ownership" were the determinants. There was little pushing for financial success. Money was scarce; many people seldom saw a coin. Goods were exchanged through barter.

The community, to quote further from *Man and Resources*, "had considerable vitality and self-sufficiency. It was well-adapted to the semi-arid environment of the Rio Grande. The centering of the settlers in the [village] was based on kinship . . . a uniformity of belief and custom."

Life had a slow, even, rhythmic roll, geared to routine labor, to nature, in a sense to eternity punctuated by the seasons of the year with their church festivals. It was "backward," "primitive" in today's view, but gracious, an echo of Spain (via Mexico). Those living it did not aspire to anything different. The conquistador type of person had had almost nothing to do with its unfolding through the centuries. A humble and meager civilization of the common people, created by themselves in their highland isolation, having something of grace and contentment, but leaving out the element of change, it could not last undisturbed indefinitely.

But much of it lasted for decades after the region became part of the United States. It is not entirely gone yet.

In 1848, under the Treaty of Guadalupe Hidalgo, the Spanish-speaking people were given their choice of citizenship, and one year in which to make up their minds. Mexico offered them land grants below the Rio Grande, but the majority preferred to stay where they were, where their families had lived for one or two hundred years, and to become citizens of the United States, whose government, they heard, promised to recognize their land holdings. In the preceding half century the Spanish and Mexican administrations had degenerated; some of the people, tired of petty corruption and abuses, thought life might be better under the new regime.

Since then their number has approximately doubled. Out of three hundred thousand all but some thirty thousand are in New Mexico. About two thousand Old Spanish families live in southern Colorado. Texas and Arizona have several hundred families each. In California—

In San Pedro, the town at Los Angeles Harbor where I lived back in the 1920s, I often watched an aloof, aristocratic old man riding on a gleaming black horse. There was something in his bearing and manner, his garb, saddle and bridle, that stirred my curiosity. Rider and horse seemed out of keeping with the busy modern harbor scene. By and by I learned that he was the head of a family of Spanish grandees who once upon a time had owned the land on the slopes above the port, and that there were other such old families in California, some right in the Los Angeles hurly-burly but not really of it, others secluding themselves on out-of-the-way ranches.

Since the 1930s, however, the situation has changed somewhat. Once torn internally, Mexico has become a leading American country. Also recently arrived Mexican Americans have begun to play a considerable part in the civic life of Los Angeles, which is occasionally referred to as the largest Mexican city outside of Mexico. Now the Old Spanish families whose members are emerging as public figures are shifting the emphasis from "Spanish American" or "of Spanish descent" to a "pride in Mexico" attitude.

This is also true of parts of Texas.

Elsewhere in the Southwest, though, and more conspicuously in New Mexico, a subtle withdrawal or aloofness still characterizes—with large exceptions—the Old Spanish element. They are old-line Americans, the oldest there are next to the Indians. But generally speaking they are *Spanish* Americans with stress on the "Spanish." In New Mexico and parts of Texas and Colorado they call themselves Hispanos. But this is a comparatively new term. "When I was a boy," S. Omar Barker, a writer living in Tecolotenos, New Mexico, tells me, "the old-time natives called themselves *Mejicanos* and thought nothing of it, just as they called us newcomers Americanos. Political 'education' brought about the use of 'Spanish American' and 'Hispano.' Common people used to take it for granted that they were American citizens and were not sensitive in general about terminology. Many, of course, had been Mexicans, that is, citizens of Mexico." Now the majority resent being referred to as Mexicans or "Mexes," indeed some don't like to be called Spanish Americans, preferring "Americans of Spanish descent." Technically they are full-fledged citizens of the United States, actually they are as patriotic as any other group in the population when it comes to buying war bonds or going into military service or dying at Bataan, as many did in 1941-1942; but—

The *but* is complex and obtrusive, particularly in New Mexico, where the 270,000 Hispanos about equal the Anglos numerically. Before the opening of oil fields and potash mines and the introduction of commercial cotton-growing which increased the Anglo population the Hispanos outnumbered them.

The Hispanos' presence in so great a proportion makes New Mexico one of the most dramatic states in the Republic. It is the only state with a bilingual administration and legislature. One need not know English to serve on a jury there. In large part this is to be ascribed to the influence of Octaviano Ambrozio Larrazolo, a native of southern Chihuahua, Mexico. He came to Tucson at the age of eleven in 1870 as a protégé of Bishop J. B. Salpointe who five years later became the archbishop of Santa Fe and took the boy along.

At eighteen Larrazolo went back to Tucson as a teacher; at twenty he was a high school principal in El Paso County, Texas; at twenty-one the district clerk at El Paso. At twenty-nine he was admitted to the bar, and two years later was elected district attorney of western Texas. In the middle 1890s he moved back to New Mexico, settling in Las Vegas and becoming a full-fledged politician in the Democratic Party, an outspoken champion of the native Spanish-speaking population, and an orator in Spanish and English well known throughout the Southwest. Lansing B. Bloom, in the *Dictionary of American Biography*, describes him as "tall, of vigorous frame, and handsome, with the proud, courtly and punctilious bearing of a Spanish gentleman. . . . An ardent patriot of his adopted country," he ran for Congress in 1906, '08 and '10, losing each time by a few hundred votes. The Republican Party was riding high in that period; so he switched over to it, thinking he might thus have more of a chance to benefit the Hispanos and himself. He was a bit of a demagogue.

Just then New Mexico was preparing for statehood and, according to P. A. F. Walter in the *New Mexico Historical Review* (April 1932), Larrazolo was mainly responsible for the strong provisions in the State constitution "guaranteeing the rights of the Spanish-speaking voters against disfranchisement and protecting them against discrimination on account of language or . . . descent. It assured the use of the Spanish language officially, together with English, for years to come." At the state Republican convention in 1911 Larrazolo proposed a native New Mexican for governor, but his candidate was not nominated. In 1918 he was elected to that office himself; ten years later to the United States Senate. Although he was almost reactionary in some ways, with his death in 1930 "one of the most effective representatives of the native people of the Southwest" departed from the American scene.

The political and cultural accommodations and compromises between the Anglos and Hispanos in New Mexico are interesting, even impressive. But the provisions in the state constitution which Larrazolo had meant as a protection for Hispanos against discrimination have not penetrated into all phases of New Mexico's life—partly because the Hispanos have neglected to take advantage of them.

Many of the older Hispanos speak no English either because they don't know it or because they prefer not to. Here and there their language is in a very limited way the classic Spanish of Cervantes (analogous to the Chaucer English spoken in isolated mountain districts in Tennessee and the Carolinas). The older Spanish women usually know no English at all. Since the 1930s, when a state law was enacted making the teaching of English compulsory in all schools, a majority of the younger people have learned English, but they continue to be conscious Hispanos. They use Spanish at home and, to a large extent, among themselves.

There is no official compulsion or encouragement for the Anglos to learn Spanish, but most of the old-timers know some. Omar Barker tells me that around where he lives Anglo "ranchmen, cowboys and merchants, especially Jewish merchants, who speak the rural Spanish idiom almost as well as they do English are as common as stray dogs. I know many an Anglo lawyer in New Mexico who can plead his case in either tongue."

But "educated" Anglos who speak Spanish appear to be proportionately fewer than "uneducated" ones. With "education" apparently goes a sort of cultural arrogance. It is especially noticeable in the southeastern sections of the state. Barker explains that "most Anglos expect the Hispanos to accommodate themselves to the United-States-ism of language, since they and their offspring will continue to be citizens of an English-speaking country." As for the "educated" Anglos, many "are simply too lazy" to learn Spanish "or too imbued with the typical American unconcern for 'foreign' languages—call it what you will. It is an attitude I personally dislike," says Barker.

The Anglo-Hispano relationship is full of subtleties and contradictory facts open to various interpretations, depending on one's attitude toward over-privilege and under-privilege, on whether one is an Anglo or a Hispano, conservative, liberal or radical.

Since about 1920 hundreds of Hispanos have gained local prominence in New Mexico, a few through the Southwest, a few in Washington, a few in the country as a whole. Some have come from the comparatively small number of well-to-do Old Spanish families, others from the large masses of poor people.

Perhaps the best-known contemporary Hispano is United States Senator Dennis Chavez of Albuquerque, a figure in Democratic Party politics. One of New Mexico's two current congressmen-at-large is Antonio M. Fernandez of Santa Fe, also a Democrat. There is a kind of gentlemen's agreement that, insofar as it can be worked out, Hispanos and Anglos share evenly in the state's delegation to Congress. In some of the counties and towns where the two elements are about equally divided this is true also in local politics. State offices are open to Hispanos and Anglos alike, but because of their greater aggressiveness and their economic superiority Anglos fill them rather oftener than Hispanos.

Miguel Otero was governor of New Mexico (before it was a State) under McKinley and a personal friend of the President. His half-Hispano son of the same name, former district attorney and state commander of the American Legion, is a high-ranking wartime officer in the United States Army.

Manuel B. Otero, a noted football player in the Southwest during the early 1900s, ran several times for the governorship; he was defeated along with his party, not because he was Spanish. For a time he was collector of customs at El Paso. The Oteros are a well-to-do ranching family.

Here is the career of Felix Martinez, a native of Taos: At fourteen around 1875 he went to work in a store in Trinidad, Colorado. In his twenties he was in business on his own in Las Vegas, New Mexico, where he later published a Spanish-language newspaper. He was elected to the territorial legislature in 1888, to the senate in 1892. Later he moved to El Paso and became a successful banker and realtor and a civic leader. He took the initiative in organizing the Rio Grande Water Users' Association and in promoting the Elephant Butte Dam, built by the United States Reclamation Service. Shortly before his death in 1916 he served as regional director of the Federal Reserve Bank of the El Paso-Dallas district.

Pascual Martinez, supervisor of the Carson National Forest at Taos, has been an official of the United States Forestry Service for over twenty-five years.

Fabian Garcia, adopted child in a poor family, brown as a Yaqui Indian, was for forty-odd years professor of horticulture at the New Mexico Agricultural and Mineralogical College—"beloved throughout the state by Anglos and Hispanos alike," I am told by an Anglo who has known him for decades.

Luis E. Armijo, district judge, and his brother José, district attorney, both at Las Vegas, come of a moderately well-off family which has long exercised political influence in the state. José's wife is an Anglo from Washington, D. C.

Antonio Lucero, a Democrat, was elected secretary of state in a year when the majority of Spanish votes were Republican, indicating that Anglo votes turned the balance in his favor. His daughter, Aurora Lucero White, is active in New Mexico's educational world.

José D. Sena of Santa Fe was clerk of the New Mexico Supreme Court for nearly thirty years, and a sponsor of the Santa Fe Fiesta in which he often played a Franciscan monk in the De Vargas pageant.

Ernest Maes, formerly secretary of the National Indian Institute, of which John Collier was president, is chief of an educational mission to Bolivia, a cooperative project of the Office of Inter-American Affairs and the Bolivian government.

Manuel A. Sanchez, son of a substantial *paisano* (rural) family, is an ex-Surveyor General of the United States Land Office and a leading member of the Santa Fe bar.

Another Sanchez—George I.—an authority on Latin American education, formerly at the University of New Mexico, is now with the University of Texas; author of *Forgotten People* (1940), a scholarly

study of the Hispano in New Mexico, especially in Taos County. In this book and in papers submitted to the White House Conference on Rural Education (1944) and other educational gatherings, Professor Sanchez has underlined the unfortunate fact that educational practices in New Mexico, "patterned after those developed in the Middle West and in the East for peoples and conditions vastly different from those obtaining here" are "a ridiculous procedure"; and criticized the inequitable distribution of educational funds in favor of Anglo-populated counties.

Andrew R. Cordova, native of Las Vegas, descended from people who have continuously lived in New Mexico for over two hundred and fifty years, is an outstanding agricultural economist; a co-author of *Man and Resources*.

The Espinosas of Socorro and Albuquerque—thirteen brothers and sisters: lawyers, doctors, public officials, teachers—are perhaps the best-known Hispano family in New Mexico. Like the Oteros and Armijos, they are among the socially élite in the state.

On the other hand, a majority of Hispanos do not enjoy the full benefits of citizenship because of "race" and language. Marginal people, poor and unaggressive, somewhat darker than the unsunburned Anglos, most of them live in isolated villages, where they run their own life more or less as they want to, as they have for centuries. When they leave the village, however, and come in contact with strategic economic factors in the Anglo-dominated larger towns, they run into discrimination. This is especially true in the southeastern counties where the Anglos are comparative newcomers from Texas, Oklahoma and the Middle West. Here and there the average Hispanos discover that some of the well-to-do and educated Hispanos whose immediate economic interests are tied up with those of the Anglo owners are closer to the latter than to them.

Omar Barker, who is of the more conservative persuasion, admits that "there is some segregation, apparently by mutual consent, in the social life of the two 'races' (I don't like this word), but that does not mean that one is treated any different from the other in all matters of citizenship. Anglo doctors and dentists give Hispano patients the same consideration as Anglos. Barbers cut their hair. Clerks wait on them in stores, waiters serve them in restaurants, bankers handle their accounts, and so on. In fact, except for the medical and dental professions, in which Hispanos are scarce, so many Spanish Americans are intermingled in the services of daily living that to say they are treated as second-rate citizens is to say that they so treat themselves."

There is something to this, but I think not quite as Barker means it.

Why are Hispano students excluded from fraternities at the state university?

Psychologically, as already noted, the mass of Spanish Americans have nothing in common with the aggressive conquistadores of four hundred years ago. They have been no match for the Anglos who, to quote from an article in the December 1944 *Survey Graphic* by Professor Quincy Guy Burris of New Mexico Highlands University at Las Vegas, "came from the East with purpose in their eyes, commerce in their minds, and a drive in their temperaments which roiled the clear waters of Hispano tranquility." With these new conquerors came "new customs and new laws: taxes had to be paid in money, not in kind; a new and exact system of land titles speaking ownership rather than communal use; money trading, great cattle enterprises; land speculation, dry farming, home-steading, and cash crops."

"Ruthless politicians and merchants acquired their stock, their water rights, their lands," says George I. Sanchez in *Forgotten People*. "The land grants became involved in legal battles. Was the grant genuine, . . . was it registered? Who were the grantees, who the descendants, where the boundaries, and by whose authority? Defenseless before the onslaught of an intangible yet superior force, the economic foundations of New Mexican life were undermined and began to crumble. As their economy deteriorated so did the people, for their way of life was based on and identified with the agrarian economy which they had built through many generations," whereas now business—high production and sale at a good price—became the center of life in New Mexico. Nearly everything was subordinated to it.

"The codicil of the treaty of 1848," continues Mr. Burris, "assured holders of land grants of their security if the grants could be proved valid. In 1854 the United States Government seated a Surveyor General in Santa Fe. For sixty years his office fought to disentangle the coils of titles in the mazes of casual boundaries and clouded definitions. [The Spanish American], without cash, sold a piece of land. He sold another piece of land to pay the new taxes. In eighty years he lost two million acres of his private lands.

"Of his communal lands, used freely [before the Anglos arrived] by entire communities for grazing, he lost 1,700,000 acres in the same eighty years. The Federal Government took vast tracts for national forests and for the encouragement of railroads. The State took eight hundred thousand acres for the support of education"—mostly, as it has worked out, for the education of the Anglo children.

Land changed hands similarly in other southwestern states. "By force, by cajolery, by politics," says Robert West Howard in his book

Two-Billion Acre Farm, "Yankee realtors cleared the *Californio* ranch owners off their wastelands and began to develop homesites." They bought up properties running into tens and hundreds of thousands of acres at twenty-five and fifty cents an acre.

But in California this procedure touched only a few hundred Spanish Americans; there were a mere twelve hundred there all told when the region became a state in 1850. Also, by and large, the new owners in California did develop the land, did make it productive where it had not been before; in New Mexico, with its large Hispanic population, the process had—with many exceptions of course—an undermining effect. Since the 1870s widespread overgrazing by profit-eager Anglos has reduced sections of the once useful land to—or almost to— wasteland.

Hispano families retain most of their agricultural acres along the Rio Grande and its tributaries but have lost nearly all their grazing lands. In a vast majority of cases the present individual holdings are too small for families to maintain themselves on a sound economic level. They live in the same old villages, in adobe huts—a life still marked by considerable charm and wisdom based on a sense of values and proportions harking back to the pre-Anglo period, but whose limitations are too obvious for wholehearted intelligent enthusiasm.

It would be pointless to argue who is to blame, the Anglos or the Hispanos. The authors of *Man and Resources*, which covers the reduction to virtual wasteland of the Middle Rio Grande Valley, attribute it chiefly to economic and physical factors. Without underestimating these factors, I think that is too simple. The situation must be ascribed in considerable part to the ill-enacted drama of ethnic differences—so far much of it deplorable because played in unequal roles, but astir, I believe, with desirable possibilities.

In 1939 Daniel T. V. Valdes, then with the WPA Program of Adult Education and Recreation in Colorado, sent me his mimeographed study "The Spanish-Speaking People of the Southwest" which noted the differences between the Anglos and the Hispanos (or Latin Americans, to use his phrase) that revolve around physical appearance, religion, language, institutions, personal intuitions and character molds, philosophical perspective and outlook on life. "The Anglo," he says, "is the servant of time; to the Latin there is time for everything. The Anglo is practical and wants organization. The Latin is theoretical and individualistic. The Anglo is supreme in science because he places economic well-being and wealth above everything else. The Latin excels in human relations; friendship is the most important element in his life. To him work is an auxiliary of life, not the main objective. He is more interested in who you are than in what you are. He knows how to play; a recreation program such as ours, for example, in Mexico would be unnecessary. After making a study of these . . . differences, one can see the true causes of the main perplexing problems which arise when the Anglos and the Spanish Americans live in the same towns, trade at the same stores, work in the same shops, go to the same schools—"

Since the middle 1930s a good many people in New Mexico, both Hispanos and Anglos, and a few outside the state have done some serious if inconclusive thinking about all this. Some are people of influence and ability. Some are on the faculties of the state university at Albuquerque, Highlands University and the State College of Agriculture and Mechanic Arts. A few are with the Indian and Forestry Services, the Farm Security Administration and other Federal agencies working in the Southwest. They are groping for a program through which to repair the damage both in itself and in connection with other problems.

Some Anglos lately awakened to it all sentimentalize about the Hispano, bend over backward to glamorize him, to rhapsodize about New Mexico's Spanish past. But they are too unrealistic to be of much help. They are perhaps no better than the Anglos who deny anything is amiss, who say the Hispano is well off in his meager villages: why not leave him alone?

The realistically intelligent New Mexicans of all backgrounds—and like-minded people elsewhere (John Collier and William A. Brophy, for instance, the former and the present commissioners of Indian Affairs in Washington; Carey McWilliams, a native of Colorado now in Los Angeles; and Allan G. Harper, executive officer of the Interdepartmental Rio Grande Board at Albuquerque in 1942)—know that general economic conditions in New Mexico are at the core of the problem. From whatever angle they view the Anglo-Hispano tensions, they see the incongruities: the twentieth-century United States and sixteenth-century Spain and Mexico; wealth and poverty; town and village; natural beauty and the erosion run-off; the "Sunshine State's" healthy climate attracting the ill from the East and Middle West and the prevalence of disease among the Hispanos born in New Mexico. Some feel that once the economic problem is solved the ethnic one will largely disappear; that the thing to do is to bring on equality of job and business opportunities. Others believe that the economic and ethnic interplay is more complex, that both aspects call for simultaneous attention, that at some points the ethnic problem comes first.

There are stubborn facts about the Hispano of New Mexico. "The will to do sleeps in Juan," says Professor Burris. "He wants better things, better ways, but he has no drive toward them. . . . Midwives deliver all his children. Two lie under a cross in the graveyard by the church. The five who live have a three to two chance of becoming adults. All five have already weathered rickets. . . . Diphtheria comes hand in hand with the late winter months. Smallpox may touch the village; typhoid strikes mysteriously and without warning. Measles, chicken pox, and whooping cough keep the children from school. . . ." No wonder his will to do sleeps! There is need, to begin with, of an adequate health and preventive-medicine program. There is need of an integrated economic-social project like the T.V.A.

The Hispano believes in education but, in view of the Anglo-dominated setup, distrusts its effects. According to Burris, "he has seen . . . children leave the village and come back bitter." What's the use, he thinks, of educating his? Their chances for white-collar jobs are limited. Most Anglo employers don't inquire into their qualifications; the fact that they are Hispanos rules them out. What's the use of a schooling which opens their mind and vision to a world of wider horizons, when their opportunities to enter that world remain closed. As things go, it is perhaps better for one's children to stay uneducated workers and peasants. For that is what a lot of the Hispanos are— peasants in the European sense, with more and more of them living on inadequate acreage.

The 1940-1945 wartime manpower crisis lessened the Hispanos' employment predicament but, it is to be feared, only temporarily. The probability is that a few years after the war the group will once more be limited to work on road and section gangs, as cowhands, sheep-shearers and house servants.

To say, as Anglos often do of Hispanos, "They're getting along all right; at that they're happier than we are," begs the question. The Hispanos' disinclination to push or fight their way, commonly regarded as "indolence" or "apathy," more surely indicates a different scale of what is worthwhile. Their reluctance to fight for advantages may be called "Lazy faire," or it may be linked to an innate sense of dignity. The Hispanos are philosophical. With all their material disadvantages, they are more firmly rooted—they "belong" much more—in New Mexico than the Anglos.

I said that some of the facts about the Hispano are stubborn, an adjective which fits him rather generally—or its synonym "indomitable," depending on whether one is irritated or admiring. Some Anglos consider him stupid partly because he is reluctant to exert himself in ways that impress them. Actually he is likely to be a pretty wise *hombre*. He has been called simple; he isn't really; no peasant is. Bound to a long experience which happens to be at odds with the present, he is deeply complicated.

The Hispano's local community, much as it has changed in the last fifty years, still has a strong hold on him; it is the place where he feels utterly at home. "Most of the villages are still isolated," says Carey McWilliams in *Brothers Under the Skin* (1941). "Many of them are extremely difficult to find and can only be reached by barely passable roads." They have no telephones, no electric light, few automobiles; some have no mail service. "Old water-driven stone mills, incredibly ancient and crude, are still in use. In many of these villages may be found some of the most interesting specimens of church architecture in America. Some of the villages are indescribably picturesque and lovely," but also scenes of sordid economic conditions. They issue, says one of my Anglo correspondents who is a native of New Mexico, "from the commercial uses to which the land and the streams and the minerals have been put by modern industrialists. I know dozens of villages which practice a way of life that is incompatible with modern industrial America. The land around the hamlets is worn out, the population is too great for anything like a successful standard of living. . . . In many cases whole villages are exploited by some member of the Hispano group."

Vaguely on the defensive, the Hispano is extremely reticent, a man apart. But there is much more to him than meets the average Anglo eye. He descends from men who, says Professor Burris, "have for three centuries withstood drought and flood, tilled the land faithfully, adapted their building to the contours and rigors of the country, maintained the solidarity of their families." He has a "staying power we can ill afford to throw away." He does not propose to see it thrown away. He is an American, and my guess is that, way down in him somewhere, perhaps not consciously, he is determined to become part of his country—on American terms which have no relationship to the worst features of the present-day dominant Anglo attitude.

In fact, as I have said, the Spanish American is a deeply-rooted part of the country.

His ancestors introduced Colonial-Spanish architecture. The Monterrey house is in evidence with various modifications in many parts of California. The Mexican hacienda, built around a center patio, is increasingly popular. Santa Barbara, California, has several distinctive public buildings designed under the Spanish influence. The newest buildings at the University of New Mexico—including some which house fraternities that bar Hispanos and Indians from membership—combine Spanish and Indian styles.

Thousands of place names in the Southwest are Spanish.

"The American cowboy," comments Professor H. E. Bolton of the University of California, "inherited his trade, his horse, his outfit, his lingo and his methods from the Spaniard."

In an article in *New Mexico Magazine* (December 1942) dealing with the "lingo" part of this contribution, Omar Barker writes: "Just as the cowboy 'borrowed' much of his traditional 'riggin'' from the vaquero, and adapted it to his own needs, so, too, he borrowed freely from this vaquero's word supply, which he also adapted. He borrowed 'by ear,' of course, and so plentifully that today much typical western terminology owes its origin to Spanish, however little it sometimes resembles the original either in spelling or pronunciation." Ramon F. Adams' *Western Words: A Dictionary of the Range, Cow Camp and Trail* (1945) is full of adapted words. "Vamoose," for example, comes from the Spanish *vamos*, "savvy" from *Quien sabe?*, "stampede" from *estampida*, "hoosegow" from *juzgado* (hooth-gah'oo), "lariat" from *la reata*, "cinch" from *cincha*, "hackamore" from *jáquima* (hah'ke-mah), "chaps" from *chaparejos*, "ranch" from *rancho*. Many were adopted outright, some only with a change in accent: *corral, pronto, pinto, loco, adobe, cañon, mesquite, bronco, rodeo, mesa, arroyo, bolero, sombrero, amigo, hacienda, patio, adios, fiesta, siesta, plaza*—

Gradually, encouraged by an understanding of his position and worth on the part of a growing number of Anglos, and inspired by the emergence of some Hispanos who neither repudiated nor exploited him as they rose to prominence, the Hispano is beginning to stir, to aim his long-dormant powers at present problems and at the future. He will not want to be pushed around any more. Nor will he want to be pushed into sudden "progress." He says "*poco a poco*," and does *poco a poco*.

But his horizons are expanding; he is done with isolation. His sons have died at Bataan and elsewhere in the Pacific, in Africa, Italy, France and Germany. Men of his own background have spoken words that ring true to him, linking his predicament to the problems in the country as a whole, in the hemisphere and the world. Senator Chavez said in 1942: "Our nation is now involved in a tremendous war for existence and in this titanic struggle most of the Latin-American nations are allied with us. We are all brothers in the fight for the four freedoms. How, therefore, can . . . equality of opportunity be denied us within the United States?"*

* Dennis Chavez, a man of humble beginnings, means business. Deeply versed in the difficulties of his own people in New Mexico, he has consistently fought to get a fair deal for the Puerto Ricans. In the summer of 1945 he stayed in the struggle for a Fair Employment Practice Committee when no other Senator would lead that cause.

In the final chapters of *Forgotten People*, George I. Sanchez makes several recommendations: for the adaptation of education to Hispanic needs, for the modernization of agricultural techniques, and for the facilitation of buying and selling through setting up cooperatives. "Medical clinics," he goes on, "are an urgent need. This is an area where socialized medicine is certainly justified. Private practitioners cannot serve these small, poverty-stricken New Mexican communities and make a living. Credit associations that will help tide small farmers and craftsmen over periods of economic scarcity need to be organized. . . ."

Sanchez is soundly interested in "the proper incorporation of the [Spanish-speaking] New Mexican into the [larger] American fold. That incorporation requires that the New Mexican be fitted to make his contribution to American civilization. His ability to contribute, and the nature of his contribution, is suggested by the tenacity with which he has maintained himself, his economy, and his social structure on this forbidding frontier for more than three centuries. That contribution might well embody worthy elements of his culture—language, music, folklore, architecture, foods, crafts and customs. The New Mexican's filial respect, his love of home and of country, and his fortitude in the face of adversity are potential resources to Americanism. The democracy inherent in New Mexican culture bespeaks . . . preparedness to enhance American life. . . . Released from the handicaps of his present environment, he need no longer be a problem child, a culturally unassimilated subject, but a respected and self-respecting American. . . ."

Efforts to bring this about are scant and unintegrated but serious and encouraging. The authors of *Man and Resources* refer favorably to the Taos county project which aims to "bring the needs of the villages . . . into touch with the public and private agencies in position to render practical and constructive aid in social as well as economic matters. Centering in the Harwood Foundation at Taos, the project has encouraged local leadership in . . . programs of self-help in developing water, correcting erosion conditions, organizing health co-operatives, improving schools, etc. A conspicuous success has been the traveling 'Bookmobile' which has succeeded in taking much needed reading matter to the scattered and isolated villages. . . ."

Early in 1939 I received a large four-page bilingual leaflet entitled "Call to the First Congress of the Mexican and Spanish American Peoples of the United States on March 24, 25 and 26, 1939, at Albuquerque." It was addressed to "all labor organizations, fraternal and cultural and religious groups, civic and social and political clubs, and Mexican honorary commissions." It read in part: "Today more than two million Mexican and Spanish American people in the United States are facing the consequences of increasing economic and cultural poverty. Their conditions of work, housing, health, education and opportunity menace their very existence. . . . In scattered localities through the Southwest various groups have focused their attention on the issues with varying degrees of success. The experience of these groups has demonstrated that only concerted discussion and action can achieve progress toward a significant improvement of these conditions. It is recognized that the problems of the Mexican Americans may differ somewhat from those of the Spanish Americans, and the problems of the non-citizen may differ from both the other groups. Nevertheless these are differences of degree rather than of kind. . . . All three groups face essentially the same discrimination, the same restriction of opportunity, the same condition of employment and living. Only the unity of all three and the cooperation of other progressive Americans in constructive thought and action will bring about positive advances." The agenda included discussions of labor, farming, housing and health, education, discrimination, and youth problems. The call was signed by scores of Hispano, Mexican and Anglo leaders in New Mexico, Texas, California, Colorado, Arizona and elsewhere.

But the Congress was not held. For one thing, its organization was not well handled. And perhaps the attempt was a little ahead of its time. Essentially it was a capital idea and something like it is bound to be tried again. Programs of action are sure to develop during the postwar period under the common sponsorship of all the groups involved, not forgetting the Indians. They will succeed in proportion to the sincerity with which the groups accept each other's differences, and to their mutual consciousness that they all, with their diverse outlooks and mental-emotional tempos, are integral parts of the population; that they can enrich the life of the Southwest and the United States only if they seek and find the common ground that indubitably exists, that is part of the essence of America.

Under the Treaty of Guadalupe, the Rio Grande flowing east by south from El Paso (Juárez) to its mouth on the Gulf at Brownsville became about three-fifths of the 1,600-mile boundary between the United States and Mexico; the rest is a line zigzagging westward from El Paso to Tijuana.

There can be no doubt that in the second half of the nineteenth century not a few people crossed over from Old Mexico, but no one can say how many. Nor do we know how many stayed and where they settled in the immense, sparsely inhabited territory which now forms nearly one-third of the United States. They probably merged into the pre-1848 Spanish population or into the Indian tribes, depending on whether their Spanish or Indian ancestry showed more clearly in their faces.

Motion pictures of the 1910s and '20s emphasized again and again that "bandits" or "desperadoes"—portrayed as evil characters—came over the border to raid the American pioneers. Actually, many of these rough fellows were Mexican patriots—of the Robin Hood type—who resented the United States' seizure of territories which had been Spanish and Mexican for centuries. Some of them came from the Spanish element on the United States' side of the border who did not accept the Treaty. These "desperadoes" operated with the "bandits" from across the line.

The movies never showed the plain folk arriving less dramatically with a less spectacular mission than the desperadoes'. They were the ordinary mestizos in whose veins coursed as yet somewhat confusedly a mingling of Spanish and Indian blood; confusedly because they were descendants of both conqueror and conquered, the feared and the frightened. Besides, they were Mexico's downtrodden and pushed-around. Propelled by the idea, however vague, of earning enough to eat and live, or to get away from local violence, they went over the line—in many cases without realizing there was a line.

They just walked or rode north as people from Mexico had been going north for centuries. They were not immigrants in the usual sense, conscious of leaving one country for another. They experienced no thrill of reaching the New World after a stormy voyage from the Old. There was no Statue of Liberty—no Castle Garden or Ellis Island, no Immigration Service. The Indian side of their background was old in the New World, their Spanish strain was not exactly new here, either.

Born and raised in primitive villages huddling in out-of-the-way canyons of Sonora, they had not taken in the fact of the new 1848 border between their country and the domain to the north. Many were still under the impression that the United States' Southwest was still part of Mexico, at least for all practical purposes. To most of those who had heard of it, the "border" was a fiction; it was not systematically patrolled until the middle 1920s. And so, back in the late nineteenth century and the early twentieth, there arose the "border complex," as Carey McWilliams calls it—defining it as the psychological heart of "a very colorful life and a dubious traffic."

From the beginning, the human traffic has been a two-way business. The Mexican migratory workers have been coming over and going back, coming over again. The early ones, say from 1850 to 1905, were mostly cowboys, shepherds, sheep-shearers and all-around ranch laborers hiring out seasonally to both Spanish and Anglo ranchers. Others were just people with hands and stomachs ready to do anything that turned up. Then, the work season over, the majority returned not so much from the United States to their native land of Mexico as from where they had worked to the village they called home. The Mexican government had no more interest in this traffic than had the American government. It just went on.

From the time the two-way migration began, the psychology of the Mexicans has been that of a conquered, abused people, and the Anglos of Texas, New Mexico, Colorado, Arizona and California assumed a superior attitude toward them. This attitude still is the reference point of relationship between most Mexicans and most of the English-speaking people in the United States who come in contact with them. Too few Anglos realize that behind his humble, often shabby exterior the Mexican migratory worker takes much pride in being Mexican. Measured against U. S. American standards, the Mexican has more than his share of flaws and weaknesses; but like the Hispano he possesses also a firm personal integrity and codes of behavior and aspirations that in relative worth may be at least equivalent to those of the Anglos. He has a case of his own.

For a while the Mexican two-way migration was a matter of many driblets, of individuals and families and small groups arriving and departing with the work seasons. The Mexican revolutions prior to 1911 had been largely palace upheavals, clique against clique. Now, with the second decade of the twentieth century, a real revolutionary wind blew hard and strong over the high-plateau country and through the long-dormant minds of its people, ninety per cent of whom were peasants and workers. It was a fierce storm beating against oppression, poverty, ignorance, backwardness. But the changes which it brought dislocated large numbers of people. "Thousands lost what little they had," says Daniel T. Valdes in the study to which I have already referred, "and began to roam from place to place, then finally were attracted by the peace and security offered by the United States. As they began to pass in great numbers into the states of our Southwest, they were joined by thousands of others who were tired of facing danger and death, and preferred to seek refuge across the international border. . . ."

This dovetailed into the agricultural expansion in the United States, where "farmers began to look . . . for cheap labor to harvest their crops of cotton, sugar beets and fruit." Labor contractors were sent "into the northern states of Mexico to lure the hundreds of thousands of peons who were still unwanted children of the revolution. . . . Hand-bills and posters eloquently telling of the wonders of the country to the north and its resplendent opportunities went out by the millions from Spanish-set presses." The railroad companies, which also wanted cheap labor, got in on it too. "Transportation was offered free. . . . *Reenganches*, freight and broken-down passenger trains loaded with hundreds of Mexican families became a familiar sight in all of the railroad centers of the Southwest."

Labor shortages in the United States during World War I, together with continued instability in Mexico, further stimulated this migration. Except for the depression years of 1920-1921, the movement increased after the war, growing in volume when the so-called quota law cut off a free flow of immigration from Europe and reduced the reservoirs of easily exploitable labor. It reached its peak in the period of Coolidge Prosperity ending in the crash of 1929.

The quota law did not apply to Mexico. Given the nature and length of the border and the accompanying "complex," it would have been next to impossible to enforce. Nor did the southwestern agricultural and industrial interests with their powerful lobbies in Washington want it applied. Only a few migration controls were established.

Even before World War I, small trickles of Mexicans had begun to run from the Southwest into the Middle West and toward the north. By the middle 1920s they flowed in streams, and toward the end of the Coolidge era Mexicans were noticeable elements in and around Chicago, in Kansas City, in St. Paul and Minneapolis and many other centers. Mexican agents in San Antonio and elsewhere in the Southwest were taking "orders" for labor also from farmers' and food processors' associations in Arkansas and Missouri, Montana and Idaho, Nebraska and even Michigan; from cotton planters in Tennessee and Alabama where the Negro labor supply was dwindling because of colored migrations north.

Late in the 1920s not less than a million and a half Mexicans were north of the border. Well over half were in families; perhaps one hundred thousand children had been born in the previous few years. Over a million lived in the Southwest, mostly in Texas and Southern California, but large groups were also in New Mexico, Colorado, Arizona and central California. Wherever they went, they did most of the seasonal agricultural work. Thousands found employment in lumber yards, canneries and packing houses.

With sub-standard wages, no unions and almost no legal protection, they were generally abused by both employers and labor contractors. On agricultural jobs they worked, as the Negroes say in the South, "from can to can't"—from the time you can see in the morning till you can't at night.

Seasonal agriculture jerked them hither and yon. This month they worked "in nuts" in Ventura County, next month "in tomatoes" or "in melons" scores or even hundreds of miles away. One week they were in a section gang near Barstow, the next in a sewer ditch on a Los Angeles subdivision. Some traveled in special labor trains, busses or trucks in charge of labor agents; others free-lanced it—in jammed jalopies, afoot, by interurban trains or trolleys.

While "in lettuce," "in oranges" or "in beans," they lived in dangerously unsanitary, inhumanly isolated labor camps, or in their prehistoric Fords and Chevvies, or in leaky lean-tos or obsolete railroad cars on sidings, under bits of canvas or simply under trees or the open sky. Between jobs, which meant mainly the winter months, hundreds of thousands filled the slums of Los Angeles, San Antonio and the border towns between.

Few Mexicans took out naturalization papers. For one thing, they still felt the "border complex." By now they were aware of the line all right; they had to go through the United States Immigration Stations or evade the patrols. But the old idea that the Southwest was an extension of Mexico persisted in them. That their children born in San Antonio or El Centro were officially citizens of the United States did not register its significance.

The families' constant moving about made for haphazard education. Besides, many Mexican parents had small use for education in general, and American education in particular—it alienated their children from them.

Wherever the Mexicans went they carried their own culture. This was a matter of the Catholic religion (although not practiced too faithfully and formally), the Spanish language as they spoke it, Indian fatalism, endless and rather elaborate family observances, very close family affection and mutual protection, emphasis on friendship, unfailing courtesy, a deep human warmth and, underlying some behavior which looked like shiftlessness to the Anglos, a resistance to pressures aimed at making them into something they are not. Catching glimpses of their life in and around Los Angeles during 1922-1929, I often thought that the Mexicans, scarcely touching the bottom rung on the social-economic ladder, were culturally and morally superior to many U. S. Americans climbing furiously up the ladder.

Others have come to the same conclusion. "As a high school boy in Illinois back in the 1920s," a man wrote to me in the early '40s, "I peddled papers in the factory workers' section of our town, and discovered that the Mexicans could be trusted much more than the 'Whites' to pay for the paper. If they couldn't afford to keep up their subscription they almost invariably told me so before it expired, while many 'White' subscribers just stalled off paying week after week."

"In a spiritual sense," a Los Angeles Anglo said to me in 1942, "the Mexicans in California are more civilized than the Anglos. Their Catholicism is unique: an amalgam of the old native Indian faiths and the Roman. Their religion is like a third foot to them: they're just born with it. An Irish Catholic fights over any smear of his faith; a Mexican only shrugs or grins. He is rarely if ever anti-Semitic or anything like that. . . . Mexicans are not bothered by trivialities that give Anglos actual neuroses. They are born artists to a degree we cannot approach. They have a sense of form and color, and the awful curse of 'keeping up with the Joneses' does not afflict them."

Too much cannot be said about Mexican courtesy, and I can't refrain from quoting a passage from Charles Macomb Flandrau's delightful classic *Viva Mexico!*: "I have heard a half-naked laborer bent double under a sack of coffee-berries murmur, 'With your permission,' as he passed in front of a bricklayer who was repairing a wall."

The Depression of 1930-1939 cut the Mexican migrants to the quick. For lack of markets fruit dropped off trees, vegetables rotted or were not planted. Railroad section gangs shrank down to a foreman and a couple of "White" laborers. And having lived from hand to mouth even in so-called good times, the majority of Mexicans had no reserves; so now they went either on relief or back to Mexico.

Not that none had returned to Mexico during the late 1920s; many thousands had crossed and recrossed the border several times a year. Some had gone back home for good because of the prejudice against them in the United States, and also because economic, social and political conditions in Mexico had much improved. Now, however, between three and four hundred thousand left in a few years.

"Dilapidated passenger trains filled to overflowing with Mexican families," writes Mr. Valdes, "again became a familiar sight in the Southwest; only this time the engines were turned southward. . . . Hot, puffing Fords, hardly recognizable because of their great burden of humanity and belongings, filled the border towns waiting to recross the bridge. . . ."

During the previous decade, Mr. Valdes continues bitterly, these people "had made uneconomical industries pay huge profits. . . . They had done the hard, backbreaking work shunned by the more fortunate Americans. But they had not prospered. City and state agencies, ever anxious to get rid of public charges, offered free transportation and food as far as the border. To encourage them to return home, the Mexicans [here and there] were denied relief. Newspapers and patriotic organizations raised the cry, 'Send them back to Mexico! American jobs for American workers.' . . . The Mexican government, cooperating with American cities and relief agencies, sent trains to the border towns to transport its impoverished nationals to their homes."

But over a million Mexicans remained north of the border.

Among them were hundreds of families with children who were natives and therefore citizens of the United States. Some families had managed to acquire homes; a few held onto them. Thousands stayed on relief for years. They were unwilling to return even to a progressive homeland; some because they felt that relief was due them in the United States where they had worked for so long at low wages; others because they liked it here in spite of discrimination and believed the country would come out of the Depression and need them again, or because they had not lost their traditional feeling that anyhow the Southwest was their country too.

In the Mexican sections of San Antonio, Los Angeles and other cities they could continue their customs and festivals, like *Las Posadas* at Christmastime, and speak their language without much interference from Anglos. Also, now and then they discovered that there were Anglos who had no desire to exploit them but, on the contrary, wished to help them improve their position.

Among these Americans were some social workers and visiting teachers. A few schools with heavy Mexican enrolments worked out programs that succeeded in drawing entire Mexican neighborhoods, children and parents, into a wider communal life. This led many Mexican adults to take out citizenship papers and adjust in other ways to American life without sacrificing anything valid in their Mexican heritage.

The best example of creative school-community action known to me first-hand began in the mid-1930s at the Central Junior High School in Los Angeles through the initiative and direction of its principal, M. E. Herriott, in whom patriotic imagination, a sense of tact and proportion, and a lot of practical ability combine into an effectiveness that benefits the whole city. Assembly programs to which Mexican and non-Mexican parents are invited are partly in Spanish. Sometimes the school organizes pageants with Mexican themes in which Mexican and non-Mexican pupils take part. Costumes and props of professional quality are made by pupils in regular classes. The school paper *The Central Idea* often features articles and linoleum cuts presenting life in Mexico and the Mexican's life in the Southwest. Mexico as a country and as one of the two closest neighbors of the United States is studied in history and current-events classes. Aspects of Mexican culture are encouraged and "preserved" through classes in Mexican folk dancing and music (attended not only by Mexicans but also by youngsters of Anglo-Saxon, Chinese, Italian, Japanese, Negro and mixed descent). Mexican feast days and patriotic anniversaries such as September Sixteenth, *Cinco de Mayo, Las Posadas* and *Día de los Reyes Magos,* are observed in assembly programs and pageants which are not trumped-up shows on the tourist plane but actual celebrations of significant occasions, a true participation in the neighborhood's Mexican life. This helps to keep the younger and older generations in sympathy and understanding with each other, and helps the Anglos to understand and appreciate facets of the Mexican character and customs that otherwise might baffle them and cause friction between the school and the community. Also drawing school and community together is the school's policy of employing on its faculty and clerical staff as many people as possible of Mexican background and origin.

The 1940-1945 wartime industrial and agricultural boom, coupled with the serious manpower shortage, lured thousands of migrants across the border. The total number of Mexican Americans and Mexican aliens in the United States early in 1945 was estimated at better than two and a quarter million. Texas alone had over one million, California between seven and eight hundred thousand.

The Mexicans are a principal labor force in sugar beets, fruit, most vegetables; in cattle and sheep raising; in packing and canning; along the railways. And they were not inconspicuous in the new war industries of California and Texas. Large colonies exist in Chicago and the closeby Indiana steel towns, in Detroit and Toledo. In many places their wages still are lower than those of other workers for the same work; by and large, however, their labor has brought them a substantial part of their share of wartime prosperity.

Many have invested surplus earnings in war bonds and in improving their living conditions. Tens of thousands, citizens and aliens, were in the United States armed forces. Several—José Martinez of Colorado, José Lopez and Macario Garcia of Texas, Silvestre Herrera of Arizona, Manuel Perez of Chicago—were awarded Congressional Medals of Honor.

The probability is that by the end of 1945 the combined Hispanic and Mexican elements in the United States will exceed two and a half million, and that over two million of both elements are here to stay.

The postwar period will not be easy for the country as a whole; no problem will be solved overnight; and it is not to be expected that the

Anglo-Hispanic and Mexican-migrant difficulties will vanish at once. It is urgent, however, that they gradually improve. As Carey McWilliams and others have been emphasizing through the early 1940s, the success of the United States' foreign policy in reference to Latin America hinges on the American people's—and first on the Anglo Southwesterners'—ability to reorient themselves toward our Hispano and Mexican elements. In February 1944 former Under Secretary of State Sumner Welles wrote that "recently a high official of the Mexican Government was refused service in the restaurant of a leading hotel in one of our Southwestern states," and pointed out how embarrassing such incidents are to the White House and the State Department. But much more serious in the long run is the fact that, where there are large numbers of Mexican workers, prejudice forces them to live under slum conditions. And in the Southwest—next door to Mexico—Mexicans usually and sometimes Hispanos are not classed as "White" and are therefore discriminated against wherever they appear, in eating-places and movie theaters, streetcars and railways.

All this will not be easy to change, particularly should there be a postwar economic slump. The change will depend at least seventy-five per cent on the Anglos—on the leading, articulate people among them allowing themselves to soak up the facts of the long Hispanic-Mexican story in North America; on their developing a sense of its vitality and continuity from the sixteenth century to the present and a sense of its interpenetration with the general story of the United States, and then transmitting that sense to the wider Anglo public. It will depend on reactions like this:

"Once," Omar Barker writes to me, "two Spanish American members of the American Legion were refused service in a Carlsbad, New Mexico, restaurant during a state convention. Another Carlsbad resident appeared before the convention; in apologizing, he damned the offender by name; his remarks were approved by unanimous resolution, and Anglo Legionnaires returned with their Spanish-speaking comrades to the restaurant and were served with great alacrity. I was one of them."

Gradually a deep unrest is getting hold of Spanish-speaking Americans. A great many are becoming dissatisfied with themselves, with their own shortcomings in the Anglo civilization. Some are reaching out for acceptance in community integration. As I say, many of the young men have gone to war; now, coming back in 1945, they are different than when they left. In the Army a good many were accepted on a level of equality.

These boys are looking around, seeing that something is seriously wrong. They now speak English as readily as Spanish. They used to be unhappy about their parents who could not comprehend why it was necessary to register the birth of their children, to register death, to pay taxes and local assessments, to join unions, to fill out various kinds of blanks. Now they are talking things over with them, among themselves. Their families are proud of them, eager to do almost anything they consider right or necessary.

A Los Angeles teacher of my acquaintance—who keeps in touch with "the Mexican situation" also in other cities—early in 1945 received a number of letters from young Mexican Americans, veterans of African, European and Pacific campaigns. They are troubled letters, telling of prejudice in civilian life. One bumped into it in a barbershop, another in a cafeteria; a third had got into an argument with a priest who was pro-Franco, perhaps a Falangist. What is a fellow to do in such instances? One asks: How can he prepare himself to help his people? . . . "I feel these young men," the teacher writes to me, "will serve as a liaison between the isolated community life of the Mexican American and the bigger community—not only in Los Angeles and San Antonio, but also (I hope) in Detroit, Chicago, Kansas City and Pittsburgh. I think the Mexican Americans' cultural isolation is beginning to break. . . ."

I have similar reports about returned Hispano soldiers in New Mexico.

There is the story of Louis Rodriguez, born in Chicago of Mexican parents. In 1934, when asked why he had quit grammar school and did not want to go to high school, he shot back: "What good will it do me? It didn't do anything for any of the 'Mex' kids I know. High school, no high school, they're laborers just the same." In the middle 1930s he was somewhat of a problem on Halsted Street. Some ten years later, in June 1944, he was killed in the invasion of Normandy. Now young Mexican Americans born in Chicago talk about him: "Louis died for the country that had made him think it was no use for him to try get educated—"

During the war years a few Mexican Americans have emerged as leaders of their own people. One of the most noteworthy is Frank M. Paz of Chicago. He knows the situation and has succeeded in finding ways to deal with it. A resident of Hull House, he devoted many hours of his time to establishing and supervising Mexican youth clubs. He organized a fair employment practices group among the Mexicans in Chicago and consistently worked for better job opportunities for his people. Realizing that the problem required attack from various angles, he joined the Chicago Council Against Racial and Religious Discrimination and the National Public Housing Conference of Chicago.

Finally, there is the later immigration from Spain—about 175,000 in all since 1820, when the United States government began to keep immigration figures. Three-fourths of them came after 1900; many to stay only a few years. (These figures do not include the Basques who have a separate story.)

In 1945 the United States has perhaps no more than fifty thousand citizens and aliens born in Spain, and a like number of their native-American sons and daughters. They make up fairly sizable colonies in New York City and California, and smaller ones in Florida, northern New Jersey and Pennsylvania, the remainder being sparsely distributed over much of the rest of the country. Most are Roman Catholics; "the first generation immigrants, however," says an official 1943 United States government analysis of the group, "are predominantly and violently anti-clerical."

This immigration reached its height during World War I, when unskilled Spanish newcomers were readily employed in Eastern munitions plants and shipyards. Small settlements grew up in various manufacturing centers such as Waterbury and Bridgeport, Connecticut, Chicago and Cleveland. Some Asturian miners went to work in the West Virginia coal mines. About two thousand Spaniards served as sailors on American merchant ships. They were—still are—a large part of the working force in the Tampa, Florida, cigar factories.

After World War I those Spanish immigrants who did not return to the old country went into different industries and little businesses. Many opened restaurants specializing in Spanish cooking. A friend of mine apparently will never forget the pompano prepared by a Spanish chef which he consumed in Tampa years ago. "It was poetry," he says.

About half the immigrants from Spain are naturalized. Nearly all were anti-Franco. They have numerous fraternal, social and cultural associations and clubs. The Spanish Benefit Union has branches in most colonies. La Prensa, published in New York, is the largest Spanish-language paper, addressing itself mainly to the recent-immigrant element.

The best-known contemporary American of Spanish and part-Spanish stock is George Santayana, Harvard philosopher and teacher, author of many books on esthetics, an influence on a long generation of intellectuals in the United States. He came here as a boy; in the 1930s he went to live in a convent in Rome, finding that "in solitude it is possible to love mankind."

Others are José Iturbi, pianist and conductor; Xavier Cugat, orchestra leader; Salvador Dali, Julio de Diego, Federico Castellón and Luis Quintanilla, painters; José de Creeft, sculptor.

Since the middle 1910s a large number of Spanish intellectuals (excluding refugees from Franco's rule) have arrived. Many teach Spanish in universities, colleges and high schools in various parts of the country.

Dr. Joaquin Ortega, a native of Ronda, Spain, seems a link between the recent immigrants from Spain and the Hispanos and Anglos in the Southwest. He teaches Spanish and directs the School of Inter-American Affairs at the University of New Mexico in Albuquerque. He has studied at first hand the culture of the Spanish-speaking population in the Southwest, and has a common-sense approach to the Hispano-Anglo difficulty. "Fraternity among the various groups in the Southwest may be impossible," he says. "Human nature is recalcitrant. Let us strive just for the good old American principle of equal opportunity, which today hardly exists. That will be a sufficient goal." He holds that "New Mexico is destined to be the bridge between the two Americas. This state is the shortest route to Mexican good will. To work in close harmony with Mexico and heal the open sore created in the Pan-American body by the distressing situation of Mexican citizens and Mexican descendants in the midst of our vaunted democracy is more important now than ever, for Mexico is a key country . . . exerts a profound intellectual influence in Latin America. . . . The job is at once of intrinsic social justice and sound international politics."

It would be a little more accurate to say that New Mexico is a part of a potential "bridge between the two Americas." "The true test of our friendliness with the peoples of Latin America," says Mrs. Marie M. Hughes of the Los Angeles County school system, "is our acceptance of the Mexican American as an active citizen in all affairs of life in the United States, whether he be found in New Mexico, in Los Angeles, in Pittsburgh, in Detroit, or in San Antonio."

III: AMERICANS FROM FRANCE

ONLY a few decades after the Discovery—when "de Soto had not yet started for his burial in the Mississippi," as John H. Finley put it in his book *The French in the Heart of America*, when "the fathers of the Pilgrim Fathers were still in their cradles," when "Captain John Smith was not yet born," when "Henry Hudson's name was to remain obscure for three quarters of a century"—French explorers and adventurers began to come over in small expeditions.

I have already mentioned the Italian navigator Giovanni Da Ver-

razano who, in the service of King Francis I of France and with a predominantly French crew, sailed along the coast from North Carolina
to the Penobscot in 1524. In the middle of the 1530s came Jacques
Cartier with sixty-two men on two ships; then Jean Nicolet, René
Robert Cavelier de la Salle and others. In their cockleshell craft they
entered the Hudson and St. Lawrence Rivers. And their cartographers
turned out lovely maps entitled *Nouvelle France*. For a century little
more than curving lines traced on parchment, this "New France" was
the beginning of the French empire in the New World. But the
earliest French navigators and explorers were not empire-builders.

Cavaliers with wonderful-sounding names and titles, fascinated by
the newly determined fact that the world was round, they were in the
grip of the great impulse to follow the downing sun in order to arrive
at where it rose. Like Columbus who had originally sailed west from
Spain with the idea of blazing a new route to India, they were intent
on surmounting the barrier the Discoverer had run into and on finding
the northwest passage to civilized Cathay, or China. They thought
the St. Lawrence might be it, or an approach to it.

A group of them under Jean Nicolet, reaching the Great Lakes, were
told by the Indians that just beyond the rim lived a bald and beardless
race. Chinese! Certain that Cathay must be just beyond all this water,
or within a manageable distance of the western edge of the American
continent, which could not be far from the Great Lakes, Nicolet and
his fellow explorers donned resplendent Chinese silk robes and man-
darin hats. These they had brought along from France where interest
in China was high.

There is something typically French in this incident. The *voyageurs*
had none of the severe reticence and stern unconformity of the English
Pilgrims and Puritans. Theirs was a deft, imaginative conformity. They
were out to make a gesture in the grand manner, punctiliously, with
every observance of elegance and form. They meant to arrive in style
at the court of the mandarins. Their instinct was to show respect for
the ways and frills of another civilized people. In view of what lay
ahead, the average American of today would regard them as a bit too
fancy and elaborate, even somewhat absurd, yet they are very pleasant
to contemplate through the mist of centuries.

Of course they did not find China; only another tribe of Indians . . .
and the Wisconsin River . . . and the undulating prairies of the Mississippi Valley.

This led the brothers-in-law Groseilliers and Radisson to discovering
the headwaters of the Mississippi, to being the first white men in
Minnesota. It led to the explorations by Louis Jolliet and Père Mar-

quette of the Mississippi and Illinois Rivers; to the incredible voyages of La Salle, "Prince of Explorers," who, also China-bound, sailed along the whole shore of Lake Ontario, found the Allegheny and the Ohio, probably touched on the present site of Louisville, Kentucky, reached the Mississippi itself, went up to its source and then with his faithful Tonti way down to the Gulf.

La Salle claimed for Louis XIV all the land he had seen and all that he could imagine being drained by the rivers pouring into the Mississippi. In honor of the king he named the territory Louisiana.

Almost simultaneously another thread of the French story began to unwind out of the Old World's religious schism.

In 1562, a band of French Protestants called Huguenots, escaping persecution in Europe, seeking freedom of worship, came to what is now South Carolina, then moved to Florida to start a colony on St. John's River. By the end of the third year the community numbered several hundred. Then suddenly Counter-Reformation and power politics reached over from the Old World, and the Spaniards—under the command of Pedro Menéndez de Avilés (see p. 37)—slaughtered all but a few "as heretic interlopers and not as Frenchmen." Two years later on his own initiative a Catholic French nobleman, Dominique De Gourgues, invaded Florida and hanged "not as Spaniards but as murderers" all the Spaniards he and his task force of 185 men could lay their hands on.

There is also something typically French in De Gourgues' action. The motive of the Catholic French nobleman's revenge for the slaughtered French Protestants was kin to the ideal whose homeland is France—an ideal well expressed two centuries later by Voltaire: "I do not agree with a word that you say but I will defend to the death your right to say it."

On the maps for sale in Paris early in the seventeenth century "New France" stretched north and south from Labrador to the mouth of the Delaware and presumably as far westward as the unknown continent extended. In 1603 the king sent over a viceroy, Pierre Du Gast, Sieur de Monts, a Protestant, whose expedition included several competent and intrepid men. One, the mapmaker Samuel de Champlain, lost no time in laying the basis for his subsequent fame as explorer and colonizer.

Within a few years Champlain traveled over most of the coast of what was to be called New England. Penetrating inland, he found the great lake now named for him. From Lake Champlain he first caught sight of the green mountains to the east and cried, "*Voilà les Monts*

Verts!"—thus naming the subsequent colony and state of Vermont. He was instrumental in establishing the first European settlements in the northern part of North America: Quebec and St. Croix. He sailed the St. Lawrence, reached Lakes Ontario and Huron, fought the Indians, became governor of Quebec. More than an adventurer, Champlain realized that here was something to get one's teeth into—an immense new reality in the human world, greater than even the wildest, most ambitious French imagination had been able to conceive. His approach to the new reality tended to be practical, concise, realistic.

But—strangely enough, if we bear in mind the French reputation for practicality and realism—this approach did not prevail in French exploration and colonization. Most explorers plunging into the limitless country south of the Great Lakes were too excited, too much in a hurry to reach China, too tied to the vanity of their successive kings whose policy with respect to the New World and its colonization was unintelligent. They were too closely linked with the narrow purposes of the Mississippi Valley Company and the West Indies Company which held royal monopolies in the French portion of the New World.

These companies were not interested in populating the territories, but in exploiting them for people who stayed at home—one reason for the introduction of slave labor in the French West Indies and the Lower Mississippi Valley. They did not encourage the emigration of independent colonists, preferring to deal with strictly disciplined royal functionaries whose main duties were to protect them from unfriendly Indian tribes. The colonists who came over independently and refused to accept the rules of the authorities had no choice but to become *coureurs de bois* and be on their own. Their settlements had no feeder lines connecting them with Quebec and the homeland.

This policy and the monopoly system it created, influenced by the general conflict of interests between France and Britain, and by the clash between Reformation and Counter-Reformation then ripping Europe from end to end, prevented any considerable number of French people from emigrating to America. Most of those who went were not agriculturists and artisans but adventurers and exploiters.

When Champlain first arrived, the Catholic-Protestant question was of no great moment in New France; in fact, as I have mentioned, Du Gast, the viceroy, was a Protestant, and in the next two decades many of the leading men in Quebec were Huguenots who had extremely strong reasons for leaving France and for trying to create a new homeland in America. But later the powers dominant in France decided not to run any risk of allowing New France to become a Protestant community and Huguenots were barred from coming over.

Meantime the sharply anti-French and anti-Romanist English had started to colonize right under the noses of the French. The English king had determined to contest France's claim to North America based on the right of discovery. Soon Sir William Alexander arrived with a royal grant to Nova Scotia, where French Catholics had begun to settle. Sir William brought with him a number of able Huguenots who had been living as refugees in England and were eager to help take over as much of New France as possible in order to make the New World safe for Protestantism and themselves.

Thus began the long, bitter struggle between the French and English in America, incidental to their conflict in Europe. For more than a century it flared up intermittently in the American wilderness. In the long run the Anglo-Saxons, with their cooler, more obstinate purpose and methods, won out. Although not exactly of one mind about religion, they were all Protestants who had left Europe in many cases because their particular kind of faith or dogma was not tolerated there, and as such they had the sympathy and help of the Huguenots. There were other circumstances favoring the English. The majority were farmers and artisans who brought their families and whose inclination was to entrench themselves firmly in the rock-strewn soil of their New England beachhead before venturing into the interior. Unlike the French, they did not extend themselves too far, too quickly and too thin.

But at first, in fact through most of the seventeenth century, the struggle appeared to be going in favor of the Catholic French. They lost but regained their Quebec beachhead, then held onto it with so fierce a determination that it precluded their consistent interest in any other part of the coast. And their main interest was not even in Quebec; it lay diffused deep in the heartland of North America.

Beginning in the 1630s and during the rest of that century and some decades of the next, only a few hundred Catholic Frenchmen came over each year. There were relatively few women, for New France had little to attract them; most of the women who did come in response to one lure or another went no farther than Quebec. The men were a mixed crowd: more or less educated, individualists on their own, with a plexure of unfocused ideas and fitful personal urges and goals. They had no effective leadership that might have coordinated them and given them stability and a tenacious long-range purpose.

For a time in the late 1570s and 1580s the energetic, imaginative and heroic La Salle—like Champlain before him—tried hard to endow New France with some sort of tangible future. He realized that successful colonization called for more than explorers, the French flag, and proclamations read in the name of the king to the breezes and tornadoes blowing over the Mississippi Valley. But he got nowhere partly—to repeat—because circumstances in France precluded any realistic attempt to induce sound, solid, hard-working people to emigrate and partly because his own character had serious defects. He was haughty, unstable, inconsiderate of others. In the end his men mutinied and shot him.

During La Salle's wide-ranging explorations, he was accompanied and followed, occasionally preceded, by small groups of assorted Frenchmen. They were restless noblemen and unrooted commoners of all kinds— woodsmen, hunters, trappers and fur traders; priests, many of them Jesuits who, like the Spanish padres in the southern sections of the hemisphere, wanted to convert the Indians to the Catholic faith. All were in the grip of a vagrant, disjointed motivity of epic sweep. Spreading themselves so thin over the interminable Mississippi territory that their presence at any one place was negligible, they were incapable of building a real New France. But they were destined to leave their autograph on the civilization that was to flow westward from New England, Pennsylvania and Virginia under the military, political and cultural auspices of the more disciplined Anglo-Saxons.

If the west-bound Anglo-Saxons of the eighteenth century are the pioneers, then their French precursors deserve to be called pre-pioneers. "Pioneer of pioneers" is the phrase which the historian Francis Parkman applied to Étienne Brulé who came over as a boy with Champlain and later was the first White man to see Lake Superior and Sault Ste. Marie.

Next to exploring, trapping and fur trading were the early Frenchmen's biggest enterprises. These pursuits brought them into close contact with the Indians whom they exploited economically but treated rather well otherwise—much better certainly than the Anglo-Saxons treated the eastern tribes or the Spaniards those in Florida or New Mexico. Frenchmen mated with Indian women, fathering so-called half-breeds. Entering into alliances with Indians, they used them as guides and as warriors in their ever more frequent conflicts with the westering Anglo-Saxons and hostile Indian tribes.

This dramatic and colorful life existed essentially unchanged for well over a century. Operating southward from the St. Lawrence and the Great Lakes, northward from the Gulf, and eastward and westward from various points along the Mississippi, the French discovered, named and mapped all the important waterways. They traversed some of the illimitable prairies of what is now the Middle West. Several got into the Rockies, into present-day New Mexico and Arizona. At the mouth of the Mississippi they founded New Orleans, the capital of the Province of Louisiana, which they intended to make the Quebec of the south—a greater Quebec, for the St. Lawrence at whose mouth the Canadian city arose was ice-bound in winter.

They created a far-flung, haphazard network of forts and trading posts some of which, scattered at strategic points in the wilderness, were for many decades nothing more than tiny stockades built of logs. Niagara, Detroit, Sault Ste. Marie, Michilimackinac, Green Bay, Dubuque, Joliet, Des Moines, Duluth, St. Joseph, Vincennes, St. Paul, Racine, La Crosse, Prairie du Chien, and Forts St. Antoine, St. Croix, Perot and St. Louis are among the earlier of these French outposts. Now there are nearly three thousand cities and smaller communities, counties, lakes and rivers in the United States (to say nothing of Canada) whose names—some Anglicized, others adjusted to English speech, but many still in the original French—remind us of the significant and picturesque role played in North America's early civilization by explorers, missionaries, hunters and trappers, and other pre-pioneers from France who were pathfinders and trail blazers rather than empire builders. "They preferred to trap," says Fred L. Holmes in his book *Old World Wisconsin* (1944), "to wander in wilderness solitudes, and to puff a pipe at night around the fire, while telling other loiterers of the incidents and exploits of the day. Their observations on the cunning of wild animals, the ingenuity of the beaver, the wariness of the muskrat, interspersed tales of their own courage and fearlessness."

Except for the Province of Quebec, Catholic "New France" is now a phrase in quotation marks; and Quebec too, of course, is part of the predominantly English-speaking and Protestant Dominion of Canada.

Longfellow's *Evangeline* tells the early story of the Acadians—French Catholics banished by the British from Nova Scotia during and after the 1750s. Some four thousand of them found refuge in the Province of Louisiana; now over three hundred thousand of their descendants form a distinct group in the southwestern part of the state of Louisiana. Usually referred to as Cajuns, a good many know no English and speak a French very unlike that heard in present-day France or Quebec.

The Louisiana Purchase in 1803 was the greatest real estate transaction in history; also the greatest bargain. It came about in this way: France lost Louisiana to Spain under the Treaty of Paris in 1763. At that time the French population was very small. There were few colonists, officers and soldiers, and agents of monopolies. During 1789-1795, however, a great many French planters in the West Indies, obliged to flee from upheavals there, found refuge in Louisiana. In the late 1790s France again entertained colonial ambitions. Talleyrand was particularly thinking of the West Indies and Louisiana. He decided to send an expedition to Santo Domingo, which might become the jumping-off place to recover Louisiana. By the secret treaty of San Idelfonso, Spain yielded Louisiana to France, but the American government was informed and protested vehemently, even threatening war if the French landed in New Orleans. Negotiations were started and got nowhere. Suddenly Napoleon Bonaparte (then First Consul, not yet Emperor) changed his plans, gave up colonial ambitions in America, and offered to sell Louisiana to the United States. The American plenipotentiaries accepted although they had no instructions covering such an eventuality; President Jefferson, who originally had wanted only the island of New Orleans, approved.

The other thread of the French story in America has a different quality.

Most of the Huguenots massacred by the Spanish on St. John's River in 1565 had come over as refugees directly from France. Late in the sixteenth century the so-called Dispersion began—Huguenots escaping from the growing intolerance directed against them in France and seeking refuge in England, Holland and Germany where the Reformation managed to stick. And so most of the French Protestants arriving in early New England and New Netherland during the second quarter of the seventeenth century and later came from those countries, bringing with them the additional experiences and skills acquired as refugees. Some had already been partly absorbed into English, Dutch and German life, but they remained essentially French, tactful and adaptable. Now they were eager to conform, to be integrated into the life of the English and Dutch colonies in the New World. They came in families with all their possessions, to stay.

Impressed by their civilized qualities and their farming and artisan abilities, the Dutch of New Netherland received them rather more readily than did the Puritans of New England who at that time distrusted everything French as well as everything gay, and whose laws pertaining to newcomers were generally inhospitable. By and by, however, the Huguenots began also to be accepted in New England to which, writes one historian, "they brought a buoyancy and a cheerfulness that must have been contagious amidst the pervading austerity." They went in for the cultivation of flowers because they like to have flowers in their homes. They planted vineyards along Narragansett Bay. They assimilated rapidly, intermarrying with the English, taking their characteristics into the main streams of colonial life. And most important, unlike some of the Anglo-Saxon New Englanders, their passion for freedom included a tendency to accept people of other backgrounds.

By 1685, when the Edict of Nantes was revoked and the plight of the Protestants in France went abruptly from bad to worse, the Huguenots were welcome by-and-large throughout the British Colonies, which by then had absorbed New Holland. That they were barred from "New France" was their special recommendation, but during the intercolonial wars what was left of the anti-French feeling operated to side-swipe them every once in a while.

By 1700 some four thousand Huguenot immigrants and their American-born children were scattered through New England. And "their genial presence," said Lucian J. Fosdick in *The French Blood in America* (1906), ". . . was like the influx of a gladdening river into a thirsty land, carrying joy wherever it goes. . . . What did the Huguenots contribute to the change in English character? All the lighter, happier, more refining and spiritual qualities, the joyous temperament. It found speedy expression in New England in commerce and in devising new subjects of manufacture and exportation. . . . The Huguenot was devout, less ambitious than the Englishman, affectionate of heart, artistic, cultivated, and also highly endowed with the commercial instincts and skilled capacities. He brought to America the arts, accomplishments and graces of the highest civilization then known, together with a sweet cheerfulness all his own. Not a colony or class but was ameliorated by his influence."

In the first half of the eighteenth century a few hundred Huguenots came over every year to settle in Massachusetts, Rhode Island and Maine. Boston had a substantial number. There were the Faneuil brothers, Jean, André and Benjamin, leading merchants and colonial patriots commanding widespread esteem, which found expression at André's death in 1738. Eleven hundred people followed his body to the cemetery—one of the largest funerals in pre-Revolutionary Boston.

André left his business and fortune to his nephew Pierre who in spite of his consistent pursuit of the gay and good life achieved a position in Boston's mercantile world second only to John Hancock's. In the end he gave the city Faneuil Hall, "the cradle of liberty" in the Revolutionary period. That period brought to prominence other French Americans, Paul Revere, for example: Boston-born son of a Huguenot immigrant from the Island of Guernsey who had spelled his name Rivoire.

The Faneuils had come to New England from La Rochelle along with several other Huguenots—among them, Pierre Baudouin, whose grandson James Bowdoin became one of Samuel Adams' and John Hancock's fellow agitators for a revolution, later president of the Massachusetts Constitutional Convention during the Revolution, and finally governor of Massachusetts. Bowdoin College in Maine, where the family had large holdings, was named for James Bowdoin. His son, also called James, was a merchant and diplomat in the early years following the Revolution.

From the start the Huguenots had a definite place in New York (New Amsterdam). Many of the original "Dutch" settlers were really Walloons from Belgium whose background was French Huguenot. For a while New York was called Neu-Avesnes after Avesnes, a town in northern France, the birthplace of Jesse de Forest, an early Protestant leader. The first physician in New Amsterdam was Dr. Johannes La Montagne, a Huguenot who came from Leyden, Holland. The first white child born in New Netherland, in 1625, was Sarah, daughter of George Janses de Rapelje, an expatriated Huguenot who had emigrated first to Holland, then to America. A Frenchman born of refugee parents in Holland, Bartholomew LeRoux was one of the early silversmiths in New York; he also played a political role in the New York Colony for a few decades after it had passed under the English rule. His son Charles LeRoux was a well known silversmith and engraver in New York in the first half of the eighteenth century. In 1688 about two hundred of New York's families, one-quarter of the population, were Huguenots. As in New England, they had their own churches and schools. They started a settlement on Staten Island, another at New Rochelle, which was for a while a center of French culture.

The Huguenots in Pennsylvania came there in the late seventeenth century, largely by way of Germany. Later some spread to Maryland, Delaware, New Jersey, Virginia. Owing to the prevailing attitude toward anything French, in none of these colonies were they immediately and completely accepted; but everywhere, sooner or later, they won the respect of other groups and merged into the general population.

In the 1680s there was initial objection to the Huguenots in South Carolina also, although the king of England himself provided the ship which brought them over. But in time they were taken in, and decades before the Revolution they became an extremely valuable element, especially in Charleston where, prospering, they built whole streets of lovely homes reminiscent of houses in France. To them is due in large part Charleston's renown as a beautiful city.

Altogether, perhaps no more than fifteen thousand Huguenot immigrants had arrived by 1789, but Appleton's *Encyclopedia of American Biography*, published that year, contains the names of 589 men of Huguenot descent. In the modern *Dictionary of American Biography* approximately every tenth life-sketch contains some such phrase as "of French-Huguenot heritage" or "his original American forebears were Huguenot refugees from France."

John Jay, the first Chief Justice of the United States, was of Huguenot stock. So were the Reverend Jacob Duché, who opened the first
Continental Congress with prayer; Henry Laurens and Elias Boudinot,
who served as presidents of that body; John Laurens, son of Henry, who
was an aide-de-camp of George Washington's; Michael Hilligas, the first
Treasurer of the United States; the mothers of John Greenleaf Whittier
and Alexander Hamilton. So are the Deweys and the La Follettes.

The Roosevelts are partly descended from the New York Huguenots.
Franklin D. Roosevelt was part-French on both his paternal and
maternal side. He was also part-English, part-Swedish, part-Dutch, and
part-Scottish. Early in 1942 I heard him remark in the presence of
Winston Churchill that his talent for bargain-driving was to be ascribed
to the Dutch and Scottish strains in his makeup. Perhaps his buoyancy
of temperament which made it possible for him to endure the Presidency longer than any other man, and during the country's most critical
period, should be credited to the French strain. His mother was a
Delano. The founder of that family was Philippe de La Noye, a Huguenot who affiliated himself with the English Puritans while they were in
Holland and accompanied them to America in 1621. One of his direct
descendants, Amassa Delano, was a notable ship captain around the
year 1800.

During the decades just before the Revolution, Anthony Benezet and
Michel Guillaume Jean de Crèvecoeur were two very interesting Frenchmen in North America.

Born at Saint-Quentin, in Picardy, and partly educated in London
where his family had moved after the revocation of the Edict of Nantes,
Benezet arrived in Philadelphia in 1731 when eighteen years of age.
In London the Benezets had come under Quaker influence; now they
joined the Friends and Anthony eventually became a teacher in their
school now called the William Penn Charter School. In 1756 he took
a keen interest in some five hundred Acadians expelled from Nova
Scotia who came to Philadelphia, and he helped to settle many of them
in Pennsylvania and New Jersey. Then in his middle age he began to
read everything he could get hold of on the subject of slavery. He was
filled with pity for the slaves and with indignation over the trade in
human beings. This led him into a voluminous correspondence on
various injustices and stupidities in the world. He addressed himself to
such men as Benjamin Franklin and his friend John Woolman of New
Jersey, then one of the foremost American authorities on the question
of slavery; to the Abbé Raynal in France, Granville Sharp in England,
the queens of England, France and Portugal, and to Frederick the

Great. In 1766 the publication of his little book entitled A *Caution and Warning to Great Britain and Her Colonies on the Calamitous State of the Enslaved Negroes* created a stir along the Atlantic seaboard. Shortly before his death in 1784 he became passionately interested in the plight of the Indians. His name continues to be a source of inspiration in Quaker circles of southeastern Pennsylvania.

Crèvecoeur was a Norman who received some of his education in England. He came to New France in the middle 1750s when not yet twenty, and in the next five years journeyed through the Great Lakes and Ohio River regions. During the early 1760s he traversed the colonies of New York, New Jersey and Pennsylvania. He was naturalized a British colonial subject, married and settled on a farm in Orange County, New Jersey. There he began to write a series of essays which were destined to appear in book form in London in 1782 as *Letters from an American Farmer*. They are one of the most graphic records of life in the period preceding the Revolution.

Although essentially a common man, Crèvecoeur somehow did not go along with the Revolution. Apparently he regarded himself as an aristocrat and was outraged by what looked to him like chicanery on the part of some of the so-called patriots, and he decided to be a Loyalist. He went to France in 1780, returning to America three years later as the French consul at New York, to find his wife killed by the Indians and the house on his farm burned. In connection with this tragedy he experienced a great deal of kindness in New Jersey and New York, and eventually he became rather pro-Revolution. At any rate, he exchanged letters with Washington and Franklin; Jefferson attended the wedding of his daughter, whom he had named America-Francès. But in 1790 he left the United States for good and died in his native land twenty-three years later.

Crèvecoeur considered himself a farmer as well as an aristocrat. Nowadays he might be called an amateur agricultural economist, for he made himself an expert on land titles, mortgage problems and farming equipment. He took pride in having introduced into America several kinds of plants.

Of his essays, the best known and the most significant is "What is an American?" "Whence come all these people?" he asked. "They are a mixture of English, Scotch, Irish, French, Dutch, Germans and Swedes. From this promiscuous breed, that race now called Americans have risen. . . .

"In this great American asylum the poor of Europe have by some means met together, and in consequence of various causes. To what purpose should they ask one another what countrymen they are? Alas, two-thirds of them had no country. Urged by a variety of motives, here they came. Everything has tended to regenerate them. In Europe they were so many useless plants, wanting vegetative mold and refreshing showers. They withered and were mowed down by want, hunger, and war; but now, by the power of transportation, like all other plants, they have taken root and flourished! . . .

"What, then, is the American, this new man? He is neither a European nor the descendant of a European; hence that strange mixture of blood, which you will find in no other country. I could point out to you a family whose grandfather was an Englishman, whose wife was Dutch, whose son married a French woman, and whose present four sons have now four wives of different nations. *He* is an American who, leaving behind him all his ancient prejudices and manners, receives new ones from the new modes of life he has embraced, the new government which he obeys, and the new rank he holds. He becomes an American by being received in the broad lap of our great Alma Mater. Here individuals of all nations are melted into a new race of men, whose labors and posterity will one day cause great changes in the world. . . ."

The best known French name in American history is that of Marie Joseph Paul Roch Yves Gilbert Motier, Marquis de Lafayette. Fired with enthusiasm for the colonial Revolutionary cause young Lafayette flouted the official French policy, crossed the Atlantic and offered his services to George Washington. Congress made him a major general. He participated in the battle of Brandywine, was invaluable to Benjamin Franklin in his negotiations for French aid, and commanded in the campaign that brought about Cornwallis' surrender at Yorktown. He is the subject of several biographies. Many towns, a few counties, numerous streets and the college at Easton, Pennsylvania, are named for him. With the Statue of Liberty which came from France in 1886, the well-remembered name of Lafayette is a spiritually vital tie between the United States and France. At his tomb in Paris on July 4, 1917, one of General Pershing's staff officers exclaimed: "Lafayette, we're here!" When American troops entered Paris in the summer of 1944, one American soldier's widely reported remark was: "Lafayette, here we are again!"

Very different from Lafayette (who, as Jefferson said, had "a canine appetite for popularity and fame"), Jean-Baptiste Donatien de Vimeur, Count de Rochambeau is less well known, but his service to the Revolution was almost as great. In July 1780, when American hopes were very low, he brought over more than four thousand French volunteers.

Among the leaders and heroes were also Count de Grasse, Charles

Louis Jean Berthier, Louis Antoine de Bougainville, Marquis de Chastellux, Duke de Saint-Simon, Viscount de Noailles—all unknown to the
American public 160-odd years after their providential visit to America.

When Clemenceau was in the United States in 1922 and with his
companion, Stephen Bonsal, the American diplomat and writer, paused
at some of the scenes of the American Revolution, he was chagrined to
note that the role of the French troops, including the great march made
by Rochambeau's large force from Narragansett Bay to the capes of
Virginia and Yorktown, had been practically forgotten. He proposed
a sentimental journey to follow their trail on his next visit, but old age
and illness prevented his return. Mr. Bonsal made the journey alone,
and told of it in *When the French Were Here* (1945).

Most Frenchmen who survived the American Revolution returned
to France, some with significant ideas. Mr. Bonsal recalls the youthful
Saint-Simon who reflected that "in itself the war did not interest me,
but its object interested me very deeply and I willingly took part in its
labors. I said to myself: 'I want the end. I must therefore accept the
means.' . . . I felt the American Revolution marked the beginning of a
new political era; that this Revolution would necessarily set in motion
progressive currents in our general civilization, and that it would before
long occasion great changes in the social order . . . existing in Europe."
Years after the French Revolution, another returned Frenchman, Count
Philippe Paul de Ségur, noted in his memoirs that when they had
crossed the Atlantic to help the Americans "we were all dreaming of
Liberty. No one thought of a revolution in France. We all wanted to
fly to America in the name of philanthropy, and we were destined to
bring home the germs of an ardent passion for emancipation and independence."

Of those who remained in the new United States, Pierre Charles
L'Enfant stands out. His enthusiasm for the American cause had
brought him to the embattled Colonies at twenty-three after he had
received some training in architecture and engineering. Commissioned
a first lieutenant of engineers late in 1776 and eventually promoted to
major, he was wounded in the assault on Savannah and captured at
Charleston, to be exchanged in 1782. Following the Revolution he
designed the eagle which symbolizes the spirit of the United States, and
he drew the plan for the city of Washington that later was carried out
piecemeal and reluctantly by others. He remodeled New York's old
City Hall on Wall Street into the Federal Hall, reconstructed numerous
fortifications, designed many public and private buildings in different
cities.

A contemporary, W. W. Corcoran, described L'Enfant as "a tall, erect man, fully six feet in height, finely proportioned, nose prominent, of military bearing, courtly air and polite manners, his figure usually enveloped in a long overcoat and surmounted by a bell-crowned hat—a man who would attract attention in any assembly." The trouble with him was that he was a little over a century ahead of his time. He based the plan for the city of Washington on his vision of the country's future. It wasn't fully accepted until 1901. Today Washington, D.C., is essentially as he visualized it.

This delay in approval was in a measure due to L'Enfant's own nature. He was a generous, extravagant man, often impatient with others, uncompromising, apt to make immoderate demands. On the other hand, the government's recompense for his services was niggardly. He passed the last years of his life in extreme poverty. When he died in Washington in 1825, the value of his personal effects—a few engineering instruments, books, maps—amounted to $45.

In 1909 L'Enfant's bones were dug up out of his unmarked grave, laid in state at the Capitol, honored by President Theodore Roosevelt and other notables, and reburied in Arlington Cemetery. Engraved on the slab over the new grave is his plan for the city which in the early 1940s became one of the most important centers in the world.

Another French architect and engineer, Joseph François Mangin, designed (in Louis XVI style) and built the New York City Hall.

Born in Bordeaux, a ship's captain and international trader at twenty-three, Stephen Girard came to North America in the middle 1770s. After the United States was formed, he went into foreign trade again, also into banking, real estate and insurance (with farming as an avocation), and succeeded in all of them.

Unattractive in his person, almost blind, extremely unhappy in marriage (his wife went insane), he studied the philosophers, particularly Voltaire, and named his ships for them: the Voltaire in 1796, the Rousseau in 1801, the Montesquieu in 1806. A unique man from a number of angles, he did the work of ten ordinary people with good eyesight ("to rest is to rust"). He loved to plant fruit trees imported from France. He worked day and night as a nurse during yellow-fever epidemics. He aided French refugees. He helped save the United States Treasury in 1811. He handed out millions of dollars in his lifetime. He founded Girard College in Philadelphia, providing $6,000,000 in his will for educating poor white orphan boys. "So large a funeral, it is believed," said the National Gazette on December 29, 1831, "was never before known in this city."

A revealing document, his will required that the orphans admitted to Girard College "shall be fed plain but wholesome food, clothed with plain and decent apparel (no distinctive dress ever to be worn) and lodged in a plain but safe manner. . . . I would have them taught facts and things, rather than words and signs. And especially I desire that by every proper means, a pure attachment to our Republican institutions and to the sacred rights of conscience . . . shall be formed and fostered in the minds of the scholars." He further required "that no ecclesiastic, missionary, or minister of any sect whatsoever shall ever hold or exercise any station or duty whatever in the said college, nor shall any such person ever be admitted for any purpose, or as a visitor, within the premises appropriated for the purposes of said college. . . . My desire is that the instructors and teachers in the college shall take pains to instill into the minds of the scholars *the purest principles of morality* [his emphasis], so that, on their entrance into active life, they may, from inclination and habit, evince benevolence towards their fellow citizens, and a love of truth, sobriety and industry, adopting at the same time such religious tenets as their matured reasons may enable them to prefer."

The French Revolution and the Napoleonic period dislocated the lives of many people, impelling some thirty thousand to come to America. They were noblemen escaping with their skins, members of revolutionary factions that had not reached the top, army officers, and persons trained to serve the French upper classes—dancing and fencing masters, costume designers, hairdressers, perfumers, barbers, cooks. These last deeply influenced American taste and manners.

Many went into business in Philadelphia, New York and Boston. The restaurants which they started and into which they introduced new dishes, became very popular. Early in the nineteenth century in Boston, for example, one Jean Baptiste Julien, who had opened a small eating-place at the corner of Congress and Milk Streets, acquired fame with a concoction called *consommé Julien*. Most of the large hotels engaged French chefs. Their effect on American cooking is beyond over-emphasis.

And other kinds of Frenchmen came around that time.

In 1792 there arrived a young seminary student Stephen Theodore Badin, a native of Orleans, who resumed his education in Baltimore and on May 25, 1793, became the first Roman Catholic priest ordained in the United States. He worked as a missionary among the Indians and ended up as a peripatetic priest in what is now the Middle West, moving from one priestless colony of Catholics to another.

The Du Pont family emigrated in 1799 after the Jacobins had put them out of the publishing business in Paris. Within five years they were manufacturing gun powder on the Brandywine River four miles from Wilmington, Delaware. In making their start they were helped by Alexander Hamilton, who asked favors for them of the Delaware legislature, and Thomas Jefferson, who as President promised Irénée Du Pont orders from the government. During 1804-1810 the Du Pont profits averaged $7,000 a year; in 1811 they jumped to $43,000. The war with England put the business on a solid bottom. Then came the need for endless quantities of powder to blow up millions of stumps, to blast out tunnels, to quarry stone; today the Du Pont products range from plastics to machines, and the Du Ponts are near the top of the small list of families that dominate the United States industrially and financially. Several are multi-millionaires. Their enormous interests are the center of Delaware's economic and political life. Du Ponts have been soldiers, naval officers and diplomats; one, Henry Algernon Du Pont, was a United States Senator during 1906-1917.

In 1792 the French Revolutionary court indicted Joseph Jacques Ramée, architect and landscape engineer, as a political suspect. He fled the country and spent the next twenty-four years in Germany and Denmark designing palaces and public buildings, laying out the grounds around them. In 1811 he visited the United States, staying a dozen years during which he drew the plans for a number of estates and city parks and the Union College campus at Schenectady, New York. Union was the first American college to be built from an architect's plan.

On Lafayette's recommendation, two able French military engineers —General Simon Bernard, a former aide-de-camp to Napoleon, and a junior officer named Claude Crozet—entered the United States Army Corps of Engineers in 1811. Their contributions toward improving numerous fortifications on the Atlantic seaboard and enhancing the science of military engineering, which till then had been elementary in America, were great. Bernard returned to France; Crozet remained as state engineer of Virginia. In the late 1850s he was chief assistant to Captain (later Brigadier General) Montgomery C. Meigs in the construction of the aqueduct supplying Washington, D.C., with water from the Great Falls of the Potomac.

In 1816, mainly in consequence of the Napoleonic collapse, Elie Magloire Durand, a chemist from Mayenne who had been a pharmacist in the French Army, landed in New York. Eventually, after much moving about, he opened a drugstore in Philadelphia that created a

sensation. There were marble counters, mahogany drawers, huge porce-
lain jars, French bottles and other imported glassware. But what mat-
tered more was that Elias Durand, as he came to be called, was an
exceptional chemist. He subscribed to foreign journals, kept up with
pharmaceutical advances, and introduced Philadelphia physicians to
new medicines some of which he originated himself. He also innovated
the bottling of mineral water in the United States. His store at Sixth
and Chestnut Streets was a sort of doctors' club; it influenced the drug
business throughout the country. He was also an outstanding botanist
and wrote many articles on botanical and chemical subjects. He died at
eighty, one of the best loved men who ever lived in Philadelphia.

Many Frenchmen who emigrated in the early nineteenth century
were not propelled by political changes occurring in France.

In 1816 thirty-year-old Laurent Clerc, who had been a student and
later a teacher at the Institute for the Deaf and Dumb in Paris, came
to Hartford, Connecticut, to help start a similar school. For the next
three decades he pioneered in the education of the deaf in the United
States.

Octave Chanute, born in Paris, arrived with his parents in 1838 when
he was six; thirty years later, without any formal training in engineering
(little was available), he was a leading civil engineer specializing in
bridge and railroad construction. Then, suddenly, he took a deep interest
in aerodynamics and by the late 1890s, when well past middle age, he
was making significant experiments with gliders. At sixty-two he said:
"There is no more delightful sensation than gliding through the air.
All the faculties are on the alert; the motion is astonishingly smooth."
He invented the Chanute biplane, a forerunner of the first glider built
by the Wright brothers who recognized him as one of the great pioneers
in the field.

In the 1850s, after knocking about as a successful trader in Latin
America and California, one Louis Bonard, forty-odd years of age, a
native of Rouen, settled in New York and flourished in the real estate
business. On the side, he invented such contrivances as a circular loom
for weaving hats and a machine for casting iron. Something of an
eccentric, he lived penuriously in a tiny apartment, cooking his own
meals. He shunned people, but helped those in extreme straits. He
loved animals of all kinds and was roused to high indignation whenever
he saw them mistreated. Scorning formal religion, he once confessed to
a faith "based upon justice and humanity." He approved very much of
Henry Bergh, founder of the American Society for the Prevention of
Cruelty to Animals, and at his death in 1871 left to that organization

all his property, about $150,000. His will was contested by relatives in France, but the A.S.P.C.A. won, creating an important precedent for such cases.

The Louisiana Purchase added to the United States not only a vast territory but some remarkable people and a touch of French intellectual culture.

In *The Growth of American Thought* Merle Curti gives a few facts about that culture. In 1800 the village of St. Louis, for example, had 669 inhabitants with fifty-six heads of families who owned a total of 1,350 French books, many of them on engineering, medicine and other sciences; others were by Voltaire, Diderot, Rousseau, Descartes and, in translation, Locke and Goethe.

A leading figure at St. Louis then was Dr. Antoine François Saugrain de Vigni, in his sixties, a hero-survivor of Indian warfare, a naturalist and philosopher, chemist and physician. He manufactured and sold ink, matches, thermometers and other such items of civilization difficult to procure on the frontier. When he became a United States citizen, he was experimenting with electricity. In 1809 he offered the first smallpox vaccine virus in St. Louis.

In the same period down in Ascension Parish, Louisiana, a humble pioneer-surgeon named François Marie Prevost, a native of Pont-de Cé, began to perform successful Caesarean operations on Negro slave women —at a time when such operations, at the hands of famous surgeons in New York, London and Paris, were almost invariably fatal to both mother and infant. Prevost usually operated in dimly lit Negro cabins without anesthetics, asepsis and adequate instruments. He sought no credit for this, never wrote up his work; all he required was that if the patient recovered she and her offspring should be freed from slavery. One of the girls so born was named Caesarine.

Other names crowd the chapter of the French story in the United States which gets under way early in the ninteenth century:

In 1804 the nineteen-year-old John James Audubon—born at Les Cayes, Santo Domingo, of a Creole mother and a pure-French father who had served the cause of the American Revolution—claimed the estate called Mill Grove, near Philadelphia, which his father had bought. Thirty years later he was hailed as the foremost naturalist of the United States. With his famous pictures which were at once art and a signal contribution to ornithology, Audubon, as has been said, "introduced us to the birds of America." His name now is identified with the movement to preserve the country's wildlife.

One spring day in 1831 Alexis Charles Henri Clérel de Tocqueville, a young French aristocrat whose aunt had been guillotined in the Revolution, arrived to study political institutions in the United States. The result was the two-volume work *Democracy in America*, published in Paris in 1835—one of the two really good books on the subject, both by foreigners, the other being of course Lord Bryce's *The American Commonwealth*.

Late in 1848 a French shoemaker named Bernard Saint-Gaudens brought over his Irish wife and their Dublin-born baby Augustus. When the boy was thirteen, his father—one of the wisest parents on record—asked him what he wished to do in life. Augustus said he would like to be an artist, so he was apprenticed to a stone-cameo cutter. At nineteen in 1867 his father gave him the money to go to Paris and Rome. This was the genesis of one of the world's great sculptors. His work is all over the country. It is worth traveling a long distance to see his poem-in-bronze on the grave of Mrs. Henry Adams in Rock Springs Cemetery, Washington, D.C.

During the hundred years beginning about 1830, a thin but continuous stream of immigration trickled over from France. One, two, three thousand a year; seldom more than that. In the decade from 1891 to 1900, when immigration from most of Europe was assuming the proportions of a tidal wave, only 30,770 of the newcomers were French. The explanation is that during the nineteenth century, in spite of the Franco-Prussian War in the 1870s, France was the pleasantest country in the Old World—cultured, civilized, progressive—and her people had no reason to leave.

The few who came distributed themselves very thinly over the country. As an element in the population, they are at once permeant and intangible.

In the nineteenth century and early in the twentieth, many affluent American families employed French governesses, whose influence on manners in this country was very considerable. And there was the French "lady's maid"—often superior to the lady in looks, intelligence and character.

The 1940 census of the United States enumerated 349,050 persons as of French stock; 102,930 were immigrants and refugees, the rest native Americans with at least one parent born in France. It is a rare community of more than ten thousand inhabitants that hasn't one or two French-immigrant families. The largest concentrations of French immigrants, naturalized and alien, and their native-American sons and daughters and grandchildren are in New York City (40,000), Chicago (12,000) and Philadelphia (6,500).

The two large colonies in San Francisco and Los Angeles (about 10,000 each) include some third- and fourth-generation Americans whose forbears reached California as early as 1849.

Then there are about 1,500,000 other French Americans and aliens. Some of the citizens among them are very old-line Americans.

I have mentioned the Cajuns of Louisiana whose number runs into hundreds of thousands. The Creoles, a mingling of early French and Spanish strains, are another group very much evident in Louisiana, particularly in and around New Orleans, whose present population also includes many descendants of refugees from the upheavals in the French West Indies between 1789 and 1795. In Texas are thousands of descendants of Napoleonic refugees most of whom got there via New Orleans.

Along the American shores of the Great Lakes live an undetermined number of people whose forefathers settled there in the period of New France. "Paul Bunyan the Mighty Lumberjack" of the North Country, the hero of perhaps the greatest American folk epic, derives from this element, which—along with the French from Canada across the lakes —supplied much of the timber labor back in the 1850s and 1860s, before the Swedes and Finns began to arrive in large numbers.

And the New England textile, shoe and other industrial centers teem with the fairly recent French Canadian arrivals, nearly all of whom told the 1940 census-takers that their mother tongue is French. A good many resent being called French Canadians, insisting they are old-line French Americans. Like the Mexicans in the Southwest, many are not particularly impressed by the border; some move back and forth two or three times a year, following employment opportunities.

The French and French Americans who do not stem from the early Huguenots are mostly Catholics or of Catholic background. They have numerous newspapers and cultural, economic and historical societies. Most of the immigrants from France are naturalized. Since 1940 many have been intensely concerned about France and have supported various Free French organizations. This goes, also, for some of the millions of Americans with part-Huguenot ancestry.

After the Franco-Prussian War there was a brief influx of immigrants from Alsace-Lorraine. Many went to California; among them Eugene Meyer, father of Eugene Meyer, one-time head of Federal Reserve, now publisher of the Washington *Post*.

French Americans have been distinguishing themselves in American wars ever since the Revolution. Major Raoul Gervais Victor Lufbery, born in Clermont, department of Oise, who first fought in France as a member of the Escadrille Lafayette and later as an officer of the United

States Army, was one of the leading World War I "aces." In World War II Major James P. S. Devereaux (part Irish) was the gallant Marine commander of Wake Island when it was taken by the Japanese in 1941. Major Louis Huot, son of an old-line Minnesota-French family, a former New York and Paris newspaperman and radio expert, distinguished himself as commander of a small group of American officers who in October 1943 opened a perilous clandestine supply route between the Allied base in Bari, Italy, and Marshal Tito's Partisans in Yugoslavia. Major Huot told the story of that operation in his book *Guns for Tito* (1945). Lieutenant General Leonard T. Gerow, commander of the United States Fifteenth Army in France and Germany in 1945, is of Huguenot stock.

One of the most effective American weapons in World War II was the Garand rifle, invented by a French American speaking a very broken English, John C. Garand.

In normal times immigrants from France and their American-born sons and daughters engage in all sorts of work, but perhaps a majority pursue trades in which their skill is traditional: the manufacture and sale of perfumes, silk goods, dresses, lingerie and hats, cosmetics, jewelry, artists' materials, food and wine. As was true in the 1820s and '30s, many are chefs, headwaiters, hotel managers. They are at the center of the influences which enhance the amenities of American life and the appearance of American women.

The late Pierre ("Poppa") Laffitte was at once unique and representative of many of these people. The son of an Alsatian farmer, he arrived in New York in 1889 and went to work for the famous restaurateur Henri Mouqin. In 1915 he opened the Restaurant Laffitte which he ran successfully in the classic tradition until Prohibition. Insisting that a man had a moral right to sell fine wines, he refused to obey the law and was arrested twice in one day. Then he closed the place and retired. The retirement lasted as long as the Eighteenth Amendment. Immediately after Repeal, he walked into the office of Bellows & Company in New York and said: "I am Laffitte. I understand you are going to sell fine wines. I will be your wine expert," and he was until his death in 1944.

French names stand out in the arts and the entertainment field. There are Lily Pons, Claudette Colbert, Adolphe Menjou, Charles Boyer. There are René Clair and Julian Duvivier, screen directors; Louis de Rochemont, producer and director of the "March of Time" and other documentary films.

Louis Meyer, a native of Vincennes, a Paris suburb, who died early in 1945, was the publisher of *The Theatre Magazine* and the co-founder of New York City's first French bookstore.

Whoever has not yet read Charles Macomb Flandrau's *Viva Mexico!* has a treat in store. Other American authors of French origin or descent come to mind: Jacques Barzun, who is also a historian and educator; Meridel Le Seur, short-story writer and novelist, and Albert León Guérard, with a number of books on France and international problems.

There are a large number of French and French American university and college professors—most of them teaching French, French civilization, philosophy and music: Gilbert Chinard at Princeton, Curt John Ducasse at Brown, André Morize at Harvard, Albert Gabriel Feuillerat at Yale, Armand William Forstall at Denver—and public and private school teachers who, individually and as a group, contribute much to the culture of the United States by spreading the French language and French ideas and values.

In 1944 the name of René J. Dubos, of the Rockefeller Institute for Medical Research and a native of France, got into the headlines. He discovered tyrothricin, which exists in common soil and is effective where sulfa and penicillin fail. Early in 1945 Professor Vincent du Vigneaud, head of the department of biochemistry at the Cornell University Medical College, announced the synthesis of new chemical substances that deprive several species of disease-producing bacteria of biotin, a powerful vitamin without which they cannot live.

Other French Americans who are or were prominent: Carl Engel, Louis Hasselmans, Jacques Thibaud and Pierre Monteaux, musicians; Emil Blais de Sanze and Etienne Bernardeau Renaud, educators; Paul Philippe Cret, Edward Raymond Bassange, J. André Fouilhoux, Ehrick Kensett Rossiter and Emmanuel Masqueray, architects; Jules André Meliodon, Leonard Crunelle, Raoul Jean Josset, sculptors; John Lafarge, Louis Bouché and Victor Semon Perard, artists; Raymond Fernard Loewy, industrial designer; Emile Gauvreau, journalist.

Gauvreau's ancestors came to Quebec in the seventeenth century. He himself was born in Connecticut, where his father, a former soldier in the Citadel at Quebec, had migrated in the 1890s. In the early 1930s he edited the New York *Daily Mirror*, a Hearst paper. One day Franklin D. Roosevelt told him the United States was going to recognize the Soviet Union. So that summer Emile Gauvreau took a long vacation in Russia and in 1935 he published a book which pled for a better understanding of the Russians and what they were doing. As soon as the book appeared, on five minutes' notice, Hearst discharged him. Gauvreau then became a special agent of an investigating committee of the United States Congress and obtained the material for his book *The Wild Blue*

Yonder (1944), an exposé of the cartel menace to American air power. His interest in that subject dates back to his reportorial and editorial days when he covered the courtmartial of General Billy Mitchell, the great air prophet, who died, as Gauvreau told me, "practically in my arms asking me to carry on the fight."

Robert G. LeTourneau of Vicksburg, Mississippi, is the world's largest manufacturer of bulldozers and other earth-moving equipment, and a leading lay Christian evangelist who regards himself as "God's partner" in everything he does. He is old Huguenot stock.

Luther Burbank was part French—

"Americans"—to quote further from Crèvecoeur's essay "What is an American?"—"are the western pilgrims, who are carrying along with them the great mass of arts, sciences, vigor and industry which began long since in the east. They will finish the great cycle. . . ."

IV: AMERICANS FROM HOLLAND

ONE evening in 1939 I found myself listening to an American of Dutch birth whose parents had brought him as a twelve-year-old boy from Holland in 1904. The family had settled in Schenectady, New York.

"At that time," he was saying, "the chances are the population of Schenectady did not include more than a hundred people born in Holland. But our family felt at home right away, though none of us knew English. I think it was because Schenectady is a 'Dutch town' from way back, and proud of it.

"It started as an outpost of The Netherlands' colonial empire in America. It is steeped in a tradition of war, massacre and pioneering which the school books set forth as heroic, romantic and just.

"Open the local telephone book at the V's and you'll find several columns of names beginning with 'Van.' And whether or not they have a 'Van,' a good many Schenectady people preen themselves on their Holland ancestry.

"When I was a boy going to school, I received an unreasonable amount of attention. Sixty per cent of the pupils were either foreign-born or of immigrant parentage but my teachers would boast about the 'cute little Dutch boy' in their classes. They were irritated by the Polish and Italian youngsters, most of whom spoke smoother English than I, but they thought my accent was delightful. They used to encourage me to wear my wooden shoes at assembly programs and to bulldoze my mother into cooking old-country dishes for school parties. And I had to strain my imagination to describe the life and scenes I had known in The Netherlands. . . . When we read that the Dutch were a very clean people, all the eyes in the classroom turned on me. I was clean, I suppose, but I seemed to remember that not quite everybody in the old country was.

"They asked me to tell the story of the heroic boy who saved Holland by plugging a hole in the dyke with his thumb. I'd never heard of the story, and I think I offended the teacher a little—certainly I embarrassed her—when I said a dyke was much too big to be plugged that way. But still, I was Dutch and they thought I was wonderful.

"My father warned me not to let all this go to my head; besides, some of the things that went with it were absurd. Anyhow, I don't think I ever felt superior toward my classmates who were Polish or Italian or something else that wasn't Dutch. But had it not been for my father, I might have. The Dutch were played up so much in the textbooks and in the classroom, almost as much as the Anglo-Saxons. All that the Italians, Germans and Poles got was a line or two about Columbus, von Steuben, and Pulaski and Kościuszko; and 'Kościuszko' always brought a laugh because not even the teachers could pronounce it.

"My father also found things easy in Schenectady. Once he began to speak passable English he was accepted in the American community with a sincere cordiality that some of his Italian contemporaries have yet to experience thirty-five years later."

The early Dutch—or New Netherland—era has for some time been relatively well covered in American history books. Yet the average American is still rather vague about what happened in New Netherland from 1624 to 1664. Often he is unaware that such a colony ever existed. Only the most historically minded know that when Henry Hudson, the English navigator for whom the Hudson River and Hudson Bay are named, made his historic Half Moon voyage in 1609, he was in the service of the Dutch East India Company; that his crew was predominantly Dutch; that he had drawn upon the knowledge of his friend and interpreter, Jodocus Hondius, the expert mapmaker of Amsterdam.

Nor has it often occurred even to history-conscious Americans that New Netherland disappeared when it did partly because in the first half of the seventeenth century Holland was the best run country in Europe; and that, conversely, the English colonies succeeded where the Dutch settlement failed partly because Britain was then misgoverned. In a sense, a large part of the early North American development issued out of European weakness and imperfections. People came to the American wilderness not so much because they specially wanted to as because they wished to leave the Old World and its problems, or else were forced to leave in punishment or as indentured servants.

Holland was then the European state least likely to drive its citizens to America. It was a small country whose population was only about two million. A mantle of greatness had lately descended upon it when its people, led by the military genius Prince Maurice of Orange, defeated the Spanish, whose king, hereditary ruler of The Netherlands, had aspired to suppress Luther's heretical teachings, which had found fertile ground in the Low Countries, and to keep the Dutch under an absolutist rule. After that victory, the Dutch had a larger degree of religious and political freedom than any other nation. The persecuted of all other lands were welcomed; in fact Holland was the safest asylum for religious and political refugees from the rest of Europe, including Britain. Commerce and agriculture, education and science as well as the arts flourished. It was the Golden Age of The Netherlands, the period of Rembrandt and Spinoza; of Huygens, who theorized about light, and Leeuwenhoek, the pioneer physiologist, inventor of the microscope.

Amsterdam was the richest city on earth. Dutch ships carried much of the world's trade. Dutch explorers ranged the seas. They named Australia, New Holland, and New Zealand after the Dutch province of Zeeland. At home, abroad and afloat, all sorts of go-getting, clever, ambitious men emerged.

In 1623 a few of these formed the Dutch West India Company, a trading-colonizing corporation patterned after the old Dutch East India Company. The new outfit, chartered by the States-General of Holland, had monopolistic rights on the American continent so far as Dutch citizens were concerned; it absorbed the United New Netherland Company that had been trading in furs around the mouth of the Hudson.

In the next three years (1624-1626) the West India Company started four main trading posts: Fort Orange where Albany, New York, is now; Fort Nassau on the Delaware; Fort Good Hope on the site of Hartford, Connecticut; and Fort Amsterdam. From the latter grew New Amsterdam (New York City) after Peter Minuit bought Manhattan Island from the Indians for twenty-four dollars' worth of trinkets.

The British, who had recently begun a similar enterprise in North America, did not like this Dutch colonization project wedged between their northern and southern settlements, but for some forty years they did nothing definite about it. Their relations with France and Spain were tense; and as already suggested, an unhappy internal situation existed in Britain.

So for forty years there was a New Netherland governed by the quasi-official Dutch West India Company. Its territory lay along the banks of the lower Hudson, now in the states of New York and New Jersey. Its population was never purely or even preponderantly Dutch. Of the Netherlanders, some were Frisians (from Friesland, The Netherlands' province on the North Sea) whose language was akin to Old English. Scandinavians were brought in as expert lumbermen. At the height of the colony eighteen tongues were spoken in New Amsterdam, giving it a very cosmopolitan atmosphere.

New Netherland never had any future. When late in the 1630s it attained its maximum population of about ten thousand—perhaps not half of it actually Dutch—New England already numbered thirty thousand and was growing steadily. The poor, the idealistic and non-conforming of England had strong incentives for leaving the homeland; the Dutch had almost none. The poor of Holland were safeguarded against abuse of authority by the ruling classes, and a chance for education was open to them. Religious experimentation was officially forbidden but allowed in practice. With this freedom went a trend toward a spread of prosperity. Few of Holland's citizens had any compelling reason to emigrate.

From the middle 1620s to the early 1660s only an average of two hundred came over every year, some in families. Many liked it well enough to stay and to write home in this fashion: "Here we found beautiful rivers, bubbling springs flowing down into the valleys; basins of running waters in the flatlands, agreeable fruits in the woods, such as strawberries, pigeon berries, walnuts and wild grapes. The woods abound with acorns for feeding hogs, and with venison. . . . Had we cows, hogs and other stock fit for food (which we daily expect in the first ships) we would not wish to return to Holland. . . ."

Cattle and hogs were imported at great expense, and some of the colonists settled on the land. At first they lived in temporary "cellars" or sod-houses, like the pioneers of New England; later they built stone and wooden dwellings. Not enough of the colonists, however, were willing to till the soil. The majority were eager for quick returns through trade. This did not make for strong communities. Differing from some of the English colonies, there was no sharply focused and intelligently outlined vision of the future, no continual reaching toward the probable, the possible, the lasting.

Nor did those in authority have the long-range fixity of purpose that in retrospect and by comparison seems to have made New England's leadership strong and able. The West India Company's successive directors, who doubled as colonial governors, were not the best of public servants. They too were out for quick returns, exploiting the trappers, farmers and other producers in the process.

On the one hand, the company did not permit enough latitude for individual action so vital in a new and raw land, and on the other it failed to provide sufficient guidance for communal work or group enterprise. Only the patroons had a free hand.

Closely tied up with the company, the patroons were feudal lords the like of whom had disappeared in Holland long before. They regarded the people on their huge landholdings as bondsmen, taking as much as sixty to seventy per cent of their produce. (A hangover of that system brought on the sensational "Tin Horn Rebellion" in New York State in the 1840s, a highly significant episode in the rise of American democracy. It concerned many tenant farmers of Dutch ancestry, along with the descendants of one of the first and biggest patroons in America, Kiliaen Van Rensselaer, who still owned 1,152 square miles of land on both sides of the Hudson at Albany and wanted to collect some four hundred thousand dollars in back rents. The farmers organized "to take up the ball of revolution where our fathers stopped it and roll it to the final consummation of freedom and independence of the masses." That was on July 4, 1839. The sheriff, the governor, the courts were on the side of the landlords, but the farmers took to arms and to the hills; a veritable war ensued; by 1844 the Anti-Renters won, adding another reinforcement to the American spirit and tradition of freedom from oppression, and furnishing Henry Christman, himself born and raised on leasehold land, the wonderful material for his book *Tin Horns and Calico*, published early in 1945.) . . .

All in all, there is reason to think that the West India Company was never really interested in colonization, only in profits, and that it came close to resembling what nowadays would be called a racket. Here and there anti-company plots and movements cropped up to thwart its fur trade and other monopolies.

In New England religion was an insistent—in fact, a bigoted—social, political, cultural force. In New Netherland it was no force at all. For four years the colony had no minister; then Jonas Michaëlius came to serve the widely separated settlements. In 1632 the energetic Dominie Everardus Bogardus arrived. Partly because he opposed the official policy toward the Indians which sometimes was contemptuous and overbearing, and because he did not like the patroons, he was in hot water much of the time. He built the first church in the colony, and the Dutch Reformed Calvinist Church got a foothold, but the accompanying clash of personalities only added to the erratic character of life in the territory. New Netherland never got around to creating a public education system. The keen intellectual and artistic life in Holland occasioned but the faintest echoes on this side of the Atlantic. By 1664 the colony found itself too sparsely populated, too weak, too unintegrated to withstand New England's expansionist pressure. Succumbing without any serious struggle, its territory and most of its population became part of the stern, spreading English colonial realm.

For a long time the people of the former New Netherland continued to exert an influence, mainly for good, upon their surroundings. Their views and attitudes were instrumental in moderating the Puritan-Calvinist austerity and rigidity of the northern English colonies. New Englanders who moved to New York softened, relaxed in the cosmopolitan atmosphere, particularly in New York City, for many Hollanders and their neighbors of other nationalities had come to believe in having a good time. They had acquired the habit of tolerance in religious and other matters, welcoming dissenters from New England (including Anne Hutchinson), and had protested against Peter Stuyvesant's attempts to enforce religious conformity. They liked to spend part of the day in taverns and visit together in grog shops, to drink (some to excess), to eat well and to dance. They loved to race their boats and carriages, to skate and sleigh in winter. New Netherland colonists introduced these pastimes to America; also the game of *Kolf* (golf). And the new land became familiar with the Dutch feast-time specialties of colored Easter eggs and a species of doughnut called the cruller.

For a long time after the demise of New Netherland the Dutch retained economic and social dominance in communities they had founded. The patroons kept their immense estates.

In some of the smaller New Jersey and New York localities the descendants of the Early Dutch are still among the leading people. A woman who lives in Bergen County and works in Passaic County, New Jersey, tells me that in both places "the Dutch streak, going back to the 1660s, persists to this day. They still have their Dutch-language churches and schools. My grandmother, whose folks all arrived before 1700, wrote only Dutch. My late gardener's background in America reached back to 1650; he understood but could scarcely speak English."

New Netherland had several picturesque characters; the careers of some of them extended beyond the colony's. There was old peg-leg Peter Stuyvesant, its last governor, a stormy fellow, for whom a New York high school and a telephone exchange are named. Cornelis Steenwyck, a wealthy merchant, was active in politics during both the

Dutch and English periods. Frederick Philipse (or Felypsen), a powerful landowner and trader who had started as a carpenter, founded Yonkers. Bastiaen Jansen Krol, a colonial official at Fort Orange, is remembered for his friendly relations with the Indians. Jacob Boelen became one of the best early silversmiths in New Amsterdam and New York City. A businessman, Jacob Steendam, irritated by the slow growth of commerce and industry, turned poet and in 1659 wrote his "Complaint of New Amsterdam in New Netherland to Her Mother"; in '61 he penned a high-flown eulogy of the colony's attractions and potentialities.

The term "Knickerbocker," used interchangeably with "Dutch," was popularized by Washington Irving, who attributed the authorship of his *Knickerbocker's History of New York* (1809) to a fictitious writer of this name. The name was brought to America from Holland in 1674 by Harmen Jansen Knickerbocker.

The most consequential settler in New Netherland, however, was a peasant named Klaes Martensen van Roosevelt. The probability is that no one took much notice of him until long after he was dead. According to different genealogies, he arrived from Holland in 1644 or 1649 and became the common ancestor of eight presidents of the United States: James Madison, Martin Van Buren, Zachary Taylor, William H. Taft, Ulysses S. Grant, and Theodore and Franklin D. Roosevelt; also of Jefferson Davis, the president of the Confederacy during the Civil War; also of Eleanor Roosevelt.

It is fairly well known that Walt Whitman was part-Dutch; not so well that Herman Melville's mother was of Early Dutch stock.

The *Dictionary of American Biography* contains hundreds of biographies of significant men and women who came, or whose ancestors came, from Holland in the seventeenth century. The 1943-1944 *Who's Who in America* lists about 175 names beginning with "Van," many of whose owners—industrialists, financiers, professors, writers, generals, admirals, lawyers, clergymen, physicians, artists—count the Early Dutch among their forebears. There are as many more whose names do not begin with "Van." The facts about Carl Van Vechten, the novelist, may be representative of many. "My Dutch ancestors," he writes to me, "landed here in 1638 and settled in the Catskills. There are ever so many traces of them throughout the state of New York and I believe there is (there certainly was) a Van Vechten Hall in Albany. My father was born in the town of Denmark, New York, in 1839. He attended Columbia and expected to be a lawyer. However, he met my mother [whose maiden name was Fitch], married her and went to live with her family in Michigan. His elder brother, Giles Fonda Van

Vechten, had gone even farther west and established a chain of banks, including one in Cedar Rapids, Iowa, where he induced my father to join him and where they both continued to live until they died. I was born in Cedar Rapids in 1880, but came right back to New York (or you might say New Amsterdam) as soon as I could manage it and have stayed here ever since. All Van Vechtens in this country stem, I believe, from the original pair who landed in New Netherland in 1638."

Early in May 1945, twenty-year-old First Lieutenant Augustus Van Cortlandt III died of wounds received in battle in Germany. His original American ancestor was Olaf Van Cortlandt, who arrived in New Amsterdam in 1638. His father, the Manhattan socialite Augustus Van Cortlandt, Jr., is the last of the line. The family once owned eighty-two thousand acres in New York City and Westchester County, including the vast Van Cortlandt Park in the Bronx, sold to the city in 1889.

Between the conquest of New Netherland and the War of Independence, Dutch immigration to America was light and sporadic.

A number of sympathizers of the Society of Friends came over with the Quakers and founded new homes in the Colony of Pennsylvania. Among them was Reiner Jansen, a lace merchant who arrived in 1698 to become the first operator of a Quaker press in America.

Philip Schuyler led frontiersmen and Mohawks in the Anglo-French wars in the last quarter of the seventeenth century. Other Schuylers were prominent in the Anglo-French wars (with their Protestant-Catholic implications) of the eighteenth century.

Early in that century New York and Amsterdam worked out lively trade connections. Hollanders visited America, several marrying into old Dutch families in New York City and "Dutch" towns up the Hudson.

Most of the patroons were pro-English, a few actively counter-revolutionary, while other people of Holland stock played their proportionate role on the American side in the Revolution. One native of Holland, John Philip De Haas, rose to the rank of brigadier general in Washington's Army. During the first two post-Revolutionary decades sixty Dutch Americans served in the United States Congress.

By the time America had declared its independence, the mantle of greatness had slipped off Holland's shoulders; its Golden Age was over. Its politics had become confused. Europe in general was struggling around in a welter of controversies and crosscurrents, great and small. So in the early 1780s there arrived in America a few uneasy Dutch

merchants who, apparently seeing possibilities in the newly-formed
United States, wanted to bolster their fortunes. A few others who came
were skilled artisans and settled in New York, Philadelphia, Savannah
and elsewhere. A few became farmers.

Late in the 1780s the United States received a group from Holland
called the Patriot exiles, leaders of a movement for popular rights
which collapsed after the 1780-1784 war between The Netherlands and
Great Britain. In that war the new American Republic and Holland
were virtual allies, and the Patriots had the support of John Adams,
the first United States' Minister to Amsterdam.

The most notable of these émigrés was Francis Adrian Van der
Kemp, a classical scholar whom circumstances in Holland had made
a political pamphleteer. When he arrived in New York in 1788, George
Washington offered him the hospitality of Mount Vernon. He turned
to farming, failed at it, and ultimately, on the invitation of Governor
DeWitt Clinton of New York, translated into English the records of
the New Netherland colony. He filled twenty-four huge manuscript
volumes. But they were lost, together with the original records, in
1911 when fire destroyed the capitol at Albany.

Another Patriot exile, Adam Gerard Mappa, a friend of Van der
Kemp's, a type-founder by profession, came to the United States in
1789. Urged by Thomas Jefferson, he brought a complete font of
letters. He set up the first type-foundry in New York but, unable to
get anyone to help him, had to give it up. Then he joined a real estate
promotion agency aimed at attracting Hollanders to the Dutch settlement at Oldenbarneveld, near Albany; but that too did not prosper.

Both "failures," Van der Kemp and Mappa died the same year,
1828, but left a warm impression on all who had known them. In a
letter to the New York *Statesman* in 1820, Governor Clinton told how
he once chanced on these "two venerable men angling for trout in a
copious and pellucid stream." Clinton regarded Van der Kemp as "*the
most learned man in America* [his emphasis], cultivating, like our first
parent, his beautiful and spacious garden with his own hands—cultivating liturature and science—cultivating the virtues which adorn the
fireside and the alter . . . and blessing with the radiations of his
illumined and highly gifted mind all who enjoy his conversations, and
who are honored by his correspondence."

In the early decades of the nineteenth century, conditions in The
Netherlands went from bad to worse. The last remnants of the old
Dutch sea trade had disappeared. Dutch industry was in complete

decay. Those in positions of responsibility seemed paralyzed by the crisis.

Dutch workers received barely enough to hold body and soul together. Living in hovels, they and their wives and children died like flies of tuberculosis and other diseases. Rural economics slumped. Many people were afraid they would lose what little they had.

The Napoleonic occupation over, the House of Orange was restored in the person of William I. Working hand in hand with the special interests, he assumed first indirect and later undisguised control over the established church, disregarding its old democratic constitution and forms. This perverted the traditional basis of the best features of Holland's national life. It distressed and grieved the more intelligent and energetic of the younger churchmen, who started or joined secession movements for a "pure Christianity" that would not permit itself to be used by the State power. A few of these clerics also had a sense of the economic and social realities. They were persecuted, fined and jailed. Their churches and meeting-halls were raided by police and military troops, their congregations driven out in the middle of the services.

Two clergymen stand out in an especially dramatic fashion: Albertus Christiaan Van Raalte and Hendrik Peter Scholte. In the late 1840s both led their followers to the United States, setting off the New Immigration from Holland.

Van Raalte, in his mid-thirties, was then pastor of a church within the separatist movement headed by his brother-in-law Anthony Brummelkamp, who held that what the Dutch Reformed Church needed was a "second Reformation." In 1845 Van Raalte heard members of his congregation discuss the possibilities of escaping from their economic and religious straits by emigrating. Perhaps the discussion was prompted by letters from people who had gone to the United States earlier. One writer had reported that the different boarding houses where he lived were "wonderful. I have a room of my own; coffee three times a day, or tea with sugar, bread, butter, meat, fish, potatoes, greens, and now since Easter, many eggs. Also beer, cider and other drinks are here in abundance." Another had written that in Decatur, Illinois, "ordinary people are as good as rich folks . . . there are good churches here and many of God's people . . . the schools are free . . . you do not need to lock your door."

Van Raalte knew of the Reformed Church in the United States maintained by the descendants of the Early Dutch; he knew it was not wound up in the religious dispute besetting the homeland. So he drafted a letter to "The Faithful in the United States" explaining the situation and requesting advice and help should he and his people decide to come over.

Van Raalte entrusted the letter to an emigrant bound for the United States who delivered it to somebody who showed it to the Reverend Isaac N. Wyckoff, pastor of the Second Reformed Church in Albany. Mr. Wyckoff took prompt action. An immigrant-aid society was formed, and after a while he wrote to Van Raalte not to hurry too fast; the society needed time to work out plans for help.

Mails were slow and uncertain, and Wyckoff's reply did not reach Holland till after the Van Raalte band had decided that as many as possible should go to America at once, before their meager resources were entirely gone. Earlier, in the spring, they had sent a few families as "spies" to see if America was really what it was talked up to be, and back had come at least one enthusiastic letter, from a woman whose family tried out Boston: "Nearly all people eat meat three times a day. . . . And everyone is kind. They help us out with everything; what we do not have, they lend us. . . . They sleep with a feather bed underneath and a straw ticking on top; but quite correct and nice; Arnhem can't compare with it. One sees no poor here, no beggars, nor any collection or poor boxes. . . . One sees great luxury, magnificent buildings; doors have silver knobs. . . . The finery is great; one cannot discern any difference between a cobbler's wife and the wife of a prominent gentleman. . . . Washings hang out on the line all night, nobody steals here . . . no sentries in front of houses; no night watchmen . . . only a few policemen, who look more like gentlemen, but their hats are marked in front with the word: Police. . . . Evenings everything is quiet—"

In October 1846 Van Raalte, his family and fifty-three other men, women and children sailed from Rotterdam on a New York-bound brig. They were probably the more financially substantial in the group, those able to pay for their passage and contribute to the general expense of the venture. The poor were to be helped across later. The group had heard that the United States government was giving away land in the West, or selling it at a very low price, and the tentative plan was that Van Raalte should acquire enough for thousands of Hollanders to settle on. The leader's own dream was to create a great community of Dutch people where he would help them be strong in their faith, guard them against strange influences, and guide them toward a moderate degree of material well-being.

Throughout the seven weeks' voyage on the crowded brig the Van Raalte passengers did little but pray and sing psalms. Each family had its own food supplies and did its own cooking, as was customary on immigrant ships in those days and, decreasingly, for about thirty years thereafter. Six of the party died of illness and were buried at sea.

The group reached New York in mid-November. A Dutch Reformed preacher there, the Reverend Thomas DeWitt, was most helpful, getting everybody safely off on a Hudson River boat for Albany, where Pastor Wyckoff and his immigrant-aid society also did all they could.

The newcomers stayed in Albany a week. Wisconsin loomed large in the Eastern imagination as a place for pioneers. Should they go there? Or to Iowa or Louisiana? Michigan! Somehow, Van Raalte and his advisers decided that that was the place; and most of the contingent entrained for Buffalo (fare $2.50 each), where they took a boat to Detroit.

With Detroit as his base—where his people earned part of their subsistence that winter, with the Albany immigrant-aid society providing the rest—Van Raalte roamed the southern sections of lower Michigan inspecting available land. He realized that an isolated "Little Holland" was out of the question; his people would need the aid of the earlier settlers experienced in the ways of the New World.

In Ottawa County, along Lake Michigan and almost directly west of Detroit, he made friends with leading citizens of Grand Rapids, then a village of 1,500, and of Kalamazoo, also already well established. Impressed by his earnestness and eager for more population, they formed special committees to help the Hollanders get off to a good start. A number accompanied Van Raalte on his explorations of the country. He considered the climate, the tree growth, the water supply, the quality of the soil. Finally, "in all honesty, before God," he recommended to his people some tracts of state tax land along the Black River and Black Lake, slightly southwest of Grand Rapids and northwest of Kalamazoo. The tracts were very cheap and available on easy terms. His choice was approved by the group.

In February 1847 Van Raalte and his advisers decided on the exact site for their community which they named Holland.

Meantime other detachments of Van Raalte followers had arrived from The Netherlands and were waiting in the East to hear from him. When word came most of them headed for Michigan.

Spring was all the more welcome that year for its lateness. The village of Holland was started under the hazards usual to the pioneer experience of the middle nineteenth century.

More and more Hollanders reached Michigan: farmers, artisans, tradespeople, working men and women with their children; mostly mindergegoeden—people of small means, as well as some too poor to pay their own fare. For a long time, the majority were of the Van

Raalte persuasion and settled in Holland. Other secessionists wanted communities of their own. By 1849 there were six new villages besides Holland in the Grand and Kalamazoo River Territory: Groningen, Zeeland, Drenthe, Vriesland, Overisel and Graafschap, with 629 families. The majority engaged in farming.

Van Raalte was the foremost Hollander in Michigan until his death in 1876. Having had some medical training, he was now not only his people's preacher but also their physician, obliged to cope with a series of near-epidemics during the early years. The last twenty years of his life he was ill himself, but his terrific will power and his sense of responsibility kept him going. He never wavered in the face of danger or adversity, and was patient with others whose fabric of character did not match his own. He kept the community alert in economic matters, started a religious journal in the Dutch language, and served as the main liaison between the new Dutch churches in Michigan and the old Reformed organization in New York State. His perpetual emphasis on education led to the founding of Hope College, a co-educational institution, and of a theological seminary, both in the town of Holland. His initiative was behind new post offices, new roads and rural mail routes, and nearly everything else which could benefit his people.

During the Civil War, the four thousand Michigan Hollanders gave the Union Army 420 men.

After the war the town of Holland grew swiftly. In 1940 its population was fifteen thousand, mostly of Dutch and Frisian origin or descent. The names on store signs and office windows are Dutch and Frisian three to one: Van Verst, Masselink, Sterenberg, De Vries, Van der Velde, Westrate, Harms, Van Raalte, Vandenberg, Bos, Tiesenga. Dutch and Frisian are habitually spoken in hundreds of homes, including some lived in by fourth-generation Americans, but the custom is beginning to wear out.

Holland is the scene of the much publicized annual Tulip Festival which begins on the Saturday nearest to May 15th, the approximate date when the three million tulips planted throughout the town burst into bloom. The festival lasts eight days and attracts throngs of visitors from the lower Great Lakes region. The townspeople don the *klompen* (wooden shoes) and full breeches and skirts and lace caps their grandparents and great-grandparents wore back in Marken, Volendam and Zeeland. Then, as a main feature of the celebration, they usher in the traditional Dutch spring-cleaning by scrubbing the streets with brooms and brushes and pails of soapsuds under the supervision of the mayor—

the *Burgemeester*—and other worthies, all rigged up in Rembrandtian garb.

The festival is linked to a chief industry in the community, the growing of some four hundred varieties of tulip bulbs. A good many farmers around Holland also grow little cucumbers which the Heinz branch factory in town promotes into I don't know how many varieties of pickles.

The near-by town of Zeeland, with its twenty-five hundred population, is nationally famous for its chicken hatcheries.

In the 1870s Hollanders, both foreign- and Michigan-born, began to settle in Grand Rapids because of the opportunities for work, notably in furniture factories. During the 1890s Dutch and Frisian immigrants poured in. Now forty thousand of the city's 164,000 inhabitants are of Dutch and Frisian birth or descent—the backbone of the furniture industry. This is the largest and most cohesive urban concentration of the Holland element in the United States. It is the center of Dutch Calvinism, organized ecclesiastically in the Reformed and the Christian Reformed denominations. The latter, a power in the city, adheres to a rigid orthodoxy and maintains Calvin College and Seminary. School societies, largely of Christian Reformed memberships, support seven primary schools and a high school.

Perhaps the outstanding contemporary Grand Rapids native of Dutch stock is United States Senator Arthur H. Vandenberg, Republican, who in 1945 emerged as a key figure in the country's swing from the hangovers of prewar isolation to international participation.

Many Hollanders have also gone to Detroit and Flint to work in the automotive industries; and there are colonies of them all over Ottawa, Kent, Muskegon, Allegan and Kalamazoo counties in Michigan.

No close connection existed in the homeland between the Van Raalte and Scholte groups, but their emigration motives were identical.

Hendrik Peter Scholte, in his early forties, was a natural leader, lofty in intellect and spirit, dramatic in personality, and with a background which included business and art as well as theology. He seems to have reached the conclusion that emigration was the only escape from the doldrums of Holland about the same time as Van Raalte.

In 1846 at Utrecht, the center of his movement, he formed a band of prospective emigrants called The Association (later renamed The Colony) consisting at first—as in the Van Raalte movement—largely of well-to-do followers. After they decided to go to America, Scholte very systematically prepared for the departure. He knew English and read everything about America he could lay his hands on. He corresponded with Van Raalte and others already in the United States. He inspirited his congregation with sermons on a tiny Christian sect which had fled from Jerusalem in A.D. 66, when the city was besieged by Romans to put down a revolt of the Jews, and had found refuge in Pella, a little town on the Jordan in Agrippa. They too, he told them, were going to Pella—a new Pella in the New World where they would worship according to their own convictions. He persuaded everybody to sell all belongings that could not be taken along.

In May 1847, the Dominie and his family and servants and a few others reached Boston on a "fast" vessel which had taken only a month to cross the Atlantic. A few weeks later four other ships carrying some eight hundred passengers arrived in Baltimore.

Meantime Scholte had visited Albany, to confer with leaders of the Reformed Church, and Washington, to inquire about lands open to settlement. Deciding against Michigan because he felt Hollanders would do better on the prairies than in wooded territory where they would have to clear the land, he chose Iowa; and during June and July he and his people traveled nearly half the width of the continent. The colony paused briefly at St. Louis while Scholte and four other men went ahead to pick the location of their Pella between the Des Moines and Skunk Rivers in newly formed Marion County. They bought eighteen thousand acres.

When the rest of The Colony reached the place, they beheld a sign reading "Pella" which the Dominie had painted on a rough board and stuck into the ground beside a cabin abandoned by an earlier settler.

To help the town achieve a self-continuing civil government in line with American principles and customs, and in order that they might vote in their local elections even before attaining full-fledged citizenship, Scholte secured permission from the Federal government for all the adult males, about two hundred, to forswear publicly their allegiance to the king of The Netherlands and pledge their loyalty to the United States. "No tribute," wrote an American eye-witness in the Burlington (Iowa) *Hawk-Eye*, "could be more beautiful and complimentary to our institutions than to behold the men of Pella coming up in their strength on the Prairies of America, and there . . . with brawny arms upraised to heaven . . . eschewing forever all allegiance to the tyranny of king-craft."

After the first few primitive years, which most of the settlers spent in sod-houses and tents when they were not hard at work in the fields, Pella gradually grew into a handsome little town laid out according to a plan drawn by Scholte. The streets were named for the ideals and virtues which the Christian, the Separatist, the Hollander and the American in the Dominie deemed important—Independence, Liberty, Peace, Inquiry, Perseverance, Reformation, Gratitude, Experience, Patience, Expectation, Confidence and Accomplishment.

Pella had its crises of course: an unusually severe winter in 1848 when some inadequately housed settlers and many animals died; later in succession, a flood, an outbreak of cholera, a locust invasion. By the middle 1850s, however, the town was on firm economic feet. A couple of hundred new immigrants added to its numbers each year. Some old-stock Americans moved in or onto nearby farms. Roads were built; railroads followed.

Just as Van Raalte was the big man among the Michigan Dutch, Scholte was pre-eminent among the Dutch of Iowa. "He was a gentleman farmer, owner of saw mills, and brick and lime kilns, land agent, notary, printer, editor and publisher, dealer in farm implements, attorney, as well as clergyman," writes his grandson John Scholte Nollen, "and through all these activities in a rapidly growing community he contrived not to amass a fortune. He built a church at his own expense and preached in it without a salary."

During the 1850s, as more and more immigrants arrived and were naturalized, Scholte rose to power in Iowa politics. A delegate to the 1860 Republican National convention, he voted for the nomination of Lincoln, who later became his friend and whom he once visited in Washington. During the Civil War a normal proportion of Iowa Hollanders served in the Union forces. When word of Lincoln's assassination reached Pella, Scholte, then in his early sixties suffered a heart attack. He never quite recovered and died in 1868.

For decades Dutch and Frisian immigrants continued to come to Pella and its vicinity. Others only paused there on their way northwest to settle in and around Sioux City. They founded Orange City, still chiefly a Dutch town.

Visiting Pella in 1939, I found it a quiet prosperous community, the economic and religious center of a farming area with a radius of twenty-odd miles, largely inhabited by Hollanders. The descendants of the Scholte group were third- and fourth-generation Americans, but—in common with the second generation and the immigrants—the majority still referred to themselves as Hollanders, distinct from "Americans," and they spoke Dutch (or a kind of Dutch) in addition to English. Some wore the *klompen* while working in their backyards or dairies. Most of them were back in the Reformed Church, which ran the local Central College, a liberal arts school. The original Scholte separatism was gone, for religious liberty and the separation of State and Church being actualities in the United States, that cause had waned during the Dominie's lifetime. But a good deal of division over theological ideas remains. Religious arguments are a favorite Dutch indoor sport.

Pella also puts on an annual tulip festival beginning in mid-May which brings crowds from all over Iowa and Nebraska.

For decades Dutch-American historians have argued whether the Van Raalte and Scholte motives for emigration were primarily religious or economic. I am impressed by the Hollanders' letters to their people in the old country, both before and after the departure of the two groups. The majority stressed how much better one ate in the United States than in Holland. There is no doubt, however, that in both Michigan and Iowa religious convictions were a deciding factor in holding the immigrants together, and in the development of their communities.

Though the Van Raalte and Scholte movements spearheaded the New Immigration from The Netherlands, it would of course have begun sooner or later anyhow. In the 1850s and '60s and later, the word "America" throbbed in the imagination of more and more people in various parts of Europe. The "America letters" were read eagerly and passed around.

Whatever the immediate cause, the last half of the nineteenth century and the first part of the twentieth saw vast numbers of men and women and children go from Holland to the United States. They were not organized; they just up and left.

This set off a heated debate in Holland: were the emigrants foolish or wise? In due time the pro-America arguments won. In 1855 Everardus Johannes Potgieter, then one of Holland's literary figures, published a paean to the United States in his journal De Gids: ". . . Our eyes rest with pleasure upon you, you swiftly expanding, happy, free State, without king, nobility or ecclesiastical caste; you who hold the nations in a magic spell : . . whose prosperity draws all those in Europe, not singly but in great numbers, who are weary of the old days."

Evidently America's attraction was largely political and even more largely economic. Tales of industrial expansion and of the ever-receding frontier excited the Hollanders as they did the German and Scandinavians.

While many immigrants of all nationalities experienced nothing but kindness at the hands of Americans when they first arrived, many faced hostility and crookedness. They were preyed upon, to quote Scholte, by "kidnappers and deceivers who storm each incoming ship

. . . like bands of hungry wolves." For some newcomers in the 1850s and '60s, America was as much a wilderness as the coast of New England or Virginia had been to the English in the 1620s.

But nothing could discourage the Great Migration or dim the American Mirage. Official Dutch figures have it that on the average 2,250 people annually left Holland for the United States in the five years from 1846 to 1850. Perhaps half of them had been inspired by the Van Raalte and Scholte pioneers. The remainder were not connected with those movements. In 1848, for instance, over a hundred Roman Catholic Hollanders migrated to the Green Bay region of Wisconsin, where their leader, a Dominican priest, Theodore J. van der Broek, had been a missionary among the Indians, and where they started a community called Hollandtown. A little later a Protestant group also plunged into the Wisconsin wilds and founded the town of Alto. Between 1847 and 1853 small contingents of Frisians came to live in Lafayette and Goshen, Indiana, and Lancaster, Pennsylvania. Some of these people were Mennonites and the equivalent of modern conscientious objectors.

Soon, according to contemporary records, tiny colonies of Hollanders, recently arrived from various parts of The Netherlands, were noticeable in New York, Boston, Albany, Rochester, Buffalo, Cleveland, Detroit, Chicago, Milwaukee, St. Louis, Keokuk, Burlington, Davenport, Dubuque. Their abilities, inclinations and opportunities led these newcomers into diverse occupations. Ever since, newly-arriving Dutch immigrants have dispersed through much of the country. Probably twenty per cent have settled on the land, some in Minnesota, the Dakotas and in the state of Washington.

Chicago contains one of the oldest, largest, most persistent bigcity Dutch settlements. It started in a small way in the late 1840s about fifteen miles from the present Loop district. Through the '60s and '70s it sprawled toward the expanding city. At different times, even at the same time, it was called South Holland, High Prairie and Roseland.

A Cook County historian writing in the middle 1880s describes Roseland as a picturesque place resembling villages in The Netherlands. Its inhabitants were "sturdy, phlegmatic, industrious"; doing what, is not clear. Then gradually the aggressive city engulfed them and converted their community into a booming industrial center which attracted immigrants of other national origins. Now there is no trace of the colorful Dutch village of the '80s. But many people living in Roseland and adjacent sections of metropolitan Chicago are still consciously "Dutch" to the fourth generation. Among themselves they speak a revised Dutch language and adhere to the Reformed and Christian Reformed Churches.

For a long time thousands of Chicago's Hollanders have been working in the Illinois Central and Pullman shops, the International Harvester plants, the Sherwin-Williams paint factory. Hundreds own grocery stores and meat markets. Others excel as mechanics in the building trades. Some families have been in the teaming and trucking business for generations, at first with horse-drawn drays, later with trucks. Several one-time teamsters now head excavating and hauling companies. A few have gone into the real estate business. The young people work in downtown offices and stores.

Dutch Americans are as a rule rather conservative and not very active politically. In Chicago attempts to organize them as the "Dutch element" for political ends have not succeeded. One of them said after an election defeat: "Hollanders are a funny crowd. When one of us runs for office, all the others say in chorus, 'He's only a Dutchman, he can work for a living like the rest of us. He isn't too good to work. If he thinks he is, then he's no good at all.' So they all vote for some good-for-nothing Irish politician."

But they are not averse to organizing culturally into Knickerbocker Societies and forming religious associations. In New York, in 1921, Franklin D. Roosevelt, Edward Bok and Hendrik van Loon took the initiative in organizing the Netherland-American Foundation to further Dutch arts and sciences in the United States, and to perpetuate the friendship between the two countries. The Frisians have several social and cultural bodies known as *selskippen*; in 1943 they founded a Frisian Information Bureau in Grand Rapids.

In Chicago, as in Grand Rapids and a few other places, the religious Dutch Americans maintain separate "Christian schools." Their churches are well attended; in only a few are the services still in Dutch.

Except for one or two in Michigan, Dutch-language newspapers have had hard sledding since about 1930.

I have referred to a favorite Dutch indoor sport—debating theological concepts. Within the frame of their Calvinist background, they conduct their discussions on the basis of logic welded to literalness. In mundane matters too their minds are literal, reasonable and consistent. But they can be illogical and self-contradictory. In the 1920s, for example, the majority—both clerics and laymen—were opposed to Prohibition because it ran counter to their ideas of liberty; on the other hand, in Zeeland, Michigan, there are no licensed premises for selling liquor. Nor are there any movies. The last proposal to license a movie house was turned down early in 1945.

Many a Hollander is unbendingly antagonistic toward any sort of fluidity in moral concepts and practices. In this he follows the teachings and public policy of his church. Once a Calvin College professor was tried by the Synod of the Christian Reformed Church in Grand Rapids and expelled, as his partisans put it, for openly attending a movie. Those defending the expulsion say that it occurred not because he openly attended a movie—"that would have been absurd," one wrote to me—but because "he could not see his way clear to subscribe to the stand of the Christian Reformed Church" which holds that "Hollywood, on the whole, distributes products which are intellectual and cultural tripe and which, with their preoccupation with sex and gangsterism, are degrading." Some of the older folk still hold the movies in such disfavor that the younger ones have to sneak off to them.

But this Dutch and Frisian ultra-conservatism has been breaking down for some time, although not fast enough to suit the impatient. At Calvin College in the early 1900s music was not tolerated except for congregational singing with organ or piano accompaniment; now the college's music department sponsors a choral society.

Not that any kind of radicalism is in the wind. In Grand Rapids the dominant church is traditionally opposed to "neutral" (non-religious) labor unions and has been accused by C.I.O. organizers of being a "company religion," of helping the furniture factories keep wages down. In 1930, in an effort to prevent unionization of the plants, some of the church leaders tried to sponsor a Christian Labor Association based "on the principles of the word of God" and "obedience to the constituted authorities," which, according to one of my correspondents, implicitly included the employers. These church leaders, who represented a majority of the Dutch, felt so strongly about the worker's giving a good day's work (for whatever wage) that they seemed incapable of considering other aspects of an industrial civilization.

Work, hard work, is an integral part of many a Dutch American's religion. Most of the immigrants have always firmly believed in it, but some of their children and grandchildren believe in leavening it with humor. In 1940 a young man wrote me from Grand Rapids: " 'Laziness is the Devil's headpillow,' says a Dutch proverb. 'In the sweat of thy brow thou shalt earn thy bread,' says the Bible. And the literal-minded Dutch have taken both very literally. If by sweating we can earn our bread and circumvent the Devil, well, that's killing two birds with one stone. . . .

"The Dutch who are not employed in furniture factories here are plasterers, painters, masons and janitors; and, man, do they work! It's nothing short of wonderful. But—well, too many just don't see there is anything else to life than hard work and religion.

"Several Hollander contractors have done all they can to keep the trade unions weak. They've pushed the wage scale down several notches. But there is nothing intentionally evil in all this; it is just that work, work, WORK, comes before anything else. Our good parents and grandparents who were poor peasants in Holland brought this passion with them in their very souls. And the Grand Rapids papers and the Chamber of Commerce, allied with the furniture factories, praise them to the skies as the 'proud, industrious sons of old Holland, the homeland of so many solid virtues'; while the non-Dutch radicals and labor leaders, not so certain that hard work and long hours are good things in themselves, growl that they are 'stupid,' and 'reactionary.' From their angles, both are right. But I side with the unions as against the Dutch church and a lot of the Dutch community. If my father knew this!

"About 1935 when the Depression was bad it was interesting, though not very inspiring, to watch this Dutch passion for work tighten into desperation. If you were a petty contractor, one way to get work was to underbid the other fellow. You might lose on the deal, but perhaps you could fix that by working yourself and your men like all-get-out. . . ."*

* In April 1945, this section was sent for comment to a few Dutch Americans in Michigan; two approved of it as true, a third wrote:

"The implication that the Christian Labor Association was organized as a method of depressing wages, a kind of plot on the part of Church leaders who were also employers, simplifies the situation far too much. Doubtless those motivations were present, human nature being what it is. Although I have no love for the extreme conservatism of such people and have opposed them all my life, I give them credit for more sincerity than that. These neo-Calvinists, scores of thousands of them, have always believed that they are 'ever in their great Taskmaster's eye,' and they believe passionately that their Calvinistic religion should permeate all their social institutions—including labor organizations, business firms, community projects, political parties. When they organized a Christian labor union, I am convinced the motivation was at least primarily religious and in what they conceived to be the interests of the workers themselves.

". . . The worship of work for its own sake as a good in itself is not confined to the Hollanders; it runs all through nineteenth century Victorianism, with Carlyle as its high priest.

"As for the attitude of the Grand Rapids newspapers, I think the young man whose letter you quote does them an injustice. I have known personally many of those newspapermen. They did, and do, 'praise them [the Dutch] to the skies as the "proud, industrious sons of old Holland, the homeland of so many solid virtues."' But the charge implied in the phrase 'allied with the furniture factories' again is too great a simplification. Any newspaperman is likely to speak well of any large block of readers, no matter what their background or way of life. An editor who knew that he was speaking to a single block of some forty thousand in his own town, to say nothing of many more thousands in surrounding communities, would be a fool not to speak them fair. It is not necessary to assume that those editors were intent on keeping wages down. I am not suggesting that your correspondent did not have facts, merely that his interpretation is inadequate."

This situation exists to a marked degree not only in Grand Rapids, but in nearby Kalamazoo as well, where the papermill stockholders have benefited by cheap labor. And it exists because the immigrants who came during 1890-1905, the height of the influx, were peasants escaping from the farming crisis and near-starvation in Holland. Thousands were contract laborers, their passage paid by representatives of furniture companies. Some companies took unfair advantage of their employees, exploiting their peasant virtues of hard work and thrift. By this system at least two Grand Rapids factories rose to the summits of success.

But the system is on the way out. The anti-union tradition is weakening. During the late 1930s and early '40s some of the Christian Reformed diehards tried repeatedly to get the Church to take an official stand against the C.I.O. and the A. F. of L., and failed each time. Since about 1937 thousands of members of the Christian Reformed Church in Michigan—and not only those who moved to Detroit and Flint—have joined C.I.O. and A.F. of L. unions.

The 1940 census reported a total of 372,384 immigrants from Holland (most of them citizens) and second-generation Americans of Dutch descent. The figure probably is too low. Americans partly descended from the Early Dutch are beyond even approximate computation; their number may well be in the millions. Most of them live in the East, the rest are pretty well scattered. In the middle of the nineteenth century a band of Early Dutch descendants pulled up stakes in New Jersey and settled in the vicinity of Peoria and elsewhere in Illinois.

President Harry S. Truman is remotely of part-Dutch descent.

Of the latter-day Dutch and Frisian Americans, the minority live in more or less cohesive groups in the towns already mentioned and also in Sheboygan and Marathan Counties, Wisconsin, and at Terra Ceia, a tulip center in Beaufort County, North Carolina. The majority are thinly spread about the United States, and in their work, interest and ideas are all but indistinguishably merged with the local population, be it in Philadelphia or Los Angeles. Many belong to no Dutch organization or church, but support wider American movements and societies. Few outside the larger groups are what might be called professional Dutchmen. Prior to 1940 no considerable number were interested in Holland; since that fateful year many have felt concern for the old country, have been reading the printed matter sent out by the Netherlands Information Bureau, an agency of the Dutch government in New York, and found relief in the fact that Franklin Roosevelt was partial to Holland's interests.

Other traits of the Dutch and Frisian Americans (of course not copyrighted by them) are loyalty to what they are convinced is right; love of home and of flowers; stubborn perseverance in the face of hardship; general solidity of character and personality. Quiet, not shy but undemonstrative, they don't care very much if some fellow Americans of other backgrounds consider them dull. They in turn are everlastingly shocked by American wastefulness. To whatever they attempt they usually bring trained ability, a sense of economy, and personal and professional pride and discipline.

I have already suggested that outstanding performance in special fields has not been rare on the part of Dutch and Frisian Americans. A few more examples:

Joseph Raphael De Lamar, an Amsterdamer, arrived in Vineyard Haven, Massachusetts, in 1867 and became a ship contractor. Five years later, at twenty-nine, he created a sensation by raising a submerged liner. Then he went West, acquired some mining properties, sold them for two million dollars, turned capitalist and eccentric. When he died in 1918, his will divided ten million dollars among the Columbia, Harvard and Johns Hopkins medical schools.

David Christiaan Henny, a young graduate of the Polytechnic School at Delft, landed in the United States in 1884. He went to California; fifty years later he had the firm reputation of being the leading American expert on dam-building. The "Henny shear joint," an essential device in the construction of massive concrete dams, is his invention. He was either the construction or a consulting engineer on most of the big dams built in the West during his lifetime, which ended in 1935.

Born in 1839 and brought to Grand Rapids as a child, Martin Luther D'Ooge was a professor at the University of Michigan, a scholar of distinction specializing in ancient Greek life and thought, and until his death in 1915 one of the noteworthy teachers of his time.

The young immigrant Adolphus Julius F. Behrends rose to eminence as an American clergyman. Son of a Lutheran family, he changed first to the Baptist, then to the Congregational Church, and served in Cleveland, Providence and Brooklyn. When he died in 1900 an editorial in the Outlook called him "one of the not large number of truly great preachers."

His family brought Edward Bok, aged six, to the United States in 1870. The boy knew no English when he started to school in Brooklyn. To help make ends meet at home, he washed windows in a bakery for fifty cents a week, then sold newspapers and books from house to house. He worked as a telegraph messenger boy, a newspaper reporter and later, still in his twenties, as a magazine editor. Cyrus H. K. Curtis of Philadelphia made him editor of the *Ladies' Home Journal*, which had got off to a lame start some years before. The young Dutchman, applying his keen instinct about the American people to magazine publishing, introduced many innovations, still the basis of mass-circulation periodicals addressed to women. He sponsored or endorsed such causes as slum-clearance, woman suffrage, and the elimination of billboards, public drinking-cups and venereal disease. In 1892 his announcement that the *Ladies' Home Journal* would accept no more patent-medicine advertisements led to a terrific uproar among the nostrum manufacturers and ultimately to the Food and Drugs Act of 1906.

A classic case of American success, Edward Bok married his boss' daughter (incidentally "boss" came from the Dutch word *baas* for master) and acquired a large interest in the Curtis Publishing Company. When he quit the editorship in 1919, the *Ladies' Home Journal* had a two-million-plus circulation and carried over a million dollars worth of advertising. Bok had revolutionized the business and, in many respects, is the father of the modern American slick-paper magazine. In 1920, fifty years after he landed in the United States, he published his autobiography, *The Americanization of Edward Bok*, which received a Pulitzer Prize and sold nearly a quarter of a million copies. From about 1900 to his death at sixty-seven in 1930, his name was almost a household word.

During his final decade he was one of the country's leading philanthropists. He supported the Philadelphia Symphony Orchestra. He created the $10,000 yearly Philadelphia Award for community service, endowed another fund of six annual $1,000 prizes for outstanding work by policemen, firemen and park guards, set up the Harvard Awards to encourage higher standards of magazine advertising, and the Woodrow Wilson Chair of Government at Williams College. In 1923 he announced the $100,000 American Peace Award, and when that failed in its purpose, he continued his peace propaganda through the American Foundation established in 1925 to carry on his various public interests. He spent his last years at Lake Wales, Florida, where he established the well-known wildlife sanctuary with its "Singing Tower," a great attraction for tourists. He is buried in a crypt under the tower on which appear, hewn in stone, his Dutch grandmother's words: "Make you the world a bit more beautiful and better because you have been in it."

Daniel De Leon, a young man of Jewish-Dutch origin, arrived in New York about 1874. In the next forty years he became one of the world's most vigorous radical thinkers and propagandists. Active in the American labor movement, he founded *The People* (still coming out) and the Socialist Trade and Labor Alliance (later the Socialist Labor Party) and helped found the International Workers of the World (I.W.W.). A highly controversial figure during most of his life in the United States, De Leon received his major recognition some years after his death when Lenin declared early in the 1920s that his pamphlets —notably *Socialist Reconstruction of Society* (1905)—contained the germ of the Soviet governmental system.

Gerrit J. Diekema (1859-1930) is the top American political figure of unmixed Dutch blood (President Roosevelt was and Senator Vandenberg is of mixed heredity). Born in the town of Holland, he graduated from the University of Michigan Law School, immediately entered politics, and served his apprenticeship in the state legislature. He also became one of the most successful lawyers in the Middle West. He was in Congress from 1907 to 1911; he was a member of the Spanish Treaty Claims Commission. In 1929 President Hoover named him Minister to The Netherlands, where he served with distinction partly because of his native eloquence and his fluent knowledge of the language.

The Gargantuan figure of Hendrik Willem van Loon, a native of Rotterdam, will long linger in the memory of New York's literary circles as well as among American book readers and lecture audiences. *The Story of Mankind, The Story of the Bible, Tolerance, America, Life and Times of Rembrandt van Rijn, The Arts,* and some twenty other volumes sold in millions of copies all over the world. And no wonder. Excitingly written with a sharp slant toward contemporary America and illustrated with his own drawings, they were the envy of other popular and would-be popular authors. An extraordinary, vastly complicated human being, Hendrik van Loon wrote and drew with a graphic simplicity that communicated itself instantly to a wide variety of readers. Consider the opening sentences of *The Story of Mankind,* accompanied by a picture of a huge rock: "High up in the North in the land called Svitbjod, there stands a rock. It is a hundred miles high and a hundred miles wide. Once every thousand years a little bird comes to this rock to sharpen its beak. When the rock has been worn away, then a single day of eternity will have gone by."

Paul de Kruif worked during his early years as a bacteriologist at the University of Michigan and Rockefeller Institute, but is better known for his best sellers *Microbe Hunters, Hunger Fighters, Seven Iron Men, Men Against Death* and *The Male Hormone.* He was born in Zeeland,

Michigan, founded by his great-grandfather Jannes Van der Luyster, who paid the fare across the ocean for many an immigrant. Paul de Kruif has done a tremendous job of popularizing medical information in the United States.

Other American writers of Dutch origin are Pierre van Paassen, author of the best seller *Days of Our Years*, also the chief Gentile champion of Palestine as the Jewish homeland; Arnold Mulder of Kalamazoo College, of whose four novels about the Dutch in America *The Outbound Road* and *The Dominie of Harlem* are the best known; Adriaan J. Barnouw of Columbia University, author of two books on The Netherlands, now working on a history of the Dutch in America; Sara Elizabeth Gosselink, whose *Roofs Over Strawtown* is a tale of early Pella; Wesley Smitter, who wrote *F.O.B. Detroit* and *Another Morning*. Among those of Frisian descent are the brothers de Jong—David C., whose novel *Belly Fulla Straw* (1935) upset its subject, the Hollanders and Frisians of Grand Rapids; and Meindert, with several volumes for young people; Feike Feikema, whose novel *The Golden Bowl* (1944) is a story of people and conditions in the Dust Bowl.

Among musicians these Dutchmen have emerged in recent decades: Willem van Hoogstraten, Richard Hageman and Hans Kindler, conductors; Willem van de Wall, pioneer in the application of music to social problems; Cornelius van Vliet and Willem Willeke, cellists.

Since the early 1930s Dykstra has been a big name in the United States. Clarence A. Dykstra, once city manager of Cincinnati, then president of the University of Wisconsin and adviser to numerous governmental agencies, is provost of the University of California in Los Angeles. Ralph R. Dykstra of Manhattan, Kansas, is a leading authority on veterinary medicine. Theodore P. Dykstra is the famous potato expert, formerly with the United States Department of Agriculture, who since 1942 has been adapting American (Irish) potatoes to Chinese soil and thus making a major contribution toward solving the food problem of China.

Amry Vandenbosch, dean of the Political Science Department at the University of Kentucky, author of *The Dutch East Indies*, *The Neutrality of the Netherlands During the World War* and *The Dutch Communities of Chicago*, was the Office of Strategic Services' and the State Department's expert on Dutch East India during 1941-1943 and one of the secretaries of the Committee on Trusteeship at the San Francisco world security conference in 1945.

Cornelis Bol, a Dutch-born scientist at Stanford University, invented the "midget sun," a tiny mercury vapor lamp hardly bigger than a match whose brilliance clearly illuminates objects five hundred feet away and enables one to read a newspaper at a distance of a mile. Manufactured by General Electric, the Bol lamp is used for movie projectors, searchlights, photoengraving and other purposes requiring strong, concentrated light.

John Roukema is well known as a skater. John Vander Meer is the no-hit, no-run pitcher of the Cincinnati Reds.

Saco Rienk De Boer, planning consultant for Denver and other cities in the Rockies, and Jacobus Leonardus Gubbels, director of urban planning with the Texas Highway Department, are two of the better known American landscape architects; both natives of Holland.

Dr. Joseph R. Sizoo, originally of The Netherlands, now pastor of the Collegiate Church of St. Nicholas, has long been one of New York's widely known clergymen. He often quotes this Confucian saying: "It is better to light one small candle than to curse the darkness."

Leon Adrian Versluis, born in Michigan, is the founder and head of the Grand Rapids' Associated Broadcasting Corporation (ABC), which in 1945 became the fifth coast-to-coast network in the United States.

Jan Schilt, who immigrated in 1925, is head of the Rutherfurd Observatory and the department of astronomy at Columbia University. In 1935 he submitted photographic proof that individual stars of the Pleiades cluster were following slightly divergent movements, contradicting previous observations which suggested that the movements within the group were equal and parallel. This discovery facilitated the measurement of gravity among the Pleiades cluster. In 1939, after years of studying the parallaxes of stellar bodies, Professor Schilt announced that over five thousand stars centered about the sun were between two and three times closer to the earth than had hitherto been believed. He is the inventor of the Schilt photometer.

There is scarcely an observatory in the United States without an astronomer of Dutch origin or descent. And there is hardly a university or college that hasn't one or more professors of the same stock. At Harvard, J. A. De Haas teaches foreign trade and international relations; J. G. Dusser de Barenne is a professor of physiology at Yale; Samuel Abraham Goudsmit, professor of physics at the University of Michigan, is the co-discoverer with G. E. Uhlenback of the "spin of the electron"; Arie Jan Haagen-Smit, bio-organic chemist, once of Harvard, later of the California Institute of Technology, achieved the isolation and synthesis of plant hormones—

It is the general run of Dutch and Frisian Americans, however, who in the aggregate total up to long-range effectiveness—people like the girl described in the following letter which I received in 1939 from an old-stock American woman living in a Midwestern city:

"When I was little my mother once hired a maid named Augusta Bosma. She came from Friesland, but we thought of her as "Dutch." She spoke English with a heavy accent. She was only sixteen, plump, with thick yellow hair, red cheeks, blue eyes, perfect teeth; glowing with health and good humor. We took to each other at once.

"Augusta's name in the old country was Aukje in Frisian and Auwkie in Dutch, but she'd changed it because no one here could pronounce it. She told us about her family. There were fifteen children. Her father and mother had recently come to America and were dairy farmers. They owned a place near the city.

"At first Augusta could not understand our joking ways. One day Dad with an armful of wood met Mother at the swinging kitchen door and both refused to budge an inch. Whereupon Augusta said to Mother: 'Vait, I let you troo.' She grabbed my father and fairly lifted him off his feet. To brace himself, he took hold of the stove. Augusta pulled harder and Dad, wood, stove and stove pipe came down. 'Now,' she panted to Mother, 'you come troo.' . . . Dad never got tired of telling this story.

"Once at a party on a visit home Augusta met a newly arrived young Dutchman. He bragged that if he had a wife he would make her do thus and so and if she refused he would slap her down. 'Oh yes?' said Augusta, 'If anyone tried that with me I'd slap him down.' The crowd egged them on. Augusta threw him, sat astride him and, holding his arms pinned under her knees, slapped his face alternately with each hand, crying 'say nuff,' slap, 'nuff,' slap, 'say nuff!' The crowd roared. Released at last, the young man slunk off without speaking to anyone, or even stopping to get his hat and coat. He was later reported to have gone back to the old country.

"Augusta went to night school and, following an older sister's example, decided to become a trained nurse. In a few years she was one of the best surgical nurses in town. Later as a public school nurse she used to cover her district in her own car. She spent several summer vacations in Holland. Then she married a young dentist and is now living in a small place in Indiana."

V: AMERICANS FROM SWEDEN

SAVE for a few scattered adventurers who came to New Netherland and New England in the early years of the seventeenth century and of whom very little is known, the first Swedes reached the American continent in the spring of 1638. They landed on a spot called "the Rocks" within the present city of Wilmington, Delaware. They had crossed the Atlantic in their own Mayflowers—two windjammers, arriving together: the *Kalmar Nyckel* (Key of Kalmar) and the *Fogel Grip* (Bird Griffin).

The newcomers were led by Peter Minuit, a cosmopolite whom various historians have put down as a Walloon, a Frenchman and a Prussian. Years before while in the service of the Dutch he had purchased Manhattan Island from the Indians for the equivalent of twenty-four dollars. Now, employed by the Swedes as an expert on how to get along in America (but soon to perish in a storm at sea), he negotiated another remarkable real estate deal. For some trifling merchandise brought over from Europe, five sachems of the Delaware Indians scratched their marks on a deed selling "as much of the land in all parts and places of the river, up the river and on both sides, as Minuit desired." Eventually this meant a considerable territory comprising regions in four of the Thirteen Original States, Pennsylvania, Delaware, Maryland and New Jersey.

One of the first things the colonists did was to build a fort. They named it for twelve-year-old Queen Christina, daughter of Gustavus Adolphus II, Sweden's great king who had died of battle wounds in Germany six years earlier—after he and his chancellor, Axel Oxenstierna, and a Dutch promoter named Willem Usselinx had worked out the idea of starting a "Nova Suecia" (New Sweden) in America.

It wasn't a bad idea, but it was a little late, and when it was put into effect it was later still.

In the preceding quarter of a century while Gustavus Adolphus, the champion of Protestantism, was fighting wars in Russia, Poland, Germany and Bohemia, three other European powers had taken over nearly all the Atlantic seaboard of North America. When, after many delays, New Sweden finally was founded on the one likely spot not yet firmly claimed by any other country, the French, English and Dutch—as we have seen—were already established in New France, New England and

New Netherland. And what with Gustavus Adolphus dead and Oxen-stierna, young Christina's chief regent, having his hands full of the Thirty Years' War (1618-48), Sweden was unable to overcome the handicap of a late start.

Additional settlers came over sporadically, several hundred in all, among them many Finns—"Swedish Finns"; but that was not enough to count in the long run so far as New Sweden's political future was concerned, especially since over half the Swedes returned home after a few years. The colony while under Swedish government never had a population above four hundred, including Hollanders, Finns and others.

"Nova Suecia" as such lasted only seventeen years. In 1655 the Dutch, themselves on the chute, took it over with no effort at all, incorporating it into New Netherland. Nine years later the English easily absorbed the Dutch and continued to sketch the general pattern for America's future civilization.

But, short-lived as was the Swedish rule, the colony itself turned out to be the first permanent White settlement in the Delaware River Valley, and its settlers and their descendants made a definite contribution to the development of North America during the seventeenth century. The Swedes, helped by the Hollanders, Germans and Finns who had come over with them, established a few little communities which continued to attract occasional settlers long after the colony ceased to exist. One settlement, Wicaco, they started within the present site of Philadelphia in 1643—a year before William Penn was born. They and the Finns introduced a sturdy type of wooden house common in Sweden and Finland and destined to become famous as the American log cabin—the dwelling of westering pioneers, a symbol of American hardihood, the favored starting point of many a political career.

The Swedes and Finns were good farmers, tough and persevering, capable of rolling back the wilderness and then living on its edges. In this respect they were at least equal to the better known settlers of New England. When in 1682 William Penn arrived to establish the Quaker colony of Pennsylvania, he marveled at the spade work in civilization he observed throughout the lower Delaware Valley, and could not overpraise the settlers' personal qualities and large families.

That they succeeded so well was due in large measure to their attitude toward the Indians, whom they treated equitably, regarding them— with a good deal of sincerity—as "the rightful lords of the country." Unlike the New Englanders, the Dutch and the Spanish, the Swedes did not fight the Indians; on the contrary, they enjoyed their good will and cooperation.

William Penn became deservedly famous for his humane policy toward the Indians. But with the best of intentions he would not have been able to institute it except for the Swedes' record of fair dealing in Pennsylvania during the preceding two generations. "The Indians," writes Amandus Johnson in *Swedes in America* (1938), "would not have had confidence in the white man, had they been treated by the Swedes as they were treated by the English and the Dutch. William Penn's interpreters were Swedes, and the Indians relied on their word when they assured them that William Penn was honest and would treat them justly."

The Delaware Swedes were a friendly lot, partial to the ideal of freedom not only for themselves but for others as well. This traditional trait went back to their Scandinavian homeland. Planning New Sweden in the middle 1620s, Gustavus Adolphus had stressed freedom as one of its main aspirations. The colony was to be an asylum for the persecuted everywhere, dedicated to the principle of security of person and property.

In contrast to some of the Anglo-Saxon colonies, slavery and the slave trade were not allowed in New Sweden—another tradition going back to good old Gustavus Adolphus, who had had this to say on the subject: "No slave should burden the soil. Slaves cost a great deal, labor with reluctance and soon perish with hard usage. We shall gain more as a free people with wives and children."

The story of the Delaware Swedes is peppered with interesting personalities. During New Sweden's career as a colony the biggest man in it—in more ways than one—was its first real governor, Johan Bjornsson Printz, who arrived in 1643. Nearly seven feet tall and weighing four hundred pounds, he was called the Big Swede—"Big Belly" by the Indians, not disrespectfully. He had a Brobdingnagian appetite, the voice of a bull, and the first private yacht in the New World. His picturesque profanity echoed through all the settlements of North America. The earth shook under his step.

A veteran of the Thirty Years' War in which he had served now one ruler, now another, sometimes as a patriot, sometimes as a mercenary, but always without violating loyalty to his own country, Printz was an experienced, intelligent man, a natural empire-builder. A few years before, while in the Swedish Army, he had been court-martialed and only partially exonerated of the charge of improper behavior as an officer; now he was determined to make good in New Sweden, to make something of the colony, and for ten and a half years he did his best. He introduced the jury system. He tried to keep everybody steamed up; erected a few more forts which were also trading posts; started a brewery; built a wharf, a shipyard, a blockhouse, a gristmill. But it was not enough to sustain the colony. He needed more people, which the homeland would not provide. During the middle and late 1640s Sweden, too distracted by the endless warring in Europe, gradually lost interest in New Sweden. The Big Swede fumed with rage. He clashed with the Dutch and the English. He drank barrels of fire-water. He became tyrannical and finally hanged the leader of a movement that wanted to get rid of him. Then in 1653 he realized it was no use. There was scarcely anything to New Sweden; what there was, was hopelessly deranged as a political entity; its years were numbered. He resigned and returned home. One day ten years later he was thrown off a horse and killed. In 1937 the state of Delaware named a boulevard for him.

His daughter Armegot Printz was probably the first "modern woman" in America, a Lucy Stoner who two hundred years before Lucy Stone shook the frame of respectability in the United States by insisting on retaining her maiden name after her marriage. Two years after coming to New Sweden, Armegot married one Johan Papegoja, but remained known as Miss Printz. Almost as forceful a character as her father, she enlivened the territory with one rumpus after another till 1676, when she too returned home.

Another leading figure in New Sweden was the Lutheran minister Johan Campanius. He arrived with Governor Printz in 1643 and became the first Christian missionary among the Indians. To proselytize the Indians was part of Swedish official policy, also laid down by King Gustavus Adolphus when the colony was still only an idea. Campanius, a scholar with a scientific bent of mind and a man of considerable scope, studied the Delawares' folk ways, learned their language, and won their affectionate respect. He was mostly responsible for the fact that the Indians called the Swedes *Netappi* ("our people"), in contradistinction to the English and the Dutch. Campanius farmed a sizable piece of land, built a church, and for three years kept detailed weather data. He was the first meteorologist in America.

Ministering to the Swedish, Dutch, German and Finnish inhabitants of New Sweden, Campanius laid the foundation for the religious life of the region which continued in the Lutheran tradition long after Swedish authority was displaced. In fact, Swedish-Lutheran life on the Delaware really flowered, in a modest way, during the century and a half following the painless conquest of New Sweden by her neighbors. While readily accommodating themselves to the Dutch and English wherever it was necessary, the Swedes also built churches (five of which are still standing) and sent to the old country for ministers.

Between 1660 and 1780 about forty Swedish ministers came over; among them, a handful of remarkable men who influenced cultural progress along the lower Delaware and made scientific and literary contributions. Israel Acrelius, a minister in the province of New Jersey in the middle of the eighteenth century, assembled botanical, zoological and geological collections and notes, and wrote his *History of New Sweden*, published in 1759.

This was going on at the same time that the tiny Swedish group spread over the large territory was being linguistically and biologically absorbed through succeeding generations into the dominant population pattern. How the absorption occurred is suggested by the family tree of Franklin D. Roosevelt who had among his ancestors from many countries a Swedish great-great-grandmother, Cornelia Roosevelt, the granddaughter of an immigrant Swedish carpenter named Benson who is said to have arrived about 1648.

Thousands of men descending from the early Swedes participated in the Revolution. Two played outstanding roles.

John Hanson, a great-grandson of Johan Hanson who lived in New Sweden in the 1640s, was instrumental in organizing urgently needed military units in his native Maryland, and in 1781 was elected "President of the United States in Congress Assembled."

The other Founding Father of part-Swedish heritage was John Morton of Pennsylvania, whose great-grandfather, Morten Mortenson, had settled in New Sweden. A simple, modest, self-made man, Morton served in the Continental Congress from 1774 till his death in 1777; during 1776 as chairman of the Pennsylvania delegation. In July of that year he voted with Benjamin Franklin and James Wilson (Robert Morris and John Dickinson misjudged the situation and stayed away from the session), putting badly divided Pennsylvania on the side of the Revolution by a majority of one.

A large number of Swedes, many of them born in Sweden, served as officers in the American and French military and naval forces during the Revolution. Among them was Count Axel von Fersen, who had lived in France and become a favorite of Queen Marie Antoinette. He came over as aide-de-camp to Rochambeau and distinguished himself at Yorktown.

In the half century following the Revolution only a scattering of Swedes arrived in the United States. Some settled in New York, others pushed on to pioneer in Ohio and Illinois. Then in the 1840s there came three small groups led by idealists and intellectuals which are now regarded as spearheads of the mass influx from Sweden that began in the '50s and grew during the '60s and '70s, to reach its climax in the '90s and the 1900s.

The first group started a settlement named New Uppsala (after the historic university town in Sweden) at Pine Lake, Wisconsin, in 1841. It was led by Gustav Unonius, a well-educated man, and it failed largely because the settlers—many of them adventurers—were not capable of making a living at farming. But soon after it was established, Unonius wrote a letter to the Stockholm newspaper *Aftonbladet* which created a stir in Sweden.

In contrast to Europe, Unonius discovered "the people here are *everything*"—he underlined the word. Wisconsin Territory "is beautiful, adorned with oak woods and prairies broken by rivers and lakes swarming with fish. . . . The soil is the most fertile and wonderful that can be found and usually consists of rich black mold. . . . As far as we are concerned, we do not regret our undertaking. We are living a free and independent life. . . . I am partial to a republican form of government, and I have realized my youthful dream of social equality. . . . It is no disgrace to work here. Both the gentleman and the day laborer work. No epithets of degradation are applied to men of humble toil: only those whose conduct merits it are looked down upon."

This was one of the earliest of the "America letters" which were so important in stimulating emigration from Sweden to America, and which Professor George M. Stephenson of the University of Minnesota, a third-generation Swedish American, collected and translated into English. Gustav Unonius wrote many more, telling about conditions in the United States, offering advice to would-be emigrants.

Inspired partly by Unonius' epistles, the second group—in 1843—also made for Wisconsin and set up a farming community along Koshkonong Lake. The reports of this place which reached Sweden stressed the hardships, but they stirred interest in America still further. Its leader was Thure Ludvig Kumlien, a young graduate of the University of Uppsala where he had been a favorite pupil of the Swedish botanist Elias Fries. Developing into one of the leading frontier naturalists in the United States, he did pioneer work in ferns and mosses, insects and birds. His collections are preserved in museums in Sweden, the British Museum in London and the Smithsonian Institution in Washington.

The third group—arriving in batches during 1846-1847—consisted of some fifteen hundred so-called Jansonists, members of a religious-utopian sect led by Eric Janson, a wild prophet at variance with the established Swedish Church who at some points verged on charlatanism. His agent had picked Knox County, Illinois, for the sect's New Jerusalem, and there a colony was begun called Bishop Hill—a translation of Biskopskulla, Janson's native parish in the province of Uppland.

The town was organized on communistic lines. There was disagreement in Bishop Hill right off, and many members broke away. The majority, however, remained, generating a good deal of sincere idealism, and in the next few years through "America letters" and by other means the place attracted more colonists. In spite of his lopsided character, Janson was not a bad manager; his people possessed a variety of skills; there was endless willingness to work hard in the fields, at the looms and mechanics' benches; and within a few years their communal holdings exceeded ten thousand acres of wonderful prairieland.

In 1849 cholera hit Bishop Hill, later Janson died, there was no one to take his place, troubles and discord mounted, and once more settlers moved away. But again the bulk of the "communists" stayed and the expanding town (3,329 population in 1890 and 6,114 in 1900) gradually turned into a rather typical Illinois community, except that it was preponderantly Swedish. Giving up Jansonism, which had never been much more than its leader's personality, the people became Methodists, Mission Friends, Seventh-Day Adventists or followers of Robert Ingersoll, the agnostic evangelist of that period. In 1939 Stuart David Engstrand, an American writer of Swedish descent, published a novel on the early years of Bishop Hill entitled *They Sought for Paradise.*

In common with immigrants from other lands in the 1840s and after, Swedes generally came seeking for paradise. America, says Professor Stephenson in *The Religious Aspects of Swedish Immigration,* loomed up as the far-off but attainable land "where the dignity of the human soul was recognized, where work was honorable, where class distinctions were levelled, and where the future beckoned on to a status of economic independence. . . . In America there existed no scorn for the common man, no rejoicing over seeing him sweat while others were idle; there were no haughty gentlemen, no uniforms, and no privileged classes."

So the Swedes arrived—on the average of 1,690 a year during the 1850s; 12,245 annually during the 1860s; about fifteen thousand every twelve months in the 1870s. The figure rose rapidly till it reached forty-six thousand in 1887. They were the poor, the least favored of Sweden, the uncomfortable and restless, the exceptional in initiative and courage. They were both pushed and pulled—pushed by bad circumstances at home, pulled by America's promise of a better life.

It was a veritable exodus from Sweden where, as in other parts of Europe, social, economic and political conditions were a matter of depressions, near-famines and undemocratic government. Since 1850 Sweden—a country of about six million—has sent to the United States well over a million people, more than one out of every six; and, although many had intended to return home, a high majority of them stayed. At present the American population includes over two million men, women and children of Swedish or part-Swedish stock. According to the 1940 census, close to half a million were born in Sweden; these and over three hundred thousand of their American-born sons and daughters claimed Swedish as their mother tongue.

In the second half of the nineteenth century most Swedes came in families, often together in several related families. In the 1880s many a Swedish village was suddenly minus half its inhabitants; and, fearing that a majority of the nation might succumb to "the America fever," and that they might lose the most vital part of the population, panicky clergymen and State officials tried various stratagems to arrest the movement. But America by then was so firmly fixed in the imagination of Sweden's common people as framtidslandet (the land of the future) that scare-tales of immigrants being herded from Wisconsin and Minnesota to Siberia to freeze to death had scant effect.

Every mail brought more "America letters" to be read and re-read by entire villages. Here is what a Swedish immigrant wrote from the Middle West to his family back home in 1850 (translated by Professor Stephenson): "No one need to worry about my circumstances in America because I am living on God's noble and free land; nor am I a slave under others. . . . Nor is my cap worn out from lifting it in the presence of gentlemen. . . . Americans do not have to scrape their effects together and sell them in order to pay heavy taxes to the Crown and pay the salaries of officials. There are no large estates whose owners can take the last sheaf from their dependents, then turn them out to beg. . . . I sincerely hope nobody in Sweden will foolishly dissuade anyone from coming to the Land of Canaan."

Some of the letters stressed the fish swarming in the lakes of Wisconsin and Minnesota, the abundance of deer and prairie chickens and other kinds of game. Many varieties of wild fruit were mentioned —cherries, plums, gooseberries, thimbleberries, currants.

Other letters emphasized the separation of State and Church in America where, as one immigrant wrote in the 1860s, "it is the individual's own affair to worship God according to the dictates of his conscience without interference from prelates clothed with power to prescribe what one must believe in order to obtain salvation."

Flashes of life in the United States such as this were irresistible to the peasant and workingman: "The hired man, maid, and governess eat at the husbandman's table. 'Yes, sir,' says the master to his hand. 'Yes, sir,' says the hand to the master. 'If you please, ma'm,' says the lady of the house to the maid. 'Yes, ma'am,' replies the maid. . . . Today is Sunday, and at this moment what do I see but a housemaid garbed exactly as the housewife in a black silk hat, green veil, green coat, and black dress, carrying a bucket of coal! This is not an unusual sight— and it is as it should be. . . . Pastor, judge, and banker carry market baskets."

In addition, the new American railway companies, out to sell fares as well as land along their lines, sent agents to European countries where people seemed bent on going to the western states. Some of these agents were Swedish immigrants who visited the old country every now and then, representing not only railroads but land companies and the governments of states eager to increase their populations. Outstanding among them was Hans Mattson, who lost no time in learning English after his arrival in 1851. He became a terrific go-getter, a land speculator and politician, publisher-editor of Swedish-language newspapers, promoter of extensive Swedish farming settlements, and finally the author, in English, of *Reminiscences: the Story of an Immigrant* (1891).

As land speculator and politician, Mattson was partly responsible for the Swedish settlements of Red Wing and Vasa in Minnesota, where Pastor Erik Norelius—another powerful figure in the Swedish story—organized Lutheran congregations and started the first Swedish-language paper in Minnesota and a private school which later grew into Gustavus Adolphus College.

The Swedes spread out *en masse* through the people-hungry West, through Wisconsin and Minnesota, Iowa and Nebraska, Illinois and Michigan, Missouri and Kansas and the Dakotas and by and by all the way to the coast. They sprinkled thinly through the eastern states and very sparsely over the South. Groups of them settled in Texas. But, as a northern folk, they were partial to the North. "The Swedes," wrote one from Wisconsin in 1843 to his parents in the homeland, "carry the winter with them."

They moved across the United States in straight lines. The children of the early settlers in Wisconsin and Minnesota pioneered again in the building of Spokane and Seattle, in breaking the virgin sod of the northwestern wilderness. Swedish carpenters, painters and contractors moved on to new cities wherever dwellings and business blocks were needed; and reaching the Pacific, they moved down the coast to help build the boom cities of California.

Now they or their descendants are found in every section of the country, in nearly every profession and calling. They form relatively big concentrations in Chicago, New York City, Philadelphia, Detroit, Seattle, Los Angeles, San Francisco and Oakland; in Minneapolis and St. Paul, of course, and Duluth; in Worcester, Massachusetts; in Moline, Rockford and Rock Island, Illinois; in Jamestown, New York; in Omaha, Nebraska; in Des Moines and Sioux City, Iowa; in Galesburg, Illinois, the birthplace of Carl Sandburg, poet and historian and one of the foremost living Americans of Swedish descent.

With other Scandinavians, Swedish immigrants took to the land in a big way. In 1930 there were 98,589 farming people of Swedish birth in the United States—more than of any other immigrant group save the Germans. It is in farming, in the pioneer farming of fifty to a hundred years ago, that the Swedish group rendered its most substantial contribution to America's strength. In the northern Mississippi Valley they cleared and broke many millions of acres, built tens of thousands of farmsteads, started or improved innumerable farming settlements, big and small. The number of obviously Swedish place names on the North American map runs to nearly three hundred—Swedesboro, New Jersey, which dates back to the early comers; Swede Bend, Iowa; Swede Prairie, Minnesota (about one-third of them are in Minnesota); Swedeburg in Pennsylvania, Iowa, Kansas and Nebraska; New Sweden in several states.

Swedish immigration poured into the sparsely inhabited north central states partly because that territory, with its lakes and birch woods, its long white winters, was physically a good deal like Sweden, except that this new country was so much bigger, had so much elbow-room, held out such incalculable possibilities. Of course some of the immigrants who hailed from the narrow valleys of, say, Småland had difficulty in getting used to the plains of the Middle Border, where the slight heave at the far end of one's grain field formed one's physical horizon, and some never got adjusted to the new scene. A small proportion gave up farming and went to the city, or returned to Sweden. Most of them, however, came to feel at home.

As a rule, Swedish immigrants became citizens with no delay beyond the legal requirement. Politically, from the outset, they were drawn to the Republican Party. By the time they were arriving in large numbers, it was the party of the anti-slavery cause and of Abe Lincoln, a friend of the immigrant who in 1856 told an audience in Chicago: "We have among us Germans, Irish, French, and Scandinavians— men that have come from Europe themselves or whose ancestors have come hither, finding themselves our equals in all things."

The Swedish immigrants' life on the frontier was rough, almost invariably meager and ravaged by sickness, inhumanly demanding for years after they settled on some remote tract of land. Testing the spirit and the physical stamina of all who went through it, the experience was as tough on women as on men. "The Swedish women," writes Eric Englund in *Swedes in America*, "made homes in log cabins and sod houses. . . . They spun, and knitted, and wove, and made the clothing for their families. They cared for the livestock and cultivated the fields while the menfolk were away earning cash to tide the family over until the farm was producing a cash income. Their devotion to their homes and communities . . . constitutes an epic theme."

Thousands of Swedish girls and young women who did not go on the land became maids and cooks and children's nurses in cities and towns for a few years until they married, usually Swedish immigrant craftsmen.

It was the ambition of many a Swedish farm family to send one or two of its sons and daughters to one of the numerous academies or small colleges almost immediately established by the church synods in every state with large contingents of Swedish settlers. When state normal schools and state universities were established, many second-generation girls came in from the rural areas to work their way through as housemaids and later to become teachers, librarians and the wives of young men of similar background and professional training.

Through many decades hundreds of thousands of Swedish male immigrants earned ready cash by working on railroad section gangs, on bridge and highway construction crews, in iron and copper mines, in the forests. As lumberjacks and timber bosses they acquired a legendary reputation, figuring significantly in the Paul Bunyan saga. They were a powerful force in cutting millions of acres of timber. They were tall, brawny men, and the term "Big Swede," applied to Governor Printz on the Delaware in the 1640s, began to echo through Wisconsin and Oregon amid the cracking and crashing of falling pines and firs. With other Scandinavians, they got into American folk rhymes like this one, current in the Middle West about 1885:

> The Irish and the Dutch,
> They don't amount to much
> But hooroo for the Scandinoovian!

The "Dutch" here are the Germans; but with them the Swedes got along fairly well. With some of the other immigrant groups, notably the Irish, who rubbed them—and were rubbed—the wrong way, they often clashed. Old Midwestern newspaper files and obscure autobiographies bristle with accounts of fierce and bloody battles on construction jobs the country over and in the mining towns of Upper Michigan and Minnesota.

At the same time, in most places where they lived, Swedish immigrants acquired the reputation of being extremely orderly. All came armed with elaborate parish certificates giving their whole past history, usually a record of good behavior; and many were shocked when they saw the rough-and-tumble lawlessness of the American frontier.

No country gave to the United States a better kind of people than Sweden. Despite the privation undergone in the old country, or because of it, they were a hardy lot; likely to be blond, often very handsome, usually clean and neat. The interiors of their dugouts and sod-houses, later their log cabins and frame dwellings, compared well with those of the old-line American pioneers on adjacent tracts of land. Nearly all could read. Besides an elemental tendency toward the soil, they had a knack for mechanics a love of education and music—especially singing.

In 1869, on the Kansas prairie, a group of two hundred and fifty, calling themselves *jordbrukare* (land operators) and led by a Lutheran preacher opposed to State religion in Sweden, established the community of Lindsborg. Thirteen years later, on the initiative of another Lutheran minister, Carl A. Swensson, a native American, the settlers —to quench their homesickness and transcend their poverty—formed the now nationally known "Messiah Chorus." Five hundred of the town's two thousand people sing in the annual Lindsborg Easter Festival which lasts a week—a notable yearly musical event in the United States. Well known artists vie for the privilege of singing the solo parts of the oratorio. Lindsborg is also the home of Bethany College, which Carl A. Swensson started in 1881.

Other colleges founded by men of Swedish birth or background are: Augustana College and Theological Seminary (1863), Rock Island, Illinois; Gustavus Adolphus College (1862), St. Peter, Minnesota; and Upsala College (1893), East Orange, New Jersey. Junior colleges are: Luther College (1883), Wahoo, Nebraska, and North Park College (1885), Chicago.

A noteworthy fact is that while the average "no occupation" percentage for newcomers from all countries at the height of the New Immigration (1890-1900) was approximately thirty-five, it was only about fifteen for the Swedes. Some eighty-five per cent of them were either farmers and farm hands or skilled artisans: carpenters, masons, stonecutters, lumbermen, bricklayers, metal workers, even electricians

and engineers. The majority in these last categories settled, or eventually
wound up, in cities and towns. Unlike some of the other immigrant
groups, they did not concentrate in one or two industries, but entered
a great many fields.

Their part in building up the Middle West and the Northwest,
though prodigious, was neither colorful nor dramatic and it is not
easily described. It was the plodding, matter-of-course performance
from day to day which undergirds progress with stability.

Swedes are not particularly endowed with the dash, gaiety and lightness that quicken and flavor life, but those who came to the United
States added abundantly to the work of making the new country a
place in which one can live sensibly and comfortably. Solid, honest,
dependable immigrants and second-generation folk did their bit as
grocery storekeepers, minor officials, postmen and streetcar conductors,
small-town doctors, nurses and teachers. Thousands upon thousands
became teachers.

Immigrants from Sweden steered clear of private and parochial
education; they supported public schools. At one of the farm schools in
Minnesota originated the idea for the 4-H Clubs, long led by Theodore
A. Erickson, a son of Swedish immigrants.

Swedes joined parent-teacher associations and helped to develop
adult-education programs. They demanded good public housekeeping
in terms of clean streets, sewers, garbage collections, health services and
hospitals, and were willing to pay for it.

Unlike some of the other immigrant groups, they did not build
many so-called nationality halls, but they put up countless summer
cottages along lakes and in the woods, for they loved to boat and
fish and hunt and sing. They sought their recreation in the family
circle or in several families getting together, or in connection with
church affairs. They liked to picnic and favored public parks and play-
grounds.

For a time around 1920 when the United States' future immigration
policy was being debated in and out of Congress, some Swedish—
along with other Scandinavian—Americans were pleased by the emphasis the press gave to the theory of Nordic superiority. But late in
1921 Dr. Victor O. Freeburg, born in Iowa of Swedish parents, concluded an article in *The Swedish-American Trade Journal* on "Making
America More American" with these sentences:

"... It is no accident that the immigrants from Sweden have swarmed
to the prairies of the West or the forests of the Northwest. They are
by nature lovers of the open. They . . . form the strong sub-structure
of vast stretches of our democracy. Descendants of these pioneers

are now in the melting pot with other racial types, where the rugged strength of the Nordic ingredient gives solid tenacity to the new metal.

"In the end, however, it must be remembered that nothing could be more un-American than to estimate the value of one racial ingredient as against that of any other. America as a dwelling-place of clans must become a thing of the past. We believe that our country needs a brotherhood of spirit more binding than any brotherhood of blood."

One tendency is emphasized in writings about the Swedish immigrants: they became Americanized easily and quickly. This is by no means peculiar to them, but it is conspicuous. Because they came over mostly in families and to stay, because their language was second cousin to English, because they settled on the land, and because their old country was never seriously threatened, they had less difficulty than many other groups in identifying themselves with the United States, even though their clergy, Swedish-newspaper editors and other leaders strove hard (and with considerable temporary success, still in evidence) to preserve their native language and Swedish religious-cultural customs and values.

It was natural for many Swedes to take a lively interest in the broad affairs of their adopted states and of their new country, and the group produced more outstanding individuals whose functions had a general American significance than can be listed here.

In the Civil War, over three thousand Swedes (not counting the doubtless numerous partial descendants of the First Swedes) served in the Union Army; few, if any, in the Confederate forces. The Fifteenth Wisconsin Regiment was an all-Scandinavian unit, mostly Swedish; a company of Swedes from Bishop Hill was part of the Fifty-Seventh Illinois Regiment. Scores of Swedes and Swedish Americans were commissioned officers. An Illinois politician, Charles J. Stolbrand, was made a brigadier general and later went carpetbagging in North Carolina.

John Ericsson, marine engineer and inventor, immigrant from Sweden via England, arrived in New York in 1839 and became one of the chief Union heroes when in March 1862, at Hampton Roads, Virginia, the armor-clad U.S.S. *Monitor*, which he had designed and built, defeated the Confederacy's *Merrimac*. This was of epochal importance not only in the Civil War but all over the world. Ericsson's warship had the first revolving turret, to be adopted and never abandoned by naval designers. But perhaps more important still, he introduced the propeller in America, designing it in a form that proved practicable. In 1844 he built a screw-propelled ship, the *Princeton*, the first steam vessel of war with fans for inducing furnace fires. He did a lot of work on the steam-engine apart from ships, and invented a 12-inch cannon. Navy brass-hats of a hundred years ago sometimes ridiculed him as a dreamer, a crackpot; now the John Ericsson Memorial, near the Lincoln Memorial, erected by order of Congress in 1926, is one of the handsomest monuments in Washington.

The Civil War period was marked by the emergence of another American inventive genius of Swedish descent, Admiral John A. Dahlgren; his contributions to naval ordnance fill the greater part of four columns in the *Dictionary of American Biography*.

I have already referred to Hans Mattson, the Chicago and Minnesota go-getter; he became a conspicuously active patriot, and a colonel in the Union Army. He was later one of the leading Republicans in the West, twice secretary of state of Minnesota, and American consul general in India.

There have been four Swedish-born governors in Minnesota alone (Floyd Olson, governor in the middle 1930s, was American-born of Swedish and Norwegian parents). John Lind and John A. Johnson rose to rather large stature by initiating and supporting progressive legislation. Dozens of Swedish Americans have served in the House of Representatives, several in the Senate. Charles A. Lindbergh, brought over from Sweden in 1860 when a year old, was one of Minnesota's most distinguished liberal Congressmen during 1907-1917; in 1927, three years after his death, he became still better known as the father of the young mail pilot who one night made a sensational solo flight from New York to Paris. In 1944 the state of Washington elected Mon C. Wallgren, former United States Senator, to the governorship, and Warren S. Magnuson, former Congressman, to the United States Senate; both are of Swedish descent. So is Senator Edwin Carl Johnson of Colorado.

While many Swedish clergymen who came over in the early decades of the New Immigration were extraordinary in one respect or another, few projected their function and influence outside the group and into American life as a whole, but this chapter would have a serious gap if I did not mention four.

Some question exists whether T. N. Hasselquist or L. P. Esbjörn founded the Swedish Lutheran Church in America; both came over in the middle of the nineteenth century, both were exceptional characters, and each had a deep effect on the religious-cultural life of Swedish Americans. In 1860 one or the other, or both, established the Augustana Synod, whose institutions—churches, colleges, hospitals, hospices, orphanages and old people's homes, historical research institute, newspapers and magazines—are many and widely scattered, with headquarters in Rock Island, Illinois. While waning, the Synod is still the religious-cultural heart of the group. Possibly Esbjörn, in spite of his somewhat erratic nature, was the bigger man; at home not only in theology, but in mathematics, astronomy, physics, chemistry, medicine and four languages, often preaching in all four on the same Sunday.

The Hedström brothers, Olof and Jonas Gustav, came early (in fact, before the Unonius group) and in 1845 founded the Swedish Methodist Church in the United States which now has about two hundred churches, several charitable institutions and two schools.

The Swedish story in America teems with outstanding engineers, inventors, scientists, educators, artists. Some I have already named; here are a few more:

In 1775 Hans Christopher Christiansen built the first water-pumping station for municipal use, in Bethlehem, Pennsylvania.

One of engineer John August Ockerson's "greater individual achievements, undertaken in 1910," was, to quote from the *Dictionary of American Biography*, "the construction of levees to control the flood waters of the Colorado River, which threatened to overflow into the Salton Sea."

David L. Lindquist, a native of Stockholm who came to the United States in 1902 after a thorough technical education in Sweden and Germany, was greatly responsible for America's famous urban skyline. As chief engineer of the Otis Elevator Company he introduced and developed the gearless-traction electric elevator, now standard for all high buildings. In the early 1920s he and his assistants (many of them also Swedish Americans) perfected the automatic-signal control, now observable at its best—the operator merely presses buttons—in the newest and highest buildings in New York and other large cities.

Carl Axel Robert Lundin, who came to America in 1873, wound up as one of the world's foremost opticians—an expert "in cutting and fashioning glasses for great telescopes," read the Amherst College citation when he was given an honorary doctorate in 1905.

Per Axel Rydberg, a graduate of the gymnasium at Skara, Sweden, arrived in the United States in 1881, and long before his death fifty years later was given wide recognition as a botanist. Two genera (Rhydbergia and Rhydbergiella) and several species were named for him.

Otto Knut Olof Folin immigrated at fifteen in 1882 and worked his way through several universities in America and abroad, in preparation for his valuable lifelong work as a biological chemist in urinalysis, protein metabolism and related fields.

The career of Henry Reuterdahl, painter and illustrator of naval subjects, reached its height between 1903 and the early 1920s. His "Combat Between the *Monitor* and the *Merrimac*" hangs in the National Gallery of Art in Washington.

The work of geologist John August Udden with the Iowa Geological Survey, the Illinois Geological Survey and United States Geological Survey, and at the University of Texas, during the thirty-five years before his death in 1932, deeply influenced developments in both theoretical and practical geology. He is generally credited with being directly responsible for opening the major oil fields in west Texas.

Gunnar Mauritz Widforss, "the quiet Swede," "the painter of national parks," employed by the United States government, painted —"in hermitlike simplicity," as *The Art Digest* put it early in 1935— hundreds of watercolors and oils of scenes in the Grand Canyon, in Zion and Brice canyons, in the canyons of the Colorado and Yellowstone, in the Kaibab forest, at Mesa Verde, Taos, Crater Lake and elsewhere in the West.

As a horticulturalist, Gustavus A. Eisen contributed richly to fruit-growing in California, particularly of figs and grapes; as an archeologist, he wrote a two-volume study of ancient beads with forty thousand watercolor illustrations, and a ten-volume series called *Legends of the Holy Grail*.

Several Swedish immigrants did extremely well in industry and business. Shipwrecked in the Gulf of Mexico in 1838 as a young man, Sven Magnus Swenson pioneered in Texas, fled to Mexico during the Civil War owing to his pro-Union sympathies, moved to New York after the war, and established a big cotton-export business and the banking house of S. M. Swenson & Sons, which still operates in Wall Street. He died in 1896 a multimillionaire; his descendants are active in the New York financial world. Three other Swedish big businessmen: C. Eric Wickman, founder and president of the Greyhound bus concern; Charles Walgreen, of the Walgreen drugstores, and Vincent Bendix, founder of the numerous Bendix manufacturing companies.

No mere business organizer, Vincent Bendix, an immigrant's son, was also an engineer and practical inventor of high rank. A pioneer designer and builder of automobiles, he originated the "Bendix drive" making automobile self-starting practicable, and the "Bendix spring," and did essential work on the carburetor, four-wheel brakes and numerous other gadgets. He died early in 1945. The Bendix interests allegedly control some fourteen thousand patents, many of them now at the center of automobile, airplane and washing-machine production.

And there are hundreds and hundreds of small businesses owned by Swedish Americans of the first, second and third generations—building and contracting, engineering, lumbering, manufacturing, mechanical-services and merchandizing firms . . . and *smörgasbord* restaurants.

Early in the 1900s Alexander P. Anderson of Red Wing, Minnesota, invented the method of making "puffed" cereals.

On January 24, 1945, at a joint session of the American Institute of Electrical Engineers and the Institute of Radio Engineers, Dr. E. F. W. Alexanderson, originally of Sweden, now with the General Electric Company at Schenectady, New York, received the Edison Medal, the highest award in electrical engineering, "for his outstanding inventions [over 300] and developments in the radio, transportation, marine and power fields."

Half of the 1936 Nobel Prize in Physics went to Professor Carl David Anderson of the California Institute of Technology—barely thirty at the time, born in New York of Swedish parents—for his discovery of the positron.

Gustaf Stromberg, originally of Gothenburg, an authority on stellar motions and the intrinsic brightness of stars, author of *The Soul of the Universe* (1940), is with the Mount Wilson Observatory. He was listed among the foreign-born citizens who have made "outstanding contributions to American culture" on the "Wall of Fame" at the New York World's Fair in 1939-1940.

Aksel Gustav Josephson, a native of Uppsala who came to the United States at thirty in 1893, became America's top bibliographer and authority on library techniques, notably cataloguing. He died late in 1944. Another immigrant from Sweden, Adam Strohm, was long head of the Detroit Public library.

Carl Emil Seashore of the state university of Iowa, psychologist, originator of the famous Seashore tests for musical ability, is dean of American educators of Swedish stock, hundreds of whom are outstanding in their fields—Nels August Bengston (geography and geology), University of Nebraska; Thorsten Sellin (sociology), University of Pennsylvania; Ivan E. Wallin (anatomy), University of Colorado; Hugo Leander Blomquist (botany), Duke University; Franklin C. Erickson (geography), University of North Carolina; Ulric Dahlgren (biology), Princeton; Adolph B. Benson (Germanics), Rudolph John Anderson (chemistry) and Einer Hille (mathematics), Yale; Henry Johnson (history), Columbia; George M. Stephenson (history), Minnesota; Anton Julius Carlson (physiology), Chicago.

"Professor Carlson," one of his students, also a Swedish American, once wrote to me, "honors us most. He came to America as a young boy (he still speaks with a strong accent); worked as a carpenter; attended Augustana College and was to be ordained a Lutheran minister;

began to have doubts about dogmatic theology; became interested in science; gave up the ministry and studied physiology; then joined the faculty of the University of Chicago, where he has been a loved and respected member of the staff ever since. He helped organize the American Association of University Professors, of which he has been one of the most active spirits fighting for academic freedom. He is feared by politically minded college presidents, and by governors who try to introduce the spoils system into higher education. In Chicago his name is sought for all liberal movements. He is a member of the Chicago Civil Liberties Committee's advisory board. His effectiveness is due to his forthright honesty and absolute fearlessness, to be traced to his Swedish-Lutheran upbringing, as well as to a tactfulness and a wit acquired in America."

Throughout the American scientific world, Professor Carlson—seventy, as I write—is popularly known as "Ajax" and is especially famous for his habitual phrase "Vot iss de effidence?"; for proving that the heartbeat originates in the nerves, that the stomach is an independent organ, uncontrolled by the brain or the central nervous system; for his classic book *The Control of Hunger in Health and Disease* (1916), the theories in which are the main bases for modern infant feeding and gastric-ulcer diets. He has delved also into the liver, Vitamin E, the glands; has guided in their work such outstanding men, his former pupils at Chicago, as Dr. Sidney Smith, who in 1940 perfected a new way of stitching together torn blood vessels, and Dr. Andrew Conway Ivy, a specialist in gastric ulcers and the human heart in connection with parachute jumping. Dr. Carlson was a pioneer in the latter field.

In the late 1930s, as champion of teachers' independence which, he maintains, is possible only when they hold life tenure, he made a remark that went like wildfire through the American academic world. The young president of the University of Chicago, Dr. Robert M. Hutchins, announced his idea of abolishing tenure on the theory that that would "put the faculty on its toes." Said Dr. Carlson: "You are confused about your anatomy, Dr. Hutchins. It will put the faculty on its knees."

Another Swedish-American "Ajax," already referred to, is Carl Sandburg—ballad-singer, author of the best biography of Lincoln and several books of poetry and fairy tales: *The People, Yes*, which he called "a footnote to Lincoln's Gettysburg Address"; "*Good Morning, America*; *Slabs of the Sunburnt West*; *Cornhuskers*; *Rootabaga Stories* and *Rootabaga Pigeons*: a body of work closely akin to Walt Whitman. It is Midwestern expression at its very best, full of the American

Dream. His father was a Swedish-immigrant blacksmith in a railroad shop who heaved a sledge so long that he acquired a muscle-hump on his right shoulder. Sandburg once said to an interviewer: "My father and mother—how to begin? My mother lived long enough for me to realize she was a beautiful heroine, and I could tell her so. But my father died before I had become aware that in the mesh of ironic circumstances he was a heroic struggler. I would have liked to thank him for some quality of endurance—or wayward stubborness—I don't know which—that he passed on to me."

Some other well known Swedish-American writers are: Nelson Algren (*Somebody in Boots* and *Never Come Morning*), Stuart David Engstrand (*The Invaders*), Neil H. Swanson (*The Judas Tree*), Mauritz A. Hallgren (*Seeds of Revolt, The Tragic Fallacy* and *Landscape of Freedom*), Ferdinand Lundberg (*Imperial Hearst* and *America's Sixty Families*) and Oliver Carlson (*Hearst: Lord of San Simeon*).

Howard Hanson, born in Wahoo, Nebraska, of Swedish immigrant parents, is one of America's foremost "conservative modern" composers, director of the Eastman School of Music at Rochester, New York. Many believe he has done more to encourage American music than anyone else.

The sculptor Carl Milles is the foremost Swedish American artist. Among his works are the fountain group in St. Louis, the New Sweden Monument which was unveiled in 1938 on the site of the Early Swedes' first landing along the Delaware, and "The God of Peace" in the St. Paul City Hall.

In Hollywood we have Greta Garbo and Ingrid Bergman, natives of Sweden; and Chicago-born Edgar Bergen, son of immigrants, who assures me that Charlie McCarthy also "is all Swedish, except his name"—in fact, the singular dummy's original name was Kalle, Swedish equivalent of Charlie. Among the earlier Hollywood personalities of Swedish origin were: Anna Q. Nilsson, long a star; Warner Oland, the creator of "Charlie Chan," and Victor Seastrom, director.

Eric Olle Schjolin of General Motors at Pontiac, Michigan, invented a system of rear-engine operation of automobiles. He came from Sweden in 1920 to recuperate from an illness, then decided to stay.

A number of Swedish American engineers have made significant contributions to aviation; the late Philip G. Johnson, for example, was the director of experiments that resulted in the Flying Fortress and Superfortress.

Carl Gustaf ("Gus") Swebilius, who came over a sixteen-year-old blacksmith's apprentice in 1896, became early in World War II an armament manufacturer in Connecticut, specializing in the production of an anti-tank gun of his own invention.

An extremely useful citizen is the chubby-faced Ira N. Gabrielson, the "twentieth-century Noah," as he has been called, who as director of the United States Fish and Wildlife Service in the Department of the Interior manages 275 wildlife refuges whose total area exceeds that of West Virginia. "Gabe's" paternal grandfather was a Swedish immigrant.

Then there is Mary Anderson. At sixteen, late in the last century, she left her farm home near Lidköping and came to the Middle West. After a brief spell as a "hired girl," during which she started to learn English by reading newspapers most of the night after work, she got a job in a shoe factory and stayed for eighteen years. But, as she put it much later, "things didn't seem right for the wonderful America I'd come to find." She joined the International Boot and Shoe Workers' Union, became president of her local, was elected to the executive board of the international organization. Then, as an organizer for the Women's Trade Union League she traveled all over the United States and Canada and developed into the top-ranking expert on women's problems in industry. In 1920 she was appointed head of the Women's Bureau in the United States Department of Labor, and has been re-appointed to that position by each succeeding President. In 1941, a few years before she retired, Smith College gave her the honorary degree of LL.D. for having "devoted her life to improving conditions for working women throughout the country."

Two American-born women of Swedish parentage have been engaged in sincere and intelligent efforts toward solving the cultural problem which exists around the diversity of America's population: M. Margaret Anderson, editor of Common Ground, and Alice Lilliequist Sickels, formerly of the International Institute in St. Paul, where through the 1930s she directed the biennial Festival of Nations, involving the participation of the whole city and some of the rest of Minnesota; and since 1945 of Detroit, where she is working out a similar program. Mrs. Sickels' book Around the World in St. Paul (1945) tells the story of her experience.

Gunnar Myrdal is not an American citizen; he is a figure in Sweden's politics and education who has spent much time in America and who will some day, I am convinced, be regarded as part of American history. In the late 1930s he accepted the invitation of the Carnegie Foundation to direct a comprehensive study of the American Negro— the most significant project of its kind ever undertaken. A scholar of courage and imagination, Dr. Myrdal—with a large staff of Negro and White American assistants—carried it out brilliantly. His two-volume work *An American Dilemma* (1944) subtitled "The Negro Problem and Modern Democracy" is bound to have a long and far-reaching influence on the Negro-White question in the United States.

During 1942-1945 hundreds of thousands of Swedish Americans have been in the armed forces—for instance Major Richard Bong, the ace of aces, who shot down forty Japanese Zeros; Carl C. Palm, a former Brooklyn policeman of Swedish extraction, who singlehanded put five of Hitler's Royal Tiger Tanks out of action in France in 1944; Lieutenant Mae Olson of Little Falls, Minnesota, the first Army nurse on Guadalcanal; and Ensign Edward R. Sellstrom of Minneapolis, a naval hero who died in 1942 and for whom a destroyer was named in 1943.

Many high-ranking officers, including several generals and an admiral or two, are Swedish Americans, most of them born in the United States. The one that interests me most is a native of Sweden, Captain Erik G. Hakansson, chief of the Naval Medical Research Institute at Bethesda, Maryland, much of whose work will be as valuable in peacetime as it is in war. In an interview early in 1944, he declared: "A chemical process for converting sea water into drinking water has been developed and made so simple that it can be used on life rafts and in life boats. A shortage of drinking water need no longer be the fear of survivors of disasters at sea. Light, watertight exposure units which will prolong life for those who abandon ship in the cold waters of the North have been designed and found practical. Effective means of preventing the common and disabling flash burns from explosions have been found. For areas where malaria is prevalent we have developed ointments which when applied to the skin will repel mosquitoes and significantly assist in the prevention of this common tropical disease."

And there are the Borgstroms. Before the war the Borgstroms were a large family living on a ranch at Thatcher, Utah. There were six boys, four of age for military service when the Japanese attacked Pearl Harbor; three joined the Army, one the Marines. Within six months all four were casualties: one killed in Italy, one killed on Guadalcanal, one fatally wounded in Normandy, one missing in action while on a bombing mission over Europe. Said Mrs. Borgstrom, whose hair turned white during the six months: "God was good to the Sullivans. He took them all at once and their mother didn't have to receive shock after shock."

Driving through Minnesota in the summer of 1938, I happened to stop in the little town of Scandia and read the inscription on the memorial stone honoring the first known Swedish settlers in that state: "Oscar Roose, Carl Fernstrom and August Sandahl from Västergotland, Sweden, settled here about October 18, 1850, and built the first Swedish log house in Minnesota. Their countrymen erected this stone."

For decades beginning in 1948, scores of Swedish-founded towns in Wisconsin, Minnesota, Nebraska, the Dakotas and other states will be celebrating their centennials.

VI: AMERICANS FROM RUSSIA

EVERY now and then somebody declares: "We Americans are all immigrants or descendants of immigrants—except, of course, the Indians." The late Will Rogers, who was part Indian, liked to josh the descendants of the Mayflower refugees, saying that his ancestors met theirs at Plymouth Rock.

But the Indians too are descendants of immigrants—from Asia. Scientists specializing in the larger aspects of man's record on this globe were long agreed that what we now call the American continent was trodden by the first pair of human feet not much before 1000 B.C. Since the late 1920s, however, in Alaska and western Canada and along the eastern side of the Rockies in Wyoming, Colorado, New Mexico and Texas, archeologists have uncovered traces of a breed of men— collectively referred to as the Folsom Man—who between ten and fifteen thousand years ago began to come over across the Bering Strait from Siberia.

Thus, going as far back in the story of American immigration as is possible at present, we can say that the first Americans came from a territory now part of Russia. But that is about all we can say of them; we must wait for archeologists to uncover more campsites of the Folsom Man and to reach further conclusions.

But—vaulting in ignorance over a long row of millennia—we know quite a bit about the Russians' contact with America in the eighteenth century.

In 1697 Czar Peter, then only twenty-five and eventually to be called the Great, visited western Europe. He wanted to study shipbuilding and to see what other practical European skills could be introduced in old Moscovia. William Penn, who happened to be in England on a visit, made it a point to obtain an audience with Peter. His main idea was to see if he could interest the young monarch in the Quaker faith. He couldn't, it turned out, but Peter became deeply interested in America. Impressed as he was by the whole Western scheme of things, which included the establishment of colonies in the New World by England, Spain and France, perhaps this thought occurred to him: why shouldn't he too start a colony there?

To be sure, this was not necessary, for Russia was one of the biggest, most sparsely populated and least explored countries. No one knew how big it was, how far north and especially how far northeast it extended. But whatever the precise form of the Czar's idea, it had vitality. Of course no one in the world knew anything about the Folsom Man; there was, however, a dim notion in St. Petersburg that a new land, which might be part of America, existed somewhere off Siberia. It might even connect with Siberia.

Peter did not act on the idea at once; most likely he lacked the right men to take hold of it. Finally, Captain Vitus Bering, an officer of Danish origin serving in the Russian Navy, came to his notice and he straightway initiated plans for an exploratory expedition.

Peter died in 1725 just as the expedition was about to transfer its base from St. Petersburg to Kamchatka, on the Pacific Coast. But his successor, Catherine I, was in favor of the idea too, if only out of deference to Peter. Captain Bering's first voyage in 1728 was a success. He returned to the Russian capital with much valuable knowledge about the North Pacific, including the fact that Asia and America were not connected. The strait separating them, and the sea below it, were named for him. The islands he discovered were named the Catherine Archipelago for the empress, but were made famous under the newer name of the Aleutians by American G.I.'s fighting there in 1943.

In the 1740s Bering organized a second expedition which, although pursued by ill luck, blazed the way for the adventurers, hunters, fur traders, soldiers and Orthodox priests who headed for the Aleutians and Alaska, and who in the ensuing decades moved down the coast to northern California. They established military and trading posts, even towns and agricultural colonies, much as the English, the French, the Dutch, the Swedes and the Spanish were doing in the East, in the Mississippi Valley and along the Upper Rio Grande.

"Russian America" was a frail reality a quarter of a century before the American Revolution, when California and the rest of the Pacific Coast were still virtually unknown in the East. Russia claimed the territory by right of discovery, exploration and settlement; just how much of it is hard to say. The North American continent was still a fluid proposition; anything might have happened if some of the Old World directors of colonization had had a little more acumen, and if the Revolution of the English Colonies along the Atlantic had not occurred or had been postponed.

To indulge in a little more speculation: if Peter the Great had lived, the Russian foothold in America might have been much firmer. He might have sent over a better type of Russian than actually came, and might, just might, have annulled the Spanish penetration into California. If we take the American Revolution and the statesmanlike intelligence it released in the East as inevitable, the Russians of course would not have retained any of the West Coast even if Peter the Great had lived to be a hundred; but, instead of the Spanish influence, now so apparent in California, it might have been Russian influence, or perhaps a mingling of the two. San Francisco might now be called St. Petersburg or Petrograd, and Los Angeles might be New Moscow or New Vladivostok; the missions now strung the length of California might be bulbous-spired Russian Orthodox churches.

As it is, the Russian colony in California existed only till 1841, when its land was sold to a Mexican citizen of German birth named Johann Augustus Sutter. The place is now known as Fort Ross. Part of San Francisco is called Russian Hill; just north of the Bay Region are the Russian River and the town of Sebastopol. Gertrude Atherton once wrote a novel about the sad romance of Count Nikolai Petrovich Resanoff, the governor of "Russian America" who came to California in 1805 to make a trade agreement with the Spanish authorities, and Doña Conchita Arguello, daughter of the Spanish governor, who fell in love with Resanoff's "manly beauty, polished manner, accomplishments and intelligence." It seems this was one of the great love affairs. Resanoff died on his way back to Russia to seek imperial approval of the marriage, but Conchita never learned of his death, or refused to believe it. According to one account, she "continued constant and expectant, refusing other offers of marriage. Many years later, when Americans first settled in California and she had become an old woman, she remained still faithful to her love and daily scanned the Golden Gate for his approaching vessel."

Most Russians who came to California from the Aleutians and from Alaska lacked Count Resanoff's aristocratic qualities; certainly they did not enjoy his station in life. Some were convicts who had escaped after being sent from Siberia to "Russian America" as laborers. Socially, many of these early Russian immigrants were kin to the underdog elements that had been entering eastern English colonies before the Revolution. Several became Mexicanized and turned into *vaqueros*. Some moved eastward into the Indian Territory, now Oklahoma, where many Americans of today, especially those who are part-Indian, can claim them as ancestors.

All sorts of Russians, among them political refugees, kept on drifting over from Siberia to Alaska and thence south in small numbers almost throughout the nineteenth century, before and after "Russian America" had become a matter of history. Many settled in San Francisco. Some took to ranching.

By the middle nineteenth century "Russian America" was clearly restricted to Alaska and the islands off its coast. There the Russians impressed themselves so deeply during their century-long possession that their cultural influence is still evident. In the first quarter of the century that northern territory was run by Russian adventurers and missionaries, then for seventy-odd years by a semi-official trading corporation and the Orthodox Church, which in 1861 consisted of forty-two churches and chapels organized in a diocese whose Episcopal See was at Sitka. That year the Russian government took over Alaska, and six years later the United States—pursuant to the Monroe Doctrine—purchased it for $7,200,000.

This ended Russia's interest in the Western Hemisphere. In 1872 the Episcopal See was transferred from Sitka to San Francisco, which brought to California an Orthodox bishop and several priests. They built a cathedral, which was rebuilt after its destruction in the 1906 earthquake and fire, although before the 1920s the Russian population in North California was never sufficient to justify a large edifice. The explanation lies in the Russians' traditional sentiment for California.

Russia is the only country that has been contributing migrants to the American population over both the Pacific and Atlantic Oceans. But very few Russians came across the Atlantic in the eighteenth century and the first three-quarters of the nineteenth.

A man named Charles Thiel, native of St. Petersburg, a pharmacist by profession, came to Philadelphia in 1769 after he had run into trouble with the authorities of Catherine the Great. He changed his name to Charles Cist and eventually succeeded in the printing and publishing business. But his fame rests chiefly on the fact that he was one of the first men to see that "stone coal" (anthracite) could be used as fuel. When he tried to peddle it, he was threatened with mob violence as a swindler and a foreigner.

In 1792 a young fellow speaking half a dozen languages who said his name was Augustine Smith appeared in Baltimore. Actually he was a disillusioned nobleman, Prince Dimitri Augustin Gallitzin. He looked up Bishop Carroll, was converted to the Catholic religion, and became a missionary in Maryland and Pennsylvania. Tolerance of differences among people was a main theme of his sermons. At his own expense he tried to establish Catholic communities in Pennsylvania, where the town of Gallitzin is named for him. Charles M. Schwab, the steel magnate, put up a statue to him in Loretto, Pennsylvania.

In 1855 a young Russian engineer, John B. Turchin, formerly of the Imperial Staff and a veteran of the Crimean War, arrived and found an engineering job with the Illinois Central Railway. At the outbreak of the Civil War he was appointed colonel of the 19th Illinois Volunteers, which achieved fame as one of the best trained, most marched and battle-scarred Union regiments. In a personal order Lincoln made him a brigadier general. After the war Turchin wrote a book, *The Battle of Chickamauga*; in 1901, all but forgotten, he died in extreme poverty.

In the late 1860s the Reverend Agapy Goncharenko, a political refugee from Russia, got off the boat in New York. Some publicity brought him to the attention of Secretary of State Seward and other Washington officials who were anxious that the Russians on the Pacific Coast, particularly those in newly acquired Alaska, should be Americanized. The priest was sent to San Francisco where, with funds provided by the government, he began to publish the first Russian-language newspaper in this country, the *Alaskan Herald*. But the arrangement didn't work out. Goncharenko took his task too seriously. As an anti-Czarist revolutionary impressed by the republican institutions and the developing democracy of the United States, he concentrated his verbal powers on detaching the thoughts and feelings of the Russians on the Coast from the monarchical regime in Russia. Since the publication was being subsidized by the government, the Russian Ambassador in Washington protested to the State Department; Goncharenko was instructed to moderate his attacks on the Czar. He refused. Losing his government subsidy, he renamed the paper *Liberty*, continued to rip into Czarism—its political despotism, religious intolerance, class inequality, economic slavery and compulsory ignorance; and at the same time turned his criticism—only a little less savagely—on the American administration in Alaska.

Czarist Russia in the last half of the nineteenth century, as well as before and after, was a pretty impossible place for the masses of its inhabitants, but it was the last of the large countries in the Old World to send to the New anything like a mass migration. Most of the worst-off people in Russia during the nineteenth century had not even heard of the United States; the St. Petersburg regime, while never unfriendly to the American government, took good care that the people should not hear of it. But of course the news about "The Land of Promise" could not be kept from the peoples of Russia forever.

Perhaps the first group in the Moscovite empire to think of the United States as a desirable place to live in were the so-called Russia Germans. Most of them had been lured to Russia in the second half of the eighteenth century by Catherine the Great, who hoped they would become a stabilizing factor along the Lower Volga and the Don Rivers, a bulwark against the nomadic tribes that kept disrupting those territories. In return for this service the Empress offered them special privileges—cash grants, tax exemptions for ten years, retention of their language and national character, freedom from military service and religious liberty.

To some of those who responded, the last two privileges were the most appealing. They were Mennonites, opposed to military service and war; and they had been more or less persecuted in Germany ever since the beginning of their sect. Many emigrated to Russia for virtually the same reason that the Germans whose descendants are now known as the Pennsylvania Dutch had gone, somewhat earlier, to America. Their entry into Russia was on a formal business basis. A contract was drawn between each migrant and the Russian government. From 1764 to 1767 around 27,000 Mennonites and other Germans signed these contracts and built and settled small communities on the eastern banks of the Volga and the Don. Later many more followed; the movement continued until 1820. They were of all classes: farmers, noblemen, bankrupts, teachers, clergymen, mechanics. And for nearly a century the scheme worked out in a fashion. The Germans started 202 settlements, which had a marked effect on the civilization of the region. For a time the settlers had to fight the nomadic Kirghiz and various robber bands. After that many of them prospered; the group doubled, trebled, quadrupled. In a general way, the Russian government adhered to the contract—until the middle of the nineteenth century, a time of great unrest, when the Czar decided that the Germans should be Russianized and made to serve in the Army.

By then large numbers of Germans had emigrated from Germany to America, and Russia Germans, especially the Mennonites, were hearing through their contacts with the Fatherland of what sounded like Utopia. In the United States, it appeared, people with no great education, but with a touch of common sense and a readiness to work hard, could aspire with a chance of success to economic and social advancement even if they were the most recent immigrants. There religious freedom was a firm actuality that no one of any consequence challenged; militarism was openly regarded with extreme disfavor.

The late Ambrose Bierce's too-clever definition of an emigrant—"an unenlightened person who thinks one country better than another"—did not apply to the Russia Germans. America did have a better system of government and life than Czarist Russia, then ruled by Alexander II, or Germany, then dominated by the ultra-imperialistic Bismarck and on the verge of war with France.

So about 1874, in the face of strong opposition from the imperial government in St. Petersburg, the Mennonites and other German-stock settlers along the Volga and the Don, most of them natives of Russia, began to pull up their stakes, roll their bundles and head for America.

To the United States, where they were referred to as the Volga Germans, they kept coming for twenty years, between 1874 and 1894; then, after a pause of four years, again from 1898 to the outbreak of World War I—from a few hundred to over a thousand annually, most of them in families. They were good farmers and artisans; solid, restrained, hard-working folk, just what this country needed at that stage of its civilization.

The majority wanted to go on the soil again. Eventually many did, some as soon as they arrived, although by then most of the desirable government free land had been pre-empted. They made themselves a factor in the agricultural progress of Kansas, Oklahoma, Nebraska, Wisconsin and Minnesota. Thousands went into the sugar-beet industry in Colorado, wheat-raising in Washington, fruit-growing in California.

But many distributed themselves in cities throughout the country, finding work in a variety of available occupations, especially as carpenters, masons and blacksmiths. Section gangs of them helped to construct the Western railroads.

This immigration had a high proportion of young people who, according to one contemporary historian, "found themselves at home at once. They soon acquired some English words, and this produced a wonderful linguistic mixture in the homes of the Volga Germans. They eagerly aped all the customs and ways of the country. America swallowed them up as a child assimilates candy."

Today in the third generation, widely intermarried with other groups, the Volga-German Americans number around four hundred thousand. Perhaps half are Mennonites.

In 1940 an old-line American woman in Topeka wrote me: "My daughter teaches in a high school out in one of the Mennonite settlements in central Kansas, and it is heart-warming to really understand what these people's solidity and energy have added to the prosperity and welfare of our state. Ex-Governor Walter Huxman, who now lives in Topeka, is the son of a Mennonite immigrant; his mother speaks English very brokenly. In 1939 he was appointed to the United States Circuit Court of Appeals, and he chose as his clerk a brilliant young Jewish lad who worked his way through our Washburn Law School here in Topeka and is the son of a second-hand clothing dealer in another Kansas town."

Next to leave Russia for America were the Jews. And no wonder.

Nearly all the Jews within the Czar's realm lived along its western edges, in the Ukraine and in the so-called Pale of Settlement, which took in part of ancient Poland and Lithuania. They were practically barred by government decrees from agriculture, from higher education and the professions as distinct from trades; in short, they were denied the opportunity to integrate into Russian life. Their chances for advancement and their freedom of movement were rigidly restricted. But until 1881 there was no organized physical violence against them. That year a Nihilist, member of a small Russian terroristic-political party which had no connection with anything Jewish, succeeded in assassinating Czar Alexander II; whereupon hell broke loose in Russia. The government and the ruling class started repressing all groups in the empire who might have had cause to complain or to act against the existing system. This took in the Jews. There began a series of pogroms which in some districts were directly instigated by government officials seeking to divert to a new target any anti-Czarist feelings and revolutionary impulses that might exist in the non-Jewish Russian masses. In these pogroms between 1881 and 1903, large numbers of Jews were slaughtered; others fled for their lives. During the thirty-year period from 1881 to 1910 over a million Russian Jews came to America. Several hundred thousand more arrived during 1911-1914.

They too, like the Volga Germans, came in families and to stay. The great majority settled in cities, usually in the East, although they also spread westward. Close to forty per cent of the male adults were skilled artisans, mostly tailors and furriers—two trades in which they had been allowed to engage in Russia. Soon they were an energetic force in the expanding American garment, millinery and fur industries, which employed also many unskilled Russian-Jewish immigrants. The rest scattered into all walks of life, business, manufacturing, the professions, the arts and sciences.

Thousands who were peddlers in Russia resumed their peddling here, traveling about with packs containing their wares until they made enough to open a retail shop. Many of the small shops started by these Jewish pack-peddlers all over the United States eventually grew into big department stores, the world's most efficient mercantile establishments.

The Jews wrote back to Russia of the opportunities and freedom in America; the word spread out from the ancient cities over the plains of the western provinces; and, in spite of the St. Petersburg government's continued and vigorous discouragement of emigration, Slavic Russians started to cross the Atlantic. First they came in a barely perceptible ripple; then, around 1890, in increasing waves. They were Great Russians from the northwestern provinces, White Russians from the regions east of present-day Poland and Czechoslovakia, and Little Russians, now better known as Ukrainians. Some emigrated chiefly for economic reasons, others chiefly for political or religious reasons, and still others for a mingling of reasons. In 1890, ten thousand dissenters from the official Russian Orthodox Church arrived almost in a body to take over sections of government land in the Dakotas, where no one cared what they believed or how they worshipped. They, or rather their American-born children, are still there.

In the 1900s another religious group at odds with Orthodoxy, the Molokans or Milk-Drinkers, followed "the Inner Light" of their faith which led them to America and across the continent to California, where they settled on Boyle Heights, now a district in Los Angeles, also known as "The Flats" or "Russiatown." They are a distinct group there to this day. The men are still bearded, still wear embroidered Russian blouses girdled below the waist; while the women's costume consists of shawls or kerchiefs, long full skirts over starched petticoats, ample-sleeved waistcoats, and white lace-bordered aprons. Although most of them know English by now, as do all their children born in this country, their speech among themselves is still Russian. They brew tea in samovars and the interiors of their little houses, built back around 1910, contain many reminders of Old Russia. A people of sober, almost austere dignity, committed to The Simple Life, the good Molokans neither drink nor smoke. The women augment the family income by domestic service; the men work in lumber yards and at rubbish-collecting, driving their own trucks or wagons. A few with specially luxuriant beards pick up an occasional bit of easy money as extras in Hollywood films.

The Molokans came to America to create their own Zion. Like some of the German sects, they have no priests, no leaders; only elders. They are uncompromising in their adherence to their beliefs, in their opposition to evil as they see it; toward other people they are extremely tolerant. They don't maintain that theirs is the only true religion. With them in Russiatown live all kinds of people: Mexicans, Italians, Armenians, Jews and Russians belonging to other sects—such as the Jew-Subbotniks who are Slavic converts to a mixture of Judaism and Molokanism, and who, arriving here just before World War I, are to be found in several other parts of the United States.

Another Russian sect that escaped persecution by coming to the New World are the Dukhobors, or Spirit-Wrestlers. Generally they went to Canada, but—along with the Raskolniki, or Old Believers, and the Byeguni, or Holy Jumpers—little groups of them are found in the Northwest, in California, here and there in the industrial East.

Most of the Slavic immigrants arriving from Russia in the period from 1890 to 1914, however, were just plain Russians—Orthodox Russians, with a tiny admixture of Catholics. They came singly or in very small groups. At first they were mostly men, who subsequently sent for their families or girls if they decided to stay. Sixty to seventy per cent of them did. This immigration reached its peak during 1910-1914 and would doubtless have continued at a growing rate had it not been for the war.

A few were educated people getting away from the injustice and stupidity of the Czarist regime which they did not believe would be overthrown or changed for generations to come. A handful were refugee revolutionaries. Some were extreme idealists who embraced the freedom they found here as the most precious condition under the sun.

The majority were from the anonymous mass of common men of a backward, ill-governed land: workers and peasants, many without any formal education, but with plenty of physical and spiritual stamina and the terrific need to be doing something that was not fruitless on the face of it. They were "the wretched . . . lost . . . and tempest-tost"— to pull a few adjectives from Emma Lazarus' poetic inscription on the Statue of Liberty inviting just such people to America's "Golden Door."

The Castle Garden and Ellis Island doors through which the immigrants entered did not suggest anything "golden" and the preponderance of Slavic Russians who stayed—like the majority of Volga Germans and Russian Jews—never rose to very high economic and social levels as these levels are regarded in the United States. For most of them, however, the new country was an enormous improvement on Czarist Russia. With the Lithuanian and other Baltic immigrants, whose lands were then within the Russian State (as they are now again within the Soviet Union), they scattered through the East and Middle

West, becoming part of the pounding, roaring heart of the country's Industrial Revolution. They worked as coal miners, steel workers, factory hands, usually doing the most arduous tasks.

Some got into the timber lands of Michigan and Wisconsin, and thence drifted all the way to Montana and Idaho, Oregon and Washington. Others took up longshoring in New York and other eastern ports. Now many work in the automotive industries, in paper and glass and shoe factories, in the clothing and fur-dressing and shoe trades. Thousands clean the windows of our skyscrapers. Other thousands are employed in the house-wrecking and rubble-removing businesses.

Their tendency from the start has been to join labor unions. Owing perhaps to their background in Czarist Russia, they have a strong instinct for getting together with others, with anybody, to work for social progress. "The Russian is very patient and stolid," wrote Jerome Davis in his book *The Russian Immigrant* (1922). "He is willing to endure a good deal, even under bad conditions, and will work uncomplainingly for long hours at low wages. . . . His love of music and the theater is a well-known characteristic. He is very sympathetic, always willing to contribute to the need of those who are suffering. If a Russian is killed in a mine or factory, his neighbors will often care for the widow and children, though they themselves may barely be making a living. . . . He is also quickly responsive to what strikes him as a higher good, and is willing to suffer for it."

Perhaps this human quality, going hand in hand with their labor within our dynamic industrial life, is one of the Russian immigrants' main contributions to America.

Altogether, Czarist Russia sent to the United States well over four million people. There were not only Slavic Russians, Volga Germans, and Jews, but also Poles, Lithuanians, Estonians, Letts, Finns and other minority nationalities. Of the total, the Jews made up the largest single group. The various Slavic Russians come to six or seven hundred thousand. The 1940 census shows 1,040,900 natives of Russia (excluding Lithuanians and the other minorities within the Czarist empire), most of them naturalized, and 1,569,300 Russian Americans born in this country. In these figures the large majority are Jews. The Slavic-Russian immigrants are estimated at about four hundred thousand.

About thirty thousand Russian immigrants are on the land in the East and the Middle West. In sections of New England, Pennsylvania, New York and New Jersey the Russians—like the Polish, Lithuanian and other "foreign" farmers—are doing very well on land that was abandoned by Americans of earlier immigration.

In the 1890s Russians brought to the United States from their native steppes the seeds of the so-called *kubanka* and *arnautka* wheat and special Russian rye and sunflowers. Their cultivation has since been adopted in many parts of the country.

World War I, to repeat, stopped the inflow of this solid, common-man type of immigrant from Russia, as it did of course from most other countries; and practically no ordinary people, no workers and farmers, have migrated to America since. The Soviet Union, with a government building a new civilization, and fearing the attack which came in 1941, held desperately onto its working manpower.

The massive and far-reaching revolutionary upheaval of 1917-1921, however, culminating in the firm establishment of the Soviet Union, caused a vast number of people who opposed the Revolution to flee from Russia. Some had been leading men and women under the Czar: princes and princesses, counts and barons, feudal lords, big industrialists, engineers, professors, army officers, aristocrats and officeholders. Many were White Guardists who had fought the Revolution in organized warfare on the side of the Western powers; then in the early 1920s, defeated, they found themselves *émigrés* in various European and Asiatic countries. Estimates of these people run as high as two million; and in the 1920s and thereafter about forty thousand came as refugee-immigrants to the United States, landing in both eastern and Pacific Coast ports.

They were at once a glamorous and a pathetic group. The majority were moneyless archduchesses and barons, generals and professors, but they felt they must maintain the front that went with their high station in life in Russia. A few married American money. Many hoped against hope that the Soviet government would collapse and they could return to their old positions. Some spent their time agitating against the new regime in Russia. A Fascist society of these people, supporting Hitler's invasion of Russia, was disbanded only after Pearl Harbor.

Most of them discovered that the surest way not to starve in America was to go to work. So, by and by, generals of the old Imperial Army became hotel and apartment-house doormen. Princesses took to writing books and selling gloves and perfume over department store counters. Former patrons of exclusive Old World cafés made good waiters and waitresses, second cooks and even dishwashers, housemaids and butlers. One-time owners of extensive Russian estates and their wives and daughters, who had never known what work meant, got jobs in biscuit and candy factories; a few even as grave-diggers in a Brooklyn cemetery. And to their amazement, many found this new life satisfying. Some were amused to discover that Lenin's slogan: "Whoever does not work does not eat," which they had resented so much in 1919 that they fled from Russia to escape its effect, was nothing new in the world. Some three hundred years ago Captain John Smith announced the same dictum to the lace-frilled English colonists at Jamestown, Virginia. Former Czarist Army colonels, who used to shoot down strikers in Kiev, now joined unions and struck and picketed with their fellow workers.

A book published in New York in 1939, *Service Entrance: Memoirs of a Park Avenue Cook*, told the story of two of these people. The author, Kyra Goritzina, an alumna of the Institute for Noble Young Ladies in St. Petersburg, and her husband, an ex-officer of the Imperial Guards, reached New York in 1923 and after a few weeks decided— like the couple in the Broadway play *Tovarich*—that domestic service was the best means of turning pre-Revolutionary Russian manners into postwar American meals. So they hired out, and in the next fifteen years had a series of jobs on Park Avenue and in the exclusive New York suburbs. They wound up earning two hundred a month. She became a good cook; he, as an able butler, mastered his sense of class so thoroughly that he did not even wince when a guest shook his hand by mistake at a party and then instinctively made a gesture to wipe off the soiling touch.

But some of the aristocrats were quite helpless here. In the middle 1930s I knew a Russian family in New York who were adopted wholesale by their St. Petersburg housekeeper who had come with them to America. Working in a shop, she supported herself and the baron and baroness and their two sons. She sent the youngsters through high school and college; in 1943-1945 both were rather typical young American officers in the United States Army. One died fighting in Germany.

Among the *émigrés* of course were some very effective people who re-oriented themselves quickly, saw opportunities which had not existed in Czarist Russia, and started new industries, especially in the aviation field. Several achieved distinction on the faculties of our leading universities. A number of others turned into successful authors, impresarios, musicians, radio engineers in New York, movie technicians in Hollywood, poultry farmers in Petaluma, restaurateurs and hotel managers in Manhattan, Palm Beach, Hollywood and San Francisco.

After they realized that the Soviet Union would endure, and they would not return to Russia, a large percentage were naturalized. I knew an old man, a Park Avenue doorman in New York, whose uniform was probably as resplendent as the general's uniform he had worn in the Imperial Russian Army. On our first meeting he handed me his card, which read: "General So-and-so, United States Citizen."

A few of these Russians are still anti-Soviet, but fewer and fewer right along. While some have merely reconciled themselves to the permanence of the Soviet system in Russia, more have grown enthusiastic about Soviet accomplishments and the great showing of the Red Army and the Russian nation as a whole during World War II. They are proud of the old country.

Most of the common people who have come over, even those who barely escaped with their lives from pogroms and persecution, retain a warm spot in their hearts for *Matushka Rossiya* (Mother Russia). During 1941-1945 that spot has glowed bright.

The various immigrant groups from Russia have their own religious institutions, fraternal or protective organizations, and newspapers in Yiddish, German, Lithuanian and Russian. But the immigrants' American-born children and grandchildren read the large metropolitan dailies and national magazines, and tend toward the older, more prevalent American organizations.

Since 1941 hundreds of thousands of Russian, Volga-German, and Russian Jewish Americans, most of them born in the United States, have been in the military services. Early in 1945, while fighting in Italy, Private Isadore Rubin of Brooklyn won the essay contest on "What Victory Means to Me" conducted by the Information and Education Section of the Mediterranean Theater of Operations with a piece including these lines:

"At the moment, it's difficult to think of victory as meaning anything but an end to fear, to loneliness and death, and a chance to go back to pick up the strands of interrupted lives.

"Henceforth, each simple pleasure, each right we always took so lightly will take on rich meaning. We know what it cost to keep them, and we know too that we've really earned a share in them.

"But victory means much more.

"With victory, we stand on the threshold of limitless inventions and comforts. We possess the resources to extend our horizons in every field of endeavor and every aspect of human relations.

"However, ancient and stubborn enemies are still to be conquered. Enemies which must be overcome not by armies, but by minds and hearts and talents set wholly free. Such enemies are poverty, insecurity, prejudice, disunity.

"These too shall be conquered. For we have begun to think more deeply and more dynamically. And if we can sweep aside . . . obstacles to smash the most ruthlessly efficient machine of destruction ever devised, surely we possess the vision and the practical genius to organize for peace, security and a world designed for living. . . .

"With victory, we shall have destroyed those who would have enslaved the world. Our sacrifices have been great, but we have won the opportunity to emerge from the animal kingdom and enter the kingdom of man.

"I look forward to living in such a world."

Immigration from Russia has given America its share of men and women who excelled in their fields partly because of their special native talents and proclivities, and partly because the United States offered them a chance to release and realize themselves. I shall mention only a few.

About the same time that Father Goncharenko was active on the West Coast, there arrived another political refugee, Peter Demyanov— later simplified to Peter Demens, who made a dent on America. He became a successful businessman and railroad builder, and started the city of St. Petersburg, Florida. Incidentally, there are St. Petersburgs or Petersburgs in fourteen other states; and Moscows in ten, Odessas in nine, and Kremlins in two.

Still another revolutionary refugee was the architect Vladimir Stoleshnikov who is partly responsible for Carnegie Hall in New York.

In 1879 the nineteen-year-old Isaac Aaronovich Hourwich, a medical student in St. Petersburg, published a pamphlet entitled "What is Constitutionalism?" He was imprisoned on the charge of treason. Released, he decided to devote himself to law and revolution. Late in the 1880s, to evade another arrest and probable banishment to Siberia, he fled to Sweden and from there made his way to the United States, where he enrolled in political science at Columbia College, graduating in 1893. Later he became a lawyer and until his death in 1924 pursued the varied career of legal counsel, government statistician, writer and expert on immigration. In his book *Immigration and Labor*, first published in 1912 and reissued in a revised edition in 1921, he disputed the data and conclusions of the forty-one-volume *Reports of the United States Immigration Commission*, proving statistically that immigrant labor did not depress the wages of native labor nor increase unemployment; that, on the contrary, immigrant labor raised consumer demand and thus industrial production and jobs.

Born in a little Russian village in 1857, motherless from birth, Hiram N. Vineberg was brought to America by his father. Early in 1945 at eighty-eight Dr. Vineberg died in his sleep in New York, where he had practiced medicine since 1886, specializing in gynecology—perhaps the foremost pioneer in the United States in the treatment of women's diseases.

Two other well-known medical men born in Russia died in 1945 during the writing of this book: Isaac Levin, New York specialist in cancer and radiology, and George W. Raiziss, director of the Dermatological Research Laboratories in Philadelphia since 1914. In thirty years Dr. Raiziss developed one of the most powerful antiseptics known, Metaphen, an organic mercury compound used widely in hospitals and clinics; the first American bismuth compound for the treatment of syphilis after the supply from Germany was cut off during World War I; antiseptics and compounds for the treatment of streptococcic infection; and Diasone, a promising cure for tuberculosis. A pioneer also in sulfa experiments, he had a part in the discovery of sulfapyrazine, used against pneumonia.

Sophie Irene Simon Loeb was born in Rovno in 1876. Her parents brought her to America as a child. The family settled in McKeesport, Pennsylvania. When Sophie was sixteen her father died and her mother's struggle to provide for the family made a deep impression on her. Moving to New York in 1910, she went into journalism, covering the slums for The World, then became a pioneer social worker stressing the need of aid for widows with young children. The mother-care legislation now on the statute books of New York and other states is traceable to her crusade between 1910-1922. She also conducted campaigns for lower taxi fares and bonded drivers, for housing relief and safer movie theaters, model tenements and school centers. When she died in 1929, over a thousand people, including Al Smith, went to her funeral.

Born in Riga of mixed German and Lithuanian stock, Henry Romeike ran away from home at fifteen in 1870, knocked about Europe for the next thirteen years—until one day, talking with a man on a park bench in Paris who had been reading a newspaper, it suddenly occurred to him that prominent people might like to receive clippings about themselves. He tried the idea first in Paris, then in London; eventually he came to New York and scored a marked success. He died in 1903; the clipping service company bearing his name is still the leader in its field.

In 1890 thirty-five-year old Akiba Horowitz arrived in New York from Minsk, where the Czarist anti-Jewish policy had been making it increasingly difficult for him to engage in business. Changing his name to Conrad Hubert, he tried his hand successively at operating a cigar store, a restaurant, a boarding house, a farm, a milk wagon route and a jewelry store. He failed to make good in any of these enterprises. In 1898 he chanced to get hold of a new electrical gadget for lighting gas, which he thought was a good if crude idea. He invented and patented a device of his own which he began to manufacture and sell. Later he patented an electric time alarm, a small electric lamp, an electric battery. The last two resulted in the "portable electric light" containing the basic patents of today's flashlight. A modest man who almost never appeared in public, he organized the American Ever Ready Company and the Yale Electric Corporation and at his death in 1928 left eight million dollars—three-quarters of it to charitable, religious, medical and educational institutions selected by his executors, who were Calvin Coolidge, Alfred E. Smith and Julius Rosenwald.

When in 1938, shortly before his death, B. Charney Vladeck was elected majority leader in the New York City Council, one newspaper reporter pointed out that there were marks of a Cossack's knout on his face. He had come to America in 1907 after taking part in the 1905 Russian Revolution. In the next thirty years, as a militant social worker on New York's East Side and the manager of the largest non-English newspaper in the United States, the highly influential *Jewish Daily Forward*, Vladeck had become one of the best known New Yorkers. In 1938, when a Tammany politician attacked him in the Council, invoking his own American forebears to give point to his words, Vladeck smiled and said: "Let me ask Mr. Quinn where his people were when Jefferson was writing the Declaration of Independence?"—"They were not in any prison," replied Quinn, hinting at Vladeck's revolutionary past. "They were in Ireland fighting for liberty."—"Anyone fighting for liberty in Ireland who was not in prison at one time or another couldn't have been a very good Irishman," said Vladeck, evoking laughter from the galleries. "It matters very little where a fellow was born. It does not matter who he is. It does not matter whether he got here first. It does matter what he does when he gets here. The Bible says the first to arrive were the fish, the worms, the reptiles. I *was* in prison in Russia, not once, but many times, Mr. Quinn. But not for stealing, not for real estate speculation, and not for shady transactions. . . . You say your mother was born on the farm next to Abraham Lincoln's in Kentucky; well, a great ancestor of mine, Moses, was secretary to the Lord Almighty."

In 1889 his parents brought Maurice William from Kharkov to New York as an eight-year-old boy. He grew up on the eastside listening to Socialist soapbox orators, and later became "The Dentist Who Changed World History," to use the title of an article about him by Maurice Zololow in the December 1943 *Harpers*. During World War I, in the time he could spare from practicing dentistry, Dr. William wrote an argumentative book *The Social Interpretation of History* which no regular publisher thought worth bringing out. So in 1920 the author published it at his own expense. He sent free copies to prominent American radicals, but none of them seemed to read it. In fact, hardly anyone noticed it. By chance a young Chinese student at Union Theological Seminary in New York heard of the book in 1921 and sent for it. Eventually a copy landed in the hands of Dr. Sun Yat-sen, the founder of the Chinese Republic, on whom it made so deep an impression that he based many of his policies, which had far-reaching effects in Asia and the rest of the world, on Dr. William's ideas. Prior to the early 1940s, when magazines began to publish articles about this curious historical development, only a few hundred copies of the book had been distributed in the United States. The Chinese government, however, decorated Dr. William with the Order of the Jade.

In the 1930s in New York, I knew a man named Alex Gumberg. Born in the Russian Ukraine, the son of a schoolteacher, Alex had come to the United States alone in 1903 at fifteen. Working by day at all kinds of jobs and studying by night, he became a licensed pharmacist; but his future lay in another direction.

Returning to Russia in 1917 after the Kerensky revolution, just to see what was going on there, Alex chanced to meet Colonel Raymond Robins, head of the American Red Cross mission to Russia, who took him on as his interpreter and confidential advisor. Alex told the colonel months in advance that the Kerensky regime would not last and would be succeeded by a Soviet. Extremely impressed by the Bolshevik revolution which they observed firsthand, both Robins (who became President Wilson's unofficial ambassador to the Kremlin) and Alex had frequent interviews with Lenin, who made friends with them both. Early in the 1920s, back in America with the Red Cross mission, Alex organized a syndicate to purchase and send to the new Soviet Union millions of dollars worth of American cotton. This was the first substantial business transaction between the U.S.A. and the U.S.S.R. Alex could easily have made a million dollars on the deal, but he had as much when he quit the syndicate as when he created it—nothing. Following this episode, he found himself advising the Chase National Bank on Russian affairs; in 1930 he joined the staff of the Atlas Corporation, then a new outfit in Wall Street. In this capacity he was for nine years closely associated with Floyd B. Odlum in building up Atlas to one of the leading investment companies in the United States.

When Alex died, the obituaries referred to him as a "financier"—but he didn't leave anything. Money meant nothing to him. People interested him, individually and in their effect on each other. America and Russia interested him, separately and together, especially together. He knew all manner of people and always had slews around him—Morgan partners and Communists, Cabinet members and scrubwomen, United States Senators and obscure writers. He liked them all, liked to be with them and see what made them tick, and how he might help them and influence them to enhance each other. If they were able and ready to do something to improve the relations between the United States and Russia, they became something special to him. He was a passionate American and a passionate pro-Russian, and one of the best public-relations men under the sun. Having a virtually unlimited expense account from Atlas, Alex was perennially giving luncheons and dinners and week-end parties, talking, kidding, drawing people out, explaining Russia to Americans, America to Russians.

"His life," read an editorial in the Nation (June 10, 1939) the week after he died, "touched the lives of men and women who stood for different and often hostile points of view, who moved on widely separated social levels, of whom it might almost be said that their sole common denominator lay in Alex Gumberg's esteem. He managed somehow to bridge all existing cleavages and to do so, not by compromising or concealing his own views, but by shifting human values to a dimension of his own in which ordinary social and intellectual differences played no role. At his home bankers and labor leaders, Republicans and New Dealers fraternized in an atmosphere of humorous and humane tolerance. With a pleasure that seemed almost mischievous Alex Gumberg encouraged open showdowns between honest adversaries; he hated the evasion and surface politeness that comprise the ordinary social intercourse of such diverse groups as were drawn into his circle. He had one of the most sophisticated minds and one of the least calculating hearts that could be imagined. With a sharp understanding of the realities of public business, he combined an almost childlike faith in the men and women to whom he gave his friendship. He tolerated no doubts of the motives of such persons, and he gave a generous share of his energy and wisdom to the support of their fortunes and hopes.

"His public interests ranged so widely that it is hard to point to one special focus of influence. But it should be said here, because the newspapers have made little mention of the fact, that Russia has had no friend in the United States so wise and tireless as Alex Gumberg. Apart from innumerable concrete services, he did more than any other American to prepare the way for the recognition of the Soviet government.

And from the time just after the revolution, when he helped distribute American food to starving Russians until the day he died, he kept his faith that the country of his birth would survive its years of suffering and conflict and play a heroic role in the life of nations. He believed, in particular, that a successful resistance to the present threat of fascist conquest would depend in large measure on Russian leadership and collaboration."

For decades Russian immigrants of all varieties have been conspicuous in American music—Sergei Koussevitzky, André Kostelanetz, Alexander Saslavsky, Alexander Koshetz, Nicolai Sokoloff and Paul Stassevich, conductors; Max Vogrich, Vladimir Horowitz, Sergei Rachmaninoff, Bernard Alfred Mirovitch, Jascha Heifetz, Mischa Elman, Mischa Mischakoff, Leo Ornstein, Efrem Zimbalist, Josef Lhevinne, Isadore Kohon, Ossip Gabrilowitch, Vera Fonaroff, Nikolai Lopatnikoff and Leopold Godowsky, violinists and pianists; Louis Gruenberg, Nicolai T. Berezowsky, Irving Berlin and Vernon Duke, composers; Sophie Braslau, Feodore Chaliapin, Irene Pavlovska, Mari Barova, Nina Koshetz, Adolf Muhlmann, Maria Kurenko, and the Don Cossack Chorus, singers; Gregor Piatigorsky, cellist; Samuel Chotzinoff, Nicolas Nabokor and Nicolas Slonimsky, critics.

In American writing these come to mind: Mary Antin, Herman Bernstein, Abraham Cahan, Maurice Hindus, Simeon Strunsky, Max Lerner, Irina Skariatina, Nicholas Wreden, Mark Aldanov, Anzia Yezierska, Avrahm Yarmolinsky, Alexander Nazarov, Sonia Tomara, Marya Zaturenska, George Papashvily, Nina Fedorova, Joshua Kunitz, George Sokolsky, Alexandra Krastin and Vera Micheles Dean.

In painting, sculpture and cartooning: Peter Blume, Boris M. Artzybasheff, Alexander Portnoff, Boris Chaliapin, M. V. Dobujinsky, Nicolai Cikovsky, Abbo Ostrowsky, Gleb Derujinsky, Leon Gaspard, Leon Gordon, S. Souderkin, Serge Konevkoff, Louis Lozowick, Ivan G. Olinsky, Maurice Sterne, Abraham Walkowitz, Marc Chagall, Constantine Alajalov, Mischa Richter, William Gropper, the brothers Raphael, Isaac and Moses Soyer, Nahum Tschacbasov, Alexander Brook, Robert Brackman, Aaron Bohrod and Elizabeth Schoumatoff.

In acting: Alla Nazimova, Olga Petrova, Marya Ouspenskaya, Gregory Ratoff, Mischa Auer, Eugenie Leontovich, Jacob Adler.

In the film industry: Louis B. Mayer, the Warner brothers, the Schencks and many others.

In stage production: Morris Gest.

In the dance: Michael Fokine, George Balanchine, Bronislava Nijinskaya and Leonid Massine, choreographers and directors; Tamara

Toumanova, Tatiana Riaboushinkaya, Irina Baronova, Nicholas Daks and André Eglevsky, dancers. In this field the Russian influence, derived from the rigorous training in the imperial ballet, is predominant.

In philosophy: Morris Raphael Cohen, G. P. Fedotov and Morris Zucker.

In education: Saul Badanes, who devised the "insight method" of teaching arithmetic.

In physiology: Samuel J. Meltzer and S. Menkin.

In sociology: Pitirim A. Sorokin.

In zoology: Alexander Petrunkevich, the world's greatest authority on the spider.

In general scientific research: Vladimir K. Zworykin.

In archeology: Michael Rostovtzeff.

In history: Michael Karpovich, Sergei Yakobson, Helen Iswolsky and George V. Vernadsky.

In psychiatry: Boris Sidis and Gregory Zilboorg.

In marine biology: Victor L. Loosanoff.

In chemistry: Iwan I. Ostromislensky, V. N. Ipatiev, Taisa Stadnishenko, Samuel L. Madorsky—and George B. Kistiakowsky, who worked on the atomic bomb experiments in New Mexico in 1945.

In forestry: Raphael Zon.

Professors of Russian and Russian literature: Nikander Strelsky, George D. Grebenstchikoff, Alexander Kaun.

Leaders in the labor movement: Sidney Hillman and Jacob S. Potofsky* of the Amalgamated Clothing Workers of America; Samuel Wolchok of the United Retail, Wholesale and Department Store Em-

---

* According to *Time* (May 21, 1945), at the hearing on the extension of the Reciprocal Trade Agreements Act held in mid-May by a House committee in Washington, "Jake" Potofsky, representing the C.I.O., "stole the show with his eloquent argument":

"Some people say the standard of living of the American worker will be reduced, if tariffs are cut down. We do not hold this view. We think that high wages result from high productivity, imaginative and progressive managerial leadership and good union organization—and not from tariffs.

"Moreover, we think that real standards of living depend not only on what is in the pay envelope, but on what we can buy with it. The only effective protection the American worker has against so-called foreign competition is not a tariff barrier against foreign goods, but efficient production at home and a decent standard of living abroad.

"I am convinced that . . . far from threatening American agriculture, industry and labor, the Trade Agreements Act is an important element in promoting the postwar prosperity of all of them. It is one of the indispensable steps in bringing about a world order in which cooperation among nations replaces strife. We . . . are on the threshold of the first decisions that will determine whether we shall direct our efforts towards that goal."

ployees; Boris Shishkin, economist for the American Federation of Labor.

Leaders in the Socialist movement: Jacob Rombro and Morris Hillquit.

Leo Pasvolsky, economist, was an assistant to the Secretary of State.

David Sarnoff, president of the Radio Corporation of America, was a brigadier general in the United States Army Signal Corps during World War II. In 1933 Sam Zemurray became the operating head of the United Fruit Company. Samuel Rosoff is a big name in contracting and subway-building.

Russian immigrants, mostly former "White Guardists," have made a big place for themselves in aviation as executives, designers, engineers and other kinds of technicians—Igor I. Sikorsky, Alexander de Seversky, Michael and Serge Gluhareff, Illya Islamoff, Korvan Kruhovsky, Alexander Kartveli, Alexander Pishvanov, Serge Tchemesoff and George de Bothezat.

Scores of other Russian immigrants appear in Who's Who. And there are thousands and thousands of sons and daughters of immigrants from Russia who are outstanding in their fields—law, medicine, dentistry, the arts and sciences, industry, business, radio, politics, education, sports—such people as Belle Moskowitz, Al Smith's long-time co-worker and adviser; Herman Shumlin and Oscar Serlin, Broadway producers; Leo Cherne of the Research Institute of America; Norman Rosten, poet; Jan Peerce, a leading "Italian" tenor of the Metropolitan Opera Company; Jo Davidson, sculptor; Stella Adler, actress; Henry A. Davidson, psychiatrist—

But as is true in other groups, the over-all significance of Russian immigration is in the masses of Great, Little and White Russians, Russian Jews and Germans; in the millions of garment and fur workers, farmers and miners, steel workers and window-washers. Many have worn themselves out or have been killed in industrial accidents; the survivors and their American-born children are a stout spoke in a wheel of the vehicle on which the United States will ride to the future.

In his book published in 1922 from which I have already quoted, Jerome Davis pointed out that the Russian immigrants came to the United States with the huge handicap of their background in Czarist autocracy, "but also with traits which are good. Many of them have the same longing for liberty that actuated our forefathers when they founded this republic."

In 1939 I spent an evening in New York listening to a Russian American friend of mine, the late Mark Villchur, who wrote on immigration from Russia and to whom I am indebted for some of the facts in this article. In a rural Connecticut town, whence he had just returned, he had heard talk of a "dumb Russian" farmer nearby who was clearing his stony fields with his bare hands. Villchur went to see the man. "You see," explained the farmer, "I know that dynamite would do a quicker and better job, but it costs money to buy it, and I haven't any too much money. Sometimes I feel it is foolish to hope to clear all these fields. But then I look at the stone walls around my fields which were put up by people who owned this land before me, and I feel ashamed of myself. The price I paid for this farm would not begin to pay for their labor. I have been here six years, and every year I have cleared about half an acre. My horse helps to pull the big stones away; I use a lever to push up the big fellows. When I die, the next owner will find a better place here—anyhow just a little better maybe."

Mark Villchur's comment was: "To my mind, this grizzled farmer of Russian birth is as truly a member of the pioneer tribe and a follower of the 'American tradition' as if he traced his lineage to the Jamestown or the Mayflower group."

In 1944 a Russian immigrant's American-born son—Yeoman Second Class Jerry Palevsky of the United States Navy—wrote to the New York Times:

"Americanism is basically determined not by the date your ancestors came to this country or where they came from, or your accent, or your color, or your looks. It is rather determined by your ideas and conceptions of the 'brotherhood of man' and freedom and equality of opportunity; of respect for fair play and decency and dislike for bullying and narrow-mindedness. If certain people must feel like 'super' people, they are to be pitied, but not to be respected or considered good Americans. They are dangerously un-American. The fact that their ideas are probably a result of ignorance does not detract from their viciousness and destructiveness."

When in April 1945 the Fifth Marine Division cemetery was dedicated on Iwo Jima, the sermon was delivered by the division's Jewish chaplain, Roland B. Gittelsohn, Cleveland-born son of an immigrant from Lithuania when it was part of Russia, who is rabbi of the Central Synagogue of Nassau County, Rockville Center, Long Island, New York. "Somewhere in this plot of ground," he said, "there may lie the man who could have discovered the cure for cancer. Under one of these Christian crosses, or beneath a Jewish Star of David, there may rest now a man who was destined to be a great prophet. . . . Now they lie here silently in this sacred soil, and we gather to consecrate this earth to their memory. . . .

"Here lie officers and men, Negroes and Whites, rich men and poor . . . Here are Protestants, Catholics and Jews. . . . Here no man prefers another because of his color. Here there are no quotas of how many from each group are admitted or allowed. Theirs is the highest and purest democracy.

"Any man among us the living who . . . lifts his hand in hate against a brother, or thinks himself superior to those who happen to be in the minority, makes of this ceremony and of the bloody sacrifice it commemorates, an empty mockery. . . ."

VII: AMERICANS FROM GERMANY

For two centuries after the Discovery, Europe floundered in a dreadful confusion. Parts of the old continent were being loosed from the heavy grip of the Middle Ages. The disintegration of feudalism had begun. Military wars mingled with religious strife. People were exchanging ancient bigotries for new ones.

Germany, in the center of the unhappy continent, was not yet a united state. It was a collection of small principalities ruled by autocratic individuals and cliques. Poverty and frustration, persecution and defensiveness, ran all through German life. Seeking escape from a plethora of predicaments and bafflements, people groped about in spiritual realms. Here and there groups recoiling from the chaos of the times were forming new religious sects on the periphery of the Protestant movement; which in some cases called down upon their heads the intolerance of the established powers. This was especially true in the Palatinate—a fertile region around the confluence of the Rhine and Main Rivers, mostly south of the juncture—where a proud, sturdy people lived.

Cosmography was another realm that attracted German imagination. In the early sixteenth century there were several outstanding German mapmakers. Martin Waldseemueller has already been mentioned as the man who is generally credited with having invented the name "America." (See p. 19.) Gerhard Kramer, who Latinized his name into Mercator, devised the system of projection, based on the curve of the earth's surface, which has remained indispensable in nautical mapmaking to this day.

One would think that this interest, coupled with the general situation, would have led to German exploration and colonization, as did equivalent conditions in Spain, England, France, Holland and Sweden, but it didn't. Germany was not a maritime country, there were no German seafarers and explorers.

A few Teutons reached the New World in the dimness of its history as members of non-German expeditions. A man named Tyrker who came with Leif Erikson in the year 1000 from Iceland was supposed to have been a Teuton. In the 1560s several Germans (Alsatian and Hessian Protestants) were among the Huguenot colonists who tried to settle first in what is now South Carolina and later in Florida, and may have been slaughtered by the Spaniards. There were "Dutch-men," actually Germans, in the Jamestown Colony, where Captain John Smith—the popularly accepted but historically disputed leader of the settlement—regarded them highly for their skills along with the "Polanders" and Armenians. There were Germans too in New Netherland and New Sweden.

In 1660 one Jacob Leisler arrived in New Amsterdam (soon to be New York) from Frankfurt-am-Main and presently rose to prominence as a trader. Twenty years later, at the height of his business career, he got involved in the Protestant-Catholic and monarchical disputes then ripping England and the American Colonies. As a champion of Protestantism and supported by the militia, he summoned a convention which made him commander-in-chief, virtually governor, of the New York Colony. In 1690 he called the first congress of American colonial governors; nothing much came of it—but this step may furnish grounds for considering Leisler the first official American, for apparently his intention was to assert American will and authority in America. In the ensuing mixup he was declared a rebel and was hanged in 1691. Whereupon for several decades New York politics continued extremely lively: Leislerians versus anti-Leislerians. Leisler had been rather autocratic by nature, but his rebellion created a political impulse that caused his posthumous followers to fight for popular rights.

Late in the seventeenth century Franz Daniel Pastorius, who had attended five universities and was much traveled and at home in most European languages, became interested in William Penn's literature advertising Pennsylvania which was sifting through Holland and along the Upper Rhine in Germany. In the town of Krefeld, near the Dutch border, Pastorius was the leader of a group of Mennonites tending toward Quakerism. Some of his followers also became interested in Penn's Land of Promise, and in 1683 the ship Concord—"the Mayflower of German immigration"—reached Philadelphia with thirteen German families. Six years later, after clearing a lot of forest land and putting up their homes, church and school, this group formally founded Germantown, which some of them at first, keenly aware of their meager lot, called Armentown, the Town of the Poor.

Pastorius, perhaps the best educated individual in the Colonies at the time—"not forgetting Cotton Mather," as one historian puts it— was a man of ideas and ideals, and of practical purpose and ability when circumstances demanded. During the town's crucial years, he was its minister, teacher, mayor and treasurer, legal and business adviser and manager. He led the community to raise flax and weave linen, which after a while attained great commercial favor in Philadelphia. He compiled a primer—the first schoolbook printed in Pennsylvania. He started the first night school, teaching English to his fellow immigrants, which also makes him a pioneer in adult education.

In 1688 under Pastorius' leadership, the people of Germantown drew up and presented to a magistrate the first public protest against slavery in the New World. Rightly enough, no teller of the German saga in America neglects to mention this fact.

In the final years of the seventeenth century and the first half of the eighteenth, Germans came to these shores at a steadily increasing rate, mostly via Holland and England. Usually referred to as the Palatines or Palatinates, the early immigrants belonged almost entirely to Pietist sects and were at odds with the prevailing religious atmosphere, to say nothing of the social and economic conditions, in their native provinces. Many were Mennonites, followers of a Protestant leader named Menno Simons who had lived early in the sixteenth century and had preached, among other things, opposition to political oppression, war and militarism. Here, or in England before starting over, some of the Mennonites became Quakers.

In 1694 a leader named Johann Kelpius, later famous as a theologian and hymn writer, a hermit, and an all-round eccentric, brought over forty "Mystics." They settled on Wissahickon Creek near Philadelphia. There the brothers Klaus and Wilhelm Rittenhaus (Rittenhouse) started the first paper mill in America.

Some Palatines were lured across the Atlantic by English and Dutch shipowners' agents who wore fine clothes and heavy gold watch-chains and told the wretched peasants of the Rhine country that in America such attire was the usual thing. Succumbing to this advertising, moneyless emigrants obligated themselves to the agents for the fare and arrived in America as virtual bondsmen, having to work for years to pay back the cost of their passage.

Philadelphia was long the principal port for German immigrants.

From there, or rather from Germantown, which Pastorius made into a clearing station for Palatine newcomers, they spread northward into the limestone region, which has a distinct and highly agreeable "Pennsylvania Dutch" character and atmosphere even today. Some spilled across the Delaware into western New Jersey between Trenton on the south and Phillipsburg on the north. Eventually others overflowed to Maryland and, across the Potomac and through the Shenandoah Valley, to Virginia and North Carolina, to Georgia.

Some settled in Philadelphia, Baltimore and other embryo cities, but most took to pioneer farming and made good nearly everywhere. Simple, conservative, hard-working folk, they were not given to adventure and exploration as were, say, the Irish, then pushing brashly into the wilderness of western Pennsylvania. They were a practical people in everyday affairs, and where they applied their axes and plows they founded stable communities. Pennsylvania's Lancaster County, for instance, was described over two hundred years ago as a "farmers' paradise." It is still quite Pennsylvania-Dutch, as are Bucks County and sections of the Lehigh Valley.

The colonial German immigration included few Catholics. A good many, particularly those who settled in towns toward the middle of the eighteenth century, were regular Lutherans or of the German Reformed Church and in most cases readily adjustable to the local customs. This was not true of some of the two-dozen varieties of sectarians, clannish, stubborn people rigidly holding onto their religious doctrines and folk values and ways. Slightly differing sects were called Dunkers or Dunkards, Schwenkfelders, the New-Born, the New Mooners, the many kinds of Brethren, and so on. Most were, or stemmed from, Mennonites and had several attitudes and practices in common. They believed in what they interpreted to be in the Bible and nothing else. The keynote of their behavior was humility and unworldliness, which in some became anti-worldliness. They would take no hand in government affairs, least of all would they bear arms. They wanted to mind their own business and to be left alone with their beliefs and manner of life. Members of the same sex greeted one another with a kiss. They did not care how eccentric others thought them, or how conformative others wished to be. They held that the goal of man is the building of character that is socially creative and as such eternally significant.

Some of the sects had no churches; still haven't. One group, the "Old Order Amish," are found in southeastern Pennsylvania pretty much as they were two hundred years ago, but in danger of disintegrating under the pressure of powerful modern influences. They wear the plainest imaginable clothes with hooks and eyes instead of buttons; they scorn carpets and curtains in their spotlessly clean, whitewashed houses. Married men grow beards, shaving the upper lip. Like many other Pennsylvania Dutch, among themselves they speak a language which is a mixture of German with English endings and vice versa. When they speak English they retain a strong flavor of German word use and position. A friend of mine tells me of a sign he found in Lancaster over a doorbell which was out of order: "Bump! The bell don't make!"—which is German literally translated into English.

William Penn's province was the most liberal colony in America, several regions of which were rather bigoted; none the less, long after they first appeared, the Pennsylvania Germans were regarded by many English and Protestant-Irish colonists with suspicion or resentment. Benjamin Franklin blurted out some uncomplimentary remarks about them. But that did not faze them; taking the ridicule in their stride, they stuck to their language, religions, costumes and habits, and after a while the tendency was not only to tolerate but to accept and respect them. Thus they made a subtle contribution to one of the best American traditions—that of letting people alone, of not regarding nonconformity as a crime.

In 1730, having revised his opinion of the Germans, Benjamin Franklin printed—for Johann Konrad Beissel, a Palatine hymn writer, the successor to Johann Kelpius and founder of the Solitary Brethren of the Community of Seventh-Day Baptists at Ephrata—one of the first German books in America, *Goettliche Liebes—und Lobesgethoene* (Sacred Love and Praise Tunes). And another signer of the Declaration of Independence, Benjamin Rush, describing the German settlers as "industrious, frugal, punctual and just," said they were chiefly responsible for Pennsylvania's stability and prosperity in the eighteenth century.

They were not only good farmers but superb mechanics. According to Professor Carl Wittke's account in *They Who Built America*, they introduced into Pennsylvania the vast barns adapted from a barn common in parts of Germany two or three hundred years ago; and they were "probably the first to cultivate asparagus and cauliflower in America." Where they originally settled in the lonely parts of southeastern Pennsylvania, they lived—in common with most American pioneers—in caves and sod-houses. Then they began to build the now well-known and highly appreciated Pennsylvania-Dutch stone farmhouse, still very much in evidence around Doylestown, Easton, Bethlehem, Allentown, Lancaster and Reading.

As conditions got worse in Germany throughout the eighteenth century, and more and more people heard of America and that the British government did not object to their entering the American Colonies, large numbers of Germans of all kinds headed for Rotterdam and thence for England. In 1708-1709 over thirteen thousand jammed the refugee facilities in London. Riots and disease broke out, killing many. Anti-Romanism sent about two thousand Catholics back to the continent of Europe. Most of the Protestants were gradually shipped to America.

Hundreds sailed to Virginia, where the British intended to develop iron mines, and to the Carolinas, to settle on the land. Presently some of these and others who followed them penetrated to Tennessee and Kentucky.

In 1709 a German refugee leader, Joshua Kocherthal, with a group of Palatines, founded Neuburg, now Newburgh-on-Hudson. The next year, on ten ships, about 2,300 Germans reached New York; over 440 fewer than had started from England—that number having died enroute from the effects of bad food, lack of fresh water and overcrowded conditions during the voyage. But this was the usual thing for immigrants at the time and for a good while after.

These and subsequent Germans started—in some cases with British financial aid—settlements in New York, especially along the Mohawk, where they got along poorly with the Hollanders but wonderfully with the Indians, participating in their sport festivals. The names of the present-day towns of Herkimer, Mannheim and Oppenheim are reminders of German colonization in the early eighteenth century.

Among the German refugee-immigrants filling one of the disease-ridden ships which reached New York in 1710 was a boy in his teens, John Peter Zenger, an orphan whose father had died during the trip. In New York City he was apprenticed to a printer, required for years to work mainly to pay for his and his father's voyage. But his master was both a good man and a good printer; in 1733 Zenger owned a shop of his own and published the New York Weekly Journal.

It was a time of bitter political struggle in New York. The popular leader Rip Van Dam attacked the colonial governor, Crosby, calling him corrupt and tyrannical. The climax came when Zenger published a documented article damaging to Crosby, who jailed him for libel and sent militiamen to bust up his shop. But the printer-editor, aided by friends who carried out instructions given from his prison cell, continued to issue the paper and rip into the governor.

Zenger's friends got one of the most highly respected lawyers in the Colonies, Andrew Hamilton of Philadelphia, to take the case; and

Hamilton made his significant speech calling on the jury to render a just verdict and thereby create "a noble foundation for securing to ourselves, our posterity and our neighbors that to which nature and the laws of our country have given us the right—the liberty of both exposing and opposing arbitrary power, in these parts of the world, at least, . . . by speaking and writing Truth!" The verdict of "Not Guilty" was a trumpet blast betokening the future.

During the trial, Zenger's sheet published a full account of the proceedings—an extremely important document in the annals of America. The combination of a German-immigrant printer, who had spent most of his youth paying for his passage to the New World, and a wealthy Protestant-Irish Philadelphia lawyer, laid the foundation for the American tradition of freedom of the press.

Ten years later, in 1743, in Germantown, Christoph Saur published in German the first complete Bible printed in America in a European language; it went into three editions. Saur also published the first religious magazine on the continent and, in addition, Germantown's first newspaper, whose name might be Englished as *The High German Pennsylvania Historian, or Collection of Important News from the Kingdom of Nature and of the Church.* In 1771 his son started the first type foundry in North America.

In 1735 an immigrant named Hunter established in Montgomery County, Pennsylvania, the first factory for the manufacture of brick roofing tile. In 1765 at Mannheim, Pennsylvania, Henry William Stiegel started the first glass furnace. There are, in the chronicle of the colonial Germans, many other such "firsts" of great practical value.

But my favorite pre-Revolutionary German is Christian Priber (also written Pryber and Preber), a native of Saxony and a very learned man who lived long in England before coming to South Carolina in the 1730s with the idea of starting in America a perfect state called Paradise, of which he would be prime minister. According to Herbert Ravenell Sass in the June 3, 1944, *Saturday Evening Post,* Priber was a roly-poly little man in his middle years with a bright twinkle in his wide-spaced blue eyes, and full of self-confidence and high purpose. In a chest on his horse's back he carried his few belongings, which included a manuscript outlining his philosophy and plans for a perfect social order. Thus equipped, and unarmed, he plunged five hundred miles into the wild Indian country beyond the Smoky Mountains. He was at home wherever he stopped and his idea of the Republic of Paradise, and belief that he was on the verge of realizing it, were deeply convincing to most of the Indian chiefs and some of the White men scattered thereabouts. Forty years before the American Revolution, says Mr.

Sass, Priber preached that all men are born free and equal, that women are entitled to the same rights as men, that tyranny and related evils had better be expelled from this virgin continent before it was too late, before they got too firm a grip on it. Otherwise, liberty might have the devil of a time establishing itself as the core of an order fit for human beings to live in.

A tremendous forward-looker with a centuries-long telescope and with a matter-of-fact manner and much political acumen, Christian Priber came so close to organizing the Southern Indian Nations and many Whites in a formidable movement that the commanders of both the French and British frontier garrisons decided not to take any chances with him. He was captured and shut up in the strong British fort on St. Simon Island off Georgia. He lived for many years—the rest of his life—in prison, always cheerful, confident that America was potential Paradise. At first his captors regarded him as a dangerous crackpot, but they grew to respect him and his utopian conception.

Probably very few Germans in America in the eighteenth century knew of Priber's frustrated project, but many must have had occasional glimmers of his vision, of what was to be called the American Dream; for when the Revolution came thousands eagerly joined in the struggle. There were scarcely any German Tories or Loyalists; only Patriots. No doubt this was due partly to the fact that, while not doing badly on their farms and in their city shops, most Germans found themselves in inferior positions alongside the English and Dutch colonists. Many English settlers in particular still regarded them as outlandish, unassimilable foreigners, stupid and awkward, pointlessly stubborn because they insisted on doing and seeing things differently, on behaving not quite according to the dominant pattern. All this rubbed the Germans the wrong way; and since many English colonists who showed their disdain for Pennsylvania and Mohawk Valley Germans were Loyalists, the Germans just naturally supported the Revolution.

Also, by the mid-1770s there were exceptional individuals of German stock scattered through the Colonies who came close to being as acute politically as were the principal Anglo-Saxon revolutionaries; some, in fact, were more so. In the summer of 1774 the Mohawk Valley Palatines issued a statement anticipating the Declaration of Independence in which they said right out that they would prefer to die than to exist under tyranny. The next spring they created the historically important Committee of Safety in Tyron County, which sponsored the formation of four battalions. This militia, eventually commanded by General

Nicholas Herckheimer, a man of German stock, played a memorable role three years later in the operations against the British general, Burgoyne, part of whose forces consisted of Hessian mercenaries. In the crucial battle of Oriskany on August 6, 1777, of the eight hundred Palatines engaged, 245 fell. Herckheimer himself died of wounds eleven days later.

One Sunday early in 1776, a Pennsylvania-Dutch Lutheran minister, Peter Muhlenberg, ended his sermon: "There is a time for preaching and praying, but also a time for battle, and such a time has now arrived." There in the pulpit he took off his ministerial garb, revealing the uniform of a Continental Army colonel, and called for men to join his regiment. Later he was made a general; he fought in the battles of Brandywine, Germantown and Yorktown. His statue is in the Hall of Fame in Washington.

Possibly no one foreigner made a greater military contribution to the American Revolutionary struggle than Baron Friedrich Wilhelm von Steuben, a Prussian veteran of the Seven Year's War, a former aide-de-camp to Frederick the Great, who came over on the urging of Benjamin Franklin to help shape the revolutionists into a disciplined fighting force under a methodical administrative setup. In addition, he helped in the strategic jams at Monmouth and Yorktown. After the war George Washington wrote him a letter of thanks, four states voted him land grants, and Congress gave him a pension.

Many of Washington's bodyguards were Pennsylvania Germans, commanded by Major Barth von Heer. His quartermaster general was Heinrich Emmanuel Lutterloh. Christopher Ludwig, receiving a salary of seventy-five dollars a month, ran the bakeries supplying the Army. And in front of the Naval Academy at Annapolis there is a statue to General John De Kalb, who died in the Battle of Camden.

Some of the units under the Polish general, Count Pulaski, consisted largely of Pennsylvania Germans.

A big proportion of Revolutionary soldiers who stuck it out at Valley Forge during the critical winter of 1777-1778 were Pennsylvania Germans; and most of the men who went through that experience benefited from the food and clothing which the German farmers—"the Good Samaritans"—of the surrounding territory brought them. Thousands of Germans whose religious convictions precluded their serving as soldiers participated in the War of Independence as noncombatants: cooks, bakers, nurses, stretcher-bearers.

"Molly Pitcher," whose real name was Mary Heis and who carried water to the hard-pressed colonial forces at Monmouth, was the daughter of German immigrant settlers in New Jersey.

Michael Hillegas became the first treasurer of the Continental Congress; Johann Adam Treutlen, the first governor of Georgia; Heinrich Miller, whose paper, the Philadelphia *Staatsbote*, had scooped the whole American press on the acceptance of the Declaration of Independence, the first Printer of Congress; Frederick Muhlenberg, the first Speaker in Congress, to be twice re-elected.

So it went: German Americans were a vital part of American life. In 1790 their number was around 360,000 in a total White population of 3,172,000, and it kept increasing at a quickening rate.

The 1790 figure included some ten thousand Hessians who were allowed to remain here after the surrender at Saratoga. They spread through the East; many headed south and west. One named Kuester settled in Pennsylvania, to became the first American ancestor of General George A. Custer, the renowned Indian fighter of the post-Civil War period. Some of the Carolina hill-people are still called "Hessians."

A number of German states had issued anti-emigration decrees even before the American Revolution, specifically forbidding the departure of skilled craftsmen, but Germans of all kinds continued to come over. A friend of mine, the late Judge John D. Fearhake of New Canaan, Connecticut, once told me that his great-great-grandfather, a Hanoverian glass-blower named Feuerhacker, had had himself smuggled over the border into Holland as a corpse in a coffin, so he could get to Maryland where a glass manufacturer, who had sent a labor agent to Germany, needed his skill.

Around 1800 and later, American labor agents were very active in Germany, as in some other countries, starting many a German peasant and artisan across the ocean. Then, following William Penn's successful example, the governors and legislatures of some of the new states with vast unpopulated areas, Ohio and Wisconsin in particular, began to advertise their virtues abroad. Thus the New Immigration got under way. Germans came in in large numbers through every United States port, spreading themselves all over the continent; taking their proportionate part in the opening of the New West, in the rapid development of new industries and new towns. Many entered at New Orleans, then went up the Mississippi.

Early in the nineteenth century, with the almost simultaneous rise to intellectual stardom of Goethe, Schiller, Fichte and Kant, sections of the German nation experienced an abrupt flash of bright promise in their national life. A liberal, progressive ferment reached its height in the northern Protestant provinces. It expressed itself through various clubs and movements which took "Liberty" as their watchword and opposed the monarchy and rule by the few. In alarm, the reactionaries in the saddle resorted to extreme repressive measures; which in turn, and on top of successive crop failures and low wages, gave a fresh impetus to the stream pouring toward America. The frustrated revolutionary upheavals of 1830 and 1848 produced the high-points in the volume and intensity of this flow, and eventually the German immigrants arriving during the latter period were referred to as the Forty-Eighters. Highly educated men were not rare among them; and it has been said that from about 1815 to 1860 many a German heaving a pick on railroad-construction jobs, or cutting a furrow through virgin soil, recited Greek and Latin verse as he worked.

About ten thousand Germans arrived in 1832, seventeen thousand in 1834, twenty-four thousand in 1837, 951,667 in the decade 1850-1860, and close to another quarter of a million in the few years immediately before the Civil War.

Streams of them flowed into Wisconsin. Others settled in southern Ohio, in the St. Louis district of Missouri; in New York, Buffalo and Baltimore, in Chicago and elsewhere in Illinois; in Indiana, Michigan, Nebraska, Iowa, Minnesota. Some of those entering through the Gulf ports started colonies in Texas and Louisiana. The majority, however, arrived by way of the eastern ports; often as many as a dozen westbound German-immigrant trains a day left New York. Thousands joined in the gold rush to California; hundreds headed for Oregon, where a German, the elder Astor, had established a trading post at Astoria. Another German, Henry Yesler, a lumberman from Maryland, started a post farther up north, founding Seattle.

Immigrants came from almost all sections of Germany, and were of various religions and none. A small percentage were Catholics. In the 1830s Jews began to arrive in large contingents, some in flight from the anti-Semitic discrimination rising in Germany about then, particularly in Bavaria; others for the same reasons as non-Jews: poverty and political reaction.

Tens of thousands of Germans arriving between 1830 and 1860, Gentile and Jewish, were among the best educated, politically most advanced Europeans of that era. Thousands were journalists, poets, lawyers, doctors, apothecaries. Some were rich; some came with a price on their heads—Carl Schurz among them.

After they got here a good many Forty-Eighters seemed to discover that politically they were way ahead of the general American public and most of its leaders. Also, like the Catholic Irish who were pouring in at the same time, they were temperamentally at variance with the still somewhat Puritanical attitudes of the Anglo-Saxon Americans who gave the dominant note to the American ways of life. And, being pretty tautly wound up by their direct experience of revolting against German oppression, they were generally a bit aggressive—which caused impatience and annoyance, not to say resentment, all around. In fact, it was one of the reasons for the development of Native-American or Know-Nothing movements, which the Forty-Eighters fought tooth and nail. But the struggle, ending as it did in the defeat of Know-Nothingism, was all to the good—it strengthened enlightened Americanism. Historians now are agreed that the intellectual German immigrant of the middle nineteenth century was one of the most valuable elements in the New Immigration. From the 1850s on the group produced a huge number of unusually effective Americans in industry and business, politics, education, medicine, journalism, the labor movement, the Army and the arts—most of all in music.

Earlier German immigrants had pioneered in American music. The Moravian groups in Germantown and Bethlehem had begun to emphasize music in their church observances long before the Revolution; later they made Bethlehem a center of interpretation of Bach. In 1815 a German immigrant, Gottlieb Graupner, had initiated the famous Handel and Haydn Society in Boston, whose membership was almost entirely German American. In 1835 the German Americans of Philadelphia had founded the first singing society, the *Maennerchor*, or Male Choir. But prior to the 1850s, prior to the climax of the inflow of the Forty-Eighters, music in the United States had been shy, hesitant, poorly appreciated. With the Forty-Eighters, it became unashamed. They started musical societies and movements in Milwaukee, Cincinnati, New York. So-called *Saengerbuende* and *Liederkraenze* flourished almost everywhere they settled. They brought the Germania Orchestra over from the old country. It was badly received in the United States, but many of its members stayed; Carl Bergmann, for one, who in 1855 became conductor of the New York Philharmonic Symphony Orchestra—"the first important American conductor." Two other members of the Germania Orchestra, Hans Balatka and Carl Zerrahn, shone as the foremost musical figures of Chicago and Boston. Most music teachers in America during the last half of the nineteenth century were German immigrants. And of course there were Theodore Thomas and Leopold Damrosch who, on their nationwide orchestral tours, faced for decades the prevalent American indifference. They were confident that in time music would win its place in the new country; and it did. Today New York, Boston, Philadelphia, Cleveland, Chicago, St. Louis, Los Angeles and San Francisco are musical centers of worldwide renown.

My friend Mrs. John D. (Emily Rice) Fearhake, a Texas native of old-line Anglo-Saxon stock now living in New Canaan, Connecticut, remembers that the German immigrants' "flare for music was woven into the fabric of Galveston living"—during 1872-1900—"in numberless ways.

"Galveston was then the wealthiest, swankiest city in Texas, and German male choruses came there from all over the state to compete for prizes. Competition was keen, and the Saengerfeste—everybody used the word—were outstanding musical events; everybody went. As a little girl I was fascinated by the many fat, tubby middle-aged Germans among the singers getting red and purple in the face while singing, particularly the tenors.

"German homes had amateur musical evenings, men, women and children contributing. It was a privilege to be invited. Something musical sponsored by Germans was always cropping up. Nearly all the music teachers in town were German.

"All my generation in Galveston owe more pleasure than one can say to an organization called the Garten Verein. On the initiative of a number of Germans, and always dominated by them, a group of citizens bought an easily accessible city block and developed it into a private club. Any woman or child could come as guest of a member, but men had to be members to be admitted. The place was beautifully laid out—trees, shrubs, flowers, walks, tables and benches secluded among the greenery. There were a dancing pavilion, a playground for children with swings and see-saws, a restaurant, a bowling alley and a band stand. The whole place was always open, but we never missed a Wednesday evening—concert, dancing and eating.

"Germans were well regarded as businessmen. I remember a cotton firm of three immigrants—friends—who started it as young men, then married and raised large families. They had nice homes where we were often asked to musical evenings. . . . My father had great respect for them; considered them pleasant, able, honorable to work with, their word as good as their bond.

"But generally the Germans seemed clannish. They invited few outsiders to their evenings. . . . One fine old man who lived in Galveston for fifty years never became a citizen. I remember that when we talked about this one evening we were all startled and rather shocked, but not antagonistic to his evident sentiment for his native Germany. We loved going to his house; his daughter and I are still friends. My German girl friends were simple, unsophisticated, fun-loving—very charming to me."

The Forty-Eighters were a determinant in the creation of the Republican Party and the election and re-election of Lincoln; and, as already mentioned, in the destruction of Know-Nothingism. Their political background in Europe left no doubt as to which side they would take on the slavery issue. The Germans around St. Louis kept Missouri from going pro-slavery.

It was natural that the Forty-Eighters should lead the German element in the North into the Civil War on the Union side; in the South, probably a majority of the older German settlers supported the Confederacy. According to one historian, 216,000 soldiers in the Union Army were foreign-born Germans, both naturalized and alien, and about three hundred thousand more were of German descent. Several units were entirely German and the officers gave commands in German. Perhaps over a thousand Germans and German Americans were officers, among them nine major generals and several brigadier generals.

Among the soldiers was Count Ferdinand Zeppelin. Neglected by his countrymen, declared insane by his family, the man for whom the dirigible was named came over and volunteered in the Union Army. He later returned to Germany, but his first balloon ascent took place in America.

The most famous of the generals, Carl Schurz, is now widely regarded as the greatest German American to date; certainly he was one of the greatest immigrant Americans. Arriving in 1853 as a young man in his mid-twenties, with a bristling red beard and a temper to match, he went to Wisconsin, where some of the Forty-Eighters wished (as others were wishing in Missouri and in Minnesota) to set up a kind of "New Germany." Schurz had no sympathy with this idea. Almost overnight he learned fluent English, perceived the propulsions and meaning of the United States, and became a passionate American. He told his fellow immigrants to bear in mind that "we as Germans are not called upon here to form a separate nationality but rather to contribute to the American nationality the strongest there is in us, and in place of our weakness to substitute the strength wherein our fellow Americans excel us, and blend it with our wisdom. We should never forget that in the political life of this republic, we as Germans have no peculiar interests, but that the universal well-being is ours also."

The thoughtless remark sometimes flung at the foreign-born (and occasionally also at Indians), "If you don't like the way things are run

here, why don't you go back where you came from?" was supposedly
first addressed to Carl Schurz—the man who was, as a matter of fact,
an Americanizer not only of the foreign-born but of many native
Americans as well. In 1859, before he was naturalized, he made his
famous speech on "true Americanism" defending the Republican Party
against the charge of nativism.

One of the noble men of his time, he was a warm personal friend
and ardent political supporter of Abraham Lincoln. In 1861 Lincoln
made him minister to Spain; in 1865 President Johnson sent him South
to study postwar conditions; in 1877 he became President Hayes' Secretary of State. He was a Republican who in 1884, placing issues above
parties and personalities, backed the Democratic candidate, Grover
Cleveland.

After the war Schurz adopted Missouri as his state and was sent to
the United States Senate, where in addition to making some mistakes,
notably on the Southern Reconstruction problem, he also made one of
America's grand patriotic statements: "Our country, right or wrong.
When right, to be kept right; when wrong, to be put right."

His reactions to trends and events abroad were often keen and
usually sound. At the turn of the century, for instance, he wrote letters
to Mayor Seth Low of New York City, expressing his sense of outrage
over the anti-Jewish pogroms in Czarist Russia: ". . . The persecution
and maltreatment of human beings on account of their race or their
religious belief is always an offense not only unjust to the victim, but
also degrading to the offender. But the persecution and maltreatment
of the Jews as mankind has witnessed it, and is now rewitnessing it in
several countries, has been not only especially barbarous in the ferocity
of its excesses, but in a singular degree self-debasing and cowardly in
the invention of the reasons adduced for its justification."

Schurz never lost interest in Germany. His political philosophy,
which led him to back many liberal and reform movements and
measures, issued from the ideals of the beaten German revolution of
1848 and the American Declaration of Independence. For a time he
owned and edited a German-language paper. He read German books
throughout his life, was wont to address German American audiences
in forceful German, frequented rathskellers and liked to take a few
seidels of beer. He wrote the first volume of his autobiography in his
native language, since it was with that tongue that his most intimate
early memories were bound.

In 1856, at Watertown, Wisconsin, his wife, Margarethe Meyer
Schurz, started the first kindergarten (kinder means children) in the
United States. And he himself pioneered in Civil Service reform, the

protection of the Indians, the saving of our national forests. He was against excluding the Chinese from naturalization and for Philippine autonomy. He died in New York in 1906; ex-President Cleveland delivered the principal address at the memorial service in Carnegie Hall. In Philadelphia is the Carl Schurz Memorial Foundation, one of whose chief interests is the accumulation of German-Americana.

Indirectly, Carl Schurz had a lot to do with the immense wave of immigration from Germany which began about 1870. His activities here were minutely reported in the more than seven hundred German-language papers, copies of which found their way to Germany; also immigrants wrote home about him, along with news of the development of conditions in the United States favorable to foreigners not in the habit of shying away from hard work. So he was an inspiration to many Germans before they came. And they came by the tens and hundreds of thousands a year—all manner of them: Lutherans, adherents of the Reformed Church, Catholics, Jews, Free-Thinkers, and sectarians; Low Germans, Prussians, Bavarians, people of the Black Forest and the coastal areas along the North Sea; slow-moving, stubborn peasants; husky, straw-blond girls eager to work as maid-servants till they married; unskilled laborers; also whole armies of highly deft, methodical and thorough artisans; and some intellectuals and artists—all getting away from the harshness and circumscriptions of Bismarckian and post-Bismarckian Germany, from military service and the fear of future wars—all set to work hard and improve their lot in America, where

> The chaos of a mighty world
> Is rounding into form.

These new German immigrants scattered far and wide, through the cities and small towns, over the rural regions—mostly, however, in the East and Middle West. Here is a figure which tells volumes: the United States census of 1900 shows that 522,252 farmers of German origin or descent owned farms, as against 183,157 Anglo-Saxon, 176,968 Irish and 174,694 Scandinavian American farmers. Carl Wittke says that the Germans have developed 672,000 farms in all, totaling over one hundred million acres. For two centuries Teutonic agriculture has been a sustaining part of American prosperity.

The story of German immigration is not dissimilar to the stories of several other non-English groups; only it is bigger, involving more people, touching more places in America.

Between 1820 and 1940 more Germans than any other national group came over: six million from Germany itself and perhaps another million and a half from the Austro-Hungarian empire, from Russia and Switzerland, from the post-1918 republics of Austria, Poland and Czechoslovakia, from Rumania, Yugoslavia and other countries with German elements in their populations. Some returned, but the majority stayed.

In 1900 the United States had nearly 2,700,000 immigrants born in Germany and another three-quarters of a million Germans from other European countries. They were the newest part of the estimated nineteen million people of German stock then forming twenty-seven per cent of the American population. The English strain exceeded the German by but two million; and perhaps it should be noted that then both the English and the Germans were more "English" and more "German" than they are today.

The current relative proportion of Americans who may be able to claim mainly English or mainly German descent is anybody's guess. Millions are both "English" and "German," and admixtures of other strains besides. Intermarriage during the last half century—among new-immigrant groups and between them and the old-stock Anglo-Saxon elements—has been so widespread that its results are beyond accurate statistical grasp.

In the late 1930s the Hitlerites estimated that the "German element" in the United States ran as high as fifty-eight million. This was typical Nazi arithmetic. It is not too wild to say, however, that nearly one-fourth of the American population—about thirty million—is of German or part-German stock.

But it is my impression that of this estimate, only about one-fourth regard themselves as "Germans" or German Americans. This takes in, first of all, 1,200,000 immigrants born in Germany, seventy-five per cent of whom are naturalized citizens. Next there are about four million American-born sons and daughters of immigrants whose "old country" is Germany.

Three-fourths of the thirty million are, for all practical purposes, simply Americans. This goes for many who have come here as immigrants—General Walter Krueger, for example, a native of Germany, one of the highest-ranking American commanders in the Pacific war during 1944-1945; or the distinguished United States Senator Robert F. Wagner of New York, brought here from Hesse-Nassau in his childhood; Johannes Steel, author and radio commentator; George Grosz, artist; Emil Ludwig, biographer; Erich Wolfgang Korngold and Kurt Weill, composers; Bruno Walter, conductor; or Frank J. Krupp, born in Bavaria seventy-odd years ago, who since about 1910 has been the favorite military tailor in Washington, making uniforms (as he told

in an interview) "for pretty nearly anybody you want to name—
Pershing, Malin Craig, Eisenhower, Mark Clark, maybe a hundred
generals." It goes for such people as Adolf Augustus Berle, one-time
Assistant Secretary of State; Hans Kaltenborn, dean of radio com-
mentators; John Gunther, journalist; Arthur M. Schlesinger, historian;
Theodore Dreiser, John Steinbeck and Frederic Prokosch, novelists; H.
L. Mencken, critic; Claude M. Fuess, headmaster of Phillips Academy;
Henry J. Kaiser, our foremost industrial evangelist and organizer, and
many other outstanding people whose parents or grandparents emigrated
from Germany. It goes too for Clark Gable, Babe Ruth, Herbert Hoover,
Lowell Thomas, and the Astor, Waldorf, Hagemeyer, Rockefeller,
Wanamaker, Drexel, Straus, Spreckles, Kuhn, Rosenwald, Adler, Lilien-
thal, Ginzburg, Schwab (also Swope), Flexner, Loeb, Lehman, War-
burg, Lewisohn, Guggenheim, Wurlitzer, Steinway, Studebaker, Heinz,
Hershey, Kraft, Weyerhaeuser, Schiff, Bloomingdale, Morgenthau,
Chrysler, Sulzberger, Oppenheimer, Eisenhower and Stieglitz families;
and for General Pershing, whose early American ancestors were Germans named Pfoerschin.

As already suggested, German immigration has been a giant factor in
American life for well over a century; a factor in the development of
some of the country's soundest ideals and practices, and in its two world
war crises.

In 1914-1916 and again just before the United States was drawn
into World War II, some of the "Germans," under the influence of
propaganda conducted by agents of the German government, seemed
a problem. Immediately preceding our entrance into World War I,
the general American reaction against their hyphenism was intense
and, on the whole, ignorant; in some instances violent. After we got
into the war, however, the problem—apart from outright agents and
spies—largely disappeared overnight. German Americans, says Professor Carl Wittke, "responded to their country's call like any other
group . . . and met every tangible test . . . to prove their loyalty" to the
United States. Thousands were officers; many became heroes. In fact,
German American soldiers came in for specially favorable mention in
at least one confidential intelligence report from the French front
which the War Department published after the war.

In 1937-1941 Hitler's agents, some of whom had become American
citizens and others of whom were non-German old-line American
pro-Nazis, spent millions of dollars on propaganda directed at the
"German element" in the United States, and for a time there was some
reason—the German-American Bund, for one thing, with its encamp-
ments, uniforms, newspapers and Nazi salute—for feeling alarmed.

Fortunately, the country as a whole and the Administration in Washington did not get hysterical about it. There was no need to. Scores of thousands of German and part-German Americans were volunteering for the Army and Navy before Pearl Harbor, and some of the leading interventionists during 1939-1941 were German Americans. After Pearl Harbor, German Americans did what they had done in 1917—only more so, for now there were many more of them and they were even more closely integrated into the American population than they were twenty-five years earlier. The first American soldier off the boat carrying the first contingent of the second American expeditionary force to Europe, which landed in Northern Ireland late in January 1942, was Private Milburn Henke of Hutchinson, Minnesota, the son of German-immigrant parents.

As I write in 1945, perhaps one-third of the eleven million men and women in the United States' armed forces are of German or part-German descent. This includes tens of thousands who were born in Germany and thousands of German refugees who left Europe during the 1930s—such as Sergeant Klaus Mann, a son of Thomas Mann, who in 1945 wrote in the *Stars and Stripes* (Rome edition): "I am sure I speak also for other Germans now active in the various forces of the United Nations when I say that our militant resolution has a two-fold psychological and moral source: first, our natural loyalty to a new homeland to which we are deeply indebted; and second, our intimate, first-hand knowledge of the mortal danger which Hitlerism means to civilization. . . . My family and I left the Reich voluntarily, as did many other Germans, as soon as Hitler came to power. We left because we felt that a country taken over by the Nazis would be an impossible place to live in—a place where the very air was stifling and poisonous. We left because we realized that Hitler would inevitably lead the German nation to war, to disgrace and to disaster. . . . We might have thought and acted differently—in fact, we might have found that it would be more useful and more honorable to stay at home—if there had been a chance to fight Nazism within Germany. But there was no chance—especially in the case of people who were so notorious, from the Nazi point of view, as was the Mann tribe."

Late in March 1945, the headquarters of General George Patton's Third United States Army released the story of Pfc. Helmut Bollenbacher, a native of Osbach, Germany, who came to America in 1930 and now, fifteen years later, returned to his home town as an American soldier. He ran to the house of his birth and found his older brother reading a book and his mother washing dishes in the kitchen. Neither recognized him till he took off his helmet and cried, "Mama, mama!"

During 1942-1945 the citizenship of a few naturalized natives of Germany was revoked by court action on account of their pro-Nazi sentiments, a few others renounced it, but about one hundred thousand German aliens took out their papers. Two or three naturalized Germans were executed as spies and traitors, but hundreds of thousands have distinguished themselves in war production and on the battle fronts. I shall mention only two war heroes, one an old-line American of Pennsylvania-Dutch stock, the other an immigrant:

Alton Knapperberger, born near Nazareth, Pennsylvania, barely twenty years old, was awarded the Congressional Medal of Honor for singlehandedly killing sixty Germans in a few minutes during the Anzio invasion, and destroying two machine-gun nests and an antiaircraft gun. "Knappie's" family background is Mennonite and Pacifist. "I was just shootin'," is the way he explained his exploit.

Herman Bottcher, born in Landsberg, Germany, lost his American citizenship in 1938 for fighting in the Spanish Civil War as a major in the Abraham Lincoln Brigade. After Pearl Harbor he enlisted as a private in the United States Army and was sent to the South Pacific. In New Guinea he became known as "the one-man army of Buna." A sergeant in December 1942, he assumed command of an infantry company when his superiors were killed or wounded, and split the Japanese lines by smashing to the coast between the village of Buna and Buna Mission. For this action he received a battlefield commission and the Distinguished Service Cross, and had his American citizenship restored by a special act of Congress. By 1943 Captain Bottcher was a legend; when Eleanor Roosevelt visited Australia, she specially requested to meet him. In the battle down the Ormoc corridor of Leyte, he made himself "the eyes and ears" of Major General William H. Gill's Thirty-second Division. He and his company were continually behind Japanese lines getting information and destroying bridges and other installations. Few of his men were killed, wounded or captured. One of them once said: "People may think I'm crazy but it's actually fun working out there with him. It's like playing cops and robbers." But on December 31, 1944, a burst of mortar fire killed Captain Bottcher. He was awarded a posthumous Silver Star.

Through 1942-1945 sixty to eighty per cent of the names in casualty lists published in Milwaukee, Cincinnati and St. Louis were German. Possibly one-fifth of American generals and admirals, whose total number is about 3,500 at this writing, have such names as Nimitz, Wedemeyer, Spaatz, Schmidt, Krueger, Eisenhower. The last name came to America about 1700 from Germany by way of Switzerland.

In March 1940, New York newspapers published stories about a naturalized middle-aged "German Aryan immigrant living in Queens" who insisted on paying a higher income tax than the law required because he felt the country was in for a lot of trouble and would need a lot of money. He refused to permit his accountant to give his name to the press.

Early in January 1945 Otto Kalbe, a seventy-six-year-old butcher born in Germany, died in Seattle, leaving his entire estate "to the United States of America as an expression of gratitude for being granted the privileges of citizenship."

The long-range impact of the German element on America is beyond exaggeration. To return to its peacetime contributions, it added the Christmas tree and the Christmas stocking to American life, and Pennsylvania-Dutch pottery, furniture and decorative painting; hot dogs and hamburgers, pretzels and pumpernickel, sauerbraten and pig's knuckles with sauerkraut, liverwurst, Limburger cheese, Liebkuchen, potato pancakes; Bavarian bierstube, with their *Gemütlichkeit*; and the Ringling brothers of circus fame. People from Germany helped to introduce gymnastic societies, amateur theatricals, hiking clubs, bowling alleys, sharp-shooting clubs, picnics, masquerade balls, delicatessen stores (*essen*—to eat). They were chiefly instrumental in converting Sunday afternoon from a row of dour, solemn hours to a time for social calls.

Germans and German Americans have had a big hand in the glass, chemical and drug industries, in operating pharmacies, in perfecting musical and scientific instruments, in toolmaking and die-casting, in the manufacture of all sorts of machines and vehicles; and, of course, in baking and beer brewing. At one time Germans practically monopolized the latter. Such names as Anheuser-Busch, Pabst, Heurich, Blatz, Brehm, Schlitz, Ehret and Ruppert are generally familiar.

Germans and German Americans have been a direct or indirect influence in nearly every field. Perhaps thirty per cent of American physicians and surgeons and dentists are German and part-German Americans, Jewish and Gentile. In 1940, while visiting friends at Harvard, I learned that forty per cent of the faculty were Americans of German and part-German descent. Approximately the same seems true of many other leading educational institutions.

I have already mentioned several outstanding German American names in different professions and enterprises; here are a few more:

Henry Engelhard Steinweg (1798-1871) came here to build the famous pianos which bear his name, modified to Steinway.

Nicola Marschall, born in Prussia, designed the Confederate flag and uniform. Another Prussian, Colonel Heros von Borcke, was the latter-day von Steuben of the southern forces. Still another native of Germany, Christopher Gustavus Memminger, was secretary of the treasury of the Confederate States.

Rudolph Blankenburg came to the United States at twenty-two in 1865 after he had read *Uncle Tom's Cabin* in German translation in his native town of Barnstrup. He settled in Philadelphia, married an old-line American girl and went into business and local politics. A crusading Republican, he fought "the powers that prey"—his phrase, now current in the language of reform and radical politics. In 1911 he was elected mayor of Philadelphia on an independent ticket and when he died seven years later he was known as "the Old Dutch Cleanser."

In 1892-1896 John Peter Altgeld, born in Germany, reared in Ohio, was governor of Illinois. In some respects he was an even bigger man than Carl Schurz—independent, uncompromising in his social and political thinking, a champion of the underprivileged. His spirit still broods over Illinois. It is part of the progressive tradition in the country at large.

Senator William E. Borah was a descendant of Catherine von Borah, who married Martin Luther.

"Washington Crossing the Delaware" was painted by a German, Emanuel Leutze.

Joseph Seemann, born in Germany in 1845, who pioneered in the cultivation of the sugar beet, has been called "Creator of Michigan's Sugar Bowl."

In 1924 the northwestern clover-growers and seedsmen unveiled a monument to Wendelin Grimm, a humble German farmer who sixty-odd years earlier, on that very spot in Minnesota, had sown the first bagful of so-called everlasting clover seed; he had brought it with him from Germany. That clover, capable of great resistance to cold, now grows throughout the Northwest and Canada.

Wilhelm Saksdorf (1850-1932), a German immigrant, was "a nice little man, but a bit odd" to the people who saw him crawl over the slopes of the Cascades in the state of Washington, but botanists now rate him highly as a pioneer in their field.

Adolphus Bonzano arrived in Philadelphia from Wuertemberg at the age of twenty in 1850 and over the next forty years experimented with the draw-span, the turntable and other features of modern bridge-building. Besides being one of the foremost engineers and mechanical inventors of his time (he died in 1913), he was also a talented pianist, organist and choir-master.

Arriving as a young man at the end of the Civil War, Albert Arents invented the "syphon lead-well" device, very important in smelting, and added partzite to the mineralogical list. He died in 1914.

William P. Bettendorf (1857-1910), born in Delaware of German stock, invented the power-lift sulky plow, the Betendorf Metal Wheel (for wagons and farm implements) and a steel gear for farm wagons; he was an early manufacturer of steel farm implements and railroad equipment. Shortly before his death a major part of his business was absorbed by the International Harvester Company.

Julius Bien, a young Forty-Eighter, started business in New York with a small lithographic press, then gradually became the leading mapmaker in the United States, creating the standards for American cartography. He produced thousands of maps, especially of the West. He was active in American Jewish life, serving as president of the B'nai B'rith organization.

A New-York-born son of Jewish immigrants from Bavaria, Benjamin Altman became, through "ability and hard work—a lot of ability and a lot of hard work," as a fellow merchant put it, the founder of Altman's department store in New York, a philanthropist and art patron. When he died in 1913 a friend of his said, "I doubt if one hundred persons in New York knew him by sight." Of his thirty-five million dollar estate, twenty millions were represented by works of art which he willed to the Metropolitan Museum.

Other German and German Jewish Americans, some immigrants, some sons of immigrants, acquired vast wealth and, with varying degrees of wisdom and good taste, became public benefactors. One of the most intelligent of these was Julius Rosenwald, who was born in 1862 in Springfield, Illinois, across the street from Abraham Lincoln's house; which, together with his being a religious Jew all his adult life, probably had something to do with his deep interest in the underprivileged Negro people and his belief that the common sense of common men and women was uncommonly good. He made his fortune in the mail-order business, in which he was a pioneer. In 1917 he created the Julius Rosenwald Fund, whose purpose was "the well-being of humanity." There were thirty million dollars in the fund in 1929, and his will required that the capital and interest be spent within twenty-five years after his death, which occurred in 1932. The Rosenwald money has helped to start thousands of schools for Negro children in the South, and millions have gone to the University of Chicago and other institutions.

Felix Adler founded the Ethical Culture movement.

Florenz Ziegfeld, the Chicago-born son of the German Catholic immigrant who founded the Chicago Musical College, brought the musical review to the American stage. A Broadway feature for over twenty years beginning in 1907, *The Ziegfeld Follies* dominated contemporary American notions of feminine beauty. They brought forth such comedians as Will Rogers and Eddie Cantor, and had a tremendous and widespread effect on the entertainment field.

The father of Superior Court Justice Louis D. Brandeis was a Forty-Eighter.

Karl Merz, German-born grandfather of Charles Merz, now editor of the New York *Times*, was a pioneer musician in Ohio in the second half of the nineteenth century. He wrote the popular waltzes "Sounds from the Ohio" and "Pearl of the Sea." (*Waltz*, of course, is a German word.)

Adolph Ochs, who made the New York *Times* into America's leading newspaper, was the son of a Jewish immigrant from Germany. His successor as head of the *Times*, Arthur Hays Sulzberger, also is a descendant of an immigrant family from Germany.

One of the Sulzberger immigrants, Ferdinand, was a big meat packer in the 1890s and 1900s. The prominent New York dermatologist, Dr. Marion B. Sulzberger, is one of his sons.

Nathan Straus introduced pasteurization of milk in the United States and is credited with causing a sharp reduction in infant mortality. Oscar S. Straus was a member of Theodore Roosevelt's cabinet and United States Ambassador to Turkey.

The first newspaper set on the lintoype machine, the New York *Daily Tribune*, appeared on July 3, 1886. The inventor of the machine, Ottmar Mergenthaler, came over from Germany in 1872 and died in Baltimore in 1899. His grandson, Private George Ottmar Mergenthaler, was reported a war casualty in Luxemburg early in 1945.

Thomas Nast, an immigrant, may be regarded as the father of modern political cartooning. He originated the Tammany tiger, the Democratic donkey, the Republican elephant. He covered the Civil War as artist correspondent for *Harper's Weekly*; his sketches are the best means of giving one a conception of the scope of that struggle.

A marble slab commemorating Joseph Timble Rothrock, a third-generation German American who achieved the height of his effectiveness around 1900, describes him as "the Father of Forestry in Pennsylvania." His forestry program has been copied by other states.

John A. Roebling built the Niagara and Brooklyn Bridges; Gustav Lindenthal, Hell Gate Bridge; Albert Fink, the Ohio River Bridge—

all extraordinary engineering jobs in their day. Roebling invented the multi-strand wire cable which made possible suspension bridges. In 1931, according to D. B. Steinman in *The Builders of the Bridge, the Story of John Roebling and His Son* (1945), some people in Muhlhausen, Germany, proposed to celebrate the centenary of John's emigration to America, but the idea was turned down by the city fathers on the ground that he had contributed greatly to Germany's defeat in the World War. His company was largely responsible for the North Sea Mine Barrage, with its twenty-seven million feet of steel rope, which practically ended the U-boat menace. On April 5, 1945, American troops took Muhlhausen after crossing the Rhine in Alligator amphibious tanks perfected by Donald Roebling, John Roebling's great-grandson.

John Fritz, responsible for the erection of the Bethlehem Iron Works, whom Andrew Carnegie characterized as "indisputably the foremost man of his day in any pursuit," was a German immigrant's son. Steelmen Henry Clay Frick and Charles M. Schwab also were of German descent.

In 1888 the young hunchback son of a well-to-do Breslau family, named Karl August Rudolf Steinmetz, a student of theoretical physics, higher mathematics, engineering, chemistry and medicine, wrote an editorial for a Socialist paper, and had to flee Germany to avoid arrest. He went to Switzerland; then suddenly in 1889 he emigrated to the United States. Applying for citizenship, he gave his name as Charles Proteus Steinmetz, Proteus being a nickname he had acquired in his student mathematical society in Breslau. During the next twenty-five years he rose to first rank among the world's electrical engineers and was a leading Socialist in the United States. One phase of his work reached a dramatic climax in 1921 when he produced man-made lightning in his laboratory at Schenectady. Before his death in 1923 he received all the honors in his field. His inventions are the basis of countless electrical appliances.

Another German-immigrant Socialist, Oscar Ameringer, functioned as a labor editor and radical humorist. His autobiography *If You Don't Weaken* (1943) is a unique book. He defined politics as "the art by which politicians obtain campaign contributions from the rich and votes from the poor on the pretext of protecting each from the other."

Albert B. Faust's *The German Element in the United States* is the most comprehensive book on the subject; it was published by the Steuben Society of America, founded in 1919.

Hitler's rise in Germany early in the 1930s caused some eminent Germans to leave for the United States—Albert Einstein, Thomas Mann,

Oscar Maria Graf, Lion Feuchtwanger and Frederick W. Foerster among others.

Foerster, a Prussian by birth, in his late seventies as I write, is probably the foremost authority on pan-Germanism and on the German mentality in general. His book *Europe and the German Question*, published in New York in 1940, is "must" reading for all who want to think intelligently about Germany's place in new Europe.

Einstein and Mann are Nobel Prize winners—in physics and literature, respectively; other German Americans who have received the prize are A. A. Michelson (brother of Charles Michelson, public relations expert and longtime publicity director of the National Democratic Committee) and Isidor Isaac Rabi, also in the field of physics, and Karl Landsheimer, in medicine.

I have already referred to Henry J. Kaiser, whose father was a Forty-Eighter. The leading Know-How and Can-Do industrialist in the United States during the 1930s and later during World War II, he revolutionized heavy construction at Boulder, Grand Coulee and Bonneville dams, and brought mass production into shipbuilding, cutting production time to a small fraction of previous records. His organizing genius accomplished near-miracles in steel, magnesium, cement, labor-capital relations, and hospitalization.

Dr. Simon Baruch—father of Bernard Baruch, financier and philanthropist, adviser to Presidents for two generations, reputed to be one of the best practical minds in the contemporary United States—was an immigrant from Germany.

So was the father of Julius Stieglitz (1867-1937), who, like the sons of many well-to-do German immigrants, was educated in Germany. In the forty years prior to his death in Chicago, he became a leader-pioneer in modern American chemistry, specializing in qualitative analysis. His book on that subject was used in schools throughout the country. His daughter Dr. Hedwig Stieglitz Kuhn, whose mother was a German immigrant, is an outstanding ophthalmologist, practicing with her husband, Dr. Hugh Kuhn, in Hammond, Indiana. She has pioneered in industrial ophthalmology, published the first book on the subject; and the Kuhns act as consultants on eye health to most of the industries in the Calumet region on both sides of the Illinois-Indiana state line. Alfred Stieglitz, the famous photographer, belongs to the same family.

One of the most creative labor leaders to emerge in the United States just before the country's official entrance into World War II is a second-generation German American, Walter P. Reuther, an organizer and vice-president of the United Automobile Workers (C.I.O.).

In 1940 he submitted plans for increased production in the automotive industries.

A favorite of mine among contemporary Americans is Samuel C. Klein, whose mother was born in Germany and who is a garment manufacturer in St. Louis and somewhat of a statesman in racial and human relations. His office staff is mixed White, Negro and Nisei. His secretary, who meets all his customers, including several from the Deep South, is a Negro girl; and he tells me he hasn't lost any business yet. A member of his sales personnel in New York is a Chinese American girl.

H. L. Mencken is the authority on the American language.

Physicist J. Robert Oppenheimer directed the final phase of the production of the atomic bomb.

And there was Wendell L. Willkie whose sudden death in 1944 was one of the great tragedies of the World War II period.

Through his trips to Britain, to the Near East, to Russia and China, through writing his amazingly successful book *One World*, through his continual and avid pursuit of facts concerning the international situation, Willkie swiftly evolved into a massive, bold, relentless, enlightened personality. His mind and feelings caught the contemporary global rhythm which he expressed in such cogent sentences as this: "To raise the standard of living of any man anywhere in the world is to raise the standard of living by some slight degree of every man everywhere in the world."

Despite his rejection as candidate for the Republican nomination in 1944, he wielded a tremendous, and a tremendously sound, influence in America. He fought anti-Semitism, discrimination against Negroes, bigotries of all kinds. He seemed to have grasped, better than almost any other American of comparable influence, the meaning and scope, the direction and principles of successful world cooperation. His loss was a severe blow to progressive forces in America, whose struggles to shape American policy toward establishing world peace will be incomparably harder because of his death.

American as apple pie and Radio City, Wendell Willkie was consciously a German American. Whenever we met during 1942-1944, he spoke of it. He had been spiritually raised on Carl Schurz, whom his father had greatly admired, and was full of him. Politically he was patterning himself—naturally, unconsciously—on Schurz's independence about party regularity, his liberalism, his vision as to the nature, function and purpose of government and politics.

On February 4, 1941, Willkie broadcast to the German people by shortwave from London: "I am of purely German descent. My family name is not Willkie, but Willicke. My grandparents left Germany ninety years ago because they were protestants against autocracy and demanded the right to live as free men. I, too, claim that right.

"I am proud of my German blood. But I hate aggression and tyranny. And my convictions are shared to the full by the overwhelming majority of my fellow countrymen of German descent. They, too, believe in freedom and human rights. . . . We German Americans reject and hate the aggression and lust for power of the present German government."

If most Americans "of purely German descent" felt as he did, how is one to account for Nazi Germany? Willkie and I discussed this once. I told him of the theory of another friend of mine, that the Germans who came to America were a self-selected group—the unconformed, the unorthodox, the protestants, democrats and liberals. Beginning with the *Concord* in 1683, swelling their ranks after 1848 and again after 1870, they withdrew themselves from Germany, leaving the country to the goose-steppers, the potential Nazis.

Willkie swung a leg over the arm of his chair, tilted his big, tousled head, and looked at me a long time, then he said, "I hope that theory isn't true. Germany is going to be an awful problem, and we'll have to be firm and as intelligent as we can possibly be; but I hope we'll find people there who may have been brushed by Nazism but who are potential democrats, potentially decent." He fell silent, obviously thinking, then repeated: "I hope that theory isn't true. But we'll see; we'll see soon now. Let's talk about it again someday."

In the spring of 1945, with the war's end in Europe, there were some German Americans and unnaturalized German immigrants who refused to believe the well-documented accounts of the atrocities committed in Germany and German-occupied countries. Some even muttered approving words about Hitler, Himmler & Company. Several German-language newspapers abused the freedom of the country by resorting to propaganda designed to soften the fate of German war criminals and the Allies' terms to Germany, and to make difficult the path of friendly relations between the United States and the Soviet Union. In mid-May the Chicago *Sun* investigated this situation, revealing some disturbing attitudes.

The majority of German Americans, however, were as outraged by the atrocities as everybody else; many more so than most non-German Americans. I think that Judge John Gutknecht of the Chicago Municipal Court spoke for many Germans and other Americans when in an interview with the *Sun* (May 17) he discussed the problem of defeated Germany as part of the general European problem. He referred to the strange American and British policies in Italy, Greece and Spain. "You cannot restore or support fascism in these countries," he said, "and expect to wipe it out in Germany." He favored the elimination of the Nazi party in the same manner in which "it eliminated its victims." Ernest L. Klein, a former Chicago German-language newspaper editor, proposed that Germany be split into several pieces, with parts given to France, Austria, Czechoslovakia, Poland and other countries which have suffered from German aggression. He wanted "the remaining core of Germany . . . deprived of all heavy industry so that it will become an agricultural country. . . . The danger in Germany lies with two groups: the Junker officers and the businessmen in control of heavy industry. . . . We will have to watch for Pan-Germanism."

VIII: NEGRO AMERICANS

ONE-TENTH of Americans, thirteen million, are Negroes—one of the biggest groups in the population. Their story has been closely interwoven with the wider American annals from way back.

In the summer of 1944 people were startled to read in a magazine article that Duke Ellington, the famous jazz maestro, descends from "one of the first families of Virginia." His ancestors arrived in Jamestown in 1619, some ten months before the Pilgrims landed on Plymouth Rock. They were among the "twenty Negars" (in Captain John Smith's spelling) brought to Jamestown by a Dutch ship.

This is usually regarded as the beginning of the importation of slaves to the present confines of the United States. Actually black slaves were in North America nearly a century earlier—and on the same site as Jamestown, where the Spanish explorer Lucas Vásquez de Ayllón was trying to establish a colony with some five hundred Spaniards and a hundred Negroes. After Ayllón's death in 1526, his successors in running the settlement so maltreated the Negroes that they rebelled, killing a number of their masters, then escaping into the woods, probably to the Indians. Chaos seized the community and it collapsed. The surviving White colonists returned to Haiti.

Spanish explorers brought Negroes to all the points they touched within what is now the United States. I have mentioned Estevan, the dark man who contributed conspicuously to the drama of New Mexico in 1538. (See p. 40.)

But in a vital and continuous sense the Negro chronicle in North

America dates from Jamestown in 1619. Through the next two centuries the slave trade increased steadily, until in 1790 nearly one-fifth
of the United States (757,208 out of the total population of 3,929,214)
was "Negro" or "colored"—meaning everybody with any Negro blood.

The Negroes are the only major element in the American population
whose ancestors—on the black side—did not come to the New World
of their own free will as emigrants getting away from unsatisfactory
conditions in the Old World. They were brought over forcibly to
be sold into permanent servitude.

This fact is a unique aspect of the Negro group. It caused serious
uneasiness to some of the founding fathers as they put forth the
proposition that "all men are created free and equal."A bill put forward
by Jefferson in 1784, which would have excluded slavery from the
whole public domain, and limited it to the South Atlantic seaboard—
thus insuring its eventual total abolition—was narrowly defeated in
Congress. An undemocratic balance prevailed at a critical moment.
So in the next half century slavery, among other things, led to the
greatest crisis in American history, the tragic Civil War.

For two centuries black men and women were imported by the
shipload. They came of tribes as different from each other as the
various European nations. There were Arabs, Moors, Hottentots, Bantus.
The majority came from Guinea; others from the Ivory, Slave and Gold
Coasts, from French West Africa, the Niger Valley, the Cameroons,
the Congo, the Benguela.

Many of these people were physically magnificent. Many came from
civilized communities in Africa where they had practiced farming and
crafts, engaged in trade, lived under organized governments, adhered
to established religions. Some belonged to the foremost clans in their
tribes; a few were headmen and princes, captured because they simply
were not equipped to cope with the slavers' stratagems, weapons and
purposes.

On the way to and later in America, the strains became thoroughly
mixed and also absorbed much White and Indian blood, so that the
average American Negro is markedly unlike the black African. There
was in America a colored "Melting Pot" as well as a white one; the
colored one took in White and Indian blood.

Black-White mixing was especially widespread in the decades just
before the Civil War. Millions of colored Americans of today are
more Caucasian than African; some of the "best" Southern "White"
blood courses in their veins. Dr. Melville J. Herskovitz, an authority on
the subject, maintains that less than twenty per cent of the Negroes in

the United States are of wholly African stock. The rest are a new biological mixture, a new strain. In most cases their skin is not black, but ranges the gamut of browns. Some are blond and blue-eyed. One Negro writer, George Schuyler, uses the phrase "the so-called Negroes."

Their folkways too are almost totally unrelated to the customs of their African background, but also somewhat unlike the patterns of White American life. They were Christianized, but some of their religious forms vary considerably from those of the White Christians. The divergence is only natural, since their American folk ways and religion began to evolve in slavery, rather apart from the Whites—the so-called Whites, for no "White" person is really white and, come summertime, many Caucasian Americans go to great trouble and expense to be darker than are many Negroes whom they bar from bathing beaches. (I use "Negro" and "White" in this chapter for lack of other words. Inexact descriptions of color-as-color, they represent color-as-a-race-symbol, a thing full of mischief not only in America but internationally.)

The Negroes have retained no trace of African dialects. The English language as spoken by most of them has a delightful rhythmic turn peculiarly their own which through many generations has influenced the speech of White Southerners.

The story of the Negroes, as I say, is intimately interwoven with the larger American annals; they are a component part of the American population. On the other hand, slavery and color—especially color, or rather the White majority attitude toward "color" when it happens to be a permanent part of a man's skin—have made the Negroes a more sharply defined group than any other in the United States.

Slaves were first used in clearing the land for cultivation, then on the tobacco, rice, sugar, cotton and indigo plantations. As most of these industries declined around the time of the Revolution, slavery and the slave business also fell off. But for a long time the dark folk did nearly all the hard work in the South. They were, and are, a crucial factor in its economic life. Their toil has become part of the wealth of the United States. The trouble was, and is, that Negro labor created not only wealth but, under the existing system, also a small class of Whites in whom was vested the control of that wealth and thereby of the South politically.

For two hundred years—between 1660, when slavery was made official (prior to that year it was a matter of custom), and 1860—Negroes frequently conspired and rebelled against the White slaveholders. In his significant but too little known book *Negro Slave Revolts in the*

United States (1939), Herbert Aptheker opens the story with the
episode in Gloucester County, Virginia, in 1663 when a favorite slave
betrayed to his master, John Smith, a widespread conspiracy of Negro
slaves and White indentured servants, with the result that the would-be
rebels were executed and the informer was freed. Thereafter every few
years in different parts of the South, plots and incipient rebellions,
which terrified the slave-owners, were put down by hanging the leaders
or breaking them on the wheel. For some years—1730, for instance—
two, three or more such incidents are on record. Nearly every time the
conspirators and rebels were betrayed by a fellow slave who was re-
warded with his release from servitude. But the apparent hopelessness
of their struggle failed to deter new attempts, and now there is no
group in the United States with an older and more persistent tradition in the cause of liberty.

Colored freedmen living in the North participated in the Revolution.
The first American killed in that upheaval—in the Boston Massacre on
March 5, 1770—was Crispus Attucks, a mulatto sailor; his figure is
part of a monument on Boston Common. One of the three patriots in
the painting called "The Spirit of 1776" was a Negro, Barzillai Lew.
Negroes were in the battle of Bunker Hill; one of them, Peter Salem,
shot the Tory Major Pitcairn. George Washington commended the
Negroes for the fight they put up at Red Bank.

In 1793 the invention of the cotton gin changed the entire scheme
of life in the South, strengthening immeasurably the institution of
slavery, and gradually tautening North-South relations till they snapped
in the early 1860s. Imported in mounting numbers, slaves were forced
into the service of King Cotton; and, says one historian, "their breeding
in this country became almost an industry." From three-quarters of a
million Negroes in 1790 their number increased to nearly two million
by 1830. In 1863, when the Emancipation Proclamation freed four
million in the South, there were another half-million Negroes in the
North.

In 1790 two-fifths of the slaves were in Virginia. Sugar in Louisiana
and the cotton boom throughout the Deep South drew them west and
south. When the Civil War broke out, 466,000 were in Georgia,
437,000 each in Alabama and Mississippi, 357,000 in Louisiana, and at
least two hundred thousand in each of the other southern states.

In the late 1870s, when the Reconstruction state governments were
overthrown, a couple of hundred thousand hard-pressed ex-slaves set
out on a migration to Kansas. Only about one-fourth got there; the
others stopped enroute. A few continued farther west.

Most history books view the Civil War as a conflict between the White North and the White South, leaving Negroes out so far as issues and participation in the fighting were concerned. Actually the Negroes took part in both.

They were numerous and important in the far-flung prewar anti-slavery movement which took in such Whites as Benjamin Lundy, William Lloyd Garrison, Wendell Phillips and Gerrit Smith who worked in the North. The Negro anti-slavery leaders worked both in the North and in the South. In the fifties the movement depended largely on them—notably on Frederick Douglass, an escaped slave, orator and organizer, perhaps a man of genius, who became an adviser to Lincoln. The Negro leaders—including such people as Harriet Tubman and Sojourner Truth, Robert Purvis, Henry Highland Garnett, David Walter, Samuel R. Ward, J. W. C. Pennington, Martin Delaney and James McCune Smith—ran the Underground Railroad and fought with John Brown, "God's angry man," for the defense of Kansas.

In the war itself, according to different estimates, between 170,000 and a quarter of a million Negroes joined the Union Army in response to the call of Frederick Douglass. "Their conduct," wrote General Nathaniel Prentiss Banks, "was heroic. No troops could be more determined and daring."

One colored soldier, Sergeant Carney of the 54th Massachusetts Volunteers, is remembered for his classic remark: "With God's help I will bring back the colors with honor or else report to Him the reason why."

Seventy thousand colored men were killed or wounded in action.

Had it not been for the Negro troops, the North would have lost many a battle, the Civil War might have ended otherwise, Lincoln—according to his own admission—might not have had a chance to issue the Emancipation Proclamation, and the subsequent history of the United States might have been very different.

On the other hand, several thousand Negroes fought on the Confederate side, among them hundreds who were not slaves but slave-owners. C. D. Wilson, an authority on the subject, estimated that in 1860 there were 6,230 such Negroes throughout the South. Charleston, South Carolina, for example, had 132 who owned 390 slaves. These Negro slave-owners fought in the Civil War for the same reason as the White ones—to keep their chattels.

But let it be stressed that a preponderance of active Negroes were with the North, on the side of free labor as against slave labor.

With Emancipation, the four million southern Negroes—and to a lesser degree the North's half million earlier freedmen—suddenly found themselves in an extremely difficult position. No element of the American population, except possibly the Indians, started out in the modern race for self-improvement with greater handicaps than the Negroes; and for decades the country as a whole did next to nothing to help them—one of the worst examples of communal irresponsibility in modern history.

As recent slaves, without any formal education, the Negroes were individually and collectively backward. They were mostly people of the soil, but by now all the fertile land in the South had been taken up; besides, they had no money with which to acquire even poor land. As slaves they had had no opportunity to choose in most matters affecting their lives. Now they were technically free, but they were dark in a White-dominated civilization intensely conscious of color and shot through (especially in the South) with feelings of guilt and fear.

Right after the war in a few of the southern states, notably in North Carolina, colored men took part—with northern support—in establishing White-Negro Reconstruction governments, in opening schools and enacting progressive social legislation. But the reaction which set in in both the North and the South after Lincoln's assassination destroyed most of this incipient work, which was generally forgotten during the next seventy-five years—until Howard Fast published his novel *Freedom Road* (1944).

In the tense, success-mad, reactionary period following the Civil War, some of the new-immigrant groups in the North, particularly the Irish, struggling for advantage on the labor market and to gain psychological compensation for their own inferior status, turned anti-Negro, although many Irish had fought in the war that freed the slaves. Many immigrants, themselves only a few years here, went to the polls to vote down proposals for equal economic rights. "Down with the Nagurs!" was the cry. "Send them back to Africa where they belong."

Basically, the North had fought the Civil War not primarily to free the slaves but to equalize labor and industrial conditions between the North and the South, and—as Lincoln had kept on stressing—to save the Union. In 1876 the leading southern interests finally came to terms with the dominant industrial interests of the North, whereupon the White South was free to treat the Negroes as it liked.

Jim Crow was made chief of police in White-Negro relations.

With Lincoln's death, most of the intelligence and good-will among northern Whites that he had meant to harness to his statesmanlike Reconstruction program for the South degenerated into indifference and carpetbagging. The defeated White South was bitter and the victorious North did not attempt to alter that state of mind. Psychologically as much victims of slavery as were the Negroes, many White Southerners lived in the grip of fears which found expression in lynching bees and the formation of anti-Negro terrorist organizations. For decades, North or South, few Whites had any actively constructive interest in the Negroes, who were thus left largely to their own resources which, at first glance, were not many. There were few educated Negro leaders even in the North; the very few potential colored leaders in the South had been obliged to depart.

The dice were generally loaded against the colored people. For decades, below the Mason-Dixon line, their day-to-day economic position in some respects was no better than it had been under slavery.

Nevertheless, since the opening of the twentieth century the country has witnessed an extraordinary development in the race situation. Groping in a maze of present disabilities and long-range disadvantages, erring at many points, taking an occasionally outstretched White helping hand, and—most important—drawing on their own inner strength, on their own long tradition of fighting for freedom, and on the key concepts of Americanism as enunciated by Lincoln and in the Declaration of Independence and the Constitution with its Bill of Rights, the Negroes have gradually and doggedly advanced toward a measure of personal freedom and independence, education, self-improvement and self-respect, economic betterment and civic responsibility. The position of masses of them is still a long way from parity with the Whites'; some seem to despair that they will ever even approach it. In the spring of 1944 a sixteen-year-old Negro girl in Columbus, Ohio, won a high school essay contest on "What To Do With Hitler After the War" by writing a single sentence: "Put him in a black skin and let him live the rest of his life in America." But a significant point is that she won the contest. Her race does continue to make progress, partly because of the innate character of large numbers of its members, partly as a natural consequence of the good side of the American system of society, and partly because a lot of Whites, South and North, believe in the practice, not merely the principle, of equality.

Education is a keynote of Negro progress.

Before the Civil War, the South provided no schooling for slaves. Whether and what they were taught was up to their individual masters. In the North were a few schools for free Negroes but, caught in the political crossfire over the slavery question, they were not very successful. Powerful northern forces, wanting to appease the South, for a long time opposed Negro education quite as much as did the South. Shortly before the war ended, Congress created the Freedmen's Bureau in Washington, one of whose jobs was to start classes for ex-slaves; but it only partially achieved its objectives.

In the South before the Reconstruction governments were over-thrown, some of them had established free, tax-supported, bi-racial public school systems. These were now abolished, or rather changed into separate schools for White and Negro children, and the school tax funds were given more and more to White schools.

In recent decades the General Education Board (a branch of the Rockefeller Foundation), the Peabody, the John F. Slater, the Anna T. Jeannes and the Phelps-Stokes Funds have aided both Negro and White education in the South. The Julius Rosenwald Fund (see p. 189) helped several southern states and many local communities to build over five thousand rural schools for Negro children.

A few figures which speak volumes: In 1865 Negro illiteracy was ninety-five per cent; in 1945 it is under fifteen per cent. Of the approxi-mately three million southern Negro school-age children, nearly two and a half million are studying under fifty thousand Negro teachers. Although as yet only a good beginning, this is swift progress even in America.

Two Negro educators stand out: Booker T. Washington and W. E. Burghard Du Bois—the first born a slave in Virginia in 1856, the other of free parents in Massachusetts in 1868; very different in personality, background, outlook and aims, but both impressive, organic products of the highly dramatic White-Negro situation in the United States.

Booker T. Washington's mother was cook on a plantation. His father probably was White. Still a child after Emancipation, Booker got a job in a salt-furnace, starting to work at four in the morning. Later he was employed in coal mines and as a house servant. A White woman in whose home he worked taught him to read. In his mid-teens he over-heard a couple of miners speak of Hampton Institute where Negroes could work their way and learn a trade. He managed to get there and graduate. Then he taught school and later helped organize, and headed, the now well known Tuskegee Institute.

His career as a leader of his people began with a speech at the Cotton States Exposition in Atlanta in 1895. It was the first time a Negro speaker had shared the platform of a nationwide assembly with southern Whites. "No race can prosper," he said in his full, resonant voice, "until it learns that there is as much dignity in tilling a field as in writing a poem." He warned Negroes not to let their grievances overwhelm their opportunities. He urged Whites to cease discriminating against Negroes, "whose fidelity and love you have tested," and to stop looking ex-clusively to White immigration for their industrial labor supply. There was, he went on, no future "for any of us except in the highest intelligence and development for all."

During the next twenty years, evolving his philosophy of Negro education which emphasized vocational training in trades and crafts, Booker Washington was the foremost Negro in America, partly because—as his Negro critics pointed out—influential Whites in the North, apprehensive about "the color problem," built him up. Theodore Roosevelt consulted him, entertained him at dinner in the White House; Harvard and Dartmouth gave him honorary degrees; large sums of money were put at his disposal by White philanthropists, by some no doubt because they considered him the safest Negro leader in sight. He was in demand as a lecturer, and several southern Negro institutions took his Tuskegee Institute as a model; it was the easiest if not the only way to get financial support for Negro education. The emphasis on training for crafts and trades as opposed to education for professions and independent thinking made the Tuskegee idea tolerable to many southern Whites. Booker Washington bowed to Jim Crow; he never came out boldly against him. His program was bottomed on gradualism, on conciliation of the Whites.

For a generation he was the leader of the colored people, a looming figure in American life. He and the people about him built up the so-called Tuskegee Machine which for a time controlled or tried to control every phase of Negro education. But with all his limitations, the man had a touch of greatness. One day when a White shoved him off a sidewalk, he said to his outraged White companion: "No man, black or white, from North or South, shall drag me down so low as to make me hate him." When he died in 1915, the eminent editor Henry Watterson wrote in the Louisville Courier-Journal: "No man, since the war of sections, has exercised such beneficent influence and done such real good for the country—especially for the South." Washington's autobiography Up From Slavery is a significant American book. In 1943 a Liberty ship was named the Booker T. Washington and—on the insistence of the National Maritime Union, headed by Joe Curran, an American of Irish descent—put in command of a Negro master, with a Negro-White crew.

A Northerner, a dozen years younger than Washington, a Harvard man who sought education also in the South and in Europe, W. E. B. Du Bois became a professor at Atlanta University and an author. In 1903 his book The Souls of Black Folk caused a stir. Articulate in the best American intellectual manner, speaking in a deep, sincere, disciplined voice, Du Bois was among the first to oppose the segregation of Negroes which Booker Washington accepted. Challenging the older man, he called for the creation through education of a numerous intelligent Negro leadership as a prerequisite to the progress of the race, to its becoming a positive element of the American population. This, he pointed out, could not be achieved under Washington's conciliatory, gradualist philosophy and the Tuskegee crafts-and-trades program, which was inadequate even to prepare colored people for self-respecting functions in the modern industrial world of specialized and swiftly changing techniques. Through his writings, from the lecture platform, in classroom and personal contact, and by example, Du Bois continually urged young Negroes to take full advantage of their rights as Americans under the Constitution, to dodge Jim Crow and seek political, economic and social equality with their White fellow citizens, to absorb as much education as they could and, in spite of color bars, to pursue opportunities in fields that interested them. The Tuskegee Machine, backed by White philanthropists, opposed him at every step; but he persisted and finally won a response.

The clash between the Washington and Du Bois ideas has been of historic significance. Neither leader stuck to his idea one hundred per cent. Typically American in content and tactics, the struggle continues. It has been confusing at many points; its importance to the Negroes and all America cannot be overemphasized.

In 1905, when Washington was approaching the height of his influence and power, Du Bois called a conference of thirty educated Negroes who more or less saw things as he did and a rather definite movement got under way in opposition to the Washington theory of limited education, segregation, gradualism and conciliation. In 1909 the movement crystallized in the formation of the National Association for the Advancement of Colored People, in which Du Bois became director of publicity and research and editor of the official publication *The Crisis*, whose files are a primary source for the study of the thought of modern Negroes about their position in the United States.

For fifteen years or longer non-segregation and unlimited education continued to be a dual point of Du Bois' philosophy. He seemed to feel the Negroes' future lay in working together with liberal and radical White Americans—ultimately in some sort of socialistic form of society. He thought that in time the propaganda of enlightenment would triumph over White anti-Negro prejudice; that on the bare level of self-interest people would eventually discover that racial discrimination does not pay; that common sense, decency and intelligence would prevail.

Toward the end of the 1920s, however, and in the early 1930s, Du Bois was profoundly impressed by the persistency of anti-Negro prejudice among White Americans on the lower and middle economic levels, and his thinking changed. He switched to what he called "internal self-organization" within "groups of communities and farms inhabited by colored folk"; which was equivalent to segregation. It was, he believed, voluntary segregation decided upon through reason. Du Bois said in effect that a quarter of a century of endeavor by the N.A.A.C.P. and individuals like himself had been futile; Jim Crow was stronger than ever. Now, he wrote in *The Crisis* for April 1933, "we can work for ourselves. We can consume mainly what we ourselves produce, and produce as large a proportion as possible of that which we consume. There would be [White] monopoly and privilege to fight, but only stupidity and disloyalty could actually stop progress. Expel both unflinchingly. . . . We are fleeing not only from poverty, but from insult and murder and social death. We have an instinct of race and a bond of color, in place of a protective tariff for our infant industry. We have, as police power, social ostracism within to coerce a race thrown back upon itself by ostracism without; and behind us if we will survive is Must, not May."

In 1934 Du Bois resigned from the N.A.A.C.P. board of directors and the editorship of *The Crisis* on the grounds that the organization had no policy, and withdrew into academic life at Atlanta University and the writing of books. This threw the Negro American intellectual world into a crisis that did not begin to resolve until World War II. For a time Du Bois was sharply criticized by younger Negro intellectuals as a latter-day Booker T. Washington. But the debate he provoked in the early 1930s had a beneficial effect. It helped to make other Americans intensely aware of the White-Negro situation, of the American Dilemma, as Gunnar Myrdal (see p. 142) called it in the title of his book, that reached its peak during World War II.

Not that Du Bois accepted segregation in principle. The facts of life as he observed them, coupled with his independent honesty and advancing years, had driven him to this "internal self-organization" as a partial resolution of the Negro people's complex predicament. And, although he was widely criticized, his ideas had in the late 1930s a good measure of tactical intelligence. "To a degree," he admitted in *Dusk of Dawn* (1940), ". . . this is a program of segregation. The consumer group is in important aspects a self-segregated group. We are now segregated largely without reason. Let us put reason and power beneath this segregation. . . . Rail if you will against the race segregation . . . involved and condoned [in the segregated Federal-financed housing projects] but take advantage of it by planting secure centers of Negro cooperative effort and particularly of economic power to make us spiritually free for initiative and creation in other and wider fields, and for eventually breaking down all segregation based on color and curl of hair."

Du Bois has done much to show America the psychological problems involved in being a Negro. "It is a peculiar sensation, this double-consciousness, this sense of always looking at oneself through the eyes of others, of measuring one's soul by the tape of a world that looks on in amused contempt and pity," he wrote in *The Souls of Black Folk*. "One ever feels this two-ness—an American, a Negro; two souls, two thoughts, two unreconciled strivings; two warring ideals in one dark body, whose dogged strength alone keeps it from being torn asunder."

"It is difficult to let others see the full psychological meaning of caste segregation," he wrote in *Dusk of Dawn*. "It is as though one, looking out from a dark cave in a side of an impending mountain, sees the world passing by and speaks to it; speaks courteously and persuasively, showing them how these entombed souls are hindered in their natural movement, expression and development; and how their loosening from prison would be a matter not simply of courtesy, sympathy and help to them, but aid to all the world. One talks on evenly and logically in this way, but notices that the passing throng does not even turn its head, or if it does, glances curiously and walks on. It gradually penetrates the minds of the prisoners that the people passing do not hear; that some thick sheet of invisible but horribly tangible plate glass is between them and the world. They get excited; they talk louder; they gesticulate. Some of the passing world stop in curiosity; these gesticulations seem so pointless; they laugh and pass on. They still either do not hear at all, or hear but dimly, and even what they hear, they do not understand. Then the people within may become hysterical. They may scream and hurl themselves against the barriers, hardly realizing in their bewilderment that they are screaming in a vacuum unheard and that their antics may actually seem funny to those outside looking in. They may even, here and there, break through in blood and disfigurement, and find themselves faced by a horrified, implacable, and quite overwhelming mob of people frightened for their own very existence.

"It is hard under such circumstances to be philosophical and calm, and to think through a method of approach and accommodation between castes. The entombed find themselves not simply trying to make the outer world understand their essential and common humanity but even worse, as they become inured to their experience, they have to keep reminding themselves that the great and oppressing world outside is also real and human and in its essence honest."

In his seventies, W. E. B. Du Bois remains a central personality in the American Negro world. His influence has been far-reaching. Partly because of him, many Negroes are among the best educated, most intelligent contemporary Americans and tens of thousands are better educated than they would have been had he not been prodding Negro education since the early 1900s. These men and women in their fifties, forties, thirties, and middle and late twenties are now planning future progress for the race. Some are anti-Du Bois or think that he has fulfilled his usefulness. Others continue to work with him. Under the direction of Walter White, for instance, who grew up in purpose and effectiveness during the Du Bois period, the National Association for the Advancement of Colored People has become a vital organization of national—lately of world—significance. In fact, Du Bois returned to it in 1944 as director in charge of special research. He seems to have tentatively ceased insisting on voluntary segregation, which implied hopelessness of working with Whites; at any rate I have been seeing him during 1940-1945 at conferences on racial matters attended by both Negroes and Whites. In the spring of 1945 he was one of the N.A.A.C.P. representatives attached to the United States' Delegation to the United Nations Security Conference in San Francisco, with the special duty of tackling Jim Crow internationally—to induce the Conference to write into the world charter provisions for (1) the equality of all races, (2) a bill of rights for all the peoples of the world, and (3) the abolition of the colonial system in favor of an international agency to which the colonial powers would report.

At the same time (late May 1945) he published an angry little book, *Color and Democracy: Colonies and Peace*, speaking for three-quarters of a billion colored people living in the "forgotten international slums" under British, Dutch and French rule who had no representation at the San Francisco Conference. . . .

In Du Bois' time Negro higher education developed considerably. In 1900 colored college graduates numbered four thousand; in 1940 over twenty thousand. The leading all-Negro colleges are: Howard University in Washington, D.C., Fisk University and Meharry Medical College in Nashville, Atlanta University with its affiliated colleges, Dillard University, a merger of denominational colleges in New Orleans. And there are such training schools as Tuskegee and Hampton. Besides, since about the 1920s, hundreds of Negroes have been graduating from "White" institutions in the North and West which do not bar colored students.

Simultaneously with increased educational opportunities, large numbers of the younger Negroes joined the general American exodus from rural districts into cities. The movement of colored people reached a climax during World War I, when tens of thousands were suddenly admitted into urban industries, especially in the North—in New York, Philadelphia, Pittsburgh, Cleveland, Detroit, Chicago.

A few more statistics: In 1910 about twenty-seven per cent of Negroes were in cities of twenty-five hundred population or over; in 1930 about forty-three per cent (5,193,913) lived in cities. Of the total American population in 1910 forty-six per cent were in cities; fifty-six per cent in 1930. The largest urban concentrations of Negroes are in New York (Harlem), Chicago, Philadelphia and Detroit; where, however, they represent only five, seven and eleven per cent of the respective populations. Birmingham has the largest proportional Negro group: close to forty per cent of its total number of inhabitants. The Urban League, with its numerous branches, is the Negro organization focused on the colored people's position in the cities.

With many ups and downs, helped at times by one kind of Whites and obstructed by another kind, confronted by a racial-economic situation which has fluctuated between terrible and tolerable, the Negroes, South and North, have won fairly widespread recognition as a section of human America which is important and worthy of respect. Through most of the South they continue to be caught in a tangle of extremely real political, economic and social handicaps which hamper their development as citizens and human beings; in the North, however, they have attained some economic and voting power, and fill elective and appointive public offices. In eight northern states they hold the balance of power between the Republican and Democratic Parties.

The Federal government recognized the Negroes as a factor to be reckoned with in World War I. Fearing German propaganda, it hastened to act. The Secretary of State added a Negro adviser to his staff, the War Department opened a special camp to train Negro officer candidates and eventually commissioned seven hundred of them. The United States was the only preponderantly White country in that war with so many Negro officers. Most Negro troops were in labor battalions; those permitted to fight gave a good account of themselves. The 369th Infantry, a New York National Guard outfit consisting entirely of Harlem volunteers, was the first American force to reach the Rhine. The regiment was 191 days under fire, longer than any other A.E.F. unit; it never lost an engagement. Three other Negro regiments and a battalion were collectively cited for bravery. Henry Johnson, a Negro, who singlehanded killed four Germans and wounded twenty-eight, was the first American soldier to be decorated by France in World War I.

Those who read only the daily press, which has a way of emphasizing the more violent and less pleasant events, are not apt to get a rounded picture of the so-called Negro Problem (which exists, God knows; only it is not a Negro but a White-Negro Problem). They are likely to be insufficiently informed as to the valuable, positive aspects of the fact that the American population includes thirteen million Negroes. Nor is the average White American aware of the remarkable Negro individuals in American life, some of whom emerged even before the first rays of freedom touched the race as a whole.

Benjamin Banneker, son of a freedman with a farm near Baltimore, was a self-taught genius born in 1731 who before his death in 1806 became a clockmaker, construction engineer, mathematician, astronomer, surveyor, expert on bees and locusts (he calculated the cycles of locust plagues), and a writer on large social and political issues, favoring democracy, opposing war and capital punishment, and anticipating the United Nations.

Phillis Wheatley was the first Negro poet. A little African girl in a cargo of slaves brought over in 1761, she was purchased by a rich Bostonian, John Wheatley, and given as a present to his wife. Impressed by the youngster's quick mind and vivid spirit, Mrs. Wheatley decided to help her. Twelve years later, Phillis published a volume of poetry which was superior to most verse written by White poets in America at that time.

I have mentioned Harriet Tubman—the fugitive slave who came north via the Underground Railway, over which thousands of runaway slaves gained their liberty; one of the really intrepid figures in recent American history. In the face of the Fugitive Slave Law, she went back South nineteen times, bringing out more than three hundred slaves. She freed three of her ten brothers and sisters, and in 1857, in a specially perilous journey, brought out her parents. Sometimes the fugitives she helped were daunted by the dangerous trip north and wanted to turn back. Then—displaying a characteristic of many liberators—she would pull out her pistol and say, "You go on or you die." She was the only woman confidante of John Brown, and may have been on her way to Harper's Ferry when Brown struck there. She led soldiers in battle during the Civil War; was an orator and woman suffragist. Earl Conrad, a White writer who published a biography of her in 1943, places her beside Joan of Arc. After the war she set up a refuge for aged Negroes in Auburn, New York. She died in 1913; the next year the Cayuga County Historical Association placed a tablet commemorating her work in the Auburn Auditorium. Booker T. Washington was the principal speaker at the ceremony.

In recent decades these men besides Washington and Du Bois have made an imprint on Negro education: Robert R. Moton, John Hope, Julian H. Lewis, John Davis, Matthew W. Dogan, Rufus C. Clement, Mary McLeod Bethune, Charlotte Hawkins Brown, Charles H. Thompson, Mordecai W. Johnson, Carter G. Woodson, Charles H. Wesley, Benjamin Brawley, Doxey Wilkerson, Metz T. P. Lochard. The latter is editor-in-chief of the Chicago *Defender*, a firmly progressive paper. Dr. Woodson is the founder of the Association for the Study of Negro Life and History, editor of the *Journal of Negro History*, and author of some twenty volumes of Negro historiography.

Several Negroes stand out in medicine: Daniel Hale Williams, charter member of the American College of Surgeons, the first to operate successfully on the human heart; Solomon Carter Fuller, neurologist and psychiatrist; Louis T. Wright of Harlem Hospital, another member of the American College of Surgeons; Charles Richard Drew of Howard University, pioneer in plasma which has saved innumerable lives in World War II.

In science and invention: Henry Blair of Maryland, the first Negro to register a patent in the United States Patent Office—for a corn harvester, in 1834; Granville Woods, who contributed to telegraphy, the phonograph, and electric railroading; Jan E. Matzeliger, a Negro from Dutch Guiana who came to the United States as a young man and invented a machine for fastening soles to shoes—now a key instrument in the huge United States Shoe Machinery Company; Ernest Everett Just, a biologist specializing in fertilization, artificial parthogenesis and cell division; and George W. Carver, born a slave in Missouri in 1864 to become a protégé of Booker T. Washington at Tuskegee and eventually to work out several hundred formulæ for sweet potato, pecan, peanut and soy bean products, which together are of incalculable value to the United States. About a thousand patents have been registered by Negroes.

Of course color has little if anything to do, fundamentally, with one's ability or predilection in such fields as medicine, biology and invention. In the arts it is different. Most Negro artists are what they are in considerable measure because they stem in part from Africa and because their black forebears were slaves. And it may be that the colored element's second great contribution to the New World, right next to its epic centuries-long physical labor in the South, is in that realm.

Were it not for the Negroes, particularly for their folk music, American folk art would be rather barren. American Negro folk art was not brought from Africa; nothing like it exists there; it is a fresh product, distilled from the distant African background and the American environment.

Among the clearest forms of Negro folk art are the spirituals, religious music with African rhythmic and emotional bases, set in the American language, and expressing the idea of escape to Heaven from a world of unceasing labor and suffering, the world that was—to a great extent still is—the Negroes' America.

And there is jazz, also known the world over as an American art; its origins too are distinctly Negro, expressing in a unique way wide human reactions to contemporary urban-industrial civilization. The often heart-rending moans and cries of the blues, like the perfect rhythmic cadence of the work-songs and the chain-gang chants, are markedly American Negro, as is also much of the modern social dance in the United States and abroad.

The Negroes' creative impulse, which for two centuries poured itself out in folk music, is now infiltrating into all the fine arts: painting, sculpture, literature, drama, dancing, architecture and other forms of music.

The pioneer Negro painter was Edward Bannister of Providence, Rhode Island, who took a prize at the Philadelphia Centennial Exposition of 1876. He founded the Providence Art Club. Edmonia Lewis, sculptress, exhibited at the same exposition. Then came the well-remembered painter and sculptor, Henry Ossaw Tanner and Neta Warrick Fuller, both recognized in France as well as in the United States. Since 1920 colored painters and sculptors too numerous to list have emerged in Harlem, Chicago, Los Angeles and elsewhere. Among the most recent are William Edmonson, Jacob Lawrence, Selma Burke and Edward Loper.

In literature the next noteworthy figure after Phillis Wheatley was Paul Laurence Dunbar, who came along late in the nineteenth century with a definite poetic talent. In the 1900s Stanley Braithwaite stands out. During and after World War I an interesting group of Negro poets and prose writers, led by Claude McKay of Harlem, really began to speak out for their people, protesting against injustice, challenging the conscience of America. In the late 1920s the leading magazines began to publish the poems of Langston Hughes and Countee Cullen. Hughes wrote:

> I, too, sing America
> I am the darker brother
> I, too, am America.

James Weldon Johnson brought out his famous little book God's Trombones, a collection of intensely moving poems based on Negro sermons.

Since about the 1930s dozens of Negro poets, novelists and other writers have appeared; their work usually has a special quality which can be traced only to their being Negroes, to their group's creative folk impulse. I shall mention a few: Jean Toomer, Sterling Brown, Zora Neale Hurston, Roi Ottley, Margaret Walker, J. Saunders Redding, Richard Wright.

Paul R. Williams of Los Angeles is a well-known American architect.

There has been a profusion of remarkable Negroes in the theater, concert and other entertainment fields: writers, composers, performers— especially performers. Ira Frederick Aldridge's "Othello" was famous in Europe a hundred years ago. In the early 1930s two colored actors gained fame: Charles Gilpin as "Emperor Jones" and Richard B. Harrison as "De Lawd" in Green Pastures.

Who has not heard the singers Roland Hayes, Paul Robeson, Marion Anderson, Dorothy Maynor, Carol Brice? Or who can ever forget Bill Robinson after seeing him tap-dance? Who does not know Rex Ingram, Hattie McDaniel, Ethel Waters, Lena Horne, Josh White, Hazel Scott, Katherine Dunham of the stage, screen and radio?

About 1891 a barber named Buddy Bolden, who played the cornet in a New Orleans band, cut loose and syncopated in jazz style the dance music his band was playing; now we have such famous names in jazz and swing as Jelly Roll Morton, Louis Armstrong, Lionel Hampton, Cab Calloway, Duke Ellington and Meade Lux Lewis.

For a time jazz was regarded as crude or primitive music; since the late 1930s it is being recognized by serious composers, Negro and White, American and foreign, as material that gives interest and range to symphonic compositions. Its idioms and phrases now are part of the so-called higher forms of music.

In the field of classical music these Negroes are famous: Harry T. Burleigh, William Grant Still, Clarence Cameron White, William L. Dawson and Dean Dixon.

In the arts the Negroes encounter the least discrimination.

Discrimination exists even in sports where, if anywhere, fair play might be expected to prevail; Negroes are banned from professional baseball. In boxing the names of Jack Johnson and Joe Louis tell the story. Four Negroes have made All-American football teams. Some of the greatest American runners have been Negroes: at the 1932 Olympic games Eddie Tolan won the hundred-meter race and hung up a new world record for the two-hundred-meter race, while at the 1936 Olympics Jessie Owens, Archie Williams and John Woodruff won in track events.

Many Negroes have succeeded in business, most of them within their own group. Perhaps the most remarkable instance is Richard Robert Wright, president of the Citizens and Southern Bank and Trust Company of Philadelphia. Born a slave in the middle 1850s, he taught school for fifty years. He became president of Georgia State College for Negroes. "For years I kept telling my graduates to go out and get into business," he said to Webb Waldron who published an article about him in the *Progressive* (Madison, Wisconsin; March 12, 1945), "but they would come back and tell me there were too many handicaps for a Negro. I realized that the worst handicap was a firm belief among both Whites and Negroes that the Negro hadn't any head for business. I thought it was up to me to disprove that." This was in 1921 when he was sixty-seven. He induced one of his three sons, all college graduates, to go into banking with him. They could not do it in the South, so they went North. After a course in banking at the University of Pennsylvania, they opened the Citizens and Southern on an unpaved street with a capital of $125,000 and three hundred Negro stockholders. In the next fifteen years the neighborhood improved; many small Negro businesses were started under Wright's encouragement. By and by Whites began to entrust their money to the Citizens and Southern, which was one of the first in Philadelphia to reopen after the 1933 bank crisis.

Another Philadelphia success story is that of Joseph Hudson, a one-time garage helper and chauffeur, who now operates five large gas stations, a repair shop, a body and fender shop, and a paint shop—typical of many such businessmen in New York and Chicago.

The most effective Negro labor leaders are A. Philip Randolph, president of the Sleeping Car Porters, whose "March on Washington" idea in the early 1940s had a profound effect on the Negroes' future, for it helped to bring on the Fair Employment Practices Commission during World War II; Willard S. Townsend, organizer and president of the United Transport Service Employees (red caps) of America whose membership is mostly Negro but includes also White and Japanese Americans; Ferdinand Smith, an immigrant from the West Indies who in 1936 was elected secretary-treasurer of the National Maritime Union of America; Sheldon Tappes, one-time president of the Ford Foundry Local 600, one of the largest union locals in the country; and Revels Cayton, of the International Longshoremen's and Warehousemen's Union. The first two unions are almost exclusively Negro; the last three are White-Negro, and as such perhaps the more significant. But all five are at the very heart of progress for the Negro masses. Townsend is a member of the C.I.O. executive board.

Most of the mixed White-Negro unions, some of which have Negro officials, are in the C.I.O., but the A.F. of L. has a few too. Early in 1945 Maida Stewart Springer, a Negro dressmaker and member of

Local 22 of the International Ladies Garment Workers, an A.F. of L. affiliate, went to England as one of two women delegates appointed to represent the federation on a good will mission to the women workers of England.

I have mentioned the number of Negro teachers. There are two thousand Negro dentists, twelve hundred lawyers, six thousand trained nurses, eleven thousand musicians.

There are about four thousand Negro physicians, or one to every three thousand Negroes—the over-all American ratio is one physician to about 840 people. The ratio in other professions is nearly the same, except for the clergy, of whom there are twice as many in proportion in the Negro group as there are among the Whites. Twenty-five thousand Negro clergymen serve over forty thousand Negro churches, which have five million members and two hundred million dollars' worth of property. The church has been a major influence—sometimes revolutionary, often progressive—in determining the thinking of the colored population.

There are said to be only twenty-two all-Negro villages and small towns in the United States, all in the South; total population: less than 25,000. Generally, the Negroes live in communities with the Whites.

The Negroes publish scores of substantial newspapers and magazines the country over. These prints are the most important factor in processing the Negro mind. Every White citizen of the United States ought to read at least one Negro publication in order to get an occasional glimpse of developments in the White-Negro Problem from the Negro angle.* Not that that angle is one hundred per cent objective; on the contrary, it often is askew—but that is a lesser flaw than the slant of most of the White newspapers and magazines which play up the riots and overlook the intelligent creative, tactful work being done by Negroes and Whites, South and North, toward justice and cooperation, toward the time when these lines by Langston Hughes will have only historic meaning for the Negro:

> O, yes,
> I may say it plain,
> America never was America to me,
> And yet I swear this oath—
> America will be.

During World War II over eight hundred thousand Negroes were in the Army, including about six thousand officers—highest rank: brigadier general, held by Benjamin O. Davis, a West Pointer. His son,

* For a partial list of worthwhile Negro publications see p. 360.

SPANISH AMERICAN: Muskrat trapper in his camp in the marshes, Delacroix Island, St. Bernard Parish, Louisiana.

(Photo by Marion Post Wolcott. Farm Security Administration—Library of Congress)

SPANISH AMERICAN: Migratory farm worker in Texas.
SWEDISH AMERICAN: Manager of a dairy farm in Minnesota.
(Photos by Arthur Rothstein. Farm Security Administration—Library of

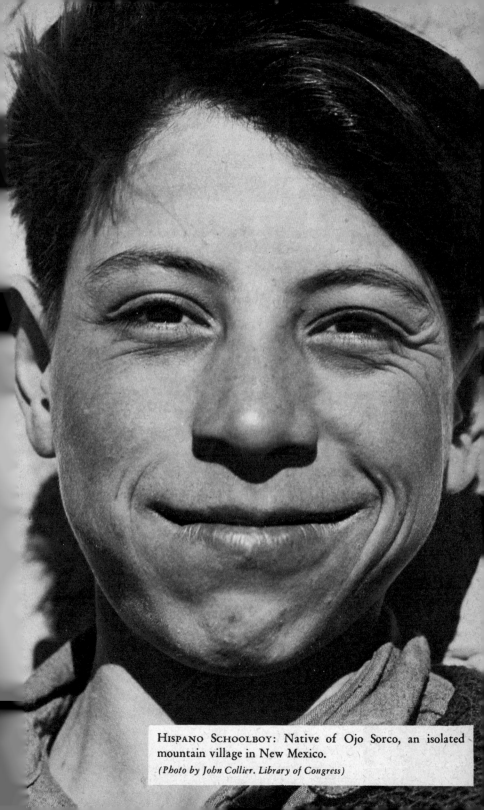

HISPANO SCHOOLBOY: Native of Ojo Sorco, an isolated mountain village in New Mexico.

(Photo by John Collier. Library of Congress)

PANO AMERICANS: The Lopez home at Trampas, New
xico, is many generations old.

oto by John Collier. Library of Congress)

GERMAN AMERICANS: Farm family in Lincoln County,
Nebraska.

*(Photo by John Vachon. Farm Security Administration—Library of
Congress)*

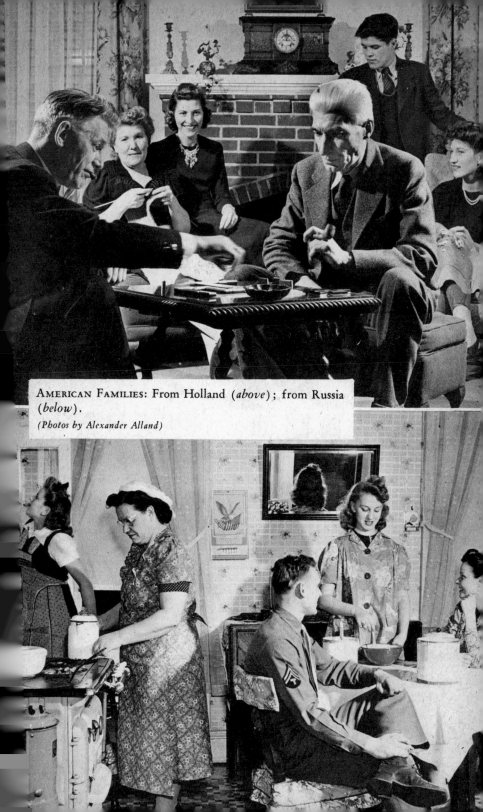

AMERICAN FAMILIES: From Holland (*above*); from Russia (*below*).

(Photos by Alexander Alland)

CLASSROOM
(Photos by Alexander Alland)
HOME STUDY

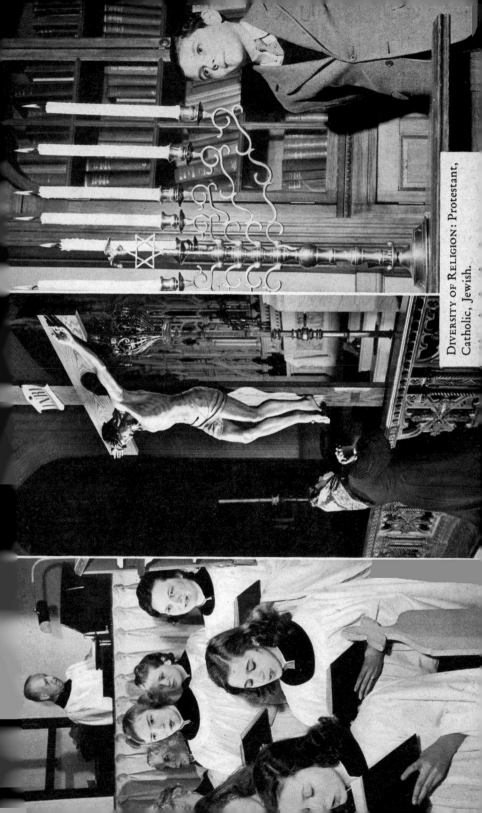

DIVERSITY OF RELIGION: Protestant, Catholic, Jewish.

POLISH AMERICAN: Louis Poleski, tobacco farmer of Enfield, Connecticut.

(Photo by Jack Delano. Library of Congress)

POLISH AMERICAN: Josephine Wotowicz, industrial worker
of Hadley, Massachusetts, who, when her three brothers left
for the armed forces in 1942-1944, took to doing also a good
deal of work on the family farm.

(Photo by Bubley. Standard Oil Company of New Jersey)

FROM GREECE: Grandfather and his American-born granddaughter with the funnies. (Photo by Alexander Alland)

NEGRO AMERICANS: Mother and children.

NORWEGIAN AMERICANS: (*Left*) Born in Norway, working for a Chicago musical-instruments firm since 1909, Edward Groe went into war work in 1941 to regulate the pneumatic motors of trainer planes. (*Right*) Of Norwegian descent, John Granrud was superintendent of the Springfield, Massachusetts, school system, pioneering in the well-known "Springfield Plan."

(Photos by Ann Rosener, Library of Congress, and Alexander Alland)

YUGOSLAV AMERICAN: Steelworker in Gary, Indiana.
(Free-Lance Photographers Guild)

IRISH AMERICANS: (*Above*) Bartender, born in Ireland, serving British
sailors in a Third Avenue, New York,
bar. (*Below*) Martin J. Farrell, mason, and Michael Gallagher, machin-
ist; both of Bayonne, New Jersey.

*(Library of Congress. Photos by Libsohn,
Standard Oil Company of New Jersey)*

His Father, a Jewish Rabbi, Came from Poland: Major General Maurice Rose, an outstanding American soldier of World War II, killed in Germany in 1945 while in command

Born in Germany: General Walter Krueger, commander of the U. S. Army liberating the Philippines 1944-1945;

ITALIAN AMERICAN: Marine Gunnery Sergeant John Basilone of Raritan, New Jersey, the first enlisted man to earn the Congressional Medal of Honor in World War II; killed on the first day of the assault on Iwo Jima.
(Official U. S. Marine Corps Photo)

YUGOSLAV AMERICAN: Captain George S. Wuchinich of the Office of Strategic Services who distinguished himself in secret operations in German-occupied Yugoslavia during 1943–44 and in China in 1945. His parents emigrated from Serbia. (U. S. Army Photo)

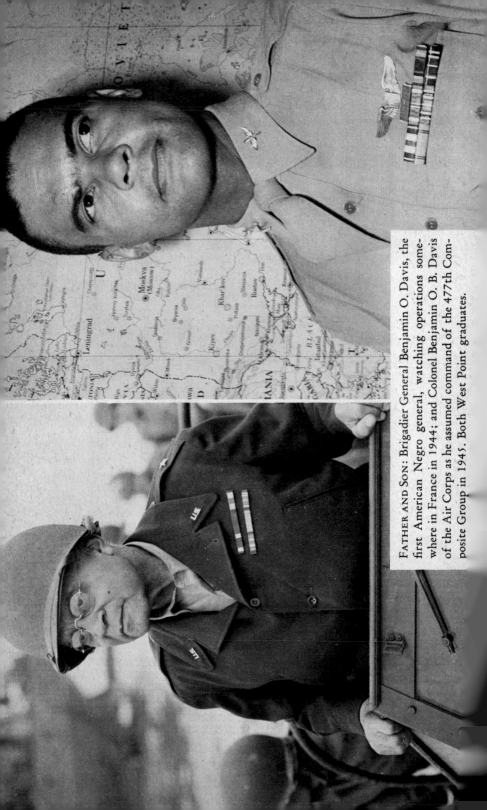

FATHER AND SON: Brigadier General Benjamin O. Davis, the first American Negro general, watching operations somewhere in France in 1944; and Colonel Benjamin O. B. Davis of the Air Corps as he assumed command of the 477th Composite Group in 1945. Both West Point graduates.

Benjamin O. Davis, Jr., a colonel, winner of the Distinguished Service Cross, commanded a Negro air squadron in North Africa and Italy and elsewhere, and in June 1945 was assigned to command the 477th Composite Group at Godman Field, Kentucky. Hundreds of other Negroes were decorated for bravery. One is Captain Charles L. Thomas of Detroit, formerly a Ford metal pourer and molder who as commander of a tank destroyer company in France early in 1945 received the D.S.C. for "extraordinary heroism in action." The action occurred in December 1944 outside the Alsatian village of Climbach which had to be taken. The mountain road leading out of it was crawling with German supply trucks. In a scout car jouncing along at the head of a task force of infantrymen, Thomas (then a first lieutenant) and his men—all Negroes—got the brunt of a burst of German fire as they reached the crest of a hill. All were wounded. Thomas grabbed the car's 50-caliber machine gun and raked the woods and the buildings ahead, ordering the men to crawl away. When he followed them, he was hit again in the chest, legs and arms, but retained consciousness and control of the critical situation. He ordered the emplacement of two anti-tank guns, called the next-in-command, and gave him cool and precise directions for bringing up other guns into position to blow out the enemy. Then he allowed himself to be carried to the rear. Climbach was taken.

In the main, Negro troops in World War II, as in World War I, served in labor battalions. The Negro found himself in the position of having to fight for the right to serve as a combat soldier, for the chance to die for his country. Largely denied that right, he performed well in the dull tasks of the labor units. A White lieutenant, a Southerner, Richard Burns, stationed in India, wrote this to Earl Conrad, a columnist on the Chicago Defender: "It has been said that for every mile of the Stilwell Road a Negro lad lost his life. . . . This road is a rock-and-mud monument to the Negro soldiers serving in these parts; it might well be heeded as a preview of what is to come at home. . . ."

Relatively few Negroes served in the Navy during World War II, but one of the earliest American heroes in this conflict was a Negro messman, Dorie Miller. For his heroic behavior during the Japanese attack on Pearl Harbor, Admiral Nimitz decorated him with the Navy Cross. Dorie Miller was later killed in action when the aircraft carrier Liscome Bay was lost in the Pacific.

In August 1944 the War Shipping Administration's Recruitment and Manning Organization in New York issued a report showing that upward of eight thousand merchant seamen were serving to expedite the shipment of war materials to the fighting fronts. Included in this number were three Negro ship captains and scores of other Negro officers of lower rank.

Several Negro scientists, most of them young men—William J. Knox of Columbia University; Sherman Carter, also of New York; and J. Ernest Wilkins, Moddie Taylor, Jasper Jeffries and Benjamin F. Scott, of Chicago—contributed to the development of the atomic bomb.

Up to 1938 most Negroes working for the government in Washington were in "custodial" employment; very few reached the clerical or professional grades. Now, however, there are some two hundred responsible officials selected for their training and ability. A few of them—such as Robert C. Weaver, an adviser to Paul V. McNutt in the War Manpower Commission—formed the "Black Cabinet," an unofficial group of officials bent on seeing that the Negroes should receive their fair share of employment during the wartime manpower shortage.

Robert C. Weaver declared in the summer of 1943 that over a million Negroes were employed in war industries. During 1944-1945 that number increased by at least a half million. *But—*

One could write a volume around this *but.*

By and large, the Negro people still live on the rough uncomfortable edges of the country's national economy. They are securely established as Pullman porters and red caps, somewhat less securely as elevator operators and household servants. Many Negroes in these occupations are college graduates barred from employment in fields for which they are trained. Outside of the service jobs, they are the first to be hit when unemployment comes.

What of the Negro worker in the postwar period when the manpower shortage is likely to become the manpower surplus?

The answer to that question will depend on a thousand and one factors—such as the general national economy, the quality of the Administration leadership in Washington, Fair Employment Practices legislation, international developments and their effect on our various population groups, the soundness of the cultural and social leadership emanating from labor unions, industry and business, schools and churches, from writers and lecturers, from the theater, the screen, the radio.

It will depend on the American public in general getting a grasp of the facts about the Negroes and the White-Negro Problem.

It will depend on the National Association for the Advancement of Colored People, the Urban League and the Southern Conference on

Human Welfare, and on the less well-known Negro, Negro-White and White organizations working in the same field.*

It will depend on the appearance of more industrial concerns such as the Electronic Corporation of America (New York) and The National Smelting Company (Cleveland) which will make a deliberate, intelligent effort toward good relations between White and Negro workers, employed solely on the basis of qualifications for the job and without regard to race.

It will depend on the quick realization by those who are trying to do something about it that the "Negro Problem" is not something apart from the country's general cultural-social-economic setup; on whether or not the American people as a whole can rid themselves of their fears, especially racial fears; on the country's ability to discard the idea that it is exclusively White, Protestant and Anglo-Saxon; on whether or not America can firmly Americanize itself.

* Commission on the Church and Minority Peoples, 297 Fourth Avenue, New York 10, N. Y. Instituted by the Federal Council of the Churches of Christ in America.
American Council on Race Relations, 32 West Randolph Street, Chicago 1, Ill.
National Organizing Committee for Negro Work, 80 Fifth Avenue, New York 11, N. Y.
Kentucky Commission on Negro Affairs, 418 South Fifth Street, Louisville. (Should be "White-Negro Affairs.")
Governor's Commission on Problems Affecting the Negro Population, State Executive Offices, Annapolis, Md. (Should be "the Negro and White Population.")
Committee for Observance of Negro History Week, Room 601, 101 Post Street, San Francisco 8, Calif.
The Interracial Council of Greater Hartford, 11 Asylum Street, Hartford 3, Conn.
Interracial Committee of Winter Park, 637 New York Avenue, Winter Park, Fla.
Youth for Interracial Solidarity, 3032 South Wabash Avenue, Chicago, Ill.
Mayor's Committee on Race Relations, 600½ South Seventh Street, Springfield, Ill.
Interracial Committee of the Gary Chamber of Commerce, Gary, Ind.
Des Moines Interracial Commission, 701 Maple Street, Des Moines, Iowa.
Student Interracial Committee, Central High School, Flint, Mich.
Joint Advisory Committee on Interracial Problems, Chamber of Commerce, Jackson, Miss.
Madison Interracial Committee, c/o Public Library, Madison, New Jersey.
Interracial Fellowship of Greater New York, 564 West 160th Street, New York 32, N. Y.
The Abraham Lincoln Carriers On Club, Little Red School House, 196 Bleecker Street, (Greenwich Village) New York 12, N. Y.
Albany Inter-Cultural Group, 518 Madison Avenue, Albany, N. Y.
Committee on Unity of the American People, 357 Portage Road, Niagara Falls, N. Y.
Mayor's Interracial Committee, 12 Locust Street, New Rochelle, N. Y.
Interracial Committee of the YWCA, Troy, N. Y.
Committee on Interracial Affairs, City Hall, Durham, N. C.
League for Human Rights, 511 Chester Ninth Bldg., Cleveland, Ohio.
Northwest Community Council of Milwaukee, 904 West Vine Street. Milwaukee 5, Wis.

It will depend on whether American democracy turns out to be an expanding or a contracting ideal; on whether Christianity and Judaism will enter into the lives of those who profess those faiths or remain mere disguises for spiritual undevelopment, decadence and corruption.

Since the 1920s it has grown clearer and clearer that the White-Negro Problem has been stuck on the horns of Dr. Myrdal's American Dilemma: "the ever-raging conflict between, on the one hand, the valuations preserved on the general plane which we shall call the 'American Creed,' where the American thinks, talks and acts under the influence of high national and Christian precepts, and, on the other, the valuations on the specific planes of individual and group living, where personal and local interests; economic, social and sexual jealousies, considerations of community prestige and conformity; group prejudice against particular persons or types of people; and all sorts of miscellaneous wants, impulses and habits dominate his outlook."

This conflict involves the future of the "American Creed."

"No Yankee will be tactless enough to mention it in so many words," says the Swedish scholar in *An American Dilemma*, "and no Southerner can afford to admit it, but the main thing happening to the South is that it is gradually becoming Americanized."

The statement that "no Southerner" (meaning White Southerner) can afford this admission is not exactly accurate. There is Lillian Smith of Clayton, Georgia, who started to work toward the Americanization of her native South years before the publication of her startling novel *Strange Fruit* (1944). There is Mrs. M. E. Tilly of Atlanta, a leader of church women, long active in the White-Negro Problem. There is Hodding Carter, Southern editor and novelist, who in *The Winds of Fear* (1944) tells from the inside "something of both the causes and the results of the fear of race which reacts upon the interchangeably feared and fearing who are its victims." There is Clark H. Foreman who organized the Southern Conference for Human Welfare.

While an undergraduate at the University of Georgia during the war "to make the world safe for democracy," Clark Foreman—son of an Atlanta businessman, grandson of an editor of *The Atlanta Constitution* —witnessed a lynching. He was terribly shocked, but could not think of anything he could do about it. After graduation he studied at the School of Economics in London, where the college paper asked him to review G. H. Oldham's *Christianity and the Race Problem*. The book contained an account of the Inter-Racial Commission in Atlanta; two years later he got a job with that organization. Then he worked for the Phelps-Stokes Fund and the Julius Rosenwald Fund. In 1933 he joined the staff of Harold Ickes, Secretary of the Interior, as adviser on race problems. In this capacity, Foreman was the first White government official to employ a Negro secretary. In 1938, as the National Emergency Council's state director for Georgia, he issued a report on economic conditions in the South, covering both Whites and Negroes, which led to the first Southern Conference for Human Welfare, held in Birmingham.

The Conference was organized on a permanent basis with a program of full employment and equal civil rights for all citizens, White and Negro. Clark Foreman has been its president since 1942. At its request, Congressman Lee Geyer of California introduced the first anti-poll tax bill in Congress in 1938. The Conference sponsored the creation of the National Committee to Abolish the Poll Tax. In 1944 Foreman served as executive secretary of the C.I.O. Political Action Committee, which was instrumental in ending a number of reactionary political careers, all of them based on the old White-Protestant-Anglo-Saxon concept of the United States.

This is a definite part of the South's Americanization.

But, as suggested before, the South is not the only part of the United States in need of Americanization. There is almost as much anti-Negro discrimination in the North as in the South; and the Americanization needed in the North is not only in reference to the Negro. The worst race riot during World War II occurred in Detroit. And most of the Whites who attacked the Negroes in that incident were Polish and other new-immigrant Americans. A friend of mine maintains that those Polish Americans were "Americanized" on the basis of the White-Protestant-Anglo-Saxon concept of the country, but I think this explanation is insufficient, and not only because Polish Americans are Catholics and as such, perhaps, anti-Protestant. Many new-immigrant Americans are anti-Negro as a psychological compensation for their own inferior status under the White-Protestant-Anglo-Saxon concept—a concept which also provides psychological compensation for the inferiorities of many White, Protestant, Anglo-Saxon Americans. It is a *Herrenvolk* concept—a main ingredient of the dynamite lying loose about the country. It is not helping us in the struggle against other *Herrenvolk* concepts.

The probability is that the democratic process and the Judaic-Christian religion and morality in the United States will go through their ultimate test in connection with the White-Negro situation.

What are the prospects?

At this writing they are better than they were, say, in 1935 or even in 1940 or 1943, but they are far from sanguine. They depend on developments in the world crisis and on alterations in the general American psychology which may or may not come about in time to strengthen the positive tendencies. The prospects depend on endless immediacies and long-term possibilities, on variable Negro and White moods, on changing national and world conditions.

Perhaps the following items, pulled at random out of our whirling, kaleidoscopic race relations, will suggest the trends among Negroes and Whites, North and South.

In 1943 a story current in the Negro world told of a mortally wounded American Negro soldier in the jungle of a Pacific island who asked a comrade to paint these words on the cross marking his grave: HERE LIES A BLACK MAN WHO DIED FIGHTING THE YELLOW MAN FOR THE FREEDOM OF THE WHITE MAN.

A letter from a Negro soldier fighting on Okinawa to the Editor of the Pittsburgh Courier (May 19, 1945):

. . . I can tell you one thing for sure about our boys: they are in this thing for better or worse. That is, they are not coming back with the idea of just taking up where they left off. We are going to have the things that are rightfully due us or else, which is a very large order, but we have proven . . . that we are people and not just the servants of the White man. And the White fellows with us, as a whole, accept this as part of America. We had fun together; we slept together, ate together, shared and shared alike, even in death.

I have talked with fellows all through my service and my belief is that most of them are going to help us gain that right which is ours—even to the young Southern White boy. We have just about forgotten the old Southern rebel, for he is through, just as Germany and Japan are through. From now on there is going to be a new spirit that is going home to take over and do what their forefathers fought to do—equalization for all men, regardless of race, color or creed.

Please pass this on to the people and America and let them know that a different American is coming home from the one who left.

A letter from a Negro soldier in the South Pacific to his family in North Carolina, published in the December 2, 1944, Durham Carolina Times:

What did they ever do with that bus driver that shot the

boy in Durham some time ago? If they let him get away with that, things aren't so good back there. It seems our fighting for America is in vain. I feel and believe every man is created equal and everybody should have equal rights, if they don't they might as well throw the Constitution away or burn it, for they are making it a lie and until the people back there come to realize it and start treating everybody equal, this war is just a sample of what is to come. I hope we are not over here fighting and suffering for nothing. If this war doesn't help things it won't do any good to fight, for after all, we are Americans. If we are going to be treated like the enemies are being treated, what have we got to fight for. I do hope and pray that we will have a democracy after this war is over so America will be a country and a place for all red blooded Americans to be proud of and a place in which everyone is treated right and all for one and one for all, and everyone will get equal breaks and jobs. That's the America I'm fighting for.

> *A report from England:*
> Two American Negro soldiers got on a Cardiff tram. Two American officers followed and one told the colored soldiers to "Get out." As they were about to leave the conductress stopped them, saying: "You are in Britain. Colored men are not banned from our cars. Stay on." And they stayed.
> When the officers were getting off one said: "You English are making it hard for us; when we get back to America we shall not be able to manage these fellows."

During 1942-1945 there were several Negro "mutinies" in the United States armed forces against Jim Crow discrimination—always behind the lines, never at the front; sometimes the Negro troops "mutinied" against not being allowed to fight the enemy. The most dramatic incidents were the hunger strike of a Seabee battalion in California in 1944, the spectacular "insubordination" case involving four Negro Wacs at Fort Devens, Massachusetts, early in 1945, the refusal of 101 Negro flying officers at Freeman Field, Indiana, to be Jim-Crowed in a separate officers' club, which led to their arrest and confinement to quarters, and later, their transfer to another post. On this latter episode George S. Schuyler commented in the Pittsburgh *Courier* (May 3, 1945):

"[The young officers'] action took high courage, and all

Americans who value character and principle should applaud them. . . . No group can fail to achieve its objectives when its educated young men are willing to challenge wrong and face the consequences. The United States Army may foolishly 'make an example' of them, but they will always be heroes to Americans with red blood in their bodies.

". . . They were entirely correct, because a Jim-Crow officers' club is a violation of Army regulations and the commanding officer knew it—or should have known it. But Jim-Crowism is the unwritten law of the armed forces and has more force than the written regulations. Only a year ago the Army with great fanfare of trumpets outlawed color discrimination in all places under its jurisdiction, but this regulation has chiefly been honored in the breach, if I am to believe the verbal and written complaints I receive from Negro soldiers all over the world.

"There has been a disposition on the part of far too many [Negro] commissioned and non-commissioned officers to play safe and Uncle Tom in the face of these violations of the Army regulations, but happily there is less of that in World War II than there was in World War I. The realization has come to an increasing number of our young men that it is better to lose one's money and rank than to lose one's soul. Every time a Negro willingly accepts a second-class status, a piece of his soul vanishes, never to return. No man with a shadow of self-respect can remain a man while accepting the status of a slave. And yet we have far too many Negroes who not only accept it, but actually defend it on the ground of expediency which some 'leaders' call 'racial statesmanship.' It is impossible for any man to be a first-class officer if constantly forced into a second-class position. The situation surrounding Negro officers is difficult at best, made that way by the refusal of his superiors, from the President of the United States down, to enforce the laws of the Nation and the regulations of the Army. When these Negro officers are humiliated before their men and their White brother officers, their position becomes unbearable. This was evidently the case with the Freeman Field officers. They came to a military post only to discover that they had entered a plantation.

"It is a pleasure to note that the War Department has had the good sense to release these young men to duty, and it is to be hoped that the High Command will take steps to see that there is no recurrence of such incidents. The regulations are quite clear and it is doubtful if any appreciable percentage of the American population wants to see Army officers humiliated, no matter what their color or 'race.' . . ."

A letter to me from a White soldier in a Texas camp, dated December 5, 1944:

My Army experience has been solely in the field of classification, and I have seen the most brutal aspects of racial segregation at close hand. . . . Higher scores on aptitude tests are required for school attendance by Negroes than by Whites. Civilian skills of Whites may be utilized, but almost never those of Negroes. At one time the Second Air Force had a critical shortage of photographers, but I was forbidden to utilize the skill of a Negro who had had 13 years of professional experience; I was told to watch for White boys who had made photography a "hobby." I blush at the discriminatory treatment which I was compelled to observe, and I am happy to have been elsewise assigned. I was ashamed to be White.

A letter to the Editor of the St. Louis Post-Dispatch, early in 1945, signed "H.C.S.":

It irks me considerably to read constantly of a shortage of women workers in the defense industries of metropolitan St. Louis. Do you realize that there are thousands and thousands of Negro women in St. Louis who are available for this type of work but are rejected for reasons of prejudice?

During the polio epidemic in New York State in 1944 a radio appeal went out for graduate nurses asking them to volunteer their services during the emergency. Miss Iva Wallace who was awaiting assignment to active duty in the Army Nurse Corps immediately wrote the State Health Department offering her services, stating that she is a Negro. On December 6, Miss Wallace received a telegram requesting her to go to Buffalo where an emergency was said to exist. On arriving at the Buffalo General Hospital, Miss Wallace was directed to the Nurses Home where the housekeeper cordially directed her to a room. Here her roommate was quite friendly and was chatting with Miss Wallace when the housekeeper returned saying there had been a mistake and that the new nurse was to be in the "other nurses home." After spending the night in a vacant ward that was under repair and being forced to eat her breakfast there, Miss Wallace was called to a supervisor's office and in-

formed that Buffalo General did not hire Negro nurses and that
the Department of Health "should have known better." The
nurse was given her expense money and returned to Brooklyn
pending her assignment to the Army Nurses Corps.

Dr. George E. Haynes, executive secretary, Department of
Race Relations, Federal Council of Churches of Christ, late in
1944:
Experience during World War I shows clearly that the rioting
and mobs in our large industrial centers had their taproot in
economic discriminations, especially in the widespread denial of
jobs to Negroes. We do not wish any repetition of these conditions, and if we are to win the peace as well as the war, both
the church and the state should uphold and protect equal rights
and responsibilities for all our people. The idea of superior and
inferior peoples with privileges and rights for the superior over
the inferior must be rooted out of every community and state
in this nation.

From a 1944 statement by Edwin R. Embree, president of
the Julius Rosenwald Fund:
Coming back from war, the whole young male [Negro]
population . . . will never again fit into the serfdom of southern feudalism or into second-class status in northern industrial
cities. It is too late ever again to keep Negroes "in their place."
If we wanted that, we should never have drawn them into war
production nor called them to the tremendous education of
the armed forces. We now have the problem—and the opportunity—to build Negroes, with all other citizens, into a common
working force, which may then produce the highest standard of
living ever known by any people; into a common culture, which
will be enriched by the wisdom and ingenuity of this race as it
has been by their art and music; into a common social and political order which may then become a true democracy.

George S. Schuyler, in the April 28, 1945, Pittsburgh Courier:
Negro leaders spent the greater part of last week eulogizing
the late President Roosevelt because "under his administration
the greatest advances for the race had been made." Such as
what? And were those "advances"—if any—greater than Emancipation by the heroism and sacrifice of a quarter of a million
Negro soldiers during the Civil War?

Said Lillian Smith, early in 1945:
The Negro wants the four freedoms that the rest of us want
and need; but he wants another. Freedom from shame. A
freedom that is his profound right to have. The Negro wants
freedom from shame for his children, yes; and I want it for ours
also. Neither his children nor ours can ever have it as long as
segregation is the way of life in America.

From the Washington, D.C., telephone directory:
Democratic Nat'l Committee Mayflower Htl   DI strict 1717
Colored Division 615 F Nw   EX ecutive 1796

*Will W. Alexander, vice-president of the Julius Rosenwald
Fund, in 1945:*
Unless the problem of segregation can be solved, there is no
hope of any alleviation of the race problem in America.

Jim Crow practices became so widespread in Portland,
Oregon, during 1944-1945 that it was reported that a prosperous
business was growing up engaged primarily in the manufacture
of "White Trade Only" signs. It was also reported that the
preoccupation of Negro citizens with this type of gratuitous
insult was overshadowing such issues as housing and employment.

Paul Robeson, in 1944:
The American Negro has changed his temper. Now he wants
his freedom. Whether he is smiling at you or not, he wants his
freedom. The old exploitation of peoples is definitely passed.

An editorial in the Macon, Georgia, News:
Strange as it may seem, it is the high school pupils who ride
the buses to and from school who are daily antagonizing and
insulting Negroes who happen to be passengers on the buses.
At times they occupy all the seats that are supposed to be reserved for the Negroes in the rear, and make insulting and
indecent remarks about the hapless Negroes, taunting them
about their color and yelling from the windows at Negroes on
the street as they pass. Indeed, one boy spat in the face of an
unoffending Negro boy on the back seat because he did not get
up and give him his seat.
If these boys who are acting so disgracefully were sons of

the lower criminal classes their behavior would be blamed on their upbringing, their environment, their parents. But such is not the case. Most of the offenders come from the best homes of Macon.

There are many parents who would hang their heads in shame and humiliation if they knew of this flouting of good manners and common decency by these children for whom they have such high hopes.

We suggest that some parents make it a point to ride a bus to or from school a couple of days and observe for themselves a situation that is fast getting out of bounds.

> In Houston, Texas, at Christmastime in 1944, Fred Stone, manager of the local Negro movie house, moved into a neighborhood which had hitherto been occupied by middle-class Whites. His neighbors raised vigorous protests; however, when Stone refused to leave, several houses were placed on sale. These structures, built at prices ranging from five and one-half to seven thousand dollars during the relatively high-priced period 1927-1930, are being sold to Negro physicians, school teachers and others for thirteen thousand dollars and up.

A letter to the editors of The Nation (February 23, 1945) from Jarmina Marton, West Hollywood, California:

Prejudice can be licked. We did it in our neighborhood. Perhaps the case of the Johnsons of West Hollywood and their victory can be taken as a pattern for similar victories in other communities. The backbone of the pattern is the militant decency of most people once they are informed, aroused, and organized.

The Johnsons—that isn't their real name—are a Negro family, and they couldn't find a place to live at any price. Finally they bought a house in our district, which is White, and moved in. Their next-door neighbors were outraged, drew up a petition, and began a campaign among the Whites to force the Johnsons to vacate. The bigots were off to a flying start. But that was as far as they got. As they circulated their petition they were astonished and dismayed to find that people refused to sign it. The Johnsons still live in their new home, and they will continue to stay there. They have not been ostracized, and they are becoming part of the life of the community.

The Johnsons fared better than the Maxwells, not because

we have fewer bigots in our district or are in any way unusual, but simply because neighborhood liberal elements were already geared to fight. This is the way we did it. Just before the last election a group of us had formed the West Hollywood Committee to help reelect Roosevelt and to further democracy. After election we enlarged our membership and tried to work at being responsible citizens—we studied local, state, national, and international affairs, formed investigating and study groups, and made our wishes known to our legislators in Sacramento and Washington.

When the Johnson incident occurred, we were prepared. Our first step was to welcome the Johnsons and assure them of our support and friendship. They were asked to join our club and did so. Next we studied the legal aspects of the case and conducted a whirlwind house-to-house campaign against the petition being circulated by the bigots. Members spoke to nonmember friends, who were also pressed into the fight. Naturally not everyone was with us, but the decent people rallied to the cause and we were able to defeat the petition. As a result the Johnsons have a home, West Hollywood has acquired another worth-while family, and the practicing democrats are welded together more firmly than ever by this common experience.

In Raiford, Florida, James William, Freddie Lane and James Davis, Negroes aged twenty-six, twenty and sixteen respectively, were electrocuted after a speedy trial in which they were convicted of the rape of a White woman. The trial was highlighted by (1) a plea for "simple justice" by an attractive and intelligent young White woman whose husband was fighting in France, (2) the feebleness of the efforts of the court-appointed defense attorneys, and (3) the rejection of evidence of the use of third-degree methods in obtaining alleged confessions.

In Abbeville, Alabama, six White youths, accused of abduction and rape by twenty-two-year-old Mrs. Recy Taylor, mother of an infant, have had no formal charges placed against them by the state. Mrs. Taylor is a Negro. A national Committee for Equal Justice for Mrs. Recy Taylor was subsequently formed. For nearly a year (1944-45) the State of Alabama was bombarded with thousands of letters and wires urging that the youths, who reportedly admitted the crime, be indicted and brought to trial.

On the evening of February 3, 1945, in Charleston, South Carolina, a Negro youth had a dispute over the fare with the driver of a crowded Belt Line bus. It was a brief argument apparently ending when the young man paid the alleged differ-ence in fare and walked quietly to the last seat on the bus. The driver, however, continued talking about the incident, using abusive language. After several minutes of this, the youth made some remark about the driver to another occupant of the rear seat. At this juncture, the driver rose, drew his gun and threat-ened to shoot the lad. A White passenger got to his feet, took out a gun, leveled it at the Negro passengers and suggested that they be taken to jail. Demanding that all Negro passengers remain on the bus, the driver drove to the police station. Here he pointed out several Negro passengers—most of whom had neither spoken nor acted—and had them arrested on charges of disorderly conduct.

Early in 1945 Will Lacey, a sixteen-year-old Negro boy of Huntsville, Alabama, was acquitted on charges of second degree murder in the death of a forty-two-year-old White man. The latter had thrown a rock at the boy. The boy picked up the rock and threw it back with such force that the man's skull was fractured when struck by it. The blow proved fatal.

At Pensacola, Florida, in February 1944, Circuit Judge L. L. Fabisinski issued a writ of mandamus ordering Ben L. Davis, Escambia County registration officer, to permit two Negroes to register and vote as members of the Democratic Party. Mean-while, State Attorney General Tom Watson, speaking at a meeting of the Florida Democratic Executive Committee— called to consider proposals for legislation among which was one that the state relinquish all control of primary elections—stated that Negro and White people are entitled to the same political rights. He urged the Committee to take the Supreme Court decision into account and admit Negroes to the primaries "or something is going to take place that will have the effect of disintegration of what we've got."

Willie Bryant, Negro, was scheduled to be electrocuted at Atlanta in February 1945 for the murder of Zach Trice, Macon White man. Another man, about to be executed for a different murder had confessed to killing Trice, but the confession had not been admitted as evidence at Bryant's second trial. Near the time set for the execution, Reginald Trice, brother of the murder victim, wired the pardon and parole board asking a commutation of sentence inasmuch as it was his "Christian duty to save Bryant's life because there was a little doubt." The board commuted the death sentence to life imprisonment. The Macon *News*, which enjoys a reputation for fairness, had earlier editorialized: ". . . Bryant may be guilty. But he may not be. And he ought not to be put to death on the verdict of a jury that knew nothing of Dixon's confession."

Early in 1945 a Negro in Atlanta, Georgia, walked down the aisle, seated himself near the center to worship in a White church. Two sets of ushers waited on him to tell him that he had to sit in the back or in the balcony. When the Negro refused to move a plainclothes officer, displaying his badge, insisted that he had to. He escorted the Negro outside and asked why he came. The Negro replied that he only wanted to worship. The plainclothesman, who it seems was also an officer of the church, at first insisted that the Negro sit in the rear or the balcony. The Negro said he would leave rather than worship in the balcony or the rear. Strange as it may seem, the officer then told the Negro he could sit in the empty front row. The segregated pattern was maintained. He could sit in the very front, the very rear, or in the balcony. He could not sit where he chose if it was in the center.

Late in April 1945 Dr. Benjamin E. Mays, president of Morehouse College, Atlanta, Georgia, filed with the Interstate Commerce Commission in Washington a complaint against the Southern Railway charging he had been refused dining car service because of his race.

Dr. E. Franklin Frazier of Howard University early in 1945:
The demobilization of the Negroes in the armed forces will throw a large number on the labor market. These men will be less disposed than the Negro in the past to remain unemployed because of race, nor will they be satisfied to be shunted into the precarious employment afforded by unskilled labor.

Perhaps many will be drawn into the radical wing of the labor movement and seek a revolutionary solution of their problem. At one time such movements on the part of the Negro could be ignored but in our urban civilization, they offer a serious threat to internal peace.

A field report:
Negro auxiliary members of the Brotherhood of Railway, Steamship Clerks, Freight Handlers, etc., were not included in invitations to hear Brother George M. Harrison, International President, when he addressed the local organization at the Hotel Peabody in Memphis on January 13, 1945.

George S. Schuyler in the April 28, 1945, Pittsburgh Courier:
Last week, Mr. Stettinius, Secretary of State, honored Louis Myers, seventy-two-year-old Negro messenger and clerk, who has served under nine Secretaries of State. Mr. Myers was given a bronze standard. Much more in order would have been a better job.

S. J. Novick, President of the Electronic Corporation of America, late in 1944, at a hearing of the New York State Commission Against Discrimination:
"[We] employ more than three hundred production workers, of whom forty are Negroes. We employ men and women of many races, religions, and national origins, but I shall devote my testimony to the condition of Negro employment because it is commonly known that the Negro, more than any other group in American life, suffers from discrimination in employment. From the very inception of our business, Negro workers have been employed on terms of complete equality with White workers, as a matter of course. Our sole criterion of employment is competence for the work required. Accordingly, you will find that our Negro personnel run the full scale of seniority, from the oldest to the newest workers. . . . We can cite two examples illustrating this policy. There was the case of the Negro stock clerk who advanced to the position of wire-man. He is now an ensign in the maritime service where he was the first Negro to be graduated from radio school. Then there was the Negro porter who went to school at night and became a draftsman in which capacity he performed satisfactorily until he entered the Army.

". . . Some people maintain that employment of Negroes causes bad feeling among the White workers and disrupts production. Our experience proves the contrary. There is complete harmony and fraternity among our workers. Negroes share in the leadership of union activities, play on our athletic teams, serve with distinction on all our labor-management committees and participate in all of our plant social functions on a plane of complete equality. There is no segregation and no ill-will."

Reginald E. Gillmor, president of Sperry Gyroscope, reported in 1945 that his company's experience with Negro workers in skilled jobs had been excellent. A considerable number of them were leaders. All of them got along well with White workers. And Negro workers in general, said Mr. Gillmor, "are neither so prone to absenteeism as other workers nor do they change or lose their jobs quite so frequently."

In 1944, under the double pressure of Negro organizations and a stringent labor market, two of New England's largest department stores, Gilchrist's and Jordan Marsh of Boston, added Negro women to their permanent sales staffs.

The first Negro permitted to take the examination for master electrician's license in Houston, Texas, passed the test in June 1945. The successful candidate: Clifford F. Smith, an ex-Seabee and one-time foreman in an electrical plant.

In February 1944 Cincinnati City Hospital announced that it would accept graduate nurses for general duty without regard to race. Formerly the institution had not hired Negro graduate nurses.

Early in 1945 State Senator Sol J. Selvin (a merchant from Toole, Utah) introduced a bill in the Utah legislature intended to prohibit discrimination on account of race, color, or creed in the admission of persons to public places of accommodation. At an open hearing on the bill, more than 200 persons, including religious leaders, returned soldiers, and the presidents of the state organizations of both the A.F. of L. and C.I.O. attended to testify on behalf of its passage. Among other things, it was pointed out that, in Utah, settled by members of a persecuted minority, it is well-nigh impossible to secure decent sleeping or eating facilities for Negro war workers or service personnel.

In December 1944, at New Bern, North Carolina, J. A. Mc-
Donald, first Negro to be elected a justice of the peace in that
state since 1898, was sworn into office. One thousand eight
hundred and ninety-five votes were cast for him, only four
hundred of them by Negroes.

Governor Simeon Willis of Kentucky announced in May
1944 that he would appoint a Negro to the State Board of
Education and would ask Attorney General Edison S. Dummit
to appoint another as an assistant attorney general.

In February 1945 Smith College, Northampton, Massachusetts, appointed its first Negro teacher, sociologist Adelaide
Cromwell Hill, a *cum laude* graduate of Smith.

> Said Federal Judge William H. Hastie, dean, Howard Uni-
> versity Law School, in 1944:
> *Millions of Americans have the common sense to be dis-*
> *turbed about the race question, but lack the thoughtfulness and*
> *courage to think and act through to conclusions. Instead, they*
> *seek some sort of middle ground, a no-man's land between*
> *justice and injustice, a working compromise between right and*
> *wrong. If there is one attitude that can be catastrophic, it is the*
> *attitude of those who cannot take sides between right and*
> *wrong when any issue is at stake.*
> *It is not a pleasant thing, but I say to you, with concern, that*
> *the Negro in America faces the future with bitterness, with*
> *cynicism, with distrust, yes, with hatred in his heart. Many of*
> *them have developed the chip on the shoulder, the undue sen-*
> *sitiveness, the finding of injury where none was intended. Those*
> *are the things which Americans should realize, should ponder,*
> *should seek the reasons for and try to correct as the values of*
> *both the souls of men and the future of our nation.*

Willard Waller, associate professor of sociology, Columbia
University; author of The Veteran Comes Back—*in 1944:*
In the postwar period intolerant movements will probably
flourish. All of us, Jews and Gentiles, Catholics and Protestants,
Negroes and Whites, should get ready to fight for racial and
religious equality in the postwar world.
If it should happen that we must at some time fight another
war, and we go into that war under the handicap of internal

oppression and hatred of minorities, which we bear at present, we shall lose that war. Tolerance of minorities is not merely a democratic duty, it is a necessity of survival. A polyglot nation, such as ours, must learn to tolerate cultural diversity or it must die.

From a statement by Dr. H. Scudder Mekeel, associate professor of anthropology at the University of Wisconsin, made in November 1944 at the annual meeting of the National Committee for Mental Hygiene:
Those of us who are White are having, and so far wasting, our last chance to be accepted on an equal basis with the other peoples of a world which is two-thirds colored. The three-hundred-year advantage we had through the industrial revolution is coming to a close as the remainder of the world becomes industrialized and capable of producing modern weapons of war.

From Riots and Ruins by A. Clayton Powell, Sr., father of Congressman A. Clayton Powell, Jr., of Harlem; published in 1945:
Nationally [the Negro] is poorer politically today than he was fifty years ago. At that time . . . there were twenty-three Negro members of the United States Congress. These men were not ignorant, either, as some of the slanderers of the race have tried to make the public believe. They were graduates of Harvard, Yale, Princeton, and Oberlin. A few of them had studied in European universities. . . . Not only have these great Negro national characters and their positions gone with the wind but *not a single bit of legislation to help the Negro in his fight for human rights has been enacted by Congress for fifty years*. . . . Congress is a political drag . . . and is absolutely dedicated to the proposition—keep the Negro down.

From an article in The Christian Century *by Eleanor Graham Nichols, a leader of Alabama church women:*
. . . Millions of our men, black and white, are engaged in battling a force which says some men are born to be masters, some to be slaves, some to hold in their hands the destinies of beings of other blood. We abhor this philosophy. . . . We think of ourselves as the champions of Christian democracy, the supporters of the "common man." But we cannot be the cham-

pions of democracy so long as there is one whit of discrimination against any . . . group in this country. Our protestations
will be an echoing mockery.

. . . Freedom is doomed to short and bitter existence unless
it is freedom for all mankind. A democracy in which a wronged
individual is unable to secure justice because of his color cannot
speak compellingly to the subject peoples of Europe and Asia,
nor can it justify the death of thousands of its sons on the
battlefield.

IX: AMERICANS FROM YUGOSLAVIA

YUGOSLAV immigrants are generally regarded as being part of the
New Immigration which reached its amazing mass proportions
during the two decades just before World War I. Certainly the majority
of Serbians, Croatians and Slovenians got here between 1885 and 1914—
before they were known collectively as Yugoslavs, or South-Slavs; when
Yugoslavia was still a political dream, not to be realized until after
the breakup of the old Austro-Hungarian empire in 1918.

In that climactic period of the great Atlantic Migration, the hundreds
of thousands of Yugoslavs who came over from southern Austria and
Hungary were lumped together as "Austrians" with the other subjects
of the Emperor Franz Josef eagerly departing from his complicated and
unhappy Dual Monarchy. They were Slovenians from Carniola, Car-
inthia, Styria, and the territory around Trieste; and Croatians and
Serbians from Croatia and Slavonia, from Istria and the Dalmatian
coast, from Bosnia and Herzegovina. At the same time small numbers
of Serbians came from the tiny Balkan kingdoms of Serbia and Montenegro which in 1918 were also included in the new Yugoslav state.

But the Yugoslav chapter in the American Story probably begins
with America's beginnings. Little doubt exists that on Columbus' ships
were cosmopolitan Croatians from the famous Dalmatian city-republic
of Ragusa (now Dubrovnik on Yugoslav maps). The Ragusan sailors
and shipbuilders of that day were among the best in the world, with a
long tradition behind them. In 1924 the Seamen's Guild of Dalmatia
celebrated the one thousandth anniversary of its existence. In the
fifteenth and sixteenth centuries its members sailed on ships of all
seafaring nations, especially, it seems, on those engaged in the India

spice trade. It is very unlikely that some of them did not get in on the great Adventure of 1492.

There is also little doubt that Ragusan ships—called "argosies" (the word comes from "Ragusa")—sailed to America during the half century immediately following the Discovery. There is a persistent Dalmatian legend, backed by some circumstantial evidence, that Yugoslav voyagers preceded by about four decades Sir Walter Raleigh's ill-fated attempts to establish an Anglo-Saxon colony within the present confines of the United States.

It is almost certain that in 1540, or thereabouts, a fleet of ships left Ragusa for America, hoping to find a region suitable for refugees streaming into the Ragusan republic from the Turkish rule oppressing the Balkan interior. And it seems that one or more of these ships were wrecked off what is now the coast of North Carolina; that a number of sailors rescued themselves on one of the islands, probably Roanoke, between the Albermarle and Pamlico Sounds; and that they then mixed with the inhabitants, who have since been known as the Croatan Indians.

In Robeson County, North Carolina, there is to this day a group of people who call themselves Croatans and claim descent from the Croatan tribes. Other descendants, I am told, live in West Virginia and in the Cumberland country of Maryland. Off North Carolina, in Cartaret County, is a Croatan Island; and the Croatan Sound connects the Albermarle and Pamlico Sounds.

Croatan Indians were found in the middle 1580s when Sir Walter Raleigh's colonies were trying to get a foothold on Roanoke Island. The name occurs in the writings of John White, leader of the Second Colony—"The Lost Colony"—and Croatans enter into most of the speculations concerning its mysterious fate.

There are scholars who are not convinced that the Croatan Indians came by their name, and partly descend, from those shipwrecked Croatian sailors; to me, however, it seems entirely plausible. Other writers—John Lawson (1714), for instance, and Hamilton McMillan (1880)—have mentioned the legend, going back to the middle sixteenth century, of shipwrecks and rescued sailors in Croatan Indian lore; while Dalmatian maritime lore has it that the Ragusan ships which sailed for the New World in the middle of the sixteenth century never returned.

But all this being as it may, the next highlight in the Yugoslav story in America occurs in 1683, when Baron Ivan Rataj, a young Croatian nobleman who had become a Catholic priest and missionary, was scalped by the Indians in New Mexico. Having arrived about ten years before, with the Spaniards via Mexico, he left valuable notes on his explorations in the Southwest.

Around 1715 some twelve hundred Croatian and Slovenian Protestants who had been living in Prussia—descendants of refugees from religious and political persecution in Austria after the anti-Reformation edict and the failure of peasant revolts in Croatia and Slovenia—came to Georgia in their search for freedom of worship and material well-being. They settled at the spot where the creek which they named Ebenezer flows into the Savannah River, and undertook the cultivation of the silkworm, which had been the family industry before their parents and grandparents moved to Prussia. For one hundred and fifty years the community throve in a quiet way, then the Civil War hit it fatally. Now only a cemetery with Slavic names on the headstones remains as a monument to this early Yugoslav immigrant group.

Through the second third of the eighteenth century, a missionary whom Spanish colonial history knows as Consago Gonzales, and also as an anthropologist, botanist, zoologist, geographer, illustrator, linguist, orator and poet, was active in Mexico and California. He drew the map of Lower California which was the only dependable guide to that region for nearly two centuries. Padre Gonzales was really Ferdinand Konschak, a native of Croatia.

Judging by their names (Gorshé, Vavtar, Vertnar, Cherne and Vidmar), a handful of Slovenian soldiers served in George Washington's Revolutionary Forces. How and why they got here, nobody knows. Also there were then in New York two Slovenians named Volk, the brothers Thomas and Abraham. Both married women of Anglo-Saxon and Dutch strains. One of Thomas' numerous grandsons, Leonard Volk, who became a well-known sculptor around 1860, was a relative-by-marriage of Stephen A. Douglas and also a friend of Abraham Lincoln, who for a while lived in the same boardinghouse with him in Chicago. His son Douglas Volk was a distinguished portrait painter late in the nineteenth and early in the twentieth century.

Another Croatian missionary, Joseph Kundek, arrived in 1838 and took a leading part in the development of a number of midwestern towns, notably Ferdinand and Jasper, in Dubois County, Indiana. Americans often have the idea that immigrants from such places as Croatia invariably came over here merely to make money to send "back home." But a little over a hundred years ago when Father Kundek began his work, people in many parts of Croatia were contributing to the "maintenance of churches and schools in America." The archives of the Archbishopric of Zagreb, capital of Croatia, show that fifty-seven thousand florins (about ten thousand dollars) were sent to the United States in the 1830s.

An exceptionally interesting immigrant was a Slovenian priest, Frederick Baraga, who in the early 1830s plunged into the wilderness of Upper Michigan and Northern Minnesota, intent on working among the Chippewa and Ojibwa Indians. Only son of a relatively well-to-do family in Carniola, he had sold his property and brought the proceeds with him. Later he sent a stream of leaflets to parishes in Slovenia appealing for money to support his projects; and for years Slovenian peasants were dropping coins in collection boxes marked "For Baraga's Indians." One of these printed leaflets is in the Minnesota Historical Society's museum in St. Paul.

Baraga learned the Chippewa-Ojibwa tongue, then worked out a grammar of it. He translated the Bible, and wrote two religious books in Chippewa.

A few years ago, on an Indian reservation in Baraga County, Michigan, I asked a sad-faced, middle-aged Chippewa what he knew of Baraga, who had died in 1868 as the first bishop of the Sault Ste. Marie and Marquette Diocese. "My father and grandfather often spoke of him," the Indian replied. "For thirty-five years he walked hundreds of miles every few months through the virgin forests of this region—often alone, sometimes with an Indian companion; sleeping in the woods like an Indian. My grandfather knew him well and used to say that Baraga moved among us as though"—lifting a hand before his face and forming the thumb and forefinger into a ring—"as though he saw something before him."

"What?" I asked. "What did he see?"

"I don't know," said the Chippewa. "Something like a light that guided him. Whatever it was, he followed it all the time he was among us. My grandfather said Baraga was completely and always good to the Indians and really wished them well and tried to help them. He respected the Indians as human beings, respected our language and customs, also our shortcomings in the strange new world growing up around us. He stood up for our rights; he went to the governor of Michigan in our behalf, and to Washington; he tried to make the corrupt Indian agents mend their ways. He strove hard to raise the level of the tribes so the White man could not exploit us, but would have to respect us too."

Baraga saw that the incursion of White people would doom the Indians unless they established permanent settlements and added agri-

culture and other pursuits to their hunting and fishing. So he spent
many years trying to teach the Ojibwas and Chippewas how to plow
and harrow and sow and reap. He started churches and schools. Some of
these he built with his own hands, even after he became bishop. A first-
class carpenter, he taught the trade to the Indians. He brought in
brother missionaries from Slovenia. A few were almost as good as he;
he made them see that "something" before them.

Here and there Baraga succeeded for a time; in the long run, however, the odds were too heavy against him and against the Red man.
He could not quell the rapacity of the new mining and timber industries which in the next three-quarters of a century turned the beautiful
and rich Upper Michigan area into a ghost region. He could not keep
out the "fire-water" that the Pale Face used in trading operations with
the Indian. Washington was unresponsive; Indian agents were too
deeply mired in corruption.

But Baraga made a profound impression; the memory of him and
some of his fellow Slovenian missionaries survives to this day. His attitude toward the Indian is now recognized as sound. In the 1930s, with
John Collier as Commissioner of Indian Affairs, the United States
government began to put into effect the policy and the practices that
Baraga started a hundred years before.

The Slovenian missionaries made America known to the plain people
in Yugoslav areas of Austria, and a few Slovenians who were not missionaries came over late in the 1840s and 1850s. Some settled on the
land in Minnesota. They participated in the founding of Brockway, a
town north of St. Paul.

Most of the others who came at that time had been pack-peddlers
in the Old World, traveling with their wares—jewelry, religious medals,
rosaries and the like—over eastern and central Europe, where no doubt
they also heard about America. They continued pack-peddling in the
United States, with the small town of Chicago as their business base.
Walking distances which they could not have imagined in the old
country, they sold their goods among the pioneers and Indians in
Wisconsin, Michigan, Iowa, Nebraska and Minnesota. Some did well;
one, John Gorshé, bought up real estate in the Chicago Loop and was
subsequently considered a millionaire. The few who knew how to write
sent letters back to Slovenia full of wonder at the size and wealth of
America and the opportunities it offered. In the 1860s and the '70s,
through pack-peddlers and priests, news about the copper and iron
mines opening in Michigan and Minnesota filtered to the old country.
This set off the first substantial flow of immigration from Slovenia
and inland Croatia.

Meantime, in fact since the start of the nineteenth century, Croatians from Dalmatia were sailing regularly to the United States in their own windjammers. New Orleans was their favorite port of call; many quit the sea there, married and settled down, and their descendants, reinforced by more recent immigrants, now constitute a sizable group along the Gulf, especially active in the fishing and canning industries.

Other Dalmatians went through the Straits of Magellan to California, which appealed to them very much; climatically and topographically it was so like Dalmatia. Indeed, it seems that a Ragusan ship had already reached the Pacific Coast by way of India at the beginning of the eighteenth century, some sixty years before the American Revolution, when few people on the Atlantic seaboard had even heard of California. The crew of this vessel is said to have settled somewhere south of what is now San Francisco.

Dalmatians joined in the Gold Rush. Then a good many took to farming and fruit-growing. In Pajaro Valley they transformed some twelve thousand wild acres into orchards, creating what for a while was known as "New Dalmatia." Jack London described it with admiration in *The Valley of the Moon.*

The famous apple industry of northern California had its start in the town of Watsonville in the 1870s when Mark Rubasa, a Dalmatian immigrant, went into business there as an apple dealer. In 1883 Steve Mitrovich of Fresno imported one thousand fig cuttings from his native village. Nine years later, at the Columbian Exposition in Chicago, his figs—called "Adriatics"—won first prize. Now they are a big business. Other Dalmatians brought to California special Dalmatian plums and grapes, the foundation of modern agricultural-industrial enterprises. A few raised apricots and lettuce on a large scale.

Still other Dalmatians went into fishing in California waters and later along Puget Sound and the coast of British Columbia and Alaska. Today their several hundred fishing vessels, for the most part owned cooperatively by the crews, supply the large tuna, sardine, salmon and mackerel canneries belonging to Yugoslav Americans. By and large, owing to the adventurous, enterprising spirit which goes with seafaring traditions, the Dalmatians did rather better by themselves than the other Yugoslav immigrant groups. Several took to shipbuilding on the Coast.

The inland Croatians, like the Slovenians and Slavonians, Bosnians and Herzegovinians, Montenegrins and other Serbians, were essentially people of the soil, slower than the Dalmatians, grubbers with toil-eager hands, inured through centuries to sparse living and endless hardship.

Arriving by the thousands annually in the 1870s, by the tens of thousands after 1880, they were drawn into the toughest jobs of the large and expanding heavy industries. Like the Poles, Czechs and Slovaks, the Russians, Hungarians and Lithuanians, they were a valuable addition to American manpower in mining, steel and iron and construction. They were mostly peasants but they rapidly picked up American production methods.

During the 1870s and 1880s most of the Yugoslavs headed for northern Michigan and Minnesota to work long hours for as little as $1.25 a day in dangerous copper and iron mines. Hundreds perished or were crippled in frequent accidents, for in that period there were few of the safety devices that protect miners nowadays. But most of them survived. After two or three years of work, many returned to the old country. Some were minus an arm or leg or lung, but carried a roll of hard-earned dollars to pay the debts on their homeland farms. Others sent for their wives and girls and began to raise American families.

Many of the Yugoslavs entering the United States during the last three decades of the nineteenth century, with the upper Great Lakes regions as their destination, stopped enroute in New York where they became dock workers and tug-boat crews in New York harbor; in Cleveland, Chicago, Joliet, Milwaukee. Instead of going into copper or iron mining, they went into a variety of industrial work, started Yugoslav "colonies" in different cities, and sent passage money to relatives in the old country.

In subsequent decades immigrants heading for Cleveland or Chicago stopped instead in Pittsburgh or in the Pennsylvania anthracite region or in the soft-coal towns of West Virginia and southern Ohio. Or they went into the coal pits of Illinois and Kansas, or into the new copper mines in Montana and Utah. Or they followed highway and railroad building all over the continent.

The 1940 census counts 161,000 foreign-born Yugoslav Americans and aliens and 221,700 native Americans of Yugoslav parentage. But these figures are low; other estimates, counting the native-American children and grandchildren, some of whom have but one Yugoslav forbear, run between six hundred thousand and a million. The Croatian group is the largest; next come the Slovenians, then the Serbians.

Perhaps two-thirds of the Yugoslav element live in and around the great industrial centers of Cleveland, Pittsburgh, Chicago, Milwaukee, Detroit, St. Louis and New York. The rest are to be found in smaller colonies in and around New Orleans and Galveston; in Biloxi, Mississippi; in the Los Angeles harbor district at San Pedro; in Los Angeles proper, in San Francisco, Fresno, Sacramento, Portland, Tacoma and

Seattle; in Bisbee, Arizona; in Butte, Helena and Anaconda, Montana; in the Utah, Colorado, Minnesota, Michigan, Kansas, Illinois, Ohio, West Virginia and Pennsylvania mining towns; in such centers as Akron and Youngstown; on farms in Wisconsin, Minnesota, Michigan and the state of Washington. In Upper Michigan, Slovenian immigrants founded a farming community called Traunik—the Slovenian word for "meadow."

Since the 1870s Yugoslav immigrants—humble people capable of physical endurance to the nth degree—have been working in all of the basic American industrial processes and enterprises, digging endless quantities of coal and ore, felling and sawing endless feet of timber, turning out endless tons of steel. Hundreds of thousands are dead now, or are old; their energy is manifest in America's skyscrapers, bridges, rail lines, locomotives, trucks, cars, machines of all kinds.

But the Yugoslav immigrants' contribution to the material greatness of this country was not only that of brawn. If mining and steel production and machines are more efficient in 1945 than they were, say, in 1885 it is partly because Yugoslav workers have invented many devices now employed in our industries. Thousands of inventions in the Patent Office in Washington are registered in Slavic names.

The names of Michael Pupin and Nikola Tesla, both Serbian immigrants, are famous. Both came here in 1884. Pupin told about his inventions in long-distance telephony, and about his personal rise, in his autobiography *From Immigrant to Inventor*, a best seller and Pulitzer Prize winner in 1925. Full of honors and financial success, he died ten years later. There is a Pupin Institute at Columbia University.

Tesla was as unlike Pupin as he could be. A modest man to whom money and public renown had no meaning, he was a sort of scientific saint, an inspired poet-physicist. Many who know his achievement and knew him personally regard Tesla as a second Leonardo da Vinci; they think him the greatest man of the Industrial Era, which was approaching a climax about the time he arrived in America in the 1880s, already a full-fledged scientist, his native genius trained in European universities. Of his inventions, seven hundred are formally credited to him; the others he did not bother to register. Today nearly everything electrical bears his touch. The Tesla induction motor runs practically everything that moves electrically. He foresaw the harnessing of atomic energy decades prior to the fateful bomb burst over Hiroshima in the summer of 1945.

Another scientist, Dr. A. B. Behrend, once said: "Were we to eliminate from our industrial world the results of Tesla's work, the wheels of industry would cease to turn, our electric trains and cars would stop, our towns would be dark, our mills and factories dead and idle. So far-reaching is his work that it has become the warp and woof of industry."

During the last twenty years of his life Tesla was almost completely ignored by the American public. In the middle 1930s the government of Yugoslavia gave him a pension. Early in 1943 he died in a New York hotel room. The following autumn a Liberty ship named *Nikola Tesla* was launched. In 1944 the first biography of Tesla was published in New York: *Prodigal Genius*, by John J. O'Neill, science editor of the New York *Herald Tribune*, who knew him for many years as a discoverer of scientific truths and one of the strangest human beings that ever lived—"unquestionably one of the world's greatest geniuses" who "created the modern era" . . . "an admixture of a Jupiter or a Thor who hurled the shafts of lightning; an Ajax who defied the Jovian bolts; a Prometheus who transmuted energy into electricity to spread over the earth; an Aurora who would light the skies as a terrestrial electric lamp; a Mazda who created a sun in the tube; a Hercules who shook the earth with his mechanical vibrations; a Mercury who bridged the ambient realms of space with his wireless waves, and a Hermes who gave birth to an electrical soul in the earth that set it pulsating from pole to pole" . . . "superman, a self-made superman" who loved pigeons.

In the field of education the name of Henry Suzzallo, one-time president of the University of Washington in Seattle, is prominent. At his death early in the 1930s he was president of the Carnegie Foundation for the Advancement of Teaching. He was born in California of Croatian parents (not Italians, as erroneously assumed by the press). His family name in the old country was Zucalo.

Other outstanding Americans of Yugoslav origin or descent, some dead, most of them living:

Croatian: Dr. Milislav Demerec, genetist at the Cold Springs Harbor, Long Island, research center of the Carnegie Institution; Matthew M. Braidech, engineer specializing in industrial water supply and stream pollution problems; Zlatko Balokovich, violinist; Zinka Milanov and Marjorie Radovan, singers; Maxo Vanka, Raymond Prohaska and Desha, artists; Mia Slavenska and Tashamira, dancers; Isaac M. Altaraz, educator; Peter Coe (original name: Knego), movie actor; Colonel Emil Antonovich, construction engineer in the United States Army Quartermaster Corps; Joe Jurich, head of the C.I.O. Fishermen's Union, covering both the Atlantic and Pacific coasts; John Rados and Joe Martinac,

Pacific Coast shipbuilders; Hugo Tomich, Chicago metal manufacturer; and Martin J. Bogdanovich, Nick Bez and Marcus Nalley, food processors. Mr. Nalley's plant in Tacoma is famous for its sound, imaginatively decent working conditions.

Serbian: Paul R. Radosavljevich, chairman of the Experimental Education Department at New York University; Nikola Terbo (original name: Trbojevich), inventor with many patents in the automobile industry, a nephew and student of Tesla's; Stoyan Pribichevich, journalist and war correspondent; Vaso Trivanovich, economist in the United States government service; Donald R. Perry (original name: Dragoslav Perishich), ex-assistant commissioner in the United States Immigration and Naturalization Service; George Perazich, industrial engineer with the United Nations Relief and Rehabilitation Administration; Savo Radulovich and Borislav Bogdanovich, artists.

Slovenian: Peter Ruppe, Arizona and Michigan mining operator; Frank J. Lausche, governor of Ohio; Harvey G. Prusheck, artist; the Reverend Francis Jager, for many years chief of the Bee Culture Division of the Minnesota Experiment Station at the University of Minnesota Farm; John Jager, Minneapolis architect and builder; Anton Subelj, singer; Anne Erste, a Federal Reserve agent; Michael Lah, movie cartoon animator; and Gus Korach, workingman and racket-buster.

Born in 1896, Gus Korach comes from the village of Vaché, Slovenia —only son of a widowed mother so poor that she barely managed to raise him. At thirteen he went to work as a *pastir*, or cowherd. Then in 1912 his mother inherited three hundred dollars in American money from a relative who had gone to the United States. She invested part of it in her son, sending him "*chez luzho*— across the pond."

Gus, now sixteen, went straight to an aunt in Marianna, Pennsylvania. Her miner husband got him a job in the pits, and Gus dug coal for a few years, quitting in 1916 because he didn't like to work underground. The next year he spent as a hobo, roaming around the United States as far west as Oklahoma. Finally he wound up in Cleveland, which had the largest Slovenian-immigrant colony in the United States. He liked Cleveland fine, and found a job. He was going on twenty-one.

Gus felt a vivid thrill when the United States declared war on Germany and Austria-Hungary in April 1917. He had been following President Wilson's ideas reported in *Glas Naroda*, *Prosveta*, *Proletarec* and other progressive Slovenian-language papers which he saw in the reading room of the Slovenian National Home on St. Clair Avenue at 64th Street—then as now the center of the Slovenian neighborhood.

Gus enlisted and went to France. But he didn't get a chance to fight; one sub-zero night while on guard duty behind the lines his feet froze and he had to go to the hospital.

Eventually he became a citizen of the United States, and after his discharge in 1919 returned to Cleveland. He got a job with White Motors which turned out to be fairly steady until the Depression in 1930. He married and had two children and acquired a little house in back of the Slovenian National Home. Gus was just another fellow, wanting little beyond a chance to work, to raise his family, to visit with friends, to see a ball game now and then—and in all probability no one except his neighbors and a few of the men at the plant would have heard of him had it not been for the rackets which during 1930-1938 infested the city of Cleveland.

In that period the annual "take" of the "mobs," part of which was turned over to police officials, exceeded thirty million dollars. Among the most successful was the "cemetery mob," so called because it sold cemetery lots through a complicated technique which involved apparently legitimate savings and loan associations and the unauthorized use of well-known, reputable names. Racketeers operated in new-immigrant districts because the thrifty "foreigners" still had money in the bank or in the mattress in spite of the Depression. Also the immigrants, not yet very familiar with American ways, were not likely to seek legal redress against the "Americans" when any unpleasantness arose.

At any rate, with thousands of other Clevelanders, Gus Korach got taken for several hundred dollars. At first the "investment" looked perfectly all right. Then people in his block began to sense that something was wrong, but nobody did anything; word got around that the "suckers" had better keep quiet. A few "suckers" who complained to the different "savings and loan associations" were given their money back just to show the business was on the level; others were thrown out if they got too insistent. If a specially stubborn "investor" started court action, he was either bought off or terrorized into withdrawing the suit. The city authorities were singularly indifferent to all this.

When Gus demanded his money back in the summer of 1936, a racketeer "official" of the "association" he dealt with told him, "You'll get it when the snow flies." Fellow victims told him to forget the whole thing: he didn't stand a chance against the racketeers who were hand in glove with the police. Rumors were being spread by the gangsters that some of the biggest people in the city—"Americans"—were "in on this" and if the "foreigners" knew what was good for them—

Gus was forty now—an awkward retiring man with a shy smile. But he couldn't stop thinking about the rackets. He figured out that the people in his block alone had been swindled for some eighty-six thousand dollars. That was a lot of money in any language for crooks to get away with.

When the first snow fell the following winter, Gus went back to the racketeers' office and said, "Well, how about it?"—pointing to the snowflakes caressing the window pane. They laughed at him.

On the way home, walking in the snow, Gus passed the Cleveland Press Building—and stopped. He had been reading the Press at the tavern where he went once or twice a week for a glass of beer. He liked old Jack Raper's column and the articles by-lined Clayton Fritchey. So he took the squeaky elevator to the editorial floor and asked for Raper, who was out; but Fritchey, a young reporter and feature writer, an old-line American, listened to Gus' story with mounting interest.

"By gosh," Gus said, "this ain't Europe—this ain't Austria. They can't treat people like this in America. Suppose I'm not very bright, can I help it? Am I supposed to be cheated because I'm dumb and a 'foreigner'—which I ain't. I mean I'm not a foreigner, I'm a citizen of the United States. Are people like me free game for the racketeers? Have all the cops sold out to 'em?"

Fritchey told Gus to come back in the afternoon. He talked with the editors and when Gus returned he said the Press had assigned him to the story.

Then they went to work. Some of the victims in Gus' block and up and down St. Clair Avenue were afraid to cooperate till Fritchey got Frank J. Lausche—Cleveland-born son of Slovenian-immigrant parents, then a judge—to persuade them to tell the truth and stick to it, regardless of what the racketeers might try to do.

The publicity brought on three grand jury investigations resulting in the arrest, indictment, conviction and long-term imprisonment of dozens of racketeers, while hundreds of others skipped town. The "mobs" were broken. Several police officials, including a captain who had received $125,000 of the "take," were exposed, tried and jailed; others resigned to forestall investigation; the police department was reorganized from top to bottom. In fact—as Clayton Fritchey, now publisher of a New Orleans paper, put it in the spring 1941 Common Ground magazine—the whole city of Cleveland was "turned upside down; on second thought, perhaps I should say right side up. . . ."

Fritchey called his article "Cleveland's Humble Hercules," and went on to say: "The general public is unaware of him, even in Cleveland; in fact, Gus' own idea of the dent he has made in his community is extremely sketchy. He asks and expects no credit for his achievement.

"It is generally conceded, however, among those who know the innermost workings of Cleveland's political life that except for Gus the city's now nationally known safety director, Eliot Ness, could never have accomplished a civic clean-up to rival Thomas Dewey's success in New York; while Harold H. Burton, Ohio's United States Senator, also owes him a debt, for without the events that Gus set in motion he could never have rolled up the majorities which made him twice mayor of Cleveland and finally sent him to Washington. And—to stretch the list no further—without Gus, *The Cleveland Press* would not have won a Pulitzer Prize in 1937."

Fritchey implied that the prize should have gone to Gus. "He worked with me in his leisure time. After doing a hard day's work, he would join me in the late afternoon and stay at my side until midnight. Day after day and week after week, we continued our investigation. It was Gus who got us into homes, who interpreted, who soothed alarms, who made it possible, finally to get coherent and effective testimony. . . . A rolling stone may not gather moss; but Gus Korach's snowflakes certainly turned into an avalanche. Only last fall [1940], in Judge Lausche's courtroom, the last of the big rackets that used to prey on the people of the city was broken by a slew of convictions."

In 1940 Lausche was elected and in 1942 re-elected mayor of Cleveland by the largest majorities in the city's history, and in 1944 was elevated to the governorship of Ohio—also partly thanks to the string of events started by Gus' disinclination to be an unprotesting victim of criminal corruption.

Hundreds of Yugoslav Americans are lawyers, doctors, dentists, teachers and local and district labor union leaders. Hundreds own grocery stores, meat markets and other small businesses. Many have excelled in baseball, football, swimming and diving, boxing, walking marathons and other sports. In the past ten years they have had at least ten All-American football players. Some of the top college athletic coaches are of Yugoslav descent.

Croatians and Slovenians are Catholics, while Serbians belong to the Serbian Orthodox Church. All three groups have scores of churches throughout the country.

They maintain a number of large fraternal-insurance organizations, started back in the last quarter of the nineteenth century when workers, particularly the foreign-born, had little social or economic security. Each of these organizations publishes a daily or weekly newspaper in the old-country language, Croatians and Slovenians using the Latin alphabet, Serbians the Cyrillic. In addition, there are hundreds of local singing, dramatic and cultural societies. The inclusive United Committee of South-Slavic Americans, formed in 1943, brings together the majority of the Yugoslav element and takes in also the less numerous Bulgarian and Macedonian American groups who consider themselves of South-Slavic background.

The United Committee came into public notice throughout the United States in connection with the general American interest in Yugoslavia during World War II. The Committee took the initiative in explaining to the government and people of the United States the forces behind the Partisan-Chetnik struggle for control of the country, and was instrumental in selling more than sixty million dollars' worth of United States war bonds among South-Slavic Americans.

About fifteen thousand Slovenians and Croatians arrived in the 1920s from the Yugoslav regions around the port city of Trst (Trieste) which international chicanery assigned to Italy after World War I. These people emigrated to escape the anti-Slavic terror which began in those territories in 1920 when Count Carlo Sforza—later well known in the United States as a "liberal"—was a leading member of the Italian government. That terror was intensified under Mussolini, but because it began in the Sforza period the Yugoslav emigrants from Italy labeled themselves "the Sforza refugees." Many barely escaped with their lives.

Most Croatian, Serbian and Slovenian immigrants are American citizens. Having come over before World War I, the majority are between fifty-five and seventy-five years of age; about fifty thousand of their children and grandchildren were in the United States' Army and Navy during 1941-1945. Numerous Yugoslav American families had between four and seven boys and girls in the service. Matt Babich of Detroit, for instance, had six in the armed forces and four working in essential war jobs.

Nearly all the American soldiers of Yugoslav background in World War I were immigrants. One of them, Captain Louis Cukela of the Marines, was the only man in that war to receive two Congressional Medals of Honor. Two other Yugoslavs, Aiex Mandusich and Jacob Mestrovich, were decorated with Congressional Medals.

Among the first American casualties of World War II was Louis Dobnikar, a Slovenian American from Cleveland, a watertender on the U.S.S. *Kearny*, the destroyer torpedoed in the North Atlantic on October 17, 1941. Two Yugoslav Americans were awarded the Congressional Medal of Honor in 1944: Peter Tomich, chief watertender of the U.S.S. *Utah*, who died at Pearl Harbor, and Lieutenant Mitchell

Paige (original Serbian name: Milan Pejich) of the Marines, who killed one hundred and ten of the enemy on Guadalcanal, then remarked, "I did what I could." In 1945 First Lieutenant John J. Tominac of Johnstown, Pennsylvania, was awarded the same decoration for exceptional heroism in France.

In a sea battle off Guadalcanal in November 1942, Lieutenant Commander Milton Pavlic, a Slovenian immigrant and Annapolis graduate, lost his life on the U.S.S. *South Dakota* after he had helped put three enemy warships and thirty-two planes out of action. A new destroyer was named the U.S.S. *Pavlic*.

Sergeant George W. Mirich, a semi-pro ball-player from Portland, Oregon, the "one-man army" of the Attu campaign in 1943, was awarded the Distinguished Service Cross for cleaning out singlehanded with machine gun and grenades seven Japanese pill-boxes defending a strategic pass. He is of Serbian descent.

On November 8, 1944, Captain George S. Wuchinich of Ridgway, Pennsylvania, son of Serbian immigrant parents, attached to the Office of Strategic Services, was given the Distinguished Service Cross "for extraordinary heroism in connection with secret military operations in the Balkans [Slovenia] against an armed enemy during the period from November 28, 1943, to July 26, 1944. Captain Wuchinich's descent by parachute into enemy-occupied territory, his leadership, and his resolute conduct in the face of great peril, throughout an extended period, in the successful accomplishment of an extremely hazardous and difficult mission, exemplified the finest traditions of the armed forces of the United States."

Early in May 1944 Lieutenant J. Luksich of Joliet, Illinois, commander of a P-51 Mustang, shot down five Nazi planes in a single afternoon. He had earlier destroyed fifteen enemy planes, eight in the air, seven on the ground. His parents are immigrants from Yugoslavia.

During World War II the bulk of the immigrants from Yugoslav lands and most of their American-born children worked in basic war industries; many of them fourteen, sixteen, even eighteen hours a day. They seem to excel especially in steel, machine tools and automotive-vehicle manufacture. They are wizards at the delicate and dangerous task of relining blast furnaces. In 1943, in the Youngstown Sheet and Tube plant at Indiana Harbor, Indiana, a crew consisting mostly of Yugoslav immigrants relined a furnace in twenty-eight days, the previous record being around sixty days. The straw-boss of the crew was John Starcevich, who had come from Croatia thirty-odd years before and whose son Max, now a high school athletic coach in Seattle, was on the All-American football team in 1938.

I am of the Yugoslav group, of its Slovenian section, and so perhaps I know it more intimately than the others. It includes some unsound elements. In Cleveland, for instance, there is a Slovenian-language paper which in 1936 urged its naturalized readers to vote Democratic because the Republicans had freed the Negroes who now competed with Whites for jobs. During the Spanish Civil War the same sheet favored Franco and in 1943-1945 supported those in Slovenia who collaborated with the Germans. In Pittsburgh a Serbian-language paper pursues a course I can describe only as Balkan medievalism gone corrupt in the service of dark forces in America and abroad. There is a faction in the Croatian group which has no relevance to anything desirable in the United States or Yugoslavia. Similar factions exist in other groups. I did not refer to them in the other chapters, or mentioned them only incidentally, because I believe they are not strong enough to win out in the long run. Being reaction gone crackpot, they are close spiritual-political kin to corresponding old-line American factions, whose adherents regard them as "foreigners." All together they will clutter up the scene awhile longer, then—

Most Yugoslav Americans are politically progressive. Their attitude toward the problems facing America and the world was stated by Nikola Tesla in 1942: "Out of this war . . . a new world must be born, . . . a world in which there shall be no exploitation of the weak by the strong, of the good by the evil; where there will be no humiliation of the poor by the violence of the rich; where the products of intellect, science and art will serve society for the betterment and beautification of life, and not the individual for achieving wealth. This new world shall not be a world of the down-trodden and humiliated, but of free men and free nations, equal in dignity and respect for man.'

X: AMERICANS FROM NORWAY

A S I SEE it, the story of the American people is primarily a saga of groups and individuals who left some situation in order to come to something they hoped would be better, and who—on the whole— have not been disappointed. Begun a good while ago, throbbing with many themes, held together by innumerable threads, the story is vast, with many chapters, all somewhat the same, but also each very different from the others, and none yet definitely ended.

The Norwegian chapter is a large one, but it is simpler and can be told in fewer words than some of the others.

Except for Ireland, no European country has given the United States so high a proportion of its people as Norway. Between 1845 and 1945 about eight hundred thousand have come to America.

The 1940 census counted 924,688 persons born in Norway or with at least one parent born there. Non-official calculations run much higher, usually around two million. In 1939, Sons of Norway, a fraternal insurance organization with headquarters in Minneapolis, issued a pamphlet estimating that there are "now in America upwards of three million people of Norwegian extraction, or as many as there are in Norway." These higher figures include third- and fourth-generation Americans, most of whom are mixed with other strains—like Harold E. Stassen, ex-governor of Minnesota, a commander in the Navy during World War II and a member of the American Delegation to the San Francisco Security Conference in the spring of 1945, who is a third-generation Norwegian-German-Czech American and as such of course also belongs in similar estimates of German and Czech groups.

The Norwegian record in the New World reaches back to the year 876 when Gunnbjorn discovered Greenland, to the year 983 when Erik the Red settled there, to the year 1000 when his son Leif Erikson came to the North American continent.

It is quite generally recognized that in the autumn of 1000 the Norse voyager Leif Erikson, sailing from Greenland or Iceland, made a landing at what is now New England and named the place Vinland or Wineland for the grapes his men found growing there. A painting entitled "Leif Erikson Discovers America" hangs in the Statuary Hall at the Capitol in Washington; his statue stands in at least half a dozen American cities, and dozens of others have named parks, boulevards and squares after this early Viking explorer. In 1930 when the Icelandic parliament celebrated its thousandth year, the Congress of the United States sent a statue of Leif Erikson to Iceland. Five years later President Roosevelt signed a Congressional resolution making October 9th the national Leif Erikson Day.

Early in the eleventh century a Norse settlement of about one hundred and sixty persons was maintained for three years somewhere in what is now Massachusetts, under the leadership of Thorfinn Karlsevne, whose wife Gudrid gave birth to the first White child in America. The colony ended disastrously. But long afterward, Norse seafarers kept coming over to "Vinland" from Iceland and Greenland.

In fact there is evidence that in 1362 one expedition made its way from "Vinland" through the St. Lawrence and the Great Lakes, or through Hudson Bay and the Nelson River and Lake Winnepeg, all the way to present-day Minnesota. The evidence is the so-called Kensington Stone with its runic inscription, found in 1898 near Kensington, Minnesota. The two-hundred-pound slab has been a controversial subject among scholars ever since, one group asserting that it is a fake perpetrated by Norwegian immigrants who settled in Minnesota in the nineteenth century. Since the early 1930s, however, there has been less and less doubt that the Kensington Stone is authentic. This conclusion is to be ascribed primarily to Hjalmar R. Holand, a careful scholar with a thorough knowledge of early Scandinavian history who has devoted most of his adult life to studying the matter and who has published two books about it—*The Kensington Stone* (1932) and *Westward From Vinland* (1940).

When the Kensington Stone was discovered in 1898, it was held fast by the roots of a felled aspen which was at least forty years old. The first Scandinavian immigrants to reach Minnesota arrived in the middle of the nineteenth century, and it is almost inconceivable that any of them was sufficiently erudite to fake an elaborate inscription in runes, even if one could imagine a motive for the hoax. The inscription has all the appearance of being centuries old. Its nine lines hint at the story of eight Goths (Swedes) and twenty-three Northmen (Norwegians) who, exploring the region, camped by a lake two days' journey from the stone. Some of the party went fishing; when they returned to camp they found ten of their companions dead. There is a prayer: "Ave Maria save us from evil" and the year 1362.

In *Westward From Vinland* Mr. Holand has it that this undoubtedly was the Paul Knutson expedition which, according to Norwegian records, left Norway in 1355 and did not return till 1364.

In 1619 King Christian IV of Denmark and Norway dispatched an expedition to find the Northwest Passage. Under the Norwegian captain Jens Munk, the party reached Hudson Bay and declared Canada a Danish possession—"Nova Dania." But this stab at colonization never developed.

About the same time some three hundred Norwegians, mostly sailors, settled among the Dutch in New Amsterdam. In the course of their assimilation many assumed Dutch names, but old Netherlander records give their Norwegian birthplaces. Several of these colonists acquired large land holdings on Manhattan Island.

The first Vanderbilt in America, Jan Arentzen van der Bilt, married a girl named Anneken Hendricks, born in Bergen, Norway. The first official midwife in New Amsterdam was Trine Jans, a Norwegian whose daughter, another Anneken, married the Reverend Everhardus Bogardus. (See p. 98.) Other "oldest families" of New York have an ancestor or two among the early Norwegian colonists in New Netherland.

A small number of Norwegians, also mostly sailors, arrived during the seventeenth and eighteenth centuries. A few settled among the Swedes in the Delaware Valley.

From 1740 on there were a good many Norwegians, Swedes, Danes and Icelanders in Philadelphia. In 1769 they formed a Scandinavian Society of which George Washington was an honorary member and whose first president, Abraham Markoe, was a Norwegian.

In the Revolutionary War men of Norwegian birth or extraction rendered, as might be expected, particularly valuable services at sea. Several fought with John Paul Jones on his famous *Bon Homme Richard*. Jones introduced one of them, John Johnson, to General Washington after the war, stating that Johnson was one of the best seamen he had ever known.

For about forty-five years after the Revolution very few Norwegians came to America. Then suddenly in 1825 there began what is now called the "modern" Norwegian immigration—a movement of epic proportions.

On October 15th of that year the New York *Daily Advertiser* ran a front-page story about the arrival from Norway, six days before, of the thirty-eight-ton sloop *Restaurationen* with forty-six passengers, including a baby girl born en route. They were led by a man named Lars Larson who, with a few of the others, had recently been converted from the official Lutheran faith to the Quaker faith. The resultant persecution by the State church was partially responsible for their emigration.

The group sailed from Norway on July 4th. The sloop—"the Norwegian Mayflower"—took fourteen weeks to make the voyage.

The party was bound for Orleans County, New York, "where an agent, who came over some time since, purchased a tract of land" on the shores of Lake Ontario not far from Rochester. The "agent" was a remarkable if eccentric fellow in his middle years, Cleng Peerson, whom many Norwegian Americans now call "the Pathfinder."

For nine years the immigrants—later referred to as "the sloopers"—tried to establish a community on Lake Ontario, but they lacked adequate means and equipment to cope with the rigorous natural conditions. Dissatisfaction set in. The colonists began to heed the lively cry then heard all over the eastern states: Go West! So in 1834

Cleng Peerson, like a sort of Moses seeking a Promised Land, walked a thousand miles westward in search of a new location.

He reached Chicago, but didn't like the dismal little village named, though few people realize it, for the wild onions which grew in the surrounding swamps. He tramped south to near-by LaSalle County and there one day, hungry and very tired, he stretched out in the tall grass on a hillside overlooking a river. After a while he thanked God for having led his calloused feet to so pleasant a place, then fell asleep and in a dream, according to a Norwegian American historian, "saw the wild prairie changed into a cultivated region teeming with all kinds of grain and fruit most beautiful to behold."

Old Cleng trudged the thousand miles back East. By then some of the "sloopers" thought him a crackpot, but the rest listened eagerly to his description of the wonders of the West. And that same year most of them made their way to what became the Fox River settlement in Illinois.

(In the early summer of 1938 driving on U.S. 52 near Joliet, I saw a sign "To Norway" at the entrance to a gravel road. It led to a tiny hamlet on a low hill, the first permanent Norwegian community in America; and sure enough, there was Cleng Peerson's vision. For miles around spread extensive grain fields dotted with substantial farmhouses, and barns like cathedrals. Many of the elder farmers were the sons and daughters of the original settlers.)

Lars Larson, the original leader of the group, stayed in New York; he built a home in Rochester. His daughter, the girl born on the sloop *Restaurationen*, went West when she grew up; she died in Chicago in 1923—the last of the "sloopers."

In the 1830s and 1840s and even much later, life in Norway was a rugged proposition in more ways than one. Three-fourths to four-fifths of the people were peasant and fisher folk who, says an English traveler writing in 1885, got somewhere in "their struggle against iron nature" only "by dogged, persistent, indomitable toil and endurance, backed up in some cases by irrepressible daring." Besides, as in many European countries, there were no large industries to absorb the surplus population; the government was unprogressive, national affairs were controlled by some of the worst people in the country.

Under the circumstances America was a magnet. By the mid-1840s, fifteen years after the start of the "modern" immigration, above a thousand Norwegians were entering the United States each year. The number rose steadily to its peak in 1882, when nearly thirty thousand arrived.

In 1837 Bishop Jacob Neumann, one of Norway's leading Lutheran clergymen, admonished the population not to be lured to America. He warned of the dangerous voyage; he cited horrible examples of what had befallen earlier emigrants; he drew on the Bible for reasons why Norwegians should stay in Norway. But he failed to impress those infected with what he condemned as "the spirit of restlessness."

People avidly read or listened to such "America letters" as this, written in 1838 by one Hans Barlien, who had been in the United States about a year: "Now for the first time I am able to breathe freely. . . . No one is persecuted here because of his religious faith. . . . Pickpockets and lawyers, unscrupulous creditors, officials and vagabonds . . . are without power to harm the people here. No restrictions are set upon freedom of occupation; and everyone secures without hindrance the fruits of his own work."

In 1837 Ole Rynning, a man of above-average education, joined a party of America-bound emigrants. A year later his book, *True Account of America for the Information and Help of Peasant and Commoner*, was published in Norway. It was a practical guidebook, but indirectly it eulogized America as a place that offered opportunities for advancement to people who were not afraid of hard work and some risks. The little volume created a sensation in Norway and gave a powerful push to what soon turned into an exodus. Thousands were afflicted with "America fever." For decades the highways and byways of Norway teemed with groups of bundle-laden men and women heading for the next ship to America. On one April day in 1853 ten emigrant ships filled to capacity left Christiania Fjord.

Out of this great migration grew a cycle of folksongs sung on the road, while waiting for ships and at sea; for instance:

> And now farewell to all my folk and parish, .
> For I am going to America,
> To seek a happier life in the New World.
> There is no help for it,
> I must cross the sea—
> Life has become too hard here for poor folk.
>
> Farewell, now, O valley of Seljord;
> Farewell to church and wood and home.
> Farewell to parson and parish clerk,
> To kith and kin, and the lovely gardens at home.
> Would to God this were otherwise!
> For the old home stands grieving there.
> Let us hasten, hasten away!

From the point of view of the United States, particularly from that of the undeveloped West, the Norwegian immigrant—like the Swedish, German, Finnish, Irish and Czech newcomer—was well-nigh ideal. The stern nature of life in the old country had given him the personal fiber to meet the West's demands for endurance, patience, continual work and thrift. As a pioneer he was made to order.

Besides the Fox River settlement, other Norwegian centers or oases were established in the late 1830s in Illinois—even in Chicago—and they became way stations of the steady influx from abroad, part of which came via the St. Lawrence River and the Great Lakes. There in Illinois' northeastern corner the migrants paused to talk with people of their own nationality and get their first orientation in the New World.

The majority only paused. They were wound up to move farther on. This impulse to follow the sunset was a fierce obsession. Few gave any thought to settling east of Chicago. Some went to northern Michigan, into copper-mining; but the larger number joined the streams of people that flowed westward on foot, in river boats, on horseback, in covered wagons—often drawn by oxen.

The streams flowed into Wisconsin and Iowa, into Minnesota and the Dakotas, there to tackle the wilderness, break virgin soil, live in sod-houses for a few years, then build dwellings and schools and steepled Lutheran churches; to turn whole regions into flourishing farm communities.

The powerful impulse that gripped these people pushed them on from Minnesota and the Dakotas to Montana and Idaho, to Oregon and Washington, to northern California, where they raised food or went into forestry and lumbering, or into deep-sea fishing on the coast. Some moved to the outermost tip of America—to Alaska with its salmon and reindeer industries. Some got to Texas. But wherever they scattered in the West, the land drew to itself from eighty to ninety per cent of the Norwegian immigrants: forlorn, futureless peasants in the old country; here, with all their ups and downs, free farmers.

Most of the rest were skilled workers or artisans: carpenters, painters, machinists, printers, masons, bricklayers, tailors. They settled in towns, where they were highly regarded for their competence. A good many artisans stayed in the East; one now finds them or their descendants in New England, in New York and New Jersey, all the way down the Atlantic rim and some distance inland. One of them wrote: "If by some magic all houses constructed by Norwegian bricklayers and carpenters should topple, some of our cities would present the appearance of having been struck by a cyclone."

Norwegian immigrants participated in the Civil War, preponderantly on the Union side. Those who settled in Texas were divided on the slavery issue. During the 1850s and early '60s a few owned slaves, but seemed uncomfortable about it. A Texas woman named Mrs. Elsie Wärenskjold wrote against slavery in 1851; twelve years later her husband was assassinated for sympathizing with the Northern cause.

Several Norwegian-born veterans of the Union Army became prominent citizens. Perhaps the foremost among them was Knute Nelson. He was brought to the United States in 1849 at the age of six and grew up in Wisconsin. In 1861, while teaching in a district school near Madison, he enlisted in the Wisconsin Infantry, later converted to the 4th Wisconsin Cavalry. He was wounded during the siege of Port Hudson. After the war he took up law, was elected to the Wisconsin Assembly for two terms, then in 1871 moved to Alexandria, Minnesota, a frontier county seat, where he combined farming with legal practice and politics. A Republican, he was the first Norwegian immigrant to be elected to Congress (1882) after he had held a number of state offices. He was elected governor of Minnesota in 1892 and '94 and went to the United States Senate in '95. By successive re-elections he was Senator till his death in 1923. An honest man, conservative throughout, his name was associated with the Bankruptcy Act in 1898, the creation of the Department of Commerce and Labor in 1902, the Prohibition law and the defeat of the League of Nations proposal.

Later on, beginning in the 1890s, came a considerable number of highly trained engineers and technicians; some on the invitation of American firms. Olaf Hoff invented a new method of building underwater tunnels, Sverre Fahm was an authority on subway construction, E. A. Cappelen-Smith stood out in the metallurgical field, Knut Dahl invented a special kind of oil-burner which was adopted by the Navy, and when Clifford Holland died in the midst of building the Holland Tunnel linking New York and New Jersey, Ole Singstad took over and finished the stupendous project. About a third of the engineers engaged in building the Panama Canal were Norwegians.

The largest urban concentrations of Norwegian Americans are in the Twin Cities, in Seattle and Chicago, and in the Bay Ridge section of Brooklyn. The latter, which is the oldest, includes descendants of "the sloopers" who did not go West with Cleng Peerson. All of these "colonies" contain second-, third- and even fourth-generation Americans. Most of the grandchildren and great-grandchildren are not of "pure Norwegian" stock. Few of the foreign-born married outside their group, but many of their American-born sons and daughters did, and do.

Native Americans of full or part Norwegian extraction are now to be found all over the United States in most occupations. They are prominent in business and industry. Nearly every American merchant ship has one or two officers of Norwegian blood, often the master or chief engineer or first mate. A large part of the Norwegian colony in Brooklyn, as of that in Staten Island or Philadelphia or Boston, consists of seafarers.

There is hardly a college or university that has no Norwegian Americans on the faculty. Several colleges in the Middle West were founded by them—by the Norwegian Lutheran Church, to be exact: St. Olaf in Northfield, Minnesota, and Luther in Decorah, Iowa, are outstanding examples. The former is the home of the Norwegian American Historical Association (one of the best organizations of its kind) and of the famous St. Olaf Choir which, under the leadership of a grand old man, Dr. F. Melius Christiansen, has made many nationwide tours and sung over wide radio hookups.

All consequential intra-group Norwegian institutions are connected with the Lutheran Church. During 1840-1925 clergymen were the group's principal leaders. The *Dictionary of American Biography* contains sketches of nine who probably were the most influential—Theodore Halvorson Dahl, Johannes Dietrichson, Elling Eielsen, Gjermund Hoyme, Erik Kristian Johnsen, Johan Nathan Kildahl, Ulrik Vilhelm Koren, Sven Oftedal and George Svendrup.

The Norwegians produced a variety of interesting men and women who gained wide notice in the United States.

After several years of musical education in her native Christiania (now Oslo), Bertha Feiring Tapper arrived in America in 1881 and became a celebrated pianist and teacher. Before her death in 1915 she was instrumental in developing the talents of many American concert performers, composers and teachers; among them Leo Ornstein, Newton Swift and Abram Chasins.

Another native of Christiania, Agnes Mathilde Wergeland—daughter of a family that produced statesmen, writers, artists and clergymen; the first woman to receive a Ph.D. from the University of Zurich—came to the United States in 1880 to accept the offer of a fellowship in history at Bryn Mawr College. She decided to stay and, after instructorships at the Universities of Illinois and Chicago, she was appointed chairman of the History Department at the University of Wyoming in Laramie—probably the first woman to hold such a position in an institution of higher learning in the United States. She published numerous historical studies in Norwegian, German and English. She died in 1914.

A fund in her memory was established at the University of Christiania to help Norwegian women students study history and economics in the United States, and a scholarship in history at the University of Wyoming was also set up in her honor. .

Alfred Owre, born in Hammerfest, Norway, arrived at fourteen in 1884. Working his way through the University of Minnesota, he received the D.D.S. degree in 1895; later an M.D. from Hamline University. He chose to become a teacher of dentistry which he called "the neglected stepchild" of medicine and surgery. In 1905 he was appointed dean of the College of Dentistry at the University of Minnesota. In 1921 the Carnegie Foundation engaged him to make a survey of dental education, in which he revealed many abuses and inadequacies. In 1927 he accepted the deanship of the Dentistry School (later renamed the School of Dental and Oral Surgery) at Columbia University. His advocacy of making dental services easily available to the lower-income groups brought repeated attacks in dental journals and at professional gatherings. In 1930 when Dr. Owre publicly approved dental and medical education and organization in the Soviet Union, and declared that "state medicine . . . or its equivalent is bound to come," his own staff at Columbia rose against him, accusing him of inefficiency and of ideas offensive to the profession. He demanded an investigation of these charges and offered to resign. During the long leave of absence before his resignation was finally accepted in 1934, the "Bolshevik" traveled in Europe and the Soviet Union. He died in 1935. Since then many of his ideas have been adopted at Columbia and other schools. He was a six-footer who kept his weight down to a hundred and twenty-five pounds by a strict diet and long hiking trips. He walked some hundred and twenty thousand miles in America, Europe, China and Japan.

Knute Rockne died in 1931, but his name continues to appear in the sports pages of American newspapers. Born in Voss, Norway, in 1888, he was brought to the United States at the age of three. As a boy in Chicago he added to the family income by washing windows, following the harvest in Wisconsin, and working on boats and in the Chicago post office. An indifferent student in high school, he was a brilliant scholar and all-around athlete at the University of Notre Dame, which took him on as an instructor in chemistry and as assistant football coach. In 1918 he became chief coach and during the next thirteen years the Notre Dame teams—operating under the "Rockne System" of speed, deception, and improved tactics in the forward pass, the shift, the spinner plays and the flexing-end play—won one hundred and five games, tied five and lost twelve.

In 1880 at San Francisco a twenty-six-year-old seaman named Andrew Furuseth, native of Romedal, Norway, fled without a cent from a British bark on which working conditions were bad but no worse than on most ships then sailing the seven seas. In the next half century he rose to almost incredible effectiveness as a fighter for improvements in the lot of seamen.

Without formal education, in most ways as ordinary as an old shoe, but full of a tremendous passion and will, Andy Furuseth acquired a thorough knowledge of "the maritime law of every country; the social conditions, the wage levels, the economic life of every seafaring nation. . . . His mind worked with the precision of a Corliss engine. He was logical, rugged, terse, quaint and fervid with conviction." I am quoting Senator Robert M. La Follette, whom he enlisted in the struggle to make the sailor a free man.

Freedom was Andy Furuseth's religion. Seamen in those days, even on many American ships, were virtual slaves; and "slaves are incapable of creative effort," argued their champion before Congressional committees and elsewhere. "They are incapable of responsibility. Sea power is in seamen; ships are tools; seamen must be free" to quit, to work like other people. . . . "No calling demands a higher mental and physical standard in the men employed. No calling has any right to higher consideration or greater honor."

But the law that he wanted "Old Bob" La Follette to sponsor and see through Congress affected powerful money interests in dozens of foreign countries as well as the United States, for it aimed to protect foreign seamen on foreign ships when in American ports no less than American seamen. When the La Follette Seamen's Act finally was passed in 1912, so many foreign governments responding to the demands of their shipowners protested against it that President Taft withheld his signature to the bill.

Furuseth did not give up. Aided by lawyers like Silas B. Axtell of New York who caught his passion, trying various approaches, he worked on individual Congressmen and other influential people till the Act was passed again, in 1915, and President Wilson decided not to heed the protests of foreign governments. He signed the bill while Andy Furuseth knelt by his desk.

The La Follette Act freed hundreds of thousands of men from serfdom—without spilling a drop of blood. Along with the ensuing amendments and court decisions, it has influenced changes in seamen's working conditions and wages throughout the world, tending to raise them in the direction of parity with American conditions and wages.

Many attempts were made to annul the Act's provisions; Furuseth fought them all, and won. He was a great liberator. When he died at eighty-four in 1938, he was called "the Abraham Lincoln of the Sea." He requested that his ashes be committed to the sea "as far from the land as possible." Now there is a monument to him in San Francisco on which the words he had uttered early in his campaign are inscribed: "You can put me in jail, but you cannot give me narrower quarters than as a seaman I have always had. You cannot give me coarser food than I have always eaten, you cannot make me lonelier than I have always been."

Born at Fredericksvärn, a fishing village in southern Norway, Hjalmar Hjorth Boyessen arrived in America in 1869 a well-educated young man of twenty-one, and became editor of a Norwegian-language paper in Chicago. By associating mainly with native Americans, he learned English very rapidly and developed the ambition to write in his adopted tongue. In 1872 he completed his first novel, Gunnar, a story of Norway, which William Dean Howells published serially in the Atlantic in '73. Thereafter Boyessen wrote several other books and many magazine stories and articles. He was at his best in writing for boys.

Ole Edvart Rölvaag was another son of Norwegian fisher folk who became an American writer. He was born on the island of Dönna, and in his late teens was himself a fisherman. At twenty he decided to emigrate; an uncle in South Dakota sent him passage money.

After his arrival in 1896 Rölvaag worked for three years as a farm hand. He had some elementary schooling in Norway and had read what books and journals were available in his village. In 1899 he entered Augustana College, a Norwegian Lutheran preparatory school in Canton, South Dakota; then transferred to St. Olaf College from which he was graduated in 1905.

The next year St. Olaf made him its professor of Norwegian—a position he kept till the late 1920s when illness and determination to devote himself to writing caused him to resign.

Rölvaag's first book Omkring Faedrearven ("Concerning Our Heritage"), published in 1922, was a collection of essays on the tragedy of immigrant life. It was a reaction to the "Americanization" campaign during World War I conducted in the main by people possessed of the idea that the United States is an Anglo-Saxon country. His subsequent conclusions on the same subject were recorded in notes and letters that his biographers, Theodore Jorgenson and Nora O. Solum, incorporated in their book O. E. Rölvaag (1939).

"Man, especially the Nordic," he wrote to Percy Boynton in 1929, "cannot tear himself loose from the soil he has been rooted in for centuries and move to a new land where even the air chills by its strangeness, without paying a great price. There is intimate kinship between the soul and the soil in which it grows. To build a Fatherland is a long process. Traditions are slowly and laboriously spun. When even the New Englander, with whom pioneering had become a habit, at times found the virgin prairies of the Mississippi Valley hard to endure, what must not these prairies have been to the non-English-speaking foreigner?

"So little of the story of the non-English-speaking immigrant . . . has yet been told in fiction. . . . Changing an Irishman, a Scot, or an Englishman into an American is one thing; transforming a German or a Scandinavian is quite another. The first leaps full-grown into American society because the speech of the new country has been his for centuries. Not so with the other.

"The giving up of one language and the acquiring of a new requires a spiritual readjustment which forever will be beyond the power of the average man, because it requires a remaking of the soul. He cannot give up the old because that would mean death to him, and he cannot master the new—the process is simply beyond his power. . . . Changing a wilderness into a sheltered abode doesn't leave one much time for language study. Acquiring a language doesn't mean just picking up words and phrases used in trade and travel—that most people can do. I have in mind the mastering of a foreign language so intimately that one's emotional life can move in the new medium freely and naturally. Not until that miracle has taken place can one feel fully at home in a new country. I call it a miracle, for then one's soul will have changed. This phase of Americanization you of English stock have no trouble to grasp intellectually, but you cannot feel it emotionally, hence you really don't understand it at all—I hope I am not offending you!

"The break between the first and the second generations of Americans of British descent may oftentimes be quite violent, due to the difference in schooling and outlook and the difference in traditions between the two countries. But in the case of, for example, Scandinavian Americans the break is oftentimes brutal, though the human qualities may be just as fine. You will agree with me, I think, that it is a tragedy for mother and child not to be able to converse intimately with each other. Her songs he cannot understand. What her soul has found nourishment in, he cannot comprehend. She seems to him a peculiar anachronism, a senseless, unreasonable being. . . . There are tragedies in life for which language has no adequate expression—this is one of them."

In 1920 at St. Olaf, Rölvaag gave a course of lectures on Norwegian immigration and Americanization based on notes like this quoted by Mr. Jorgenson and Miss Solum:

"We [Norwegian Americans] urge a cultural solidarity with the past because we desire that our people shall be made to feel at home in this new land of theirs—completely and wholeheartedly at home. The homes that have been wrested from the prairies and the forests of the Northwest have been bought with the sweat of their brows and the agony of their souls, with many long years of toil and with . . . the blood of their very hearts. There is a strange glory over those homes. We desire that our people shall be enabled to see that glory in order that they may share in a deep joy. To us those homes are and must continue to be the best and the most beautiful in the world. If our people do not cultivate the feeling of home and of kin, they will never reach the point at which they are able to sustain a true and abiding patriotism. We believe that this cultivation of love for home and heritage is the truest Americanization that any citizen may be taught.

"All the high and noble cultural values which [Norwegians] have shared down through the ages, we believe it our duty to protect and augment. All the genuine and beautiful creations, whether it be in rhythm or in thought, in word or in plastic art, we believe to be salutary factors in American life. You need it all; I need it; our children will need it. We want the spirit of the Northwest to unfold in the greatest possible luxuriance and glory."

Rölvaag resented the cultural monotony which he sensed was settling over the Northwest as a result of "Americanization" based on the concept that the United States is an Anglo-Saxon country and nothing else. His idea of how Americanization might take place was different:

"We want the most intense Americanization. We want our children to know American history from the beginning, but we think the history of their own Northwest, the region built by their own fathers, of special significance. We want a broad and deep Americanism; we think our country needs the sturdy pines and the white-stemmed birches of the North."

In one lecture he said: "I am well aware of the fact that there are many people in the United States today who do not believe in racial [or background] differences. I say that the traits are there whether you believe in them or not. Environment and teaching and training for many centuries, suffering and conditions of servitude have placed them there. And I am also well aware that many people today are seeking to blot out all [divergent] traits in this country. To me such an act is tantamount to national suicide. If richness of personal color is desirable in the individual personality, why should the monotonous gray be desirable as a national idea? I too believe in Americanization; I believe in it with all the intensity of my soul. I want every soul in America to feel that this country is the best in the world for him; and if it is not that already, it is up to you and me and to all of us to make it so.

". . . I am an American first, last, and all the time. But racially [in long-range background] I am a Norwegian. Really, I do not see how these two facts can be disputed. I am an American. That means that my whole duty is toward America. But, on the other hand, I am intensely interested in our own [group], in what it has achieved both by hand and by intelligence. I have never doubted that we ought to master the English language first of all. Yet I believe with equal sincerity that we who are of Norse parentage should have a reading and speaking knowledge of Norwegian. . . . For we cannot in the fullest sense of the word discharge our duties as Americans unless we know our . . . virtues and failings. It is more important that we are placed face to face with our deeper selves than that we gain renown among others."

Rölvaag's early writings, published in Minneapolis, appeared only in Norwegian. The climax of his literary career approached when two of his novels about Norwegian immigrant life came out in Norway— *I de Dage* ("In Those Days") in 1924 and *Riket grundlaegges* ("The Kingdom Is Founded") in 1925. Lincoln Colcord helped him to translate both, and they were issued in New York in 1927 as one novel entitled *Giants in the Earth*. The book was acclaimed both as a work of art and a social and historical document. *The Nation* (July 13, 1927) called it "the fullest, finest and most powerful novel that has been written about pioneer life in America." Vernon Parrington was impressed by its "creative realism and brooding imagination." Carl Sandburg recommended it highly. It sold over a quarter of a million copies. Essentially Norwegian in spirit, it is considered an American classic.

In 1847 a young Norwegian couple, Thomas and Kari Veblen, settled on the frontier in Wisconsin and had twelve children. The sixth, Thorstein Veblen, born in '57, evolved into one of the most interesting American thinkers. At seventeen, when he knew less English than Norwegian, his father packed him off to Carleton College at Northfield, Minnesota, where old-line American boys called him "Norskie."

For twenty years thereafter, as student and instructor, he knocked about uncomfortably in the academic world—a thin, awkward, sharp-tongued, brilliant, ill-understood individual in shabby clothes. In the '90s he began to write penetrating essays on such subjects as "The Economic Theory of Woman's Dress" and "The Instinct of Workmanship and the Irksomeness of Labor."

His first book, *The Theory of the Leisure Class* (1899), full of bitter ideas, sharp irony and fantastically constructed sentences, reached to the heart of American life and brought him sudden fame and notoriety. In the next quarter of a century he wrote a dozen more books, all slashing criticism of the capitalist system. He foresaw Fascism long before it appeared in the Italian and German forms. He envisioned a possible decent, intelligent future for humanity only in internationalism. He proposed the neutralization of merchant shipping, the neutralization of citizenship, a system of collective security.

Perhaps a century ahead of the 1945 United Nations Security Conference at San Francisco in his thinking, Veblen died near that city— at Palo Alto, in 1929—an utter pessimist. But his work has been having a sporadic influence on liberal and radical thought in the United States and elsewhere.

Among other Norwegian Americans who have made their mark are: Rear Admiral Peter C. Asserson, in his day the leading American authority on dry docks; Gunvald Aus and Kort Berle, in charge of construction of New York's Woolworth Building; Victor F. Lawson, who started the Chicago Daily News and helped to found the Associated Press; Jonas Lie, painter; Olaf Laurgaard, construction engineer; Axel Hansteen Oxholm, lumber expert; Bernt Balchen, Arctic explorer and rescuer; Ole Windingstad, one-time conductor of the New Orleans Symphony; Marcus Lee Hansen, Theodore C. Blegen and Laurence M. Larson, historians; Henry Allen Moe, secretary-general of the Guggenheim Foundation; Molla Bjursted Mallory and Ralph Guldahl, tennis and golf champions; Leola Nelson Bergmann, whose Music Master of the Middle West (1944) is the story of M. Melius Christiansen and the St. Olaf Choir; Martha Ostenso, author of Wild Geese (1925) and other popular novels; Sonja Henie, the Ice Queen; Vera Zorina, ballerina and actress; Torger Tokle, ski champion of the Western Hemisphere, killed in action early in 1945 in Italy; Governor John Moses of North Dakota; Congressman Henry Jackson of Tacoma, Washington; Brigadier General Lauris Norstad, son of a Chicago Lutheran minister, who at thirty-seven commanded the 20th Air Force, directing the B-29 Superfortress onslaughts on Tokio during 1944-1945.

The Army, Navy and Marine Corps have at least a half-dozen generals and admirals who are of Norwegian descent on both sides of their parentage, and perhaps a score who are part-Norwegian.

In 1938 the United States suddenly heard of a young scientist at the University of Wisconsin, Professor C. A. Elvehjem, whose discoveries led to the use of nicotinic acid in treating pellagra, the scourge of the South.

In 1939 Dr. Ernest O. Lawrence, of the University of California, born in South Dakota of Norwegian parents, received the Nobel Prize in physics. During 1943-1945 he had a hand in the production of the atomic bomb.

On July 2, 1943, his eightieth birthday, Dr. Ludvik Hektoen of Chicago, a son of early immigrants from Norway, witnessed the dedication of the Hektoen Institute of Medical Research at the Cook County Hospital, honoring him as one of the world's leading cancer specialists. In 1944 another Norwegian American prominent in cancer research, Dr. Conrad E. Tharaldsen, died in New York.

In 1945 Brynjolf Jacob Hovde (pronounced "brin-yuilf ya-cob huv-dah"), a former professor of history at the University of Pittsburgh and Allegheny College, became director of the New York School for Social Research.

From 1933 to 1945 John Granrud—born in Iowa of Norwegian immigrant parents—was superintendent of schools in Springfield, Massachusetts, and became nationally known for his citizenship education program called the "Springfield Plan," whose aim is to instil in school pupils an understanding and appreciation of the diversity of the American population. In 1945, when Dr. Granrud resigned from the position owing to ill health, the plan was the basis of a motion picture "It Happened in Springfield."

But enough of outstanding people—

I keep thinking of rather ordinary men and women, friends of mine in Wisconsin, Minnesota and South Dakota who, somehow, are both Norwegians and Americans. Their talk and thoughts are of day-to-day events and problems on their farms, in their communities and states, in the U. S. A.; of events on the various foreign lands where their sons were fighting and dying and winning promotions and Distinguished Flying and Service Crosses. Often too they speak of the old country. Much as the Coloradan recalls his Massachusetts childhood, they nostalgically remember how it was in Norway fifty years ago, and why they left there. They talk of modern Norway which in the 1930s became almost a model state, and of its Nazi conquest and its liberation.

I am thinking specially of one very old man. He and his bride came to a spot of untamed, forested land in eastern Minnesota in 1889. For two years they lived in a sod-house little better than a cave, while he felled trees and grubbed stumps. He sowed the newly cleared, fertile land, five or ten acres more each year, until he had a hundred and thirty under cultivation. Four years after their arrival, he built a two-story, eight-roomed house and a great barn and other outbuildings. Today, with the help of a son and the son's family, he still farms the original homestead. Sitting in their house one day in 1941 and looking at their gnarled hands and slumped shoulders, I marveled that one man and woman could have accomplished so much.

They raised four sons and two daughters, three of whom are farmers. Of twenty-odd grandchildren, nine were in the Army and Navy during 1941-1945. The old people know English, but still read their favorite Norwegian-language paper. They belong to the Sons and to the Daughters of Norway, separate but twin organizations.

"The immigrant," read an editorial published in the spring of 1925, in the Decorah *Posten*, a leading Norwegian American paper, "is above all a man of toil. He came to America for the purpose of working. Circumstances have compelled him to toil and he has never been afraid to lay hold of his task. This has in a way been his salvation. He has had a share in creating the America which we now know, and through this constant labor here he has little by little become an American. It has also been the best cure for his loneliness and his longing for all that which he has had to sacrifice to become an American."

XI: AMERICANS FROM GREECE

ONE day in 1943 I opened a newly published book which had come in the mail: *Christopher Columbus, A Greek Nobleman* by Seraphim G. Canoutas, and found it almost as fascinating as Salvador de Madariaga's *Christopher Columbus* (1939) which marshals an array of circumstantial evidence that the Discoverer may have been a Jew. Mr. Canoutas' treatise is not the first on the subject. In 1937 Spyros Cateras of Manchester, New Hampshire, describing himself as "publisher and historian," issued a tiny book called *Christopher Columbus Was a Greek Prince And His Real Name Was Nikolaos Ypshilantis from the Greek Island Chios.*

But another historian and journalist, M. J. Politis—in *One America* (1945), the symposium edited by Professors Francis J. Brown and Joseph S. Roucek—brushes all this aside as "theory." He says that the first Greek to arrive in America was a man named Theodore who according to Spanish records went to Florida in 1528 with the ill-fated Narvaez expedition. (*See page 39.*)

Juan de Fuca Straits between Vancouver Island and the state of Washington is named for a Greek mariner from the island of Cephalonia who reached it in 1592. His real name was Apostolos Valerianos;

and Mr. Politis adds that the Seattle lodge of the Order of AHEPA—an organization of Greek Americans—is also named for him.

The earliest attempt to colonize Greeks within the present limits of the United States occurred as a result of Turkish terror in southern Morea in 1767. To forestall a possible uprising, the Turks killed the archbishop and persecuted other notable people. A Scots doctor, Andrew Turnbull, who was in the British naval service in the Mediterranean and married to a Greek girl, intervened. For twelve hundred piasters he bought the privilege of saving a large number of his wife's countrymen, and some two hundred accompanied him to Florida, recently become part of the British colonial realm in North America. There in a climate supposed to be similar to that of Greece he tried to found a community called New Smyrna. The attempt failed. The Greeks who survived malaria and encounters with the Indians took refuge in close-by St. Augustine. Mr. Politis' research at the Webb Memorial Library in St. Augustine convinces him that some of the residents there in the late eighteenth century were Greeks; among them a teacher named John Giannopolis who built a schoolhouse which still draws tourists.

The Greek War of Independence in the 1820s evoked much sympathy in the United States, and American missionaries and Philhellenes—chiefly New Englanders—bought several Greek boys in the Turkish slave markets and shipped them across the ocean to be educated at Andover, Amherst and other schools. They saved other lads in various ways.

There was Alexander George Paspatis. He was up for sale in a slave market when his mother, wandering along the coast of Asia Minor in flight from the massacre on the island of Chios, saw him and bought him with her last two coins. She turned the boy over to an American missionary who sent him to Marshall P. Wilder, a Philhellene in Boston. Paspatis was graduated from Amherst in 1831, studied medicine in Europe, became a distinguished doctor in Constantinople, and finally retired to Athens, where he died in 1891.

Another dramatic story is that of Loukas Miltiades. Colonel J. P. Miller, an American fighting the Turks in Greece, came upon the child in a deserted village and adopted him. About a half century later the Greek orphan was the Honorable Lucas Miltiades Miller, a Congressman from Wisconsin.

Still another of that group of Greek boys was John Celivergos Zachos, son of a general killed in the fight for liberation. The boy was brought to America in 1830 under the protection of Dr. Samuel Gridley Howe, "the Lafayette of the Greek Revolution." At fifteen Zachos decided to relieve his benefactor by supporting himself. In 1836 he was graduated with honors from Kenyon College at Gambier, Ohio, giving the Greek oration for his class. In the next sixty years he was successively an associate principal of the Cooper Female Seminary in Dayton; an editor of the *Ohio Journal of Education*; principal of the Grammar School of Antioch College and an associate of one of America's most creative educators, Horace Mann; a nurse in the Civil War; a student of theology, later ordained a Unitarian minister and appointed a professor at Meadville Theological School in Pennsylvania; and finally curator of Cooper Union in New York, where he also taught literature and oratory. An authority on spoken English in his day, he wrote several textbooks on elocution. He got out two books on Peter Cooper—still basic material for any study of that interesting man—and two volumes of social-economic criticism. He invented a printing machine. When a heated debate on the educability of the Negro was in progress, he published a *Phonic Primer and Reader* (1864), "Designed Chiefly for the Use of Night-Schools Where Adults are Taught, and for the Myriads of Freed Men and Women Whose First Rush from the Prison-House of Slavery is to the Gates of the Temple of Knowledge," and took part in the experimental demonstrations conducted in Boston which proved that Negroes could be educated. It required courage to do this in the 1860s even in the North; Zachos, a firm believer in democracy and free education for all races and groups, did it as a matter of course.

George Musalas Calvocoresses was another survivor of the Chios massacre. He entered the Norwich Academy in Vermont, where Headmaster Alden Partridge took a special interest in him and saw to it that he received a good education before he obtained an appointment to the Naval Academy. After graduation from Annapolis, Ensign Calvocoresses was assigned to the Wilkes Expedition (1838-1842) in the South Seas and the Antarctic; in 1852 he published a book about his adventures which went into five editions. He served with distinction in the Mexican War, in the Mediterranean and along the west coast of Africa during the 1840s and early '50s, in the capture of Canton in 1856, throughout the Civil War, and finally along the west coast of South America. He was retired with the rank of captain in 1867. Five years later while returning from a business trip to his home at Litchfield, Connecticut, he was killed by some thieves in Bridgeport.

His son, George Partridge Calvocoresses, also went into the Navy. He fought under Dewey in Manila Bay and eventually rose to the rank of rear admiral and served as commandant of the Naval Academy.

American humanitarians continued to be interested in Greece through most of the nineteenth century. James Monroe and Daniel Webster made public appeals for funds to aid the Greek patriots. At one time the old South Church in Boston was the headquarters for Greek relief.

In the 1860s Philhellenism revolved around Samuel Gridley Howe. Forty years earlier he had fought for freedom in Greece; now—with a wide reputation as an educator and philanthropist—he was agitating and raising money to liberate Crete. In 1867 he sailed for Europe with the dual purpose of bringing relief to Cretan refugees in Athens and making a survey of European schools for the blind and the deaf. Two years before he had been appointed chairman of the Massachusetts Board of State Charities; he was also director of the Massachusetts School for the Blind (later called the Perkins Institution) in Watertown, Massachusetts. On reaching Athens, Howe discovered he needed a secretary to help him run the relief organization and by a stroke of luck Michael Anagnostópoulos was presented to him as a possibility.

Anagnostópoulos was of old Greek peasant stock, a native of the ancient and remote mountain village of Papingo in Epirus. The name means "descendant of the reader." Generations back, under Turkish rule, his great-grandfather was the only man in Papingo who could read. In his early boyhood Michael, tending his father's flocks on the craggy mountainsides, developed such a hunger for knowledge that, according to stories narrated after his death, he borrowed and copied by hand textbooks which his father was too poor to buy for him. His illiterate great-grandmother's reminiscences about his literate great-grandfather deeply influenced him, as did a slogan of the Greek Liberation movement: "Education is the herald of liberty." In his late teens, largely self-taught, he walked sixteen hours to the town of Janina in successful pursuit of a scholarship at the University of Athens.

The next four years he half starved while studying classics and philosophy at the University. Then he turned to journalism—a stormy profession in Greece at any time. When Dr. Howe arrived, Anagnostópoulos was thirty years old; he had just quit the editorship of a newspaper over the question of Crete.

The young Greek and the aging American Philhellene clicked at once. Their work in Athens finished, Howe invited his secretary—whom he called Anagnos for short—to come with him to the United States.

Anagnos—the form he eventually adopted as his legal name in America—soon became as indispensable to Howe at the Perkins Institution as he was in Greek relief. He married the old gentleman's daughter Julia, whose mother was Julia Ward Howe; and on Howe's death in 1876 the Greek immigrant who spoke English with a heavy accent was chosen head of the Institution. Its scope and function in the next thirty years expanded beyond anything his predecessor had visualized.

From official and private sources Anagnos extracted over a million dollars for the education of the blind. But his "real religion," his Boston friends believed, was Greece. As a memorial to his mother who had died in his childhood, he built a school in his native village. He died in 1906 while traveling in the Balkans, looking about for other things to do. His body was sent to Papingo for burial. A large memorial service was held in Boston.

The methods Anagnos introduced at Perkins form much of the basis for the modern education of the blind. In the summer of 1944, at the New England Shipbuilding Company Yards in South Portland, Maine, a Liberty ship was named the S.S. *Michael Anagnos*.

Some of the New England Perkinses are said to be descendants of a Greek merchant named Perkentzis who came to the United States by way of London in the 1780s.

Perdikaris Street in Trenton, New Jersey, is named after another early Greek-immigrant businessman.

In the nineteenth century a handful of Greek merchants went South and—with their long Old World background in the tobacco business—made themselves a factor in the rise of the American tobacco industry. But few details about them are available.

A colorful character in the American academic field in the middle decades of the nineteenth century was Evangelinus Apostolides Sophocles, classicist and neo-Hellenist. Born near Mount Pelion in Thessaly, he was educated by the monks on Mount Sinai. In the 1820s when he was in his late teens, a representative of the American Board of Commissioners for Foreign Missions helped him to emigrate to Massachusetts.

Young Sophocles went to Amherst in 1829 but ill health caused him to leave the college the following year and he apparently had no further formal education. For about a decade he held teaching jobs in minor schools in New England, then in 1842, after publishing three textbooks on the Greek language, he was made a tutor at Harvard. Twelve years later he was appointed assistant professor and in 1860 professor of Ancient, Byzantine and Modern Greek.

He published text upon text, all on the same subject: the language of Greece. Independently of other scholars, he traced the Modern Greek to the Byzantine, demolishing the theory of an Aeolic-Doric

beginning. His *Greek Lexicon of the Roman and Byzantine Periods*
(1870) became a standard work.

A unique teacher whose classes often roared at his epigrams, Professor Sophocles was a gnome-like man with a big head under a thick
shock of hair. The fierce glare of his black eyes was apt to frighten
people who met him for the first time. Actually, on the testimony of
his friends, he was gentleness itself. Children loved him. Chickens
came running when he called out their classical Greek names. An
ascetic, he spent very little on himself. Years of his salary went into
a bridge and other installations in his home town in Greece. He died
in 1883 in a bare room very much like a monk's, and left large sums
to friends and to the Harvard library.

In 1848, when 91,068 people came to the United States from Ireland
and 58,973 from Germany, one man arrived from Greece.

In terms of a mass movement the Greeks are among the newest of
the new-immigrant groups. In 1880 the country had only a few hundred
persons of Greek origin; in 1890 perhaps fewer than two thousand.

Now the computation of their number is a statistical chore.

In 1940 the census-takers found 326,762 inhabitants of the U. S. A.
who said they were of Greek stock, including those who were born in
Greece or at least one of whose parents was born abroad. Of this
number 163,252 gave Greece as the country of their birth; but tens of
thousands of other Greeks came from Bulgaria, Yugoslavia, Turkey
and Egypt or are American-born sons and daughters of Greek immigrants from those countries with Greek populations.

I have heard Greek Americans estimate their group at eight hundred
thousand, insisting that the official United States government figure
is ridiculously low. It is. Perhaps a safe compromise approximation
covering the immigrants and the second generation is four hundred and
fifty thousand. And there are probably another fifty to a hundred
thousand Americans of Greek or part-Greek descent, most of them
very young, who are the third generation. Most immigrants are naturalized citizens.

Since 1890 about half a million Greeks have arrived. The wave
touched its height in 1907 with nearly thirty-seven thousand entries,
and again in 1914 (right after the Balkan Wars) when the number was
almost thirty-six thousand. In Athens in 1937 a Johns Hopkins graduate, Basileios Balaoras, published a treatise in Greek on *The Hellenism
of the United States* which stated that from 1901 to 1930 one-tenth of
Greece's population emigrated to America.

Throughout this period the migrants were preponderantly from the

Aegean Islands and from the agricultural and pastoral sections of the
Greek mainland. The majority were young men. Often all able-bodied
males in a village packed their bundles and left.

As Professor Henry Pratt Fairchild has it in his *Greek Immigration*
(1911), the over-all explanation of the exodus was poverty, while the
direct cause were the letters received from relatives who had gone
earlier. After a few months' employment in America somebody wrote
home, perhaps boasting a bit, that he had saved, say, two hundred
dollars. The news spread through the village and to neighboring hamlets. Two hundred dollars was a fabulous sum in Epirus or Thessaly or
on Crete, Cyprus or Cephalonia, as it was nearly everywhere else in
Europe. So two, five, ten, a dozen more men and boys were off. Some
months later they in turn wrote home, perhaps enclosing pictures of
themselves dressed in their Sunday best, and their letters drew still
another group to America.

During 1900-1910 there were Greek villages where the boys grew up
with one thought: to cross the ocean. For many America was the most
exciting word in the world, a primary goal in life.

Most Greek immigrants knew just what part of the United States they
were going to and what sort of work they would do when they got there.
This was true of many immigrants from all countries. It was safer to
follow the way paved by friends than to strike out on one's own. People
naturally wanted to avoid unfortunate experiences—such as that of the
one hundred and fifty Greeks who had no sooner landed in New York in
1888 than they were picked up by labor agents for a railroad construction
job in the wilds of Canada. The company went bankrupt a week after
their arrival, and the greenhorns who knew no English were stranded
without money or food. They stuck together and made their way south,
eating berries and whatever other food they could find until they reached
a village in Maine where a man knew of some Greeks in Massachusetts.
The villagers took up a collection for their transportation to Boston.

Like other east-European groups, thousands of Greeks came with the
intention of staying only a few years; many went back, but the majority
did not. They stayed and sent "tickets" to their wives and girls. Some
returned only to come back to America with a bride.

At first they tended to congregate in and about New York City and
in New England where large Greek "colonies" were formed in Boston
and Lowell, Massachusetts, and in Manchester, New Hampshire. By
and by growing Greek settlements appeared in Philadelphia, Chicago,
Detroit, Atlanta and a few other centers. Now there is hardly a town of
five thousand population or over anywhere in the United States without
at least one Greek American.

In 1905 Greek sponge fishermen, chiefly from the Dodecanese Islands, "invaded" Tarpon Springs, a sleepy resort village north of Tampa, Florida, and turned it into a boom town, the sponge capital of the Western Hemisphere. A unique Greek contribution to America's industrial life, sponge-fishing runs into millions of dollars a year. But for the Greeks, with centuries of experience in sponge-fishing in the Aegean and Mediterranean Seas behind them, it might never have been organized and raised to its present level of success.

The sporadic trickles of Greek immigration prior to 1885 consisted almost wholly of merchants. Thereafter the majority were humble folk getting away from whatever did not suit them in the Old World. They were unskilled workers who found employment in the textile mills and shoe-manufacturing plants in New England and in diverse industries in such centers as New York, Philadelphia and Chicago. Labor agents persuaded some to go to work on railroad and waterfront construction jobs in Utah and Nevada, in Oregon and Washington, in Alaska. A few went into fishing up and down the Pacific Coast, into fruit-growing in California and Washington. A few settled on farms in Alabama, a few in the sheep country of Utah and Colorado.

The Greek immigrant seldom made a life career of working for wages. As soon as possible, particularly in the larger cities, he ventured into business on his own, opening a restaurant, a flower or fur shop, a confectionery or fruit store; and as likely as not did all right in it. Often he took advantage of a lay-off to start out as a street vendor, selling novelties or candy. Or he got himself a shoeshine stand. An individualist, he liked to be his own boss and give play to his native qualities, among the most prevalent of which were initiative, self-reliance and shrewdness. Now it is a rare town in America with over 25,000 population that hasn't a few "Greek" restaurants and a few candy stores or flower shops owned by Greek Americans.

To the confectionery and soda-fountain business Greek immigrants made vital contributions. They introduced the use of fruit syrups. One is said to have brought over nothing less than the ice-cream cone which he had thought up in London. And some Greek American historians are emphatic in crediting to Greek ingenuity the invention of the ice-cream sundae.

During the 1920s and the early 1930s a great many dance halls were owned and operated by Greeks and Greek Americans. Then gangsters began to "muscle" into the business and the Greeks gradually cleared out of it. It seems the Greek temperament and morals will have no traffic with gangsterism. I am told there have been no Greek racketeers.

Immigrants from Greece and their American-born descendants have a firm foothold in the theatrical business and the entertainment field generally. A few—the late Alexander Pantages, who at one time was the foremost independent vaudeville and movie operator, and the Skouras brothers, Spyros, Charles and George—attained marked success.

Most Greek immigrants, though, and their American-born children are like the majority of the American population, whether they have their own business or not—they are inching their way to a higher standard of living.

In his over-sociological, impatient book on the Greeks in America to 1910, presenting them as a multitudinous problem which was almost bound to get worse, Professor Fairchild made much of Greek clannishness and gregariousness. These characteristics—not unnatural ones—still exist in the group. The Greek immigrant was more consciously and definitely Greek than the average Slovenian, say, or Pole was Slovenian or Polish. A strong cultural tradition, stimulated by recent wars and revolutions for freedom and independence, was part of his makeup. The Greek Orthodox Church, whose whole history was integrated with that tradition, with everything he believed not only as a Christian but as a Greek, came over with him. In the old country his ideas and values were a mingling of nationalism and religion, of Hellenic idealism and centuries of practical experience in the face of great odds which called for caution and cunning, for sticking together and making the moment count.

In the United States the Greek immigrant's status in relation to other groups was far from sound. The situation in Lowell, Massachusetts, beginning in the 1890s is illustrative. Some of the textile mills preferred Greek immigrants to workers of other nationalities because they seemed to be steadier. This infuriated the Irish and French-Canadians who outnumbered the Greeks five to one. The sons of Hellas had to band together and rush down the middle of the main thoroughfares on their way to and from work. Overnight they holed up in their boarding and coffee-houses in the Greek neighborhood on Market Street. Finally a Greek stuck a knife into a French-Canadian who attacked him; the Greek was not arrested (presumably because the mills controlled the police); and thereafter direct persecution of Greeks in Lowell ceased. But hostility toward them continued. There were riots.

Naturally, therefore, the Greek immigrant on coming over sought out his own kind. For decades the tendency was to reproduce the old-country atmosphere as nearly as possible, to establish and patronize Greek coffee-houses and stores selling specially flavorful Greek foods.

Wherever three or four hundred Greeks settled in a city they formed an "Orthodox Community," creating a center of responsibility and mutual help.

The "Community" organization was—still is—a valid factor in Greek American life. It made the group almost self-sufficient. In times of depression few Greek immigrants applied for public aid. If a man got into extreme economic straits his relatives or friends were expected to see him through; if his plight was too much for them to cope with, the "Community" stepped in.

While perhaps an unusual case in the degree of hostility toward it, the Greek colony in Lowell was typical of others in many aspects. Employment opportunities outweighed Irish-French antagonism, and Greek immigrants kept coming to Lowell throughout the 1890s and 1900s, until its population—of approximately one hundred thousand in 1910—included close to eight thousand Greeks concentrated along Market Street. There were two newspapers with their own printing plants, two drugstores, three steamship and money-order agencies; one priest (perhaps the most important man in the colony), three doctors, one dentist, two photographers; one importing house, two cigarette factories, four restaurants featuring old-country dishes, thirty-odd grocery and meat stores, one wholesale meat market, six bakeries, one saloon, one bath-house, ten confectionery and fruit stores, many dry-goods stores, tailor, barber and shoemaker shops and coffee-houses.

Barred from other sections of Lowell, the Greeks lived in tenements which were fire-traps, though no more so than those available for other immigrant mill hands. The neighborhood was referred to as "the worst part of town." It was, however, anything but drab. For several years beginning in 1913 an amateur dramatic club gave ten modern Greek plays annually, some written in the United States. Finally the Greeks of Lowell built a Byzantine church—a source of pride to Greek Americans the country over.

For a long time (1890-1920) men outnumbered women—at first ten to one, then eight, six, four . . . to one; and in the absence of normal home life, the Greek coffee-house was the immigrants' principal day-to-day institution. "Despite its faults"—writes Theodore Saloutos, a Greek American in the history department of Oberlin College, in the January 1945 *South Atlantic Quarterly*—it was "a democratic institution wherein [gathered] Greeks from all walks of life to play cards, sip a cup of thick, black Turkish coffee, lazily draw on a narghile, or indulge in an animated discussion of politics."

In the old days the coffee-house "provided amusement and recreational facilities for the male population. Silhouettes, or what may be compared with puppet and marionette shows, strongman exhibitions, occasional Oriental floor shows, and cinema productions were staged on a . . . platform in the rear of the coffee-house. Stretched across the platform was a white sheet . . . behind which burned either candles or electric lights. The characters were usually handled by one performer [whose gestures, reflected on the screen] and rapid inflections and modulations of the voice gave them an animated appearance. . . . Silhouettes were of humorous and serious varieties, the most frequent being descriptive of the spirit of Greek independence; a Greek was always the hero, and a Turk the villain. . . ."

Thomas Burgess, who has written about *Greeks in America* (1913), says the majority had some education when they came over; probably ninety per cent could read. They had "the typical Greek genius for adaptability and versatility in business," and it may be that their most discernible contribution to the totality of American life lies in this field.

A man named Anargyros is said to have been the first Greek to roll a cigarette in America, late in the 1880s. Fifteen years later, to eliminate him as a competitor, the American Tobacco Company bought him out for a sum which made him rich.

Shortly before the Spanish-American War the Stephanou brothers, immigrants from Epirus, invested thirty-five dollars in a few pounds of tobacco. During the war they presented boxes of their cigarettes to United States Army officers. This was such effective advertising that by 1910 their firm in Philadelphia was on a sound footing. They simplified their name to Stephano.

A Greek saying has it that "Turks, not Greeks, are very fond of sweets"; but sometime in the second half of the nineteenth century a sailor named Hadzikiris, who hailed from Smyrna, discovered that Americans had a sweet-tooth too. He began to manufacture and peddle a concoction called *Rahat*—a Turkish name. In his old age he sold out and returned to Smyrna a wealthy man.

Greek importing firms appeared in New York as early as the 1880s; now too many to be counted are listed in the Manhattan telephone book. Several have branch offices in Boston, Philadelphia, Chicago; a few also in London, Cairo, Alexandria, Constantinople. They trade in black olives, olive oil, Greek cheese, wine, liqueurs, dried fish and figs, Greek and Turkish tobacco.

A subject of many jokes, Greek restaurants are well known. Few non-Greek Americans, however, realize that there are "Greek" restaurants and Greek restaurants—those for the prevalent American taste which range from awful to very good, and those serving Greek food. The latter are in every larger Greek colony, excelling—so far as I am concerned—in lamb dishes and desserts.

Greeks are also grocers, barbers, tailors, cobblers, peanut-vendors. For nearly two decades during the Coolidge-Hoover and F.D.R. periods, one of the best known Greeks in the United States was Steve Vasilakos who sold peanuts at a corner of the White House grounds in violation of street ordinances; he was protected against police interference by Presidents and members of their families. When he died early in the 1940s, his obituaries contained material for biographers of Calvin Coolidge, who bought peanuts from Steve because he liked to eat them; of Herbert Hoover, who bought them to feed them to the squirrels; of Franklin Roosevelt, who had no use for peanuts but was fond of Steve.

Here and there the Greeks "beat" the more numerous Italians in the shoeshine business. "Greeks usually do win in competition," wrote Burgess, "for in addition to their native shrewdness, they attend to business, give good return for their price, keep good-looking establishments, and are invariably polite."

"The bellboy," Burgess went on, "who respectfully carries up the grip of some great American pork-packer is in all likelihood the much more cultured man of the two." Many of those bellboys are now hotel owners or managers, captains and headwaiters. In these professions perhaps only the French excel and outnumber the Greeks. Take S. Gregory Taylor (original name: Soterios G. Tavoularis) as an example. He came over in the steerage at eighteen and got a job at the St. Regis in New York, learning the business from the bottom up. At one time he was half-owner of a candy and ice-cream factory. In the 1930s he became the owner-operator of the St. Moritz Hotel in midtown Manhattan.

I have mentioned the Skouras brothers, born in Skourokhorion (Skourasville). First to come over was Charlie. As a newsboy, waiter and bartender in St. Louis he saved enough to send for Spyros and George. All three worked in hotels and restaurants until they earned enough to buy a nickelodeon. By 1926 they operated thirty-seven—practically all—movie houses in St. Louis; in 1945, seven hundred and fifty all over the United States and four hundred and fifty more in England, Egypt, Australia and New Zealand.

In 1942, at forty-eight, Spyros became president of the Twentieth-Century-Fox empire; early in 1944 a deal with the leading British cinema interests made him a power in the international film world. When he was in London on that occasion, English reporters investigating the unpopularity in the United States of many British motion pictures asked him what was wrong with them. "Your deeksheen," replied Spyros Panayotis Skouras, whose own English diction remains profoundly influenced by Greek.

What Burgess said of Greek immigrants in general applies to the Skourases, only more so. They are extremely able, alert and hardworking men, attending to their business and trying to give the public its money's worth. The first few movie houses they acquired in St. Louis were turned into clean places with a friendly atmosphere; and movie patrons began to demand that the other film houses spruce up also, and provide courteous ticket takers and ushers. Theaters which failed to comply simply fell into the Skourases' hands.

The brothers had the old Greek traditional idea that the theater is a communal center with responsibility to its audience and to the country. Of course it is one thing to produce the great Greek tragedies in an amphitheater and another to run Hollywood celluloid in a darkened hall. But, to the annoyance of some other exhibitors, the Skouras team kept educating their managers to the Greek tradition, and the atmosphere of their houses continued to improve. Early in the 1940s, when the international crisis sucked in the United States, their numerous "units," as they call their theaters, were ready to be turned into neighborhood patriotic centers.

George, who controls a few score of "units" apart from the other Skouras houses, led off. Like Spyros and Charlie, he was disturbed by the public apathy which even Pearl Harbor did not entirely dissipate. He created a special staff to devise ways and means of rousing his patrons to the meaning of the crisis in which the country found itself, and he put a live-wire advertising man, Nick Matsoukas, also an immigrant from Greece, in charge. That this development occurred first in the Skouras theaters was due not only to George's Greek ideas as to what theaters ought to be, but also to the fact that he and his brothers had gone— even if at some distance—through their old country's agony, which had begun in 1940.

George Skouras' office made special patriotic films to stir up the people. One called "It's Up to You," employing the "living newspaper" technique, showed how everyone might help speed the war's end. It was run off first in George Skouras' houses, then in the other Skouras circuits; and finally, at government request, in some four thousand non-Skouras theaters during the next two years.

The Skouras Theatres, Inc. was the first business house apart from banks authorized by the Treasury Department to sell war bonds; and early in 1942 George's theaters, mostly in and around New York, were the first to install the Victory Booths in which young ladies sold war bonds and stamps. George paid the operating costs of these booths.

Then the other Skouras theaters all over the United States installed them, and sold millions of dollars' worth of bonds. Charlie Skouras, whose operational base is Hollywood, was chairman of the film industry's effort to stimulate the Fourth War Loan drive.

Other exhibitors eventually were forced to follow suit. For, whether or not one approved of the thing, it was a success. The Victory Booths sold war bonds—and the Skouras theaters were more crowded than ever.

George Skouras also started a local once-a-week radio program in New York called "This Is Our Cause," explaining what the war was all about from the United States and Allied point of view, and how the average person could help to win it. When the war ended, the program —under Nick Matsoukas' direction—was being handled by a nation-wide network serving two hundred and fifty stations.

In 1943 Secretary of the Treasury Henry Morgenthau directed the New York State Chairman of the War Savings Staff to "Thank George Skouras on behalf of the Treasury Department for setting a war effort example that all of us could well follow. . . . [He] is an American whose soul may well have trembled at times for the future of Europe but he has nevertheless maintained a steadfast faith in the final outcome. It is men like George and Spyros Skouras that win wars."

The Skourases are just about the hardest working men I know. Spyros, generally regarded as a wizard in finance, business strategy, knowledge of the public, and human relations, is at it eighteen to twenty hours a day, wearing out a couple of crews of secretaries and assistants in the process. Once I asked him what sort of people he employed. He thought a moment, then answered: "All kinds—Irish, Greeks, Italians, Jews, Americans of every variety. The only kind I don't want around are those who are ashamed of being Greek or Italian or Irish or Jewish or anything else. They are not what they pretend to be, are not themselves—you can't trust them."

One feels a tremendous vitality in these men. George, whom I know best, is endlessly dissatisfied with the quality of the movies. Every once in a while he goes on a spree of investigation and talks to people in all branches of the industry—production, distribution, exhibition, publicity and theater management. Then he sends out a memorandum to everybody of any consequence in the industry trying to get it come of age and participate in the serious affairs of the world. He would like to see educators become part of the industry and prepare young people to enter it.

Sometimes, feeling hopeless about the films, George goes fishing or hunting, or takes some non-movie friend to dinner and talks about Greece. He was there late in 1944, just before the British provoked the

Civil War, and what he observed made him indignant. . . . Or he talks about his nephew Athanosios Skouras, whom he had brought over in the 1930s and sent through Amherst College, in the hope the boy would return to Greece and possibly contribute to its government from a knowledge of American ideas and ideals. Meaning to devote himself to the eventual creation of a Balkan Federation, the young man did return—just in time to get into the war against the Axis. After Greece was overwhelmed, he started the first—the DOXA (Glory)—resistance group; the enemy captured and killed him. . . .

Of course hundreds of thousands of people, Greek and non-Greek Americans, contributed work and money to the Greek War Relief during 1940-1945; when all is said and done, however, it was the Skourases'—particularly Spyros'—initiative that saved no one will ever know how many Greek lives, possibly Greece itself. It was Spyros who never gave up the idea of helping Greece. To him the British blockade was just something that had to be overcome; he overcame it, and effected other complicated international arrangements for delivering American supplies on Swedish ships to German-occupied Greece. He considers this his biggest achievement.

Their interest in Greece does not keep the Skourases from being highly valuable Americans. Spyros was in the Army Air Corps in World War I; George served the United States in a special capacity in Egypt and Greece in 1944. And the energy and money of the three brothers pour into numerous organizations working to promote the intelligent development of America's domestic and international affairs.

During World War I thousands of Greek immigrants, many recent and still unnaturalized arrivals from Hellas and Asia Minor, served in the United States Army and Navy. One of them, George Dilboy who died in France, was posthumously awarded the Congressional Medal of Honor. His statue stands in Somerville, Massachusetts; an American Legion post is named for him.

In World War II thousands of American-born sons and daughters of World War I Greek veterans served in the Army, Navy, Marines, Coast Guard, Merchant Marine, Wacs, Spars and Waves. Many are officers, several with high rank, including at least one general with an Anglicized name. Many have been decorated.

Ensign Gus George Bebas of Wilmette, Illinois, distinguished himself as a naval flyer on the carrier *Hornet*. He took part in the crucial battles of the Coral Sea and Midway. He lost his life at Midway and the Distinguished Flying Cross was awarded to him posthumously. The citation read in part that Ensign Bebas "with utter disregard for his own personal safety participated in persistent bombing and strafing attacks against fleeing enemy forces. His courageous conduct and stern devotion to the fulfilment of a vastly important mission contributed materially to the victory achieved by our forces and were in keeping with the highest traditions of the United States Naval Services." On May 15, 1943, at a Boston shipyard, his mother, Mrs. Angeline M. Bebas, launched a destroyer-escort, the U.S.S. *Bebas*.

One of the finest young men I have ever known was Nick Cladakis, son of a sponge-fisherman in Tarpon Springs. In 1940, still only in his early thirties but a natural-born executive, tactful, wise, honest, unselfish and idealistic but also practical, he became leader of the turbulent milk business in the state of New York. In 1942 he left this position to accept a captaincy in the Air Force. He did not care what anybody called him, a Greek or an American; he hated tyranny, Fascism, stupidity in high places, everything that brought on wars. I will never forget the farewell party some of his friends in New York gave for him in June 1943, a few days before he went overseas. There was a lot of kidding. "Look out, Hitler and Musso! Nick is coming over!" Nick laughed, taking sips from his glass, but mostly he was serious and quiet, impatient to be off. Early in September 1943, a few days prior to the collapse of Italy, he was killed in his plane just before it plunged into the Adriatic.

Greek Americans fill—or filled—important jobs in Washington. One, with the Anglicized name of L. B. Nichols, is assistant director of the Federal Bureau of Investigation. George Xanthaky, son of Socrates Xanthaky who was publisher of the Greek-language paper *Pan-Hellenic*, was long a key official in the United Nations Relief and Rehabilitation Administration. Constantine Poulos, a native New Englander, was chief of the Foreign Language Division of the Office of War Information.

In 1944 Poulos went to the Middle East as a war correspondent and was the first American journalist to get into his father's native country after British occupation. When the curtain rose on "The Greek Tragedy" on Sunday, December 3rd, he risked his life to prevent the British-controlled police from firing at the Greek crowds parading in the streets of Athens. He was the first to tell the truth—in his Overseas News Agency dispatches—about what "liberation" meant in Greece.

John Vassos—one of the most versatile men under the sun: painter, sculptor, author, book illustrator, inventor, designer of stoves, cosmetic containers, automobile bodies, harmonicas, radio cabinets, turnstiles in the Empire State Building, Coca-Cola dispensers, and the Greek Pavilion for the 1939 New York World's Fair—was a lieutenant colonel in the Office of Strategic Services.

Other artists, sculptors, illustrators, writers and poets who have gained attention since 1920 are: Constantine Pongialis, George Z. Constant (Constantopoulos), Kimon Leckalis, Theodore Tsavalas ("who brought the Byzantine tradition to America"), Pantelis G. Zografos, Val Arms (Manolis Tsamouras), John Gulias, Theodore Giannakoulis, Aristides E. Phoutrides, Byron Vazakas and John Xeron (Xerocostas).

Greek architecture has profoundly influenced American architecture, mostly through non-Greek architects—such as Thomas Jefferson and Benjamin Latrobe (sometimes called "the father of the Greek Revival"); but three contemporary Greek American architects come to mind: Socrates T. Stathes, George N. Lykos and Stamo Papadaki.

Dimitri Mitropoulos, once conductor of the Athens Symphony Orchestra, came to America in 1936 as guest conductor of the Boston, New York, Cleveland and Minneapolis Symphony orchestras. In 1937 he was engaged as conductor in Minneapolis on a continuous basis. Now he appears to be a permanent member of the American musical world, which also includes the following Greek Americans:

Constantine Nikolaou, Odesseus Lappas and Nicola Moscona, singers; Christos Vrionides, director of the Byzantine Vocal Ensemble of the Greek Cathedral in New York; Nicholas Kouloukis and Lanbros D. Callimahos, flutists; and Lorenzo Camilieri, leader of the People's Chorus in New York.

In 1873 Anastasios Stathopoulos founded Epiphone, Incorporated, in New York City which I am told "produces the world's finest stringed instruments and has agencies in Africa and Europe." Also founded by Greek immigrants in New York, the Apollo Music Company has put out over eight hundred orchestrations in the "Apollonian Editions."

Among the fashion designers in New York are: C. Galihzato, hats; Evangelos Doukis, furs; Marie Dorros, wedding gowns.

John Callais is an interior decorator.

Emmanuel Christ Nicholides, chief engineer of the Sonotone Corporation, invented (with Hugo Lieber) the Microphone Amplifier Hearing-Aid Device. Constantine J. Nicholson (Nikolaides) originated the "Stormo-Screen," a screen in summer and a storm window in winter.

Lucas Petrou Kyrides, who came over as a youngster and worked his way through the University of Michigan, is an industrial chemist on the staff of the Monsanto Chemical Company in St. Louis, with about one hundred discoveries to his credit. Among them are the syphilis-curing drug Mercurosal and the first American process for making synthetic rubber from isoprene and butadiene. Early in 1945, when he received the Award of the American Chemical Society, he said: "Sometimes I feel that, even past sixty, my career is just getting off to a good start. There's a lot of work to be done, a lot of problems that are unsolved."

Several Greek names rank high in American medicine and surgery: George N. Papanicolau, Polyvious N. Corrylos, Lazaros Hadzopoulos, P. P. Nicholas, Leonidas Lantzounis and K. Moulinos.

In the academic field these Greek Americans have been recognized as outstanding teachers and educators: George Bouyoukos of Michigan State College, Constantine Caratheodori, mathematician of Harvard and the Universities of California and Wisconsin; Michael Choukas, Dartmouth sociologist; Dimitris Tselos (fine arts), Philip Papadakis (chemistry) and Emmanuel Broussaly (French) of New York University; Emile Malakis (French) of Johns Hopkins; Raphael Demos (philosophy), Spiros P. Sarris (medicine) of Harvard, Michael Dorizas (geography) of the University of Pennsylvania, George E. Mylonas (history of art and archeology) of Washington University in St. Louis; Kimon A. Doukas (public law and government), formerly of Brooklyn College and Indiana University, now managing editor of The Ahepan, a magazine published by the Order of the AHEPA; and L. S. Stavrianos (history) of Smith College who in 1944 published the treatise Balkan Federation, A History of the Movement Toward Balkan Unity in Modern Times.

Sports teem with Greeks: Jim Londos (Christos Theophilos), sometimes called "The Gorgeous Greek" and "the world's greatest wrestler of all time"; Jesse James (Demetrios S. Tzitzikas) of Houston, Texas, who lost only three out of more than three hundred wrestling bouts, winning the light-heavyweight title of the world in 1939; George Zengaras, George Theodoratos ("The Greek Goliath"), Steve Mamakos ("The Golden Greek") and Phil McGraw (Phillipos Karamanos), boxers; Gregory ("Gus") Zitrides and George Rassas, football players; and Alex Kampouris, the first Greek American to crash major-league baseball. Gerald Luvadis ("Jerry the Greek") was Jack Dempsey's trainer, adviser and friend.

Dean Alfange, who came over as a boy, is one of several well-known New York lawyers of Greek stock, a liberal politician, author of The Supreme Court and the National Will (1937), the originator of the much-quoted saying: "It is better that America be born in the man than the man be born in America."

Tall, bearded Archbishop Athenagoras, head of the Greek Orthodox Archdiocese of North and South America, is my idea of how a bishop should look. He suggests a figure come to life out of a Byzantine icon. His cathedral in New York City is an imposing edifice. About four

hundred churches and two hundred and fifty schools, most of them in
the United States, are under his jurisdiction. A considerable percentage
of Greek Americans of all generations are regular or sporadic church-
goers.

Greek-Orthodox churchgoing is not only religion; in many churches
it is also a very pleasant social experience. A non-Greek, J. Merle Rife
of New Concord, Ohio, described it in *The Christian Century* (October 8, 1941): ". . . They greet their friends and chance acquaintances
outside the church, inside the church, in the vestibule, in the nave, in
the choir, in the balcony, at the iconastasia, anywhere and any time.
The cantor greets them while he is chanting the liturgy, the priest
greets them at the deacon's door during services, or sends the deacon
to greet them by proxy. The men who take up the collection kill two
birds with one stone by greeting their friends as they make the rounds."

Back in 1910 or thereabouts, says Mr. Rife, "the Greek churches in
America had hardly any seats at all. . . . Many Greeks still stand during
the entire service. Clergy who first tried to introduce pews . . . were
accused of trying to make Catholics of the Greeks. The introduction
of decorum into Greek churches is part of their Americanization."

One Sunday in the early 1920s Mr. Rife, who evidently knows Greek,
took his wife "to her first and only Greek service. It was in Pittsburgh.
I stood with her on the women's side until the sermon started, but
forsook her then because I wanted to hear the sermon, the pulpit being
on the men's side. I well remember the extreme allegorizing of the
Prodigal Son we were treated to that day, but I could not have heard
a word had I remained with the women. They with their conversation
and the children with their play were creating pandemonium. Once in
a while a man would 'shoo' the noisiest of the children out into the
vestibule, but they would soon flock back. . . ."

On another occasion Mr. Rife induced a friend to accompany him
to a Greek church. "There was a large group of children on the steps
in front of the church. They greeted us with open arms. They took
us inside and presented us to their elders. The elders were just as cordial
as the children, showing us seats, giving us hymnbooks, and making us
generally welcome. Then my friend said to me, 'Well, I'll say one
thing, there's more Christianity here than in any church I was ever
in.' . . ."

The immigrants have about a score of Greek-language newspapers,
the largest of which are published in New York and Chicago. New
York's *Atlantis*, started in 1894 by Solon J. Vlastos, is the oldest; a
conservative journal edited by Vladimiros Constantinidis from Crete.

Its liberal counterpart in New York is the *National Herald* owned and edited by Basil Vlavianos who bought it in the late 1930s soon after coming to the United States. Mr. Vlavianos also writes effectively—often brilliantly—on Greek matters for liberal English-language magazines.

In Chicago, Demetrios A. Michalaros issues the *Athene*, an English-language quarterly featuring articles on Greece and her culture and on the Greek Americans. I have already mentioned *The Ahepan*, which the Order of the AHEPA issues from its national office in Washington.

AHEPA's full name—the American Hellenic Education Progressive Association—describes it. It is said to be the largest Greek American group. One of its non-Greek members was Franklin D. Roosevelt who took a keen interest in its aims to join "the choicest attributes of Hellenism . . . with the choicest attributes of Americanism, out of which the highest type of American citizen will grow. Our goal is to harmonize, foster and immortalize the thought, scope and precepts of Hellas, leader of antiquity, and America, leader of modern times." During 1942-1945 the organization, acting as an issuing agency of the Treasury Department, sold hundreds of millions of dollars' worth of war bonds. AHEPA's president, George C. Vournas, served in the Middle East as a major of the United States Army during part of World War II.

AHEPA's junior auxiliaries—Maids of Athens and Sons of Percles—restrict their membership to native Americans of Greek descent.

The Greek American Progressive Association (GAPA) is another large fraternal organization with lodges all over the country. It was started by immigrants; now it includes also their American-born descendants.

The Greek American Council with headquarters in New York takes in a large number of representative Americans of Greek birth whose minds are alive with insistent democratic, progressive ideas. On May 11, 1945, the Council sent this message to President Truman, Prime Minister Churchill and Marshal Stalin:

"At the very time fascism has been crushed in Europe we are witnessing the astounding outrage of mounting fascist terrorism in Greece . . . worse than that practiced by the Nazis in Greece. It is the greatest international scandal that the Greek people who fought the anti-fascist war since 1940 should now be victimized in hundreds of thousands by fascist outrages. Elsewhere fascist governments have fallen and the fascists have been captured, but in Greece [under the auspices of 74,000 British troops] the fascists run rampant and the democrats are being arrested and even murdered. . . ."

Earlier—on April 26, 1945—the Greek American Council had cabled to Archbishop Damaskinos, the regent of Greece:

"Continuing persecutions of democratic citizens because of their political opinions and the formation of a monarcho-fascist junta in the army with the purpose of bringing back again by force the monarchy are a bitter blow to . . . Americans of Greek descent. . . .

"Instead of moving forward to achieve a government of national unity, truly representative of the real social and political forces in Greece, a step backward has been taken through the establishment of a narrow puppet government, pulled by monarcho-fascist reaction. Only a government of national unity can command confidence and solve problems, and not accumulate new difficulties and increase chaos. Only such a government is capable of conducting an honest plebiscite. and elections, representing Greece in the family of the United Nations, and safeguarding the national rights of Greece. . . ."

In May 1945 I spoke with a member of the Greek American Council. "I am interested in what happens in Greece," he said, "partly because I was born there but also, in fact chiefly, because I am worried about democracy, even here in the United States. If democracy, the will of the people, is beaten down with terror and starvation in Greece where it originated—even if it is beaten down by so 'democratic' a power as Britain while we, the United States, look on and don't move a finger—then it is going to be tough on democracy everywhere; here too. I have two boys in the United States Army, one was wounded; we thought this was a war against fascism. My whole family is in America to stay—how can I be silent when democracy is at stake?"

Here, it seems to me, Hellenism and Americanism merge in an active perception of the interdependence of democratic peoples everywhere.

One of my favorite Greek Americans lives in a small city in upstate New York. He came to America in 1912 to escape Turkish persecution in Asia Minor. Last time I stopped in at his small confectionery store he complained that the hours were long—he was getting old and tired. I asked him why he didn't have his fourteen-year-old boy help him more. He said almost angrily: "What do you think I came to America for—to have my son grow up no better than me? He goes to school and after school he studies upstairs. I want him to go to Amherst College; lots of Greeks were educated there." His glare softened. "Do you think this country is so perfect we don't need good, educated men to make it better?"

XII: AMERICANS FROM POLAND

SEVERAL Polish American writers begin the Polish chapter of the American Story seventeen years before Columbus' First Voyage. They tell of one "Jan z Kolna" (John of Kolno), a Polish seafarer and explorer in the service of the king of Denmark who—so the legend goes —bumped into Labrador, then sailed as far south as the mouth of the Delaware. Scholars, however, find no proof of this voyage; some, in fact, are satisfied that there never was a "Jan z Kolna" except in Polish lore.

No doubt exists, though, that a number of common, run-of-the-mill men of Polish nationality were in the Jamestown Colony in Virginia early in the seventeenth century. The popularly accepted but historically disputed leader of that settlement, Captain John Smith, mentioned them very favorably in his autobiographical writing; references to them occur in other early Virginia documents.

On his own since early boyhood, John Smith—according to his own report—had knocked about the continent of Europe and knew the worth of common people. He brought a number over to America— Poles, Germans, Armenians—because, unlike many of the first English colonists in the South who were "vagabond gentlemen" wearing silk and shunning work, these men were used to continuous hard labor. Their English, if they spoke it at all even after years in Virginia, was poor; their manners lacked polish; but by Captain Smith's account they were skilled in making pitch, tar, soap-ashes and the glass beads which were used as currency in trading with the Indians.

In his book, Smith gave the Poles and the other workingmen much credit for saving the Virginia Colony. After he left the settlement, the English people in it generally regarded them and the Germans and Armenians as inferior foreigners. They were in the community, working for it, helping it to survive, fighting the hostile Indians, but they were not considered of it.

For twelve years, while the settlement swayed between success and failure, the Poles—along with the Germans and Armenians—had no political rights and were barred from participating in civil affairs. They were in effect little better than serfs.

Just how many Poles were in Jamestown is unknown. Only a few of their names have come down to us: they were workmen, the kind of people history takes little interest in. And probably not all of them were the most ideal sort of people. But whatever their number and the proportion of good men and good workers among them, they evidently realized their worth to the colony—and their power.

In 1619 they and their fellow workers of German and Armenian origin went on strike. They demanded the right to vote and full equality with the other colonists. In the tiny community this was equivalent to a major rebellion.

I have mentioned the bloody uprising of the Negroes against the Spaniards in the 1520s on the spot where Jamestown was established ninety-odd years later. The Polish-German-Armenian rebellion—possibly helped by the Irish who after 1609 were also being brought over—was the first consciously political upheaval in America for the purpose of extending rights to the common man. In it men of different backgrounds acted jointly against injustice for the first time in the New World. The future of the Virginia Colony depended on its outcome.

Too little is known about the way the strike was handled, but apparently the leading people of Jamestown realized that the community could not go on without the good will of its best workers, and the uprising came to a fortunate conclusion.

The workers' grievances were heeded by the first parliament in America, the House of Burgesses in Jamestown. According to a contemporary record, "it was agreed that they shall be enfranchised and made as free as any inhabitant there whatsoever." And in order to perpetuate their technique in making pitch, tar, soap-ashes and glass, it was further agreed "that some young men [of English stock?] shall be put unto them to learn their skill and knowledge therein—for the benefit of the country hereafter."

In the middle of the seventeenth century, perhaps after hearing how valuable the Poles were to the British colony in Virginia, the Dutch settlers of New Amsterdam persuaded others to come over from Poland to help them grow food and fight the English of New England. These immigrants too were hardy, industrious people; Governor Peter Stuyvesant of New Netherland was pleased with them.

In 1659 a Polish scholar, Dr. Alexander Kurcyusz, arrived in New Amsterdam on the Hollanders' invitation and founded an academy, the first institution of what was then higher learning in what is now New York City. In the history of American education he is known as Alexander Curtius.

In 1662 an exiled Polish nobleman named Albert Zaborowski (subsequently spelled Zabriskie) came to New Amsterdam, moved across the Hudson and became one of the first judges in New Jersey and the owner of a stretch of land along the Passaic River. He left a big family and a fortune to match it. Several of the oldest families in New York, Brooklyn and eastern New Jersey number him among their ancestors. Nearly two dozen Zabriskies are listed in the Manhattan telephone directory alone.

Poles also settled in the Delaware Valley as early as 1650. Pennsylvania archives show them to have been part of that colony in the William Penn period. There was a thin trickle of Polish immigrants into Pennsylvania and Virginia throughout the next hundred years. In 1736 John Anthony Sadowski pushed into the wilderness beyond the Alleghenies. The outpost which he established on the Ohio River grew into the town of Sandusky—that is what "Sadowski" had changed to on English-speaking American tongues.

Sadowski was killed by Indians in Virginia. His sons John and Jacob carried on their father's pioneering and worked as aides to Daniel Boone in the settling of Kentucky. They were co-founders with Boone of Harrodsburg, the oldest town in Kentucky. There is a passage about them in Theodore Roosevelt's book *The Winning of the West* (1889).

The first reliable map of the coast of New England, a useful document in its time, was drawn by a Polish surveyor, Karol Blaszkiewicz (pronounced: Blash-kye'vich).

Somewhere in the South in 1776 a man named Paul Mostowski of Warsaw tried to found a "New Poland." Scarcely anything is known of this attempt; most likely the rebuffs and obstacles which the would-be colonist leader encountered were too much for him. But it indicates that there must have been an appreciable number of Poles in America during the Revolutionary period.

How clearly and how quickly the shot at Bunker Hill was heard around the world is open to question, but an early echo did reach unhappy Poland and the Polish exiles scattered over western Europe. A young engineer named Tadeusz Andrzej Bonawentura Kościuszko (Kosh-chyoosh'ko), was among the first to arrive—on borrowed money —and offer his services to General Washington. "What can you do?" asked the American commander, according to an apocryphal story. "Try me," said the Pole. He became an aide to the Revolutionary Commander-in-Chief, and a very useful one. He had received an unusually good education in Warsaw and at military academies in other European cities, and he was a young man of character.

Military engineers were scarce in the new United States, and it may be said that Kościuszko's training and ability were tantamount to several regiments. The victory at Saratoga was credited in great part to plans he had worked out. He fortified Fort Ticonderoga and West Point. He was made a brigadier general and chief of engineers. He also excelled in other branches of military art; in fact, he acquired the title of the "Father of American Artillery."

His friend Thomas Jefferson, then Secretary of State, said: "I see Kościuszko often. He is the purest son of liberty which extends to all, not alone the rich." His superior officer, General Horatio Gates, considered him "the only pure republican. He is without any dross." Kościuszko was a founder of the Society of the Cincinnati. There is now a monument to him at West Point.

In July 1777 Count Casimir Pulaski presented himself at Washington's headquarters with a letter of introduction from Benjamin Franklin, then representing the year-old United States of America in Paris. The young nobleman was aristocratic in outlook, lacking Kościuszko's genuinely democratic personality and purpose, but Franklin accurately described him as "an officer famous throughout Europe for his defense of the liberties of his country."

During the next two years, crucial in the American Revolution, Pulaski participated in the battles at Brandywine, Warren Tavern, Germantown, Trenton and Haddonfield near Camden. He rose to the rank of general. Then after some difficulties with both his superiors and subordinates which were due at least in part to his aristocratic temperament, he organized his own Polish Legion which fought at Little Egg Harbor and Charleston and in a number of minor engagements. Ill used, he complained to Congress that he found himself "languishing in a state of inactivity," and again that there were "nothing but bears to fight." In the disastrous battle at Savannah on October 9, 1779, Pulaski was mortally wounded; he died three days later. "I could not submit to stoop before the sovereigns of Europe," read his last letter to Congress, "so I came to hazard all for the freedom of America."

Savannah erected the first Pulaski monument in 1820. Later he was memorialized by a bust in the Capitol, an equestrian statue on a square in Washington, and the Pulaski Skyway over the flats of eastern New Jersey. About a dozen towns in as many states are named for him.

Kościuszko and Pulaski are the first and only Poles to break into American history textbooks.

Haym Salomon was the subject of a movie "short" in the early 1940s which for a time made him fairly well known as one of the financiers of the American Revolution—but there is scarcely a textbook in which he rates a line. He was not strictly a Pole, but was born of Portuguese-

Jewish stock in the town of Lissa, Poland. In 1770 he was a well-educated, much-traveled man of thirty, at home in half a dozen languages. That year he threw himself into the revolutionary movement for Polish freedom. In 1772 he had to flee to evade imprisonment or death and, after a brief stay in London, he came to New York and engaged in the brokerage and commission merchant business.

The Whig movement immediately attracted him and later he responded—with all his heart—to the idea of American independence. Shortly after the Revolution broke out, the British imprisoned him as a spy, then decided to use him as an interpreter between them and the Hessians. But in this capacity Salomon is said to have secretly impelled many Hessian mercenaries to resign or desert.

In 1778 the British arrested him again, this time for his part in the plot to burn their ships and supply stocks in New York harbor, and condemned him to death.

He bribed his jailer and, leaving his family in New York, made his way to Philadelphia, where he addressed a memorandum to Congress in which he listed his services to the cause up to that date and begged assignment to some other duty. But Congress delayed acting on his petition. So, aided by leading Philadelphians who knew him as a reputable businessman, he opened a brokerage office. The new business succeeded from the start and by 1780 Haym Salomon was one of the largest depositors of the Bank of North America.

In 1785 he died—a poor man because he had put the bulk of his resources at the disposal of the Revolutionary government of the United States. He had been the paymaster for the French forces under Rochambeau and Lafayette. Out of his own pocket he had paid the salaries of government officials to keep them at their jobs during the periods when the Revolution looked to them like a lost cause. The records of Robert Morris, who was in charge of the Revolutionary finances, indicate seventy-five transactions with Haym Salomon. And various Congressional committees recognized—one as recently as 1926—that the U. S. A.'s indebtedness to Salomon totaled $658,007.43, which was a large slice of the entire cost of the War of Independence. But, in spite of the fact that a Senate committee in 1864 perceived an "undeniable merit" in his heirs' claims, no settlement was ever effected.

Besides Kościuszko and Pulaski, two other Poles contributed to American military history.

Vladimir Krzyzanowski (Kshi-zhan-off'skee), a young engineer, came to America in the 1850s. He assisted in the construction of three railroads in the Middle West, then settled down as a businessman in Washington. At the outbreak of the Civil War he joined the Union forces, organizing a militia company which included many Poles and quickly expanded into a regiment under his command. He was made colonel. The Polish Legion, as it was known, distinguished itself in the battles of Cross Keys and Bull Run. President Lincoln appointed Krzyzanowski brigadier general, but the Senate put off confirming the appointment with the excuse that none of the Senators could pronounce his name.

Krzyzanowski's reputation as a leader and fighter increased after the battles of Chancellorsville and Gettysburg and in minor engagements in Tennessee. Consistently democratic, sharing danger, hunger and fatigue with his men, he was beloved by the Legionnaires. At the end of the war they gave him a sword with an affectionate inscription. The Southerners liked him too; when he left the occupation garrison at Bridgeport, Tennessee, the residents bade him farewell with regret.

After the Civil War, General Krzyzanowski was appointed the first American administrator of Alaska. He died in 1887. His grave in Brooklyn was long neglected; in 1937 his remains were transferred to Arlington Cemetery. President Roosevelt spoke at the ceremony.

Joseph Kargé also rose to the rank of brigadier general in the Union Army. He made a name for himself in operations against "Stonewall" Jackson in Virginia and in the defense of Washington. Two serious wounds received in 1862 almost compelled him to retire, but he saw the war through. Toward the end he was assigned the task of eliminating the guerrillas in the South; after the war, he commanded a cavalry unit in Nevada.

Krzyzanowski and Kargé were part of the Polish emigration from German, Austrian and Russian Poland that got under way after the three ill-fated uprisings—in 1830, 1848 and 1863—against the rule of the three most powerful monarchs in Europe. The several thousand Polish refugees who came to the United States in that period were almost all revolutionists seeking to evade imprisonment or death.

Many possessed marked ability—Adam Kurek, believed to have founded the first brass band in the United States; Julian Fontana, a noted musician and friend of Chopin; Henryk Dmochowski-Sanders, a sculptor; Alexander Sengteller and Alexander Raszewski, steel engravers; Adam Curowski, an educator; Ludwik Sopaczek, Henryk Kolussowski and R. Tomain, physicians.

The next period, beginning in the 1870s, was mostly a matter of relatives following the refugees; then of the relatives' relatives coming to join them in the Land of Promise. For a while, many people in countries like Poland really believed that the streets in the United States were paved with gold. Polish immigration increased annually until its peak in 1912 when nearly one hundred and seventy-five thousand people from Poland were admitted.

Between 1880 and 1910 most of the newcomers were the poorest of the poor: landless peasants and urban workers whose earning power in the old country was so low that they lived almost continually on the verge of starvation.

Like other Europeans, a large proportion of Polish peasants left for America intending to earn enough to go back home and buy a piece of native soil. But whatever their plans on arrival, the majority never returned. Hundreds of thousands settled in the United States and sent for their wives and children, brothers and sisters, aunts and uncles and cousins. One of them, an old man whom I met in Chicago in 1940, explained to me why he had decided to stay: "I was only an ordinary workman in America and knew I would never be anything else, but life in the United States was so much better than what I left in Poland. I left there in 1905 when I was thirty-eight. In the old country I had hardly ever eaten meat. My mother used to split matches to make two out of one. Sometimes she had no matches at all and had to go to the neighbors with a pot to borrow live coals. . . ."

Thousands of young men emigrated to avoid serving in the German, Austrian and Russian imperial armies. One Polish American, now a successful businessman in the Middle West, told me he had decided to come here when he was nineteen because he could not bear the idea of shining Austrian officers' boots.

Polish Jews came by the tens of thousands to escape the persecutions instigated against them by the German, Austrian and Russian imperial governments. They all came to stay and, settling in the large eastern cities, went mainly into garment factories, fur and millinery shops, and small businesses. Their story is the same as that of the Jewish immigrants from Russia, told in an earlier chapter.

The majority of Slavic-Polish newcomers, both peasants and urban people, went into basic industries—mines and foundries and forests—and shoe and textile factories. Most of the rest, perhaps one-third of the total Polish immigration, went into farming; some in the Middle West, some in Texas, others all over the Northeast. In New England early in the twentieth century they started taking over farms abandoned by Yankees who believed that the soil was exhausted. With the instinctive understanding of the land and the food-growing skill they had come by in the old country, they restored hundreds of thousands of apparently hopeless acres to productivity.

These Polish farmers in New England are among my favorite groups. People to whom hard work is a religion, they succeeded where others had confessed failure. They are at once satisfying their old-country land hunger, prospering, improving neglected American soil, adding to the strength of the United States.

A small percentage of Poles who came over late in the nineteenth century went into business and professions. The qualities and achievements of some of them merit attention. There were Colonel Kasimir Stanislaus Gzowski, an engineer who was instrumental in building the first bridge at Niagara Falls; Joseph Turkolski, surveyor of Louisiana and Utah; Captain Karol Radziminski, who had a hand in establishing the United States-Mexican boundary; Leopold Boeck, reputed to have started the first polytechnical school in America; and the educators Arthur Grabowski and Joseph D'Alfons.

In their day most of these men were known not only in their own communities but in other cities as well, a few of them nationally. Their accomplishments added to the sum of American life. As intellectuals they also perpetuated the Slavic-Polish tradition in America which began in Jamestown in 1608 and which has helped the bulk of recent immigrants and their American-born children, who together now number upward of three million, to feel at home in America.

The main body of Polish immigrants and their native-American sons and daughters who are forging steel, digging coal, making motor vehicles and planes and locomotives and farm machinery, or raising food—and who were one of the principal manpower factors in the war industries during both world wars—ought not to feel any special need of hooking onto the Polish tradition created by men like Kościuszko, Pulaski and Krzyzanowski; for their own day-to-day collective achievement is so great and so necessary that in itself it should make them feel an integral part of America. The mill worker, miner or farmer, however, is often unconscious of his own direct value and contributions; he looks about for something bigger and older than himself to grasp hold of, something hallowed by history, to help him feel comfortable about his place in the American scheme of things. A Polish American farmer near the town of White House, New Jersey, finds his deepest satisfaction not in his bumper crops but in the sign "Kościuszko Road" which he put up at the entrance to the lane connecting his farm with the highway. He spends much time and energy teaching his non-Polish neighbors how to pronounce the name, and telling them the hero's story.

Most immigrants from Poland are naturalized citizens; every year many more take out their final papers. In some large cities they form a sizable proportion of the population and are politically important. In 1945 ten members of Congress were Polish Americans.

The group's greatest concentration—close to half a million—is in Chicago. They are very numerous also in Buffalo, Detroit, Milwaukee, Toledo, Cleveland, Pittsburgh, New York, Boston and several smaller New England towns; they are more or less thickly scattered outside the big urban centers of Texas, Michigan, Wisconsin, Minnesota, Nebraska, Illinois, Indiana, Missouri, Pennsylvania, New York and New Jersey.

There are over fifty towns in the United States with such names as Pulaski, Warsaw, Cracow, Polonia, Poland, New Poland.

Polish Americans have about ten thousand fraternal, dramatic, literary, musical, social, religious and athletic societies all over America. A good many are branches or affiliates of the fifty-three Polish American organizations whose total membership runs close to a million. Some of these organizations are quite old. The Gmina Polska (Polish Group), for instance, was started in 1866, the Polish Roman Catholic Union in 1874, the Polish National Alliance in 1879.

The vast majority of Poles are Catholics. There are eight hundred and forty Polish Roman Catholic parishes and eighty-odd Polish Roman Catholic missions in the United States with over a thousand priests; fourteen orphanages and three seminaries for men and three for women. There are five hundred and sixty Polish Roman Catholic parochial schools with about a quarter of a million pupils and over five thousand teachers. Perhaps one third of Polish American youngsters' go to these parochial schools, run largely by priests and nuns; the other two-thirds, to public schools.

A minority of Polish Americans adhere to the Polish National Church which does not recognize the authority of the Vatican. They support an anti-Catholic weekly newspaper, *Ameryka Echo*, which is published in Toledo and has a circulation of some twenty thousand.

There are close to a hundred Polish-language newspapers and magazines, including nine dailies; many of them issued by organizations. Some were started way back in the 1870s and '80s.

Except for a small proportion of the older first-generation immigrants, all Polish Americans—as well as the majority of alien Poles—habitually speak English. The second and third generations, of course, find it easier than Polish, whose use in churches, organizations and publications is a symbol of loyalty to their background rather than evidence that they have not readily acquired the language of the larger American community.

Polish Americans have played an interesting role in the career of modern Poland.

During World War I Paderewski and Pilsudski had the support of the Polish National Alliance of the United States.

Between the two wars the regime of Poland spent a great deal of money and effort on propaganda in the various "Polonias" all over America. The propaganda issued from the Polish embassy in Washington, from the Polish consulates in New York, Chicago, Buffalo, Cleveland, Pittsburgh and other cities. It exploited the Polish Americans' inferiority feelings in relation to the other groups in the population by stressing the virtues of Poland under Pilsudski and his successors, "the Colonels."

Many of the activities connected with this campaign to preserve and heighten Polish American interest in Poland were culturally, humanly worthwhile. No one could object to the program of the Polish Arts Club in Chicago, for instance, or to the Kościuszko Foundation in New York. The latter provided scholarships for native Americans of Polish descent in the best universities in Poland. But the campaign's general purpose was questionable—not very different from Mussolini's propaganda directed at the Italian Americans. The purpose was to make the Polish rulers, most of them beneficiaries of a semi-feudal system, synonymous with Poland in the minds of Polish Americans. There was no propaganda to counter that idea.

The result was that when the Polish crisis made front-page headlines in the United States, the Polish Americans' intense and, in large part, natural and inevitable reaction was a mixture of sound and unsound sentiments, for a time mostly the latter.

Reactionary Polish American organizations were started under the direction of Polish exiles connected with the Polish embassy, and with the support of some of the large Polish-language newspapers and the Polish Catholic clergy. They worked for the Polish government-in-exile in London, which meant that they worked against America's collaboration with Russia. About six groups were set up for this purpose. I shall mention only the fanatic National Committee of Americans of Polish Descent. Its initiator and spiritual guide was Colonel Ignacy Matuszewski, former Polish Minister of Finance who had come to America in 1941 and was violently opposed to Premier Sikorski's inclination to work out a new relationship between Poland and the Soviet Union, which would operate toward future security. The organization's American leader was M. F. Wegrzynek, the exclusive importer of Polish ham to the United States and publisher of the New York daily *Nowy Swiat* (New World), whose anti-Soviet fulminations beginning in 1939 became the keynote for many other Polish-language papers, including those belonging to the initially more moderate organizations; the fulminations also underlay the impression of the Polish "government" in London that it enjoyed a tremendous support in the United States.

Not that the impression was entirely erroneous. The Rightist pressure groups springing out of the large Polish American element found approval in the columns of the New York Daily News, the Chicago Tribune and the whole Hearst press; in hundreds of publications of the Catholic Hierarchy, among reactionary Congressmen, and in sections of the State Department. Beginning in 1942 these did their best to inhibit Franklin Roosevelt's efforts to work out a policy of friendly postwar relations with the Soviet Union. Their thesis was that Stalin was a greater enemy than Hitler; by implication they favored a war between America and Russia.

In their attempts to influence President Roosevelt, the leaders of these groups claimed that the Polish element numbered six million (with "more than a million votes"). The figure was far too high—unless it took in the Polish-Jewish Americans; which would have been rather strange because nearly all the leading Polish Americans in the Rightist pressure organizations were actively anti-Semitic. On that point, as in the matter of working toward a war between America and Russia, they were playing tag in Joseph Goebbels' favorite alley.

The progressive anti-Fascist Americans of Polish origin or descent were slow in organizing a counter movement. Professor Oscar Lange, an economist at the University of Chicago, was the first person of Polish stock to write effectively in favor of the Roosevelt policy toward the Soviet Union as it might affect Poland, and of a new Poland devoid of the prewar ruling class and capable of cooperation with her big neighbor to the east. That was late in 1943. At the same time the first anti-Rightist Polish-American organization, the Kościuszko League, was started—interestingly enough—by a third-generation American Catholic priest, the Reverend Stanislaus Orlemanski, pastor of the Polish church in Springfield, Massachusetts. It promptly evoked a strong response among the plain people in several "Polonias" who had hitherto been hearing only the Polish government-in-exile propaganda.

Early in 1944 Father Orlemanski and Professor Lange became front-page news when they flew to Moscow in response to an invitation from Stalin, who gave them important statements about the Soviet's policy on Poland and religion. Upon his return to the United States, Father Orlemanski was disciplined by Bishop Thomas O'Leary of Springfield much as the Irish straw-bosses of one or two generations earlier used to slap down "Polack" and "Hunky" and "Dago" and "Litvak" laborers under them. Father Orlemanski has not been heard of since.

Partly under the stimulus of Lange's writings and under the direct leadership of Leo Krzycki, a native American and a vice president of the Amalgamated Clothing Workers, several hundred Polish Americans, mostly second- and third-generation, all leaders or officials of labor unions, met in Cleveland in June 1944 and reorganized and reoriented their Polish American Labor Council, whose primary purpose until then had been to heighten morale among Polish Americans in war industries. The reorganization and reorientation was felt necessary because the violent anti-Russian propaganda, with its implicit attacks on Roosevelt, had begun to affect war production in Detroit, Chicago, Cleveland, Toledo, Milwaukee, Pittsburgh and elsewhere.

Among the officers of the Polish American Labor Council, besides Krzycki who was elected president, were: Larry Nowakowski of the United Automobile, Aircraft and Agricultural Implement Workers; Stanley Strobeck of the United Steelworkers; Joseph Cetnar of the United Electrical, Radio and Machine Workers; Henry Kulas of the Textile Workers Union; John Sobczak of the Amalgamated Clothing Workers; Conrad Komorowski of the United Farm Equipment and Metal Workers; Joseph Poskanka of the United Packinghouse Workers; Adolph Prywara of the Industrial and Marines Shipbuilders Workers; Dolores Pinta of the Mine, Mill, and Smelter Workers; Stanley Nowak of the State, County, and Municipal Workers; Frank Mierkiewicz of the International Fur and Leather Workers; Joseph Pyzik of the American-Polish Trades Council; Joseph Janusz of the Cooks, Countermen, and Cafeteria Workers; Maria Szymanski of the Massachusetts C.I.O.; Victor Bloswick of the Transport Workers Union, Eugene Jasinski of the United Office and Professional Workers, Albert A. Krzywonos of the Steel Workers, and John A. Zaremba of the Auto Workers. Though known to few non-Polish Americans outside the labor movement, these men and women are more representative of the majority of the Polish element in the United States than anyone else. As workers and as Americans stemming from Poland they want a progressive America and a progressive Poland living in friendly relations with Russia in a peaceful world; and as such they have more in common with, say, Walter Reuther, who is of German stock and a top leader of the Auto Workers, than with the National Committee of Americans of Polish Descent. Together with such citizens of non-Polish derivation, they have an idea how to help attain their objectives. They see the different parts and problems of the human world as interdependent. From that point of view, one of their 1945 contributions was the annulment among

Polish Americans of much of the Polish government-in-exile's propaganda; another was their sending Leo Krzycki as an observer to the United Nations Security Conference in San Francisco, where the new Poland was not represented.

Still another contribution of these Polish American officers of local unions and district labor councils is in the field of race relations. As already mentioned, several of the Whites who caused the 1943 Detroit race riot were native Americans of Polish descent who had been "Americanized" into hating Negroes. Some of those who follow the line of the Polish government-in-exile hate Negroes as well as Jews; in other words they are consistently reactionary both in reference to problems abroad and to those in the United States. The labor groups are active in reducing anti-Negro and anti-Semitic sentiments.

The Kościuszko League, begun by Father Orlemanski, merged with the Committee to Combat Propaganda Inimical to the United States Among Americans of Polish Descent, with headquarters in Detroit. In 1945 the two organizations began to issue a valuable broadside called *For the Record*, under the editorship of Thomas X. Dombrowski, featuring translations of the reactionary Polish-language editors' veiled appeals for war against Russia and analyses of the vastly complex "Polish problem" in Europe as it affects the United States.

However, the probability is that some years after this book appears the "Polish problem"—which of course is not only Polish—will have been swept away by the strong winds from the east and west, and that writers who in 1960 or 1975 tell the Polish part of American history will be torn between putting the "problem" as it existed in 1945 into a footnote or leaving it out entirely.

They will tell, instead, of the Polish Americans' role in World War II—of such men as Lieutenant Colonel Francis Gabreski of Oil City, Pennsylvania, an ace of aces; Sergeant Joseph J. Sadowski of Perth Amboy, New Jersey, whose "gallant and noble sacrifice of his life," for which he was awarded a posthumous Congressional Medal of Honor, ". . . so inspired the remainder of the tank crews that they pressed forward with great ferocity and completely destroyed the enemy forces [at Valhey, France, on September 14, 1944] without further losses to themselves"; Private John J. Wondolowski who early in 1942, at Fort Hancock, New Jersey, inspired civilian Americans to invest in war bonds by buying five thousand dollars' worth himself—the amount of his savings during the previous fourteen years as a bartender in Jersey City; and Major General Maurice Rose of Denver, who commanded the Third Armored Division, and was killed in March 1945 when captured by the enemy during one of his famous outfit's spearheading operations in Germany. His eighty-nine-year-old father, Rabbi Samuel Rose, a native of Poland, said of his death: "It is well that, since this had to be, it happened in the week of Passover. As Jehovah said 'When I see the blood, I will pass over you,' he spoke not only to the Jews but to all peoples, to the Gentiles, to Americans, to Germans, to all peoples. 'When I see the sacrifice, the blood, I will pass over you.' And so, may Jehovah accept this sacrifice, and see the blood and pass over all peoples for their sins at this Passover time. For my son's sake."

The first book printed in English west of the Rockies was written by the California pioneer Dr. Felix Wierzbicki, a Pole. The Slavic-Polish element has not yet produced an American writer of any stature, but there is little question that it will. Its background offers rich material for novels, plays, poems, biographies and historical essays. Norman Rosten, author of *The Fourth Decade* (1944), a young poet, is the son of Jewish immigrants from Poland. So is the popular radio commentator Gabriel Heatter. Sholem Asch, author of *The Nazarene* and other best-selling novels, was born in Poland. So was Arthur Kober, author of the play *Having Wonderful Time* (1937), the books *Thunder Over the Bronx* (1935) and *My Dear Bella* (1941) and numerous film scripts.

During 1942-1945 Arthur Szyk became one of the most effective cartoonists in the United States. His drawings depicting contemporary world events are often at once terrifying and beautiful, always significant.

The conductors Leopold Stokowski and Arthur Rodzinski and the tenor Jan Kiepura are Polish. Ignace Paderewski never became an American citizen but was long an especially bright light on the American musical scene.

Ralph Modjeski, the bridgebuilder, was the son of Helena Modjeska, the Shakespearean actress.

Alexander Granach, a Polish Jew well known on the European stage, came to America in the 1930s to escape Hitlerism. He appeared in several American motion pictures and died early in 1945 while playing his first Broadway role, that of Tomasino in *A Bell for Adano*. His autobiography, *There Goes an Actor*, was published after his death.

Max Kalish was brought from Poland as a child. He first attracted attention in the 1920s with his bronzes of steelworkers, locomotive engineers, loggers and drillers, and was sometimes referred to as the "Walt Whitman of bronze." In 1926 his "The Christ," destined for the Cleveland Museum of Art, created a sensation because it depicted not the gentle and mild Jesus of traditional belief, but a militant Christ, newly risen and striding wrathful through a world labeled with His name but alien to His teachings.

Casimir Funk, born in Warsaw, the "father of the vitamin," one of the great intuitive scientists of all times, arrived in America under the auspices of the Rockefeller Foundation.

James A. Dombrowski, formerly principal of the Highlander Folk School in Tennessee, is executive secretary of the Southern Conference for Human Welfare. (*See page 218.*)

M. F. Szymczak (Sim-chak) of Chicago is a member of the board of governors of the Federal Reserve System.

Finally, there is Alfred Korzybski (Kor-zib'ski), originator of a system of General Semantics, whom some of his pupils regard as one of the really important agents of human progress—in the category of Darwin, Marx, Tesla, Freud, Einstein.

Born in Warsaw in 1879, he comes of an old noble family distinguished for its scholars and scientists. Count Korzybski was trained as an engineer at the Polytechnic Institute of Warsaw; he pursued his studies in Germany and Italy, and for a time taught mathematics, physics, French and German in Poland.

He was seriously wounded in World War I, in which he served first in the Russian cavalry; then, because of his knowledge of languages and insight into human personality, in the Imperial General Staff's intelligence department. After the war he was for a while with the new Polish Army—constantly observing, thinking, studying. He reached the conclusion that the world was a madhouse run by its inmates.

Korzybski came to America on a military mission for Russia in 1915, on another for Poland after the war; then in the mid-1920s he returned to stay—with questions like these running through his mind: Why do human civilizations break down when bridges and other structures built by human beings don't break down? Both are man-made. If we can create methods for solving material problems like bridge building, why can't we invent equally effective methods for handling human problems?

In 1933, after rewriting it half a dozen times, he published *Science and Sanity*, in which he answers the last question: "But we can!" Not easy reading, the book had a slow but penetrating effect; a revised edition appeared in 1941. It goes into the enormous incongruity of the affairs of man, defines sanity and seeks ways and means of bringing it about. To Korzybski, World Wars I and II and the period between them are symptomatic of increasing and worldwide "un-sanity." General

Semantics is the method whereby humanity is invited to extricate itself from this condition which is going from bad to worse.

General Semantics, to quote from the book, is not " 'philosophy,' or 'psychology,' or 'logic' in the ordinary sense. It is a new extensional discipline which explains and trains us how to use our nervous systems most effectively. It is not a medical science but, like bacteriology, it [becomes] indispensable for medicine in general, and for psychiatry, mental hygiene, and education in particular. . . .

Korzybski's General Semantics rejects the old "theories of meaning" (which, in his view, lead to verbal hair-splitting) and favors a study and a reorientation of "evaluations," that is, of the reactions of the whole human system to signs and situations. It seeks to break up the prevailing neurologically patterned linguistic assumptions based on old linguistic systems, which result not only in endless confusions and misunderstandings in communication, but also in a state of being in which a person is incapable of perceiving intelligently what is going on in his immediate vicinity, in his country, in the world. Result: un-sanity if not downright insanity; not only personal but also communal and world.

General Semantics is a systematic effort to build up a positive theory of sanity as distinct from mere explanatory, negative theorizing about various forms of insanity.

"The task ahead," says Korzybski, "is gigantic if we are to avoid more personal, national, and even international tragedies based on unpredictability, insecurity, fears, anxieties, etc., which are steadily disintegrating the functioning of the human nervous system. Only when we face these facts fearlessly and intelligently may we save for future civilizations whatever there is left to save, and build from the ruins of a dying epoch a new and saner society. . . ."

As I understand him, Korzybski sees the core of the human problem in people's nervous makeups which are conditioned to respond to words and signs, phrases and slogans that originated long ago under conditions drastically different from those in which they live today, and that carry meanings and assumptions which have scant if any relevance to present-day realities. He has designed several "semantic devices"—too complex to describe here—which enable one to throw off the habits of infantile, primitive or unscientific evaluations.

In 1938 the Institute of General Semantics, of which Korzybski is director, was founded in Chicago. It has held several congresses and conducts courses attended by educators, industrial managers, writers, physicians, psychiatrists and laymen. Korzybski and his assistant refrain from any sort of ballyhoo; the work is supported by student fees and private contributions. Speaking in a resonant voice with a heavy accent and not always conforming to grammatical rules, Korzybski tells his classes that English is the best linguistic medium for precise, objective expression.

Korzybski is anti-dogmatist, anti-doctrinaire. He is against absolutes, fixed labels, *Herrenvolk* concepts—whether Nazi, Polish, Serbian or Anglo-Saxon. He is forever asking questions, inviting and giving tentative answers, correlating the knowledge of many hitherto separated scientific fields, trying for the maximum probability of accuracy or truth on the basis of discerned facts and facts as they become discerned and of the theories the facts give rise to, for that, says he in effect over and over again, is all we can possibly aim for in the fluid, dynamic, ever-changing world of men. He is endlessly calling for facts, facts, facts; seeking to put them together into truth-ward meaning, and urging others to do the same.

When one first confronts it, General Semantics may seem a complicated subject. Korzybski does not attempt to make it simple. Its analyses and details reach in all directions, touch almost everything human. It challenges and examines every concept, idea, notion. It is impatient with language when language does not express thought based on facts and a sense of probabilities in the whirl of events and trends. It seeks to de-departmentalize, de-specialize knowledge; to coordinate it, make it useful.

Should he hear of Korzybski, the man in the street, perennially caught in one or another un-sane if not totally crazy situation, and intent on being "practical," is likely to say, "Oh nuts! What's it to me, this General Semantics? What is this fancy Polack up to anyhow?"

Ignoring the last question, Korzybski answers that our life is greatly "dependent on the established doctrines of ethics, sociology, political economy, government, law, medical science, etc. This affects everyone consciously and unconsciously, the man in the street in the first place, because he is the most defenseless."

At sixty-five (in 1945), he believes that eventually everybody will have to come under the influence of one system of General Semantics or another.

Since the middle 1930s Korzybski has conveyed his theory and methods of gaining sanity to a few thousand people. Some of these are in strategic educational positions, working out his and their own ideas in their own ways. He encourages divergence from his system. A considerable literature on General Semantics is beginning to accumulate. Some of Korzybski's pupils are starting to tackle racism and conflict among diverse ethnic groups.

Early in the 1940s the Society for General Semantics was organized in Chicago. It publishes a review called *Etc.*

Picturesque, patently honest, immensely learned, often witty, Alfred Korzybski is still essentially an engineer. He uses engineering and mathematical terms; they are constructive, they mean what they say. He likes to quote another engineer, Walter N. Polakov of the Tennessee Valley Authority who in 1934 put his finger on what may be the central problem of man. "The youthful T.V.A.," said Mr. Polakov, "inherited the language and metaphysics of a bygone age. It encounters unprecedented difficulties in expressing new relations in terms of vanished fancies. The night fear of ghosts remains. . . . The difficulties in building the T.V.A. without a language having correspondence to reality, are not difficulties peculiar to this project. They are signs of our time— a sort of dangerous epidemic, springing out of our slow adjustment to a profoundly changed environment."

Korzybski thinks that in the inclusive world crisis which culminated in World War II "we are witnessing the death-bed agonies . . . of the old system [of dogma and doctrine] which has been applied to its deadly limit" in religion, law, government, medicine, education. "Surveying the chain of historical world tragedies as they accumulate with accelerating acceleration and intensity," he said during the Second American Congress on General Semantics held at the University of Denver in August 1941, "one naturally looks for the factors which are responsible for such cataclysms. This problem may be analyzed in many different ways, but here . . . we take frankly and explicitly an engineering point of view in which there is no 'philosophy' for 'philosophy's' sake, but we consider all those activities as products of the human nervous system, to be *applied* for its optimum efficiency. When formulated methodologically, the interrelation between science and sanity becomes obvious, and the new methods can be applied for more efficient management of our private as well as public lives, and in particular for *prevention* of maladjustments, i.e. mis-evaluations in life."

XIII: AMERICANS FROM IRELAND

A VERY fascinating story," wrote President Roosevelt in March 1940, congratulating the American Irish Historical Society on the opening of its new home in New York City, "is the story of the Irish in America, whether as related in the romantic saga of the 'Navigation of

St. Brendan' or in the later active participation of Sons of Erin in every movement from Colonial days."

Addicted as he was to maritime lore, Franklin D. Roosevelt knew of the legend—preserved in a Vatican manuscript—that St. Brendan of Clonfert in Ireland, sailing westward in the middle years of the sixth century, four hundred and fifty years before Leif Erikson, came upon a hitherto unknown land. The legend was so familiar in the Middle Ages that nearly every cartographer sketched an "Insula Sancti Brendani" somewhere in the western ocean. St. Brendan's discovery, if it actually occurred, had no consequences of any vital meaning today; it is, however, a noteworthy detail, as is the fact that Old Norse writings refer to the American continent as "Irland it Mikla" (Greater Ireland); and that an Irishman, "William from Galway," was a sailor on Columbus' *Santa Maria* in 1492.

What is especially interesting is F.D.R.'s awareness that enough "Sons of Erin" were in North America in colonial days to permit their "active participation . . . in every movement" from then on, that is, in shaping the new civilization. Such awareness does not exist in the average contemporary American whose historical knowledge is usually limited to what he learned in school. He has no inkling of the Irish story in the Colonial and Revolutionary periods.

That story is written large in early American records, in the diaries, memoirs and "lives" of many Revolutionary leaders; it formed a natural part of the annals of the early historians. Why then—and how—has it disappeared from history as written and taught since the 1870s?

To answer that fully would take a book in itself. Very briefly and much simplified, the process occurred somewhat as follows:

The writings of Jefferson and other public men in the post-Revolutionary era noted that from the moment the British government acknowledged the United States' independence, British (really English) official, mercantile and financial influence was exerted to give American ideology and polity an English aspect and, wherever possible, a pro-English direction.

This was manifest in the Hamiltonian financial measures and proposals, in the reactionary trend of the Adams administration, in the agitation for secession of the New England states; and later in English promotion of the slave-based cotton-economy which made the South dependent on English markets, in English official—not popular—support of the Confederacy, in the intrigues which long kept the U.S.A. from having an adequate merchant marine, in persistent efforts to break down prematurely the American protective tariff system.

In a competitive, free-for-all, unorganized world, these British exertions to influence American policy were natural and call for no indignation. But they need to be taken into account.

The Irish in America stood in the way of British purposes. The vast majority were Jeffersonians, in fact so sharply identified as Democrats that the promoters of the Alien and Sedition Acts and the Hartford Convention commonly used "United Irishmen" as a term of abuse for all their opponents; it was the equivalent of "Communists" as used by reactionary congressmen and newspapers in 1940-1945. Resentment of British rule in Ireland was, as we shall see, a major factor in the Revolution; it long continued thereafter as a force in American public opinion. The Continental Congress and its agents abroad, Benjamin Franklin and Arthur Lee, had identified the Irish with the American cause; and Washington wrote in 1788: "Patriots of Ireland! Champions of liberty in all lands!—be strong in hope! Your cause is identical with mine!"

In the early decades of independence, "Irish," "Hibernian" and "St. Patrick" societies flourished in the United States; at their banquets non-Irish Americans joined in toasts complimentary to Ireland often at the expense of England. The "Irish Question" was very much alive in America. It had an influential press as early as 1815. Down the years Presidents Jefferson, Jackson, Van Buren, Polk, Buchanan, Johnson, Benjamin Harrison, Cleveland, Theodore Roosevelt and Taft, as well as public leaders like Wendell Phillips, voiced sympathy with the Irish cause. Later Irish influence caused the Senate to reject treaties of Anglo-American alliance proposed by Ambassadors Pauncefote and Bryce.

In spite of such influence and sentiment, however, the spell of Britain, of England, to be more exact—the England of Shakespeare and the King James Version of the Bible and its other great books and of well-subsidized learned institutions—was natural and strong. American scholars and writers, including many of Irish descent, were specially subject to it. Snobbery and religious bigotry also had their effect. History as written by men of Protestant affiliation and marked Anglophile sentiment—John Fiske, Henry Cabot Lodge, Woodrow Wilson, Albert Bushnell Hart—omitted mention of the Irish in early America. The textbook writers naturally followed suit. When George Haven Putnam, New York book publisher and executive secretary of the Society to Promote British-American Union, declared in London on July 4, 1918, that American textbooks were being prepared to "present a juster historical account" of Anglo-American relations; when the

London *Times* on July 4, 1919, wrote that American "histories and textbooks should be revised," they were only being more diplomatic than Owen Wister who in that same issue of Lord Northcliffe's paper declared that "a movement to correct the schoolbooks of the United States has been started."

It had long been going on. Underpaid educators not unmindful of Carnegie Pensions, and coveting the distinction of training successful candidates for Rhodes Scholarships, might well have tended toward this revision of American history—for Andrew Carnegie, the great Scots-immigrant steel tycoon and philanthropist, had written in 1893: "I say that as surely as the sun in the heavens once shone upon Britain and America united, so surely it is one morning to rise, shine upon and greet again the Reunited States, the British-American Union," while Cecil Rhodes, the English "Empire-Builder," in his first will had provided a fund "for the establishment, promotion and development of a Secret Society the aim and object of which shall be the extension of British rule throughout the world . . . the ultimate recovery of the United States of America as an integral part of the British Empire." Rhodes' biographers made it clear that his final will, setting up the scholarships, pursued the same objective by subtler means.

Thus the natural orientation of American culture and American scholarship toward Britain, specifically toward England, and the fact that Britain's policy and its Anglophile supporters needed to diminish Irish influence, have combined to delete the Irish chapter from the story of the United States beginnings . . . and to emphasize Anglo-Saxon standards and values in the formulation of the concepts of "Americanism" and "Americanization."

Everyone knows that the population of this country includes millions of Irish Americans—either born in Ireland (a dwindling percentage) or wholly or in large part of Irish descent. St. Patrick's Day is an unofficial feast-day almost everywhere in America—a legal holiday for municipal employees in New York City—and millions of Americans, among them many who are not Irish, celebrate it by sticking shamrocks and green carnations in their lapels. But the general notion is that Irish immigration began only in the 1840s, or at the earliest in the 1820s, when great streams of refugees from poverty and famine poured into American ports. That they are now an integral part of the American people is not in dispute; but the fact which calls for renewed recognition, if the dynamics of early American history and of the present-day United States are to be understood, is what Franklin Roosevelt knew: the Irish are not a late-coming element that had to be integrated into the national fabric but a numerous and important part of the original stuff of the nation.

Here the "Scotch-Irish myth" intrudes. All Irish Americans of my acquaintance who have given the matter any thought call it "myth" or "legend." Whatever the word for it, it has long bedeviled historical study. It consists of attributing—where they could not be ignored—the contributions to American development made before the 1820s by anyone immigrating or stemming from Ireland to the "Scotch-Irish," not to the "Irish." In this way the Irish chapter of the American Story was watered down.

Shaemas O'Sheel of New York, third-generation Irish American, poet, prose writer, a student of these matters for forty years, has this to say about the "Scotch-Irish myth":

"The thesis that all the Irish, or at least all worth-while Irish in this country in the early days, were 'Scotch-Irish' rested originally on two propositions: that the only people who came here from Ireland at that time came from Ulster, and that all Ultonians of that period were transplanted Presbyterian Scots. These propositions are sheer fiction. I am a living refutation; my paternal forbears were in Ulster before Christ, stayed there through the English and Scots settlements, and remained Catholic. . . . But the 'Scotch-Irish' enthusiasts blandly stuck their hyphenated label on every American bearing any Irish name and deriving from any part of Ireland.

"The O'Neills, O'Donnells and Maguires were the Irish clans foremost in resisting the English-Scotch settlements in Ulster; but when some of them came to America, lo, they were 'Scotch-Irish.' O'Mahony, McCarthy, O'Sullivan and O'Brien are clans immemorially established in Munster, hundreds of miles from Ulster and from Scotland; but let any of these names turn up in American history and its bearer is pounced upon by 'Scotch-Irish historians.' Kelly and Murphy are known to all Americans as the most typical Irish names. No one has yet called the late Captain Colin Kelly, or Sergeant Charles E. ('One-Man-Army') Kelly, or Supreme Court Justice Frank Murphy a 'Scotch-Irishman'; but give these 'historians' a decade or two and they will probably file their claim—it will require no different logic than they have shown in the past.

"For three centuries up to the Battle of Clontarf in 1014 A.D., Danes, Norwegians and Swedes settled in Ireland; my maternal grandfather was a 'Dublin Dane' named Holmes. Thousands of Norman-English, Saxon-English and Welsh settlers became, as an English historian complained, 'more Irish than the Irish themselves.' In 1465 the English

Parliament 'ordeyned' that 'every Irishman . . . in the County of Dublin, Myeth, Uriell or Kildare . . . shall take unto himself an English surname of one towne, as Sutton, Chester, Trym, Corke, Kinsale; or colour, as white, blacke, browne; or art or science, as smith or carpenter; or office, as cooke, butler . . . under payne of forfeyting of his goods.' So thousands of families formerly rejoicing in Irish names complete with O' or Mac became Suttons or Chesters, Whites, Brownes, Carpenters, Smiths, Taylors, Wrights, Cookes, Butlers and so forth. Spaniards settled in the west of Ireland; later came new waves of English, Huguenots, Flemings, Hessians and Palatines; so that there are thousands of non-Gaelic names which are nevertheless veritably Irish. But let a man or woman bearing such an Irish name and known to be of Irish birth or descent win distinction in America, the 'Scotch-Irish' monopolists put in their bid. It would be equally reasonable to insist that all Americans of English descent are really 'Scotch-English.'

"In the years 1609-1611 occurred the Plantation of Ulster, the event which is supposed to have made Ulster a pure fountain of Presbyterian 'Scotch-Irish' undefiled by Catholic 'mere Irish.' It is obvious that if the Plantation resulted in any large emigration from Ulster, the 'mere Irish' would have been the ones to go. Actually, nothing of the sort happened. For one thing, three of the nine Ulster Counties were not 'planted.' The Planters numbered only about two thousand families; and many of these were English or Huguenot, not Scotch. The Catholic Old Irish by no means disappeared from Ulster. The records show that 234 of the principal Old Irish, bearing seventy-three of the old clan names—O'Neill, O'Donnell, Maguire, O'Hagen, O'Sheil, O'Hanlon, et cetera—were at the time of the Plantation assigned a total of 58,472 acres. Their tenants and agricultural laborers, all Old Irish and Catholic, must have numbered thousands. Besides, the English and Scots Planters were allowed to retain a percentage of Irish tenants, and in fact they retained more than the legal quota. Others of the Old Irish received smaller allotments of land; and many became, as an English historian puts it, 'wood-kerne'—outlaws in English eyes, Robin Hoods to the Irish.

"In 1641 the Old Irish staged a vigorous rebellion, which was suppressed; it caused little emigration either of Old Irish or Planters. But in 1649 Cromwell subdued Ireland by war and massacre, parcelled out millions of acres of Irish land (little of it in Ulster) to his soldiers (English, not Scots), causing great numbers of Catholic Irish to flee to America; moreover in the next few years the Cromwellians enslaved not less than two hundred thousand Irish men, women and children and shipped them to the West Indies, whence great numbers of them and their descendants came to the Colonies on the mainland.

"A generation later the triumph of King William over King James caused hundreds of thousands of Catholic Irish to emigrate, mostly to the European Continent but also in large numbers to America. Their room was taken by English, Hessian and Palatine followers of William. Ireland, at peace after centuries of strife, promptly began to outstrip England in woolen manufacture and other industries, whereupon the English Parliament passed laws that snuffed out Irish competition, and caused extensive emigration to America both of Old (Catholic) Irish and of later elements from the Southern and Western counties. At the same time the English, no longer needing the Ulster Presbyterians as instruments for the subjection of the Catholics, harried them with persecutions.

"Now at last extensive emigration of Ulster Presbyterians of Scots descent began, continuing for perhaps seventy-five years, until official alarm at the progress of the Revolution in America and the concurrent agitation for independence in Ireland caused the London government to adopt conciliatory measures. Dr. Robert Baird in his *History of Religion in America* and Lewis R. Harley in his *Life of Charles Thomson* state that from 1726 to 1750 an average of twelve thousand people came to America from Ulster annually, or an approximate total of three hundred thousand in a quarter of a century. One English commentator noted that a large number of Ulster Irish had arrived in America just in time to join the Continental Army which bagged 'Gentleman Johnny' Burgoyne at Saratoga!

"Abundant evidence exists that these Ulster Presbyterians—a large and honorable stream in the great flood of Irish Immigration to early America—considered and called themselves simply Irish. Every writer among the 'Scotch-Irish' myth-makers concedes that these people while they remained in Ireland never called themselves 'Scotch-Irish.' Scores of writers have produced scores of books to bolster the 'Scotch-Irish' thesis, but nowhere do we find a single direct quotation of any written or spoken passage in which any so-called 'Scotch-Irishman' used that term in Colonial or early Revolutionary times.

"A numerous minority of the eighteenth century immigrants from Ulster were certainly of immemorial Irish stock; and the Planter element, which furnished the majority, had been in Ireland three, four or five generations before turning their embittered steps toward America. Ireland was the only country they knew. Despite religious differences, there had been some intermarriage with the Old Irish; for after all many of the Planters were Highlanders, blood-brothers of the Ulster Gaels, speaking the same musical Gaelic.

"It is not strange therefore that the Masons among these immigrants set up in New Hampshire, New York and elsewhere lodges named for St. Patrick—not for St. Andrew! Nor that they named their settlements in New England, New York and Pennsylvania after towns in Ireland— Armagh, Belfast, Bangor, Londonderry—not after Scottish towns. Contemporary testimony shows that their resentment of British treatment surpassed even that of the Old Irish. It is not strange that when in 1737 twenty-six Presbyterians of Irish birth or descent met in the Presbyterian Church of the Long Lane, Boston, to form a charitable society, they met on St. Patrick's Day and called their organization The Irish Society. . . ."

Professor Wayland F. Dunaway of Pennsylvania State College attempts to give the other side of this question in his book *The Scotch-Irish of Colonial Pennsylvania* (1944). He disagrees with Joseph Smith, Protestant author of *The "Scotch-Irish" Shibboleth Analyzed and Rejected* (1898), and the foremost "mere-Irish" American historian Michael J. O'Brien, whose weighty book *A Hidden Phase of American History* (1919) really brought the issue to a head. Professor Dunaway holds their thesis "unreasonable in view of the fact that this term has been the customary usage in the nomenclature of American history and literature for so long a time, and is commonly understood by the people, that it appears to be straining a point to challenge it at this late day." He cites an English clergyman who in a letter in 1728 referred to "the Irish (who usually call themselves Scotch-Irish)" and quotes a few other such statements. Professor Dunaway does not show that the disputed term was "customary usage" in Colonial or Revolutionary times, nor for the greater part of a century following the War of Independence. It is his privilege to call the period since the 1870s "so long a time," but that does not rebut the accusation of the Irish American writers that "Scotch-Irish" was in fact a comparatively recent label, practically unknown in the time of the people to whom it is applied.

However unreasonable and strained the mere-Irish thesis may appear to the academic mind which favors "customary usage," it becomes important when one suspects that the "Scotch-Irish" tag may be intrinsic with the process of weakening the Irish part of the American Story to the benefit of the Anglo-Saxon and the detriment of the American concept of the United States, with the process of causing "Anglo-Saxon" to become synonymous with "American." It assumes at least potential significance when one is concerned with the culture and domestic and foreign policies of America; when one hears that some not unimportant American and British diplomats and journalists attending the United Nations Security Conference in San Francisco talk to the effect that of course only Britain and the United States, with their Anglo-Saxon traditions, institutions and temperament, are fit for freedom and democracy.

But aside from all that, it is an issue in some areas of the Irish American world. It is a part of the story in the New World that begins in the Emerald Isle. In this chapter all Americans who came or stem from several generations in Ireland, North or South, regardless of "racial" mixture and religion, are Irish.

David Ramsay, one of the first post-Revolutionary historians, wrote in 1789: "The Colonies which now form the United States may be considered as Europe transplanted. Ireland, England, Scotland, France, Germany, Holland, Switzerland, Sweden, Poland and Italy furnished the original stock . . . and are generally supposed to have contributed to it in the order named. For the last seventy or eighty years no nation has contributed nearly so much to the population of America as Ireland."

Regarding those "last seventy or eighty years" which included the climax of the Revolutionary period, the records unquestionably support Ramsay. It is possible that the Irish were the largest element in the early population of North America, outnumbering even the English. Responsible Irish historians, however, make no such sweeping claim.

It is generally held that the population of the Thirteen Colonies when they became states was about three million of whom one million were immigrants. It has been further estimated that fully five hundred thousand of these immigrants were Irish. The earlier Irish settlers had multiplied with characteristic heartiness so that of the two million native Americans in the year 1776 perhaps five hundred thousand were wholly or principally of Irish descent, adding up to a round million Irish Americans—one-third of the total population.

"Yet," says Shaemas O'Sheel, "not only have the later 'historians' generally concealed the extent and importance of the Irish role in the very foundation of America, but some have minimized it to the vanishing point, others have flatly denied that there were Irish here at all before the early nineteenth century. By the same technique future generations could readily be prevented from knowing that such men as Bill O'Dwyer of New York, Mayor Ed Kelly of Chicago, Jim Farley, the Sullivan brothers and Admirals Callahan and Leahy ever existed. That technique consists in simply passing over Irish names though they occur in the same pages from which these chroniclers take their other data."

There is a good deal of basis for this complaint. In 1926 William M. Clemens, the genealogist, published *American Marriage Records Before 1699*, subtitled "The First Census of the American People," in which he asserted that "this has been an English country . . . down to recent years," that "New England and Virginia were populated almost entirely by the English" and that "nine-tenths of the colonists were absolutely English." Crowding the Germans, Dutch, Swedes and other early settlers all together into ten per cent of the population was rather rough handling. As for the Irish, Clemens just ignored them.

In 1930, in examining this "census," the painstaking Michael J. O'Brien adduced scores of typically Irish names such as Brady, Burke, Callahan, Casey, Crowley, Driscoll, Fitzgerald, Lynch, McGinnis, Mulligan, O'Hogan, O'Mahony and others from the same marriage records. Clemens evidently "overlooked" them. O'Brien also cites names which are not on the face of them recognizably Irish, but whose bearers are identified in the marriage records as of Irish nativity. One was Hannah Barron, an ancestor of Calvin Coolidge.

Another was Teague Crehore, who married Mary Spur at Milton, Massachusetts, in 1688. The name Crehore is unusual, not obviously Irish, but the records show that Teague Crehore was born in Ireland. He was kidnapped by the English when a child and sold as a redemptioner. This was not an uncommon practice of the English authorities in Ireland in the seventeenth century and later. A redemptioner was one who, wishing or being forced to emigrate, turned himself over or was turned over to the master or owner of a ship who then was authorized to sell him to someone in America for a stipulated time, until he earned the cost of passage. Thousands of Irish (and thousands of other nationals, including many English) came over in this way. In the case of voluntary redemptioners, it was a form of temporary bondage entered into for the sake of eventually gaining the chance of a better life in the New World. . . .

But to return to Clemens: Irish Americans like Michael O'Brien and Shaemas O'Sheel argue that he could hardly have been ignorant of the fact that Teague or Tigue (Gaelic: Tadgh) is as Irish a name as one could find. Besides, since the record stated that Teague Crehore was a native of Ireland, Clemens was guilty of deliberate misrepresentation. If he was interested in marriages, that of Teague Crehore and Mary Spur should have fascinated him, for the first eight entries in the baptismal records of the town of Milton were those of the four sons and four daughters of this couple. One of the sons, Benjamin Crehore, made the first piano in America.

There can be no doubt that the Anglo-Saxon concept of the United States was built up in part by such writers as Clemens. Another "historian," whom O'Brien takes to task in *Pioneer Irish in New England* (1937), wrote that only two Irish names grace the New England historical records of the seventeenth century. From those same records O'Brien produces 321 indubitably Irish names, and apropos of assertions of this kind another Irish American, in a letter to me, asks these questions:

"If there were no Irish in New England, how did John Alden's descendants get the idea he was Irish? What about the fact that Priscilla, the girl who knew what she wanted, bore the Irish surname Mullins? Was John Winthrop, first Governor of Massachusetts Bay Colony, romancing when he wrote that 'Darby Field, an Irishman' had (about 1632) discovered the White Mountains?* What became of 'the Irish and Scottish gentlemen' who according to the records settled on the Merrimac River in 1634, or the four hundred Irish who came to Boston in 1654 on the ship *Goodfellow*? How did it happen that, according to the records of the General Court of Massachusetts Bay, in 1654 'some questions were stirring in ye Court whether it were not best to make some stop' to Irish immigration 'because there have come over many Irish before that time'? What strange fancy prompted New Englanders to name towns and settlements after places in Ireland—Waterford, Bangor, Belfast, Limerick and Newry in Maine; Londonderry in Vermont; Derry, Londonderry, Dublin and Antrim in New Hampshire; and Waterford in Connecticut? . . . Was it blindness or shame that prevented the 'historian' who could find mention of only two Irish in all New England in the seventeenth century from referring to 'Goody' Glover, who in 1688 was hanged in Boston on the charge of being a witch, but whose real offense was, in the words of the Reverend Cotton Mather, that she was 'a scandalous old Irishwoman, very poor, a Roman Catholic and obstinate in idolatry'? . . ."

From marriage, baptismal and burial registers; records of patentees of lands; transcripts of land grants, lists of early settlers preserved in state archives; lists of testators, executors, administrators, legatees and witnesses to wills; records of deeds and conveyances and other legal instruments; tax and rent rolls; "Town Books" or records of selectmen; records in offices of secretaries of state, county clerks and court clerks;

---

* Hailing from Slieve Bawn in County Roscommon, Darby Field named the New Hampshire highlands after his native place—*Slieve* being Gaelic for "mountain," and *bawn* for "White."

passenger lists on file at the English Public Record Office; John Camden
Hotten's *Original Lists of Persons of Quality; Emigrants; Religious
Exiles; Political Rebels; Serving Men Sold for a Term of Years; Appren-
tices; Children Stolen; Maidens Pressed; and Others Who Went from
Great Britain to the American Plantations, 1600-1700*, published in
1874—from all of these and other unquestionable sources, O'Brien,
Thomas Hobbs Maginnis (a Protestant clergyman), Martin I. J. Griffin
and other Irish researchers have drawn the names of thousands of Irish
men and women in the Colonies long before the Revolution.

An O'Brien list of only recognizably Irish names found in New
England records up to the year 1700 numbers 599. Another covering
Massachusetts (including Maine at that time), New Hampshire, Rhode
Island, Connecticut, New York, New Jersey, Pennsylvania, Delaware,
Maryland, Virginia and the Carolinas—also of only recognizably Irish
names in the seventeenth century—runs to 1,873; Vermont and Georgia
add sizable quotas; and names not Irish on their face but identified as
belonging to natives of Ireland would vastly swell the total.

The Irish element in New England was small compared with that
in Pennsylvania, Delaware, Maryland, Virginia and the Carolinas during
the seventeenth and eighteenth centuries.

By 1609 hundreds of Irishmen had been colonized in and around
Jamestown. Among them was Francis Maguire, whose description of
Virginia written in Gaelic somehow found its way into the state archives
of Spain where it is still preserved. In 1621 Captain John Smith records
that the ship *Flying Harte* reached Newport News with eighty Irish
settlers. By then the Irish must have been plentiful in Virginia, for in
that year John Brinsley, a Puritan clergyman, published in London a
book intended to help "that poor Irish nation with our loving countrymen in Virginia."

Irishmen continued to come to Virginia. The names of many appear
on the muster rolls of Colonel George Washington's regiment in the
French and Indian War. Dr. William L. Connor, one-time superintendent of education at Allentown, Pennsylvania, has shown that in
the Tidewater Counties of Virginia before the Revolution men of his
name (with its variants) appear in the records as witnesses, legatees and
executors more often than Byrds, Lees or any of the other First Families
of Virginia. Dr. Connor's great-great-great-grandfather went to school
with George Washington, who called him "Towhead Torley"—the Anglicized form of the ancient Irish name, Turlough.

George Washington was kin to a branch of the McCarthy family, of
which Daniel, Dennis, Thaddeus, Ann and Sarah McCarthy were his
second cousins. His diary shows that the McCarthys were among his

closest friends, often at Mount Vernon. When on his deathbed he dictated the list of what today would be called his honorary pallbearers, three of the eleven names were McCarthys.

But it was to Pennsylvania that the fullest stream of Irish immigrants flowed, attracted by its liberal laws framed by William Penn in the spirit of the Quaker creed and administered by Penn's agent, James Logan from Armagh. The city of Brotherly Love was a veritable magnet to the Irish who sang:

> With me knapsack on me shoulder
> Sure there's no one could be bolder,
> And I'm leavin' dear old Ireland without warnin',
> For of late I've took a notion
> For to cross the briny ocean,
> And I'm off to Philadelphia in the mornin'.

The syllables of Philadelphia had a heart-lifting ring for the Connacht peasant fleeing starvation, the Munster farmer beggared by rack-rents, the disillusioned craftsman of Leinster and the embittered Planter of Ulster. Sturdy for labor and hungry for land, they turned to with a will at such employment as offered, or poured out to the westward. Beyond the Alleghenies, James McBride was the first White man to paddle down the Ohio River and set foot in Kentucky—in 1754, while Daniel Boone was still a child. Another Irishman, John Finley, also explored Kentucky before Boone. Still another, named O'Cain, was the first English-speaking person to reach California, in 1795.

Although William Penn himself had brought numbers of Irish to his colony, by 1728 James Logan and the provincial representatives took alarm at the "crowds of foreigners . . . Irish Papists and convicts" who were pouring in. An entrance duty was levied, which the immigrant-ships' captains enabled their passengers to evade by landing them at Newcastle, Delaware, or Burlington, New Jersey.

As early as 1716 the Philadelphia and New York newspapers noted the arrival of ships from Ireland: July 1716, "Ship Cezer from Waterford . . . with seventy passengers"; the same ship "from Dublin" in September 1717 with "about one hundred passengers"; August 1716, the Dove "from Ireland . . . with passengers"; March 1718, an unnamed ship "from Cork" with fifty passengers; August 1718, the Elizabeth & Margaret from Dublin with "one hundred fifty passengers"—

A few years later Irish immigration was larger still. In 1728 fifty-six hundred Irishmen and women landed at Delaware River ports. The American Weekly Mercury of August 14, 1729, noted that during the previous week "about two thousand Irish arrived at Newcastle, Delaware, and an abundance more are daily expected." The New England Weekly Journal of March 30, 1730, reported that during the previous year 5,655 Irish had immigrated through Philadelphia, against 553 from all other countries.

In *Extracts from the Itineraries and Other Miscellanies of Ezra Stiles, D.D., LL.D.,* published in 1916 by Yale University, it appears that from Christmas 1728 to Christmas 1729 there landed at Philadelphia 267 English and Welsh passengers and servants, forty-three Scots servants, 243 Palatine passengers, and 1,155 Irish passengers and servants. Also, "in Newcastle have been landed about forty-five hundred passengers and servants, chiefly from Ireland." And in 1729 Penn's agent Logan wrote, "It looks as if Ireland is to send all her inhabitants hither, for last week not less than six ships arrived, and every day two or three also arrive."

From then until the first years of the Revolution, the pace of Irish immigration accelerated. The Pennsylvania Gazette of August 11, 1773, reported that Captain Oliffe of the ship Venus from Dublin said "that he was well informed before he left Dublin [in May or June] that upwards of eighteen thousand people had left Ireland since January last, to settle in different parts of America." That seems like a large number, but O'Brien points out that at a low average of two hundred and fifty immigrants per ship, eighteen thousand would have required only seventy-two sailings. Actually ships from Ireland arriving at New York and Philadelphia that year totaled 162; others put in at Boston, Baltimore and Charleston. On July 12, 1773, the New York Gazette and Weekly Mercury published an account taken from the Belfast News Letter reporting that during the years 1771-1772 ships with a tonnage of 17,350 sailed for America from four Irish ports, and commenting: "It may be supposed, on a moderate computation, that the number of passengers was equal to the tonnage."

The term "passengers" did not include servants and redemptioners. O'Brien concludes that their number on these same ships would at least equal that of the passengers, so that the aggregate of persons coming to America from only four Irish ports in 1771-1772 would be about 34,700. On the basis of Captain Oliffe's figures it can be estimated that up to thirty-six thousand Irish came over in 1773. Adding those sailing from ports not covered by the foregoing figures, it may be surmised that close to one hundred thousand Irish arrived in those three years.

These Irish immigrants greatly augmented the anti-English sentiment in the Colonies. Among them were thousands of future soldiers of the Revolutionary Army.

Many Irish who landed at Newcastle and Burlington settled in Delaware and New Jersey. To Catholic Maryland the Irish came in such numbers that a County of New Ireland (now Cecil County) was set up, divided into the districts of New Connaght, New Leinster and New Munster. Maryland passed through a period of Protestant control marked by rigorous persecution of Catholics, but when religious liberty was restored the Irish again swarmed in.

From the Maryland immigrants came the Carroll family, among whose many outstanding members was Father (later Bishop) John Carroll who at the request of Congress undertook a mission to the Canadian Catholics in the hope that they would join the Revolution. The life of Charles Carroll of Carrollton—a signer of the Declaration of Independence, a member of the Continental Congress, a framer of the Constitution—spanned two epochs: before the Revolution he wrote the *First Citizen Letters* which stimulated the incipient sense of American nationality, and he lived long enough to see the beginnings of a vigorous industrial growth—in fact, to preside at the opening of the Baltimore and Ohio Railroad.

In the seventeenth century the Irish were less numerous in New York than elsewhere, but John Anderson from Dublin was overseer of the Dutch settlement of Beverwyck in 1645; another Irishman, William Hayes, was a physician in New York City in 1647; and Pearson's *Genealogies of the First Settlers of the Ancient County of Albany from 1630 to 1800* contains hundreds of Irish names. Thomas Dongan, Royal Governor from 1683 to 1688, brought numbers of his fellow-Irishmen to the colony.

New York annals furnish amusing illustrations of the difficulty of determining the origins of people from the early colonial records. The overseer of Beverwyck, for instance, appears in the records as "Jan Andriessen"—a good Dutch burgher name, but the rest of the entry reads: "de Iersman van Dublingh." Willem Hogan and Jan Fyne might be as Dutch as Edam cheese, were it not that "Willem" was "van Bor in Yrlandt" and "Jan" came "van Waterfort in Irlandt"—William Hogan and John Finn from Birr and Waterford.

Other New York records illuminate a fact which has puzzled some historians—that so many of these Irish immigrants, supposedly Catholics, attended Protestant churches in the Colonies. The explanation is fairly simple. While Protestants at that time were much concerned with doctrinal niceties, religion to the Catholic masses remained a matter of faith, custom, emotion, churchgoing. Massacres under Elizabeth and Cromwell, and William's victory over James had indeed identified Protestantism with the enemy in the minds of the Old Irish, but in the new conditions of a strange world they turned pragmatist as readily as any other group. To them, church was the place for worship and for social intercourse, and excepting in Maryland and Pennsylvania there were none but Protestant churches to go to. Here and there in Pennsylvania Irish Catholics took their prayerbooks and rosaries to Protestant services.

But there was another reason for attending Protestant churches. It might be said that in those days one could only be born, baptized, married or buried through their agency. In most colonies there were no Catholic clerics to perform these rites.

This disposes of the claim that New York City could not have had more than a few Irish before 1800 because it had no Catholic churches. The claim is part of the suppression of the Irish story. Of the graves dating back before 1800, ninety-five in Trinity churchyard are still identifiable as Irish; sixty-two in St. Paul's churchyard. The extant Trinity marriage records of the same period—many have been lost by fire and theft—note the wedding of 794 people bearing Irish names. Two hundred ninety-nine children with Irish names were baptized in Trinity prior to 1800, and during only fifteen years 117 Irish children were baptized by a Trinity minister in parts of the parish outside the city. At baptisms in Trinity 329 sponsors were Irish. The records of other churches are in keeping.

O'Brien, who unearthed these figures, also found 1,479 Irish names in the New York City Surrogate's and Register's records antedating 1800.

When the Constitutional ban on the Catholic Church in New York State was lifted and the first Catholic parish was formed in 1785, men who had been active in Trinity Church's affairs promptly joined the Catholic congregation. One was William Mooney, who founded the Society of Tammany or Columbian Order from which Tammany Hall later took its name. By 1808 St. Peter's parish in New York had fourteen thousand communicants, all but a few hundred being Irish.

Most Irish immigrants were poor. Some were "convicts"—political prisoners and redemptioners. Many were indentured servants, a category just above redemptioners. Among them were scholars, schoolmasters, physicians, skilled mechanics and trained persons of other professions, ruined along with the landed gentry whose properties and industries had been confiscated after the Cromwellian conquest and the victory of William III.

Some of the Irish immigrants were extraordinarily able or aggressive men who acquired large estates or won prominence in other ways in spite of prejudice against them. George Croghan, the most noted of Indian traders, a contemporary of George Washington, owned a quarter

of a million acres. In the 1760s some of the wealthiest merchants and
shipowners were Irish, as were many public officials.

William Johnson of the Old Irish family McShane (Son of John)
was governor of all the Indians in the English-controlled territory.

In Colonial and Revolutionary days Thomas Dongan, James Clinton
and George Clinton were governors of New York; David Dunbar and
John Sullivan of New Hampshire; William Welsh and William Patter-
son of New Jersey; James Sullivan of Massachusetts; James Logan,
George Bryan, William Moore, Joseph Reed and Thomas McKean of
Pennsylvania; John Hart of Maryland; John McKinley, Thomas Collins,
John Collins and Joseph Haslett of Delaware; John Houston, John
Martin and Peter Early of Georgia; Matthew Rowan and Thomas
Burke of North Carolina; and James Moore, John Rutledge and Ed-
ward Rutledge of South Carolina.

What the governor of North Carolina said to the governor of South
Carolina has been embellished a bit. Thomas Burke was not yet governor of North Carolina, and his first cousin Aedanus Burke was not the
governor of South Carolina but its chief justice and executive head.
Thomas, colonel of a regiment at Savannah, was captured by the
British. He escaped and made his way to cousin Aedanus, ragged and
half-starved. The chief justice fed and clothed him and they sat on the
verandah with a jug between them; but Aedanus failed to pour as often
as Thomas' taste required, so after a while, with a sidelong glance at
the jug, Thomas remarked, "It's a long time between drinks."

The second thesis of Irish American historians is that in great part
the Revolution was an Irish Revolution, that it might not have occurred
and certainly could not have succeeded but for the Irish; and there is
an impressive array of facts to support it.

The Irish in Ireland were overwhelmingly for the American cause;
there was a close connection between it and the Irish cause in Ireland.
Members of the puppet Irish Parliament who concurred in the sending
of regiments from Ireland to America (which the British government
could have sent anyhow without their concurrence) were mobbed by
the people. William Pitt (Earl of Chatham) said in the British Parliament in January 1775 that Ireland was with America "to a man," and a
year later he repeated: "The whole Irish nation favour the Americans."
Matching his voice in defense of the American cause were the voices
of Edmund Burke and Isaac Barré. "The best friend you have here is
Colonel Barré," wrote Arthur Lee, agent of the Continental Congress,
to Samuel Adams from London. It was Barré who, denouncing the
Stamp Act in 1765, called the Americans "those Sons of Liberty," a

phrase—later contracted to "Liberty Boys"—which the Patriots applied to their nascent militia. Benjamin Franklin, treated with discourtesy in England, was everywhere honored in Ireland. When the war compelled the Continental Congress to suspend trade with Ireland as well as with Britain, it adopted, on July 28th, 1775, an Address to the People of Ireland expressing regret at the necessity and acknowledging their friendship. In October 1778 Franklin, then at Versailles, promised the Irish people American help in the struggle for Irish rights. All efforts of the British to raise new Irish regiments for use against the American Patriots failed, and desertions of Irish soldiers from British regiments to the Continental ranks seriously weakened the forces of Howe and Cornwallis. Many Irishmen came to America specifically to join the Patriot ranks.

Whether the American Revolution dates from resistance to the Stamp Act, the Golden Hill skirmish in New York, the Boston Massacre, the fall of Fort William and Mary, or Lexington and Concord, the Irish were in it at the start. The scholarly redemptioner Charles Thomson, translator of the Bible from the Greek, later "perpetual secretary of the Continental Congress" (still later immortalized in the name of a cigar), was the first to hint, in a letter to Franklin, that independence might eventually result from the Stamp Act. The Liberty Boys who protected their Liberty Pole at Golden Hill numbered many Irish. The Boston Massacre, said John Adams who defended the British troops, was brought on by a mob of "Irish Teagues." The capture of Fort William and Mary on New Castle Island was led by Irishmen John Sullivan and John Langdon. Irishmen were at Concord and Lexington, a whole company of them at Bunker Hill.

It has been claimed that one-half or more of the Patriot armies during the eight-year Revolution were Irish. This is probably too high; O'Brien and other responsible Irish American historians are more moderate. Muster rolls are still extant; O'Brien, counting first the soldiers and sailors who are stated to be natives of Ireland and second the names which are indisputably Irish, found that 35.83 per cent of the fighting men were of Irish birth or extraction. Aware that vast numbers of Irishmen bear names giving no hint of their nationality, O'Brien adds two per cent—a conservative amount—and arrives at approximately thirty-eight per cent as the minimum estimate of the Irish contingent in the Revolutionary armies.

But the higher estimates are not to be dismissed entirely. Joseph Galloway, speaker of the Pennsylvania Assembly, who joined the British, testified before a British commission in October 1779 that "about one-half" of the rebel army was of Irish birth. At a Parliamentary inquiry four months earlier General James Robertson, who had served in the British Army in America for twenty years, reported that General Charles Lee—second in command of the Continental Army until removed on suspicion of treason—believed that half the rebel army was from Ireland. Ambrose Serle, the British Cabinet's confidential agent in America in 1776, reported that "great numbers of Emigrants, particularly Irish, are in the Rebel Army." And the British commander-in-chief, Sir Henry Clinton, informed Lord George Germain on October 23, 1778: "The Emigrants from Ireland were in general to be looked upon as our most serious antagonists."

An incomplete list of officers shows that at least 1,492 in the Army and Navy, from lieutenant to major general, were of Irish birth or descent. Twenty-six were generals, fifteen of them born in Ireland—including Richard Montgomery, killed at Quebec; Stephen Moylan, quartermaster general; John Shee, Edward Hand and Andrew Lewis. The latter, a man of impressive appearance and extraordinary military ability demonstrated in the colonial wars, was Washington's friend and his choice for Commander-in-Chief of the Continental Army, but Lewis insisted on Washington's appointment.

Two regiments of Rochambeau's French Army were Irish, officers and men—Regiments de Dillon and de Walsh. And General Henry Lee, writing of the Pennsylvania Continentals in his *Memoirs*, said: "They were known by the designation of the Line of Pennsylvania, whereas they might have been, with more propriety, called the Line of Ireland."

The proportion of Irish seamen in the infant American Navy and on commissioned privateers appears to have been extremely large; references to them are scattered all through O'Brien's book and other works. Many of the privateers preying on British shipping were owned by Irish Americans.

When two British naval vessels ordered the people of Machias, Maine, to cut down their Liberty Pole and to deliver lumber to the British in Boston, Jeremiah O'Brien and his brothers led a band which captured both vessels and for the first time lowered the Union Jack at sea. The name O'Brien was given to a United States torpedo boat early in the 1900s, and in March 1940 to a destroyer "in honor of Captain Jeremiah O'Brien and his five brothers, Gideon, John, William, Denis and Joseph."

Tim Murphy, reputed to be the best shot in the Continental Army, saved the day at Saratoga. In the final battle there the British, led by General Fraser, were winning. The American general Morgan summoned three riflemen, one being Tim Murphy, and ordered them to get Fraser. Tim got him, as a marker on Saratoga Battlefield records. But for that bullet from Tim's gun, one is free to speculate, Saratoga might have been lost, the states cut in two, France might not have become an ally of the new country, and the Revolutionary War might have been a different story than it turned out to be.

These are samplings of the facts and logical speculations about the Irish part in the military phase of the Revolution.

The fighting revolutionaries derived by the thousands from all parts of Ireland, but principally from the South and West.

The late Senator Henry Cabot Lodge, in the days when he wrote "history" and did not need "the Irish vote" which he later courted assiduously and skillfully, was once confronted with the figures of "South Irish" names on the Revolutionary muster rolls. Like the country bumpkin who saw his first giraffe, the Senator still insisted "there ain't no such animal." He had, however, no answer at all when Michael J. O'Brien challenged him to produce any record of Cabots and Lodges in the Revolution to match the seventy-five O'Briens (with variants) on the Massachusetts rolls alone, or the 236 of that name on the rolls of all the states.

It has often been said that the American Revolution was the achievement of an "aggressive minority." This has been true of all revolutions. It seems certain that the Tories plus those who remained sullenly or timorously neutral or indifferent, were a majority of the population. Some of the same witnesses—Joseph Galloway, General Robertson, General Lee—who identified the Irish as the largest element among the armed "rebels," also asserted that not more than a fourth or even a fifth of the "native Americans" approved of separation from Britain. Their estimates may be somewhat discounted, and doubtless there were some Irish also among the timorous and indifferent. But the fact written in the pages of the early chroniclers begins to reappear: the American Revolution—without minimizing the role of other, better known, factors in it—was in considerable measure an explosion of the accumulated resentment of the Irish against the power that had invaded their homeland, imposed a harsh alien rule upon them, expropriated their soil and stifled their industry.

Integrated with the long and matchless evolution of the concept of liberty in England, English Americans as diverse as Benjamin Franklin, Samuel Adams and Thomas Paine mainly shaped the philosophy behind the Revolution (though Irishmen, as we shall see, had a big hand in that too; not to forget the Scots Patrick Henry, the Welsh Jefferson or the Italian Mazzei). But the burning resentment of recent wrongs, the thirst for revenge in the Irish who had been sold into slavery or compelled to flee from the "most distressful country," were the chemistry which transmuted the loyalty-breathing protests against the Stamp Act of 1765 into militant and armed resistance and finally the momentous resolution for Independence. The English writer Samuel Smiles summed it up: "Of the Irish colonists in America, a large proportion everywhere stood foremost on the side of the Patriots. It seemed as if Providence had mysteriously used the victims of British cruelty to Ireland, the men whom her persecution had banished from the bosom of their own land, as the means of her final punishment and humiliation on a foreign soil."

Luke Gardiner (later Lord Mountjoy) exclaimed in Parliament on April 2, 1784: "I am assured, from the best authority, the major part of the American army was composed of Irish . . . it was their valour determined the contest . . . America was lost [because of the] Irish emigrants!"

Another Englishman, J. Kent, who was in America in 1780-1782, accompanying the Marquis de Chastellux on his tour which he described in American Travels (English translation published in London in 1787) is quoted in that book: "An Irishman, the instant he sets foot on American ground, becomes ipso facto an American; this was uniformly the case during the whole of the late war. Whilst Englishmen and Scotsmen were regarded with jealousy and distrust, even with the best recommendation of zeal and attachment to their cause, a native of Ireland stood in need of no other certificate than his dialect. . . . Indeed, their conduct in the late Revolution amply justified this favourable opinion, for whilst the Irish emigrant was fighting the battles of America by sea and land, the Irish merchants . . . laboured with indefatigable zeal, and at all hazards, to promote the spirit of enterprise, to increase the wealth and maintain the credit of the country; their purses were always open, and their persons devoted to the common cause. On more than one imminent occasion, Congress owed their existence, and America possibly her preservation, to the fidelity and firmness of the Irish."

Few Irish, even those of wealth, joined the Tories.

On the other hand, General Thomas Conway, born in Ireland, was the figurehead of a cabal against Washington; and Thomas Hickey was implicated in a plot to poison the Commander-in-Chief. But most of the relations between Washington and the Irish consisted of the other kind of detail.

Among his entourage were many Irish. Stephen Moylan, Joseph Reed, Joseph Carey, John Fitzgerald and James McHenry served as his aides-de-camp. For McHenry, whom he made his Secretary of War, was named the fort at the scene which inspired Francis Scott Key, an Irish

American, to write "The Star-Spangled Banner," the third stanza of
which is violently anti-English.

Captain William O'Neill was thanked by Washington with tears in
his eyes for saving his life at Brandywine. Mrs. Elizabeth Thompson,
née Carey, spent her own funds on food for General and Mrs. Washington when they were ill, hungry and penniless at Morristown.

In its crossings of the Delaware, Washington's Army was transported
by the boats of Irish ferrymen Daniel McConkey and Patrick Colvin.
Washington Crossing, New Jersey, was first called McConkeys Ferry.

When young Alexander Hamilton came from the West Indies to
New York in 1772, he bore a letter to Irish-born Hugh Mulligan, export-
import merchant. Hugh had a brother, Hercules, also Irish-born, a tailor
and clothier, with whom Hamilton went to live, beginning a lifelong
friendship. Hercules Mulligan was a member of the Sons of Liberty and
later of the New York Committee of Correspondence. After the British
took New York, General Washington, on Hamilton's recommendation,
appointed Hercules Mulligan his confidential agent there. Pretending
to repent his former Patriotic excesses, Mulligan fitted British officers
with resplendent uniforms and Tory merchants with handsome small-
clothes, and kept his ears alert. His brother Hugh, while provisioning
the British forces, did the same. One result of their espionage was the
frustration of a British plan to capture Washington on his journey to
Newport in February 1781. To reestablish the Mulligans' reputation in
the eyes of the Patriots, the first thing Washington did on entering
New York as the British departed on Evacuation Day was to take
breakfast with Hercules.

The Friendly Sons of St. Patrick of Philadelphia, organized in 1771,
donated vast sums for the Revolutionary cause; and in 1781 George
Washington accepted "with a singular pleasure" its invitation to honorary membership, noting that it was "distinguished for the firm adherence of its members to the glorious cause in which we are embarked."
St. Patrick's Day, incidentally, was commonly celebrated in all the chief
cities by Protestants and Catholics alike; and several times during the
war Washington observed it by issuing Irish passwords and countersigns.

One of Washington's rare boon companions was Irish-born Captain
Patrick O'Flinn, a veteran of the Revolution who later kept a tavern
at Wilmington, Delaware. Retiring, modest, well educated and witty, he
was extremely congenial to Washington who, when he came to Wilmington, "made a constant rule to meet the Captain, to spend the
evening with him." The obituary notice of Patrick O'Flinn in the
newspaper *Niles' Register* (July 11, 1818) reports that Washington's
secretary, Colonel Tobias Lear, said "that in all his journeys with the

President he had never seen him so much at home in a public house as in Captain O'Flinn's, or ever with a man with whom he discoursed more familiarly." The writer adds, "There were few men with whom Washington was familiar."

George Washington Parke Curtis, Martha Washington's grandson and Washington's adopted son, presiding on July 20, 1826, at a mass meeting on behalf of the Irish cause, said of the Irish: "Washington loved them, for they were the companions of his toils, his perils, his glories, in the deliverance of his country."

A third thesis of Irish American historians is that the Irish have been among the principal shapers of American polity and society. In support of that thesis they point first of all to Thomas Dongan, Earl of Limerick, already mentioned as governor of the New York Colony during 1682-1688. He has been called "the man who invented 'the People'"; he included "the people in General Assembly" among the sources of government, thus establishing one of the primary principles on which the United States was created.

Then there was John Sullivan. His father, also from Limerick, became a New Hampshire schoolmaster after filing his application for the post in seven languages. His mother in her old age boasted that while she plowed, a future governor of New Hampshire, a future judge and a future attorney-general of that state, a future governor of Massachusetts, and five future officers of the Continental Army—all her children—tagged along after her. When she was quite old she rode horseback from New Hampshire to Boston to call on the governor, her son James. When he sent word he was busy but would see her presently, she remounted and rode home, saying that no son of hers, governor or not, could keep her waiting.

John Sullivan was one of the first agitators for resistance and independence. As already noted, he and John Langdon staged the attack on Fort William and Mary which electrified the Colonies. Because he had commanded that action, Sullivan has been called "the Father of the Revolutionary War." He became a major general in the Continental Army, governor of New Hampshire, member of the Continental Congress. And a letter of John Adams' reveals that John Sullivan was the principal author of that section of the Declaration of Independence which recites the wrongs against which the Colonies were revolting.

Four natives of Ireland—Matthew Thornton, James Smith, George Taylor and Edward Rutledge—and five men of Irish descent—Robert Treat Paine, George Read, Thomas McKean, Charles Carroll and

Thomas Lynch—signed the Declaration of Independence. Twenty-two men of Irish birth or background sat in the Continental Congress.

Robert Morris, already referred to in connection with Haym Salomon, was a principal financier of the Revolution; finally Congress made him virtual financial dictator; and many other Irishmen spent their private means for the cause of liberty. Oliver Pollock, born in Ireland, supplied the Continental Army with ammunition, financed the Lewis and Clark Expedition, and advanced over three hundred thousand dollars—a prodigious sum for those days—to the Revolutionary government. The Friendly Sons of St. Patrick of Philadelphia was not the only Irish organization to make large donations to the cause; there were many societies with such names as "St. Patrick" and "Hibernian," some of them exclusively Protestant, some admitting all faiths—all pledged to the cause of independence and freedom.

Alexis de Tocqueville, who had thoroughly studied the matter, pronounced the Constitution of the United States "an idiosyncratic document, bearing a personal stamp; one man made it, and it was Rutledge" —John Rutledge whose father came from Ireland. Part of the final draft of the Constitution is in his handwriting. Earlier, in 1780 when the British were besieging Charleston, the State's General Assembly twice voted him Dictator of his native South Carolina—the only official Dictator in American history. Later he served as Chief Justice of the United States Supreme Court.

Commander John Barry, a native of Wexford, one of the most competent naval officers in the Revolution, is sometimes called the "Father of the American Navy" by virtue of Commission Number One issued when the Navy was officially instituted during President Washington's first Administration. But his most striking, doubtless his most important action took place ashore. In the tense days after the Revolution when the Assembly of Pennsylvania could not ratify the Constitution of the United States because members of the minority opposition prevented a quorum by refusing to attend sessions, Barry gathered a few determined men who went to the absentees' homes, forcibly brought them to the Assembly chamber and held them in their seats while the vote was counted. Other states were hanging on Pennsylvania's decision—the reason it is called "the Keystone State."

Thomas FitzSimmons of Philadelphia, a friend of Washington's, was a distinguished soldier and a wealthy supporter of the cause. After the war he fought for the system of protective tariffs which was essential to American industrial growth during the first century of independence.

Her biographers have called Anna Ella Carroll of the Maryland Carrolls "the great unrecognized member of Lincoln's cabinet." She had a hand in Lincoln's nomination over Seward. She helped defeat Secession in Maryland and suggested the strategy of cutting the Confederacy in two along the Tennessee River, at the same time inducing Lincoln to promote Grant, who was on the point of being dropped. Stanton said that "she . . . did the great work that made others famous." She was one of the first women in the United States to support herself by the pen.

In the long, fierce post-Revolutionary contest between liberal and conservative ideologies, a few Irishmen of wealth and position—like Colonel FitzSimmons and New York's first mayor, James Duane—were conservative Hamiltonians. Irish Americans generally, Protestant and Catholic, were Jeffersonian liberals or democrats, forming the bulk of the progressive forces; and, as I have said, they—and occasionally their non-Irish fellow partisans—were denounced as "United Irishmen" by those of the conservative and reactionary persuasions.

I have seen unpublished treatises on the period which maintain that through the crucial Right-Left fight which followed the Revolution and which had, of course, broad and deep political and economic motives and meanings, ran the struggle between the "Anglo-Saxon" and the "Irish" elements for control of the country; that, whether they realized it or not, some Revolutionary Americans of English stock were influenced by Tories who, with or without directives from England, did what they could to make sure the United States would not assume an "Irish" character.

In my study—an incomplete one—of the post-Revolutionary era I find nothing definite enough to be called "struggle for control of the country" on a strictly ethnic basis. I don't doubt that the Irish reacted in good Irish fashion to the antagonism directed against them, but it seems to me that both the antagonism and the reaction to it were sporadic—not unimportant, yet rather superficial; sharp only when it came to specific political and economic questions, or when in everyday intermingling the Irish temperament clashed with the Puritan temperament. Religion, of course, was mixed in all this. But "control of the country" by the "Irish" or the "English" was never an open, clear-cut issue among the citizenry—at least not so one could put one's finger on it. In the period of 1780-1810 the population was already too mixed in the matter of strains for anything of that sort. People were Americans—some from England, some from Ireland, some from France . . . Holland . . . Germany, or descendants of natives of one or several of those countries—but Americans, the new breed that Crèvecoeur had defined. (See page 81.)

It may be that in the post-Revolutionary struggle for controls many

Americans of English stock were on the conservative side; while, as I say, a preponderance of Irish Americans with progressives of other stocks indubitably found their political expression through the Democratic Party, by throwing their numbers to the Welsh American, Jefferson, who led the largely successful "Second American Revolution." But, again, while full of ethnic overtones of varying sharpness, the issues were primarily economic and political.

A colorful Irish political figure vividly illustrative of those days was the "Green Mountain Boy" Matthew Lyon who got himself jailed for printing his opinion of John Adams and the Alien and Sedition Laws. While in prison he was elected to Congress, where he replied to a fellow member's insulting remark by spitting in his face, then mixing with him in a fist fight—supposedly the first in the Congress of the United States. Lyon was mercilessly attacked in the Federalist press, sometimes for being Irish. His speeches in Congress, marked by a devotion to democracy, were Americanism in direct line of the Revolution. He broke the deadlock for the Presidency between Jefferson and Aaron Burr by casting his vote for Jefferson. To render this signal service to the young country, he went against the wishes of his Vermont constituency and compromised his political future.

During much of the Revolution immigration was almost entirely suspended; at its close the influx began again. In spite of the absence of official figures, experts have been able to determine that in the thirty years from 1790 to 1820 about 225,000 people entered the United States. And most likely well over half were from Ireland.

The War of 1812 was one of the specific episodes in which the Irish were much in evidence. The British minister in Washington, a man named Foster who had done his best to avert hostilities, later testified in Parliament that the war with America had been kindled by the Irish, that among the members of Congress who voted for the war were six known members of the Society of United Irishmen.

The war was unpopular in sections of New England. Late in 1814 leaders of the anti-war sentiment met in Hartford and passed resolutions against "naturalized foreigners," recommending they "be debarred from membership in Congress and from all civil offices in the United States."

In the 1820s the Irish supported Andrew Jackson, the backwoods son of Irish immigrants who had come over two years before his birth. "Old Hickory," the great expansionist, was the first real man of the people to reach the Presidency, also the first Irish President. "Scotch-Irish" historians have claimed him, but the American Irish Historical Society

writers maintain that he was probably of "straight Old Irish descent."
He was a member of the Hibernian Society of Philadelphia, and when in
1833 he addressed the Charitable Irish Society of Boston, none of whose
members regarded himself as "Scotch-Irish," he said: "It is with great
pleasure that I see so many of the countrymen of my father assembled.
. . . I have always been proud of my ancestry and of being descended
from that noble race."

Later Presidents mostly or partly of Irish background were Polk,
Buchanan, Johnson, Arthur, McKinley, Taft and Wilson. Cleveland
and Coolidge had some Irish blood. Theodore Roosevelt, descended
from several notable Irish families, helped organize the American Irish
Historical Society. State governors and members of the House and
Senate of Irish derivation are too numerous even to begin to list.

A tide of Irish immigration set in around 1820; successive famines in
Ireland in the '40s swelled it to a flood which continued for fifty years.
During that period—1820-1870—the United States received about eight
million immigrants, of whom over three million were Irish. "Only the
old and the helpless stayed in the motherland keening for the dead
and gone."

The large majority, but by no means all, of these newcomers were
Catholics. In many sections of the United States religious bigotry, linked
to the budding exclusiveness of the Anglo-Saxon concept of Americanism—and the fear of competition in the labor market, disguised as
religious bigotry and Anglo-Saxonism—flared against them. In 1833 a
mob burned the Irish Catholic convent and orphanage at Charlestown,
Massachusetts, killing a number of nuns and children. The result of a
three-day riot in Philadelphia in 1844 was fourteen dead and forty Irish
homes, a seminary, and two churches burned. One of the churches was
St. Augustine's, to whose building fund George Washington had contributed. In 1854 and later, bloody riots took place in Boston and elsewhere.

A cult of "Nativism" arose, and the American Party—"the Know-
Nothings"—was formed with the chief purpose of barring and dis-
franchising Irish Catholics, although its ideology and program were also
directed against the German Forty-Eighters and other immigrants. (See
page 180.) In the 1850s national and local election campaigns were
punctuated by fist fights and flying paving blocks. Know-Nothing Congressmen denounced the "Catholic Irish" in the House and the Senate.
One Know-Nothing, Vice-President Millard Fillmore, became the thir-
teenth President on the death of Zachary Taylor.

The conduct of the Irish—as of the Germans—on the Union side in the Civil War was such that it helped to end Know-Nothingism and to lessen the opposition to Catholicism and immigration. But editorials like this one from The Chicago *Post* (September 9, 1868) continued to appear:

"Teddy O'Flaherty votes. He has not been in the country six months. . . . He has hair on his teeth. He never knew an hour in civilized society. . . . He is a born savage—as brutal a ruffian as an untamed Indian. . . . Breaking heads for opinion's sake is his practice. The born criminal and pauper of the civilized world . . . a wronged, abused and pitiful spectacle of a man . . . pushed straight to hell by that abomination against common sense called the Catholic religion. . . . To compare him with an intelligent freedman would be an insult to the latter. . . . The Irish fill our prisons, our poor houses. . . . Scratch a convict or a pauper, and the chances are that you tickle the skin of an Irish Catholic."

It was a fight every inch of the way; the Irish did not take anything lying down. The idea, whether correct or not, that Know-Nothingism was influenced from England, or that the English looked with favor on it, helped to keep the Irish temper taut against it.

In January 1855 Governor Henry J. Gardner of Massachusetts, in his inaugural message to the Legislature demanded that the state militia be purged of all foreigners. The only "foreigners" in the Massachusetts militia at that time were the Irish. Six years after this outburst of Know-Nothing bigotry, the Bay State was glad to enroll thousands of Irish "foreigners" in her regiments.

Shortly before the attack on Fort Sumter, Colonel Michael Corcoran of the 69th Regiment, New York National Guard, was removed from command because he refused to parade his men, all Irish, in honor of the visiting Prince of Wales. When the war broke out, he was restored to command, and led his men into battle. This regiment was recruited thrice over during the war.

So too was the 37th New York Regiment, known as "The Irish Rifles."

Many other regiments in the Union Army were wholly Irish; the 28th Massachusetts, for instance, sometimes called the "Faugh-a-Ballaghs," Irish for "Clear the way!" Several hundred thousand Irish Americans and Irishmen just off the boat fought on the Union side under a host of Irish officers. A good many slave-owning Irish in the South were of course with the Confederacy and several distinguished themselves in its service. All the Northern Irish, however, were passionately pro-Union—in part, no doubt, because England was helping the South.

Among the Irish generals on the Union side were Philip Kearny, killed in action at Chantilly; George Gordon Meade, the victor of Gettysburg; Thomas Francis Meagher, commander of the Irish Brigade whose bravery at Fredericksburg drew paeans even from the London *Times* correspondent; John A. Rawlins, Grant's chief of staff; and above all, General Philip Sheridan, whom Grant—according to Joseph Hergesheimer's biography of Sheridan—placed in "the very first rank of soldiers . . . with Napoleon and Frederick and other great commanders of history."

Not that the Irish coming over during 1820-1870—or later, for that matter—were perfection walking about on so many million pairs of legs; by and large they were no better—and no worse—than the rest of the New Immigration. In education and skilled craftsmanship they did not compare with, say, the German, Scandinavian and Czech groups. Owing to the impossible conditions in Ireland, some were illiterate. They had all the faults that the well-off and self-righteous too readily perceive in the poor. Some were unduly pugnacious. The slums into which they had to move were no more attractive than other slums. They were Catholic in a preponderantly Protestant country. They lost no time in becoming citizens, organizing into voting blocs, putting up their candidates, upsetting the political pattern of the old-line Americans of English, Scots, Welsh, Dutch, Swedish, French and early-Irish strains.

All this caused much anti-Irish feeling, which continued long after Know-Nothingism petered out. The "Scotch-Irish" label was used before this, but infrequently; now it began to be popularized. Several of my correspondents incline to the theory that in part this popularization occurred when old-stock Irish Americans, many by now pillars of American society, decided they did not want to be identified with these new "Irish."

Shaemas O'Sheel's studies have led him to believe that "the 'Scotch-Irish myth' began to be spread in the last three decades of the nineteenth century by amateur and local historians—elderly retired gentlemen who whiled away their leisure by writing the annals of their towns or counties. When they came upon references to Irishmen in the early days they were puzzled, for notice of the Irish role in our early history had already disappeared from the books they studied at school. Then they perceived that many of these intruders in the early records were from Ulster, that many bore names that might be Scots as well as Irish, and that most of them apparently were Presbyterians or other varieties of Protestants. Ignorant alike of Irish history and of the reasons why thousands of Irish Catholics conformed really or ostensibly to the reformed religions when they came to America, these chroniclers seized on the term 'Scotch-Irish' to explain the mystery. Finally it was given wide currency—deliberately—by certain general historians like John Fiske and Henry Cabot Lodge in the exercise of their God-given right to dislike Irishmen and Catholics. The cream of the jest is that all these writers were happily unaware that to any native or true scion of the 'Land O' Cakes,' the word 'Scotch' is anathema—he will take pride in Scottish nationality or Scots blood, he will drink Scots whiskey or praise Scottish heather, but never as he hopes for salvation would he pronounce the word 'Scotch.'"

Be that as it may, the new Irish came in "hordes," as the "native Americans" put it; and they were here to stay.

Most of the Irish who landed in eastern port cities remained there or moved to near-by industrial centers, like the textile towns of New England. But thousands went West, where there never was any serious prejudice against them. Many joined in the California Gold Rush—you can pick up their trail on almost any corner in downtown San Francisco.

A great number went into the mines in Pennsylvania, West Virginia, Ohio, Illinois, Michigan, Minnesota, Montana, Colorado, Utah and Arizona. The land-hungry pushed on to Nebraska and Iowa, to Minnesota and what is now the state of Washington. Their descendants may be found all over the West. They are lawyers, politicians, policemen, industrialists, doctors, contractors and builders, ranchers, skilled workers, railroad executives, priests, bishops; housewives, nuns, club women, teachers, social workers.

The Irish dug canals and manned barges. They laid most of the railroads, blasted most of the tunnels east of the Great Divide. Many of these railroad-builders were killed on the job—a saying around 1900 had it that there was "an Irishman buried under every tie."

In the East, the Irish quarried much of the marble of Vermont, granite of New Hampshire and bluestone of the Catskills. They made brick along the Hudson.

Irish laborers were a hard-working, hard-bitten, hard-drinking lot, always ready for a fight. But most of them kept an essential decency under a rough-tough surface. As I say, some arrived illiterate; many made incredible sacrifices to educate their children.

Irish newcomers to a city naturally gravitated to wherever the first Irish family had settled. Soon there was an "Irishtown." They built churches and parochial schools, and invited priests and nuns from the old country to run them. As in many other immigrant neighborhoods, there was a saloon on every other corner.

In cities where they settled in large numbers, and in proportion to the prejudice against them, the Irish developed a clannishness that their politicians, often not the best representatives of the group, exploited to advance themselves.

The Irish immigrants in the second half of the nineteenth century were in an inferior position beside the old-line Americans of Anglo-Saxon, Irish, Dutch and German strains, but they had a tremendous advantage over many of the other immigrant groups and they were not backward in seizing it. They spoke English. So they became straw-bosses, bosses and superintendents earlier than the Italians or Swedes, some of whom were their educational superiors. The Irish developed a tendency to look down on the non-English-speaking groups. This was resented, and as one Scandinavian old-timer, remembering incidents back in the 1880s, put it in a letter to me, "there was hell to pay—especially Saturday nights."

Parts of the Irish story are not to their credit. It was the Irish labor leaders of San Francisco—Dennis Kearney, Walter MacArthur, P. H. McCarthy and others, with a vast following of recent immigrants—who in the last quarter of the nineteenth century and early in the twentieth started the inhuman anti-Oriental campaign which, as Carey McWilliams shows in his important book *Prejudice* (1944), has had immense and wholly unfortunate consequences ever since. "These leaders," says McWilliams, "had been quick to realize the possibilities of uniting their . . . clannish fellow countrymen around a negative issue, namely, 'The Chinese Must Go!' It was the political rather than the economic aspects of Oriental immigration that interested these clever and resourceful leaders. Scientific evidence has always been lacking that Oriental immigrants actually ever displaced [non-Oriental] workmen in California or that they ever constituted a permanent threat to labor standards in the state. But, given the chaotic [conditions] there in the '70s, no shrewder slogan could have been devised than 'The Chinese Must Go!' At this time, moreover, Irish immigrants were being . . . abused in Eastern industrial areas. Their aggressions against Orientals on the West Coast tended to compensate for these attacks. The fact that Japan had an alliance with Great Britain merely gave them an additional reason for being opposed to Oriental immigration."

That the Catholic Irish had already become a strong political factor by the 1880s with machines and "bosses" of their own in several cities, is well known. They took to politics like ducks to water. And there is no doubt that many Irish politicians have contributed more to the annals of corruption than to statecraft. On the other hand, it is also true that corrupt politics in the United States has never been an Irish monopoly. Some of the best recent American political leaders have been of Irish or part-Irish descent—Al Smith, for one. Even the corrupt Irish "bosses" and officeholders were often closer to the people, did more for them, were more democratic in manner, than their non-Irish prototypes.

Most Catholic Irish are Democrats; the chairman of the National Democratic Committee is usually an Irish Catholic: Jim Farley, Frank Walker, Robert Hannegan.

Leadership is a strong point in the Irish character.

As already suggested, this has been true from way back. The *Dictionary of American Biography* contains the stories of nearly five hundred outstanding Americans who were born in Ireland and thousands of native Americans of Irish or part-Irish descent who made their mark in various ways. Scores in addition to those already noted were on the job when the basis for the American Way was laid; scores of others helped keep life moving on that Way. To mention a few more:

In 1766 William Prendergast from Kilkenny first aroused New York's tenant farmers to armed rebellion against the patroons. He was convicted and sentenced to be hanged, but was saved by his Quaker wife who rode eighty miles to intercede with the Royal Governor. Prendergast then moved to the freer country of western New York, where the city of Jamestown is named for one of his sons. Eighty years later the "Tinhorn and Calico" uprising (see page 98) finally put the patroon system on the chute.

General James Shields, who came over in 1826 at sixteen and who challenged Abe Lincoln to a duel when they were both young, captured Mexico City in the War with Mexico by ignoring Winfield Scott's orders, and was the only man to defeat "Stonewall" Jackson and to sit in the United States Congress as Senator from three different states in turn.

Ben Butler, who Theodore Winthrop said "abolished slavery in the United States" by his famous order to treat the slaves as "contraband of war," also fought for better hours and wages and working conditions for free workers, and curbed yellow fever in New Orleans. His much-reviled rule in that city was called by James Parton "the ablest and noblest piece of impromptu statesmanship the modern world has seen."

Ignatius Donnelly was a founder of the Republican Party, later of the Populist Party, a member of Congress, reviver of the idea that a Continent of Atlantis once existed, and contributor to the Baconian theory of the Shakespearian dramas.

The list of Irish educators in America is long. To suggest it with a few names: William Tennent, the father of Princeton University;

Thomas Hunter, pioneer of women's rights in education for whom Hunter College in New York is named; Dixon Ryan Fox, president of Union College and of the New York State Historical Society; John H. Finley, president of City College in New York, commissioner of education and long-time editor of The New York Times.

There are non-Irish lawyers who agree that Charles O'Conor was the greatest lawyer in American annals. Other legal lights: Frank P. Walsh, counsel to labor organizations and radical groups; Patrick H. O'Donnell, counsel to Sun Yat-sen in the formative days of the Chinese Republic; Supreme Court Justices John Marshall Harlan and Frank Murphy.

Bourke Cockran was a famous orator.

Dr. Ephraim McDowell performed the first ovariotomy, bringing, as Irvin S. Cobb (also of Irish descent) said, "relief and life and sanity to a million women." Dr. John Murphy, first to remove an appendix, championed asepsis.

Robert Fulton got the steamboat going. Samuel Morse invented electric telegraphy. Cyrus McCormick's reapers and harvesters opened the way for modern American agriculture. Henry Ford became the world's No. 1 pioneer in mass production. Other well known Irish American inventors, scientists and engineers: Christopher Colles, first to give New York a water system and to propose a canal linking the Great Lakes and the Atlantic; John P. Holland who perfected the first practical submarine with funds raised by Irish revolutionists in the hope of destroying the British Navy; General John J. Carty who developed improvements on the telephone; Michael M. O'Shaughnessy who is largely responsible for San Francisco's Hetch-Hetchy water system and Golden Gate Bridge; and John F. O'Rourke whose company built the Pennsylvania Terminal and tunnels in New York as well as the network of the underground electrified tracks in Grand Central Station.

A long list of industrialists and financiers of Irish extraction includes Thomas Corrigan, James J. Hill and Patrick Crowley in railroading; A. T. Stewart, William and Frederick Constable, James McCutcheon, James McCreery and James Butler (originator of the chain store) in retailing; Marcus Daly, John D. Ryan and Cornelius F. Kelly in mining; Anthony Brady, Nicholas Brady and Martin Maloney in city traction; Alexander Brown, Edward N. Hurley, Dwight Morrow and Joseph P. Kennedy in banking; William E. Corey, Elbert Gary and James A. Farrell in steel; William Mackay, founder of the Postal Telegraph and Cable system; Edward Hines, lumberman; John D. Crimmins, contractor; Humphrey O'Sullivan, originator of the rubber heel. Perhaps the ablest of this group, the most ruthless financier and the most astute political manipulator in American history, was Thomas F. (for Fortune)

Ryan, born in 1851. For nearly a generation in his late middle years he "owned" both major political parties and controlled all Presidential candidates as well as numerous governors and Senators. When he "retired" in 1908 he was on the boards of thirty corporations; some of the biggest of them he completely controlled. He died in 1928.

William M. Jeffers is president of the Union Pacific Railroad, many of whose ten thousand miles of track were laid by Irish immigrants. In fact, his own father, who had come over from County Mayo in 1868, helped to lay some of it. During 1942-1944 Bill Jeffers served as the United States Rubber Director, getting the production of synthetic rubber under way.

John Robert Gregg, born in Rockcorry, Ireland, invented the Gregg Shorthand system.

Edgar Allan Poe, Irish in both lines, whose poetry and horror tales are familiar classics, also wrote pieces for the Irish American press. An Irish ancestor of novelist Henry James and his philosopher brother William was a wealthy patriot in the Revolution. Robert Walsh was a noted American writer in the early nineteenth century. Joel Chandler Harris created Uncle Remus. Fitz-James O'Brien is remembered for his weird short stories, James Whitcomb Riley as the people's poet, Finley Peter Dunn as "Mr. Dooley," James Brendan Connolly for his sea tales, Cyrus Townsend Brady for his popular novels, Robert Dwyer Joyce for his poem "Deirdre," and John Boyle O'Reilly, editor of *The Boston Pilot* and champion of the Negro, for his Ode read at the dedication of the statue of the Pilgrim in Boston. Irish American authors also include T. A. Daly, Joyce Kilmer, Catherine Markham, Edna St. Vincent Millay, A. M. Sullivan, Padraic and Mary Colum, James T. Farrell, Joseph I. C. Clarke, Benedict Fitzpatrick, Doran Hurley, Francis Carlin, Jim Tully, Ernest Boyd, Francis Hackett, Joel Sayre, Anne O'Hare McCormick, Will Durant, Joseph Dinneen, Betty Smith, John O'Hara, Morley Callaghan, Vincent Sheean, Eleanor Rogers Cox, Robert J. Casey and scores of other novelists, poets, critics and general writers.

Irish stars crowd the American theater: The Barrymores (real name: Blythe), John McCullough, John Drew, Ada Rehan, Margaret Anglin, Maxine Elliott (McDermott), Walter Hampden (Daugherty), Chauncey Olcott and Andrew Mack, Arnold Daly, James O'Neill, Wilton Lackaye, George M. Cohan, Helen Hayes, Augustin Duncan, Dudley Digges, Sara Allgood, Barry Fitzgerald. Many of these are also film stars along with Maureen O'Hara, Geraldine Fitzgerald, Margaret Sullavan, Bing Crosby, James Cagney, Greer Garson, Spencer Tracy and Margaret O'Brien (half-Spanish).

David Wark Griffith was America's first really effective movie director.

John Ford's *The Informer*, a story of Ireland's struggle for liberty after World War I, is one of the most notable screen-plays ever made.

Eugene O'Neill is perhaps the foremost American playwright.

Isadora Duncan began her dancing career by practicing the jigs her Irish grandmother taught her.

James McNeill Whistler, Thomas Moran, Paul Daugherty, Georgia O'Keeffe, Eugene Higgins and John Costigan are a few American painters of Irish or part-Irish origin or descent. Seumas O'Brien is a sculptor, painter, poet, novelist and playwright. On the roster of sculptors are Augustus St. Gaudens (see page 90), Edmund Quinn, Andrew O'Connor, Jerome O'Conor, James O'Conor, James Edward Kelly and John J. Boyle.

James Hoban, born in Dublin in 1756 and educated as an architect, came over before the Revolution. He designed the first State House building in the United States, at Columbia, South Carolina. On July 17, 1792, the Commissioners of the District of Columbia, having together with President Washington examined competing designs for public structures in the capital, awarded a prize to Hoban for his plan for an Executive Mansion, and employed him to supervise its construction. The result was the White House, whose general lines were inspired by the then most notable private dwelling in Dublin, the residence of the Duke of Leinster (a Fitzgerald), now—still a show place—the home of the Royal Dublin Society. Hoban saw to the rebuilding of the White House after its destruction by the British in 1814 and was one of the supervising architects in the construction of the Capitol. He served in the United States' employ for about a quarter of a century, designing Federal buildings.

Louis Sullivan was the pioneer-architect of the skyscraper.

In American music, the Irish claim Stephen Collins Foster and his popular folk songs, the conductor Patrick Gilmore, the composers Edward Macdowell and James Dunn; Victor Herbert, master of musical comedy; the modernist composer Henry D. Cowell, the tenors John McCormack and Nicholas Farley; James H. Blake, who wrote the score and lyrics of "The Sidewalks of New York," the theme-song of Al Smith's political campaigns.

Horace Greeley, Lawrence Godkin, William M. Laffan and Thomas Fitzgerald are instantly recognizable names in the history of American journalism. Fitzgerald's *Evening City Item* in Philadelphia was the first paper to report baseball games. Then there were: Frank Ward O'Malley whose humor and whimsicality marked many a New York *Sun* news story in the pre-Munsey days; William F. Dillon of the widely circulated *Rural New Yorker*; Thomas D'Arcy McGee, another editor of *The Bos-*

ton *Pilot*; Peter Fenelon Collier who made a fortune peddling Catholic and Irish books on the installment plan to Irish workers and servant girls, and founded *Collier's* magazine; and his son Robert Collier who built it up into a big weekly, once a leader in the necessary muckraking of American political and social conditions in the Teddy Roosevelt era.

During World War II a young Irish American friend of mine, Delos O'Brian, Unitarian minister and newspaper columnist, became an incisive figure in the civic life of Wilmington, Delaware, addressing himself in clear, progressive terms to different groups in the city and in the country as a whole. "Since no intolerance, no bigotry, is more bitter than religious bigotry," wrote O'Brian in *Liberty* in 1945, "and since no persecution is fiercer than religious persecution, we need to build a bulwark of complete religious freedom into our postwar plans. This means freedom for every man to believe and practice and teach according to the convictions of his conscience unless he seeks to contravene the equal rights of others." My guess is that in his work and ideas he is typical of many other Irish Americans.

The Irish have supplied numerous leaders to American labor and radical movements: Terence Powderly, founder of the Knights of Labor; Patrick Collins, later Mayor of Boston; Tom Mooney; William Z. Foster of the Communist Party; Michael Quill of the Transport Workers, Dan Tobin of the Teamsters, Joe Curran of the National Maritime Union; Elizabeth Gurley Flynn, a leader in the Paterson silk workers' and Lowell textile workers' strikes in the 1910s, also a leader of the Industrial Workers of the World until she became one of the inner group of the Communist Party in the 1930s.

The roll call of Irish Americans in sports would run into the thousands. To mention only a few: Connie Mack (MacGillicuddy), John McGraw, Charles Comiskey and Roger Bresnahan in baseball; Jake Kilrain, John L. Sullivan, Jim Corbett, Terry McGovern, Gene Tunney, James J. Braddock and Jack Dempsey (part-Irish) in boxing; Johnny Farrell in golf; William Muldoon, pugilist who became physical trainer to America's eminent and wealthy men, friend of T.R., and the subject of a striking piece of literary portraiture, "The Solid Man" in *Twelve Men* by Theodore Dreiser; John Hayes the runner, Dan O'Leary the walker, Matt McGrath the shot-putter; Martin Sheridan, the Olympic Pentathlon winner—

Although the Anglophile trend of American official policy under Woodrow Wilson caused many Irish Americans to regret—mistakenly— American participation in World War I, their achievements in the armed forces during 1917-1918 more than sustained the record of their services in previous wars. The New York 69th, re-named the 165th, distinguished itself under Colonels "Wild Bill" Donovan, Timothy Moynihan, "Dynamite Mike" Kelly and Alexander E. Anderson (a major general when he died early in World War II). As chief quartermaster of the American Expeditionary Force, Colonel Daniel E. McCarthy was the first member of that Army to land in France. He subsequently compiled a list of 379 American officers and men of Irish birth or descent who received the Distinguished Service Cross, and 292 who were awarded the Croix de Guerre.

After World War I Irish Americans raised their voice in organized strength to demand that Ireland be granted independence in accordance with Wilson's principle of self-determination. This, together with the revolutionary military struggle of the people of Ireland, led to the autonomy granted Eire (the Irish Free State, comprising the twenty-six Catholic counties) in 1921. In the opinion of many Irish Americans, this new State, headed by New York-born Eamon de Valera, has not been a success domestically or internationally. Some of the older ones remember De Valera unpleasantly. His double-dealing politics in the 1920s, as one of them put it to me, "broke the unity of Irish America, freeing the British from fear of American public opinion"; which, however, is another story. Suffice it to say that De Valera has alienated many Irish Americans from Ireland. The old-country sentiment comes back to them only sporadically. The old issues have lost meaning. The old leaders are dead or heavy with years. The strength of old-line Irish organizations in the United States has steadily decreased. Most of the "Irishtowns" and "Dublins" have disappeared. The Irish newspapers are of negligible circulation and influence.

Irish Americans form the bulk of the Roman Catholic Church in the United States. Multitudes of them belong to organizations which have Irish leaders. But these organizations and leaders have become more Catholic than they are Irish; and, for the most part, they are ultra-conservative, failing to keep pace with the times. In the years when the inevitable war between freedom and Fascism was brewing, such organizations did not develop a sound orientation toward the rising forces of freedom; their ecclesiastic and lay leaders had only praise for Mussolini and Franco; and too many Irish Americans approached World War II ill-prepared to understand its issues. The majority were isolationists, some more anti-British or anti-Russian than anti-Axis. After Pearl Harbor, however, and the German and Italian declarations of war against the United States, their natural patriotism impelled them to render their full share of service to the country where the greater part of the "Irish race" now lives.

When the poet A. M. Sullivan surveyed—in *The Recorder* of the American Irish Historical Society—the Irish record in the armed forces for the fifteen months after Pearl Harbor, he was able to list eighty-four Irish Americans cited for exceptional heroism. Since then the number has multiplied many times. Before World War II exactly five hundred Irish Americans had been awarded the Congressional Medal of Honor.

I have said that the list of Irish names in American politics is very long. In 1938 the American Irish Historical Society wrote all members of Congress inquiring if they were in any part of Irish descent. Replies showed that twenty-eight Senators and ninety-nine Representatives were wholly, mostly, half or in some measure of Irish stock. Senator Harry S. Truman of Missouri indicated that his mother's mother descended from Irish settlers in Pennsylvania.

Americans of Irish descent held high positions in the Administration in Washington during World War II. Some have already been mentioned; others were James F. Byrnes, head of the Office of War Mobilization ("Assistant President") under F. D. R. and secretary of state under Truman; Admiral of the Fleet William D. Leahy, personal chief of staff of the Commander-in-Chief; Major General William J. Donovan, chief of the Office of Strategic Services, the "cloak and dagger" outfit in the Army whose activities are still little known; Grace Tully, President Roosevelt's confidential secretary; Matthew J. Connelly, secretary to President Truman.

Patrick J. Hurley, secretary of war under Hoover, major general and chief Presidential trouble-shooter in the Orient during World War II, was appointed Ambassador to China in 1944.

One of Edward R. Stettinius' grandmothers was a Reilly.

Irish Americans in the Roman Catholic Church not only form the largest block of its membership in the United States but they furnish most of its American priests. In addition to Bishop Carroll, many notable Americans have been Irish Catholic churchmen: James Cardinal Gibbons of Baltimore, honored by people of all faiths; Archbishop John Ireland of St. Paul whom some regarded as a constructive force in the Northwest; and Patrick Cardinal Hayes, who rose from the sidewalks of New York to become a power behind many constructive measures, although progressives will always deplore his leading part in defeating the Child Labor Amendment to the Constitution.

The Catholic Hierarchy has always been preponderantly Irish. Through the National Catholic Welfare Conference, whose Washington headquarters is staffed mainly by Irish Americans, it controls a vast network of organizations through which it exerts a growing influence on the Administration in Washington, on the radio and the theater, on the movies and newspapers, on local and state politics, on education and morals and ethics, on practically every phase of American life.

In the fall of 1944 *The Christian Century*, the foremost American Protestant magazine, ran a series of eight articles by Harold E. Fey under the general title "Can Catholicism Win America?" The author admitted that Protestantism was finding itself on the defensive in the United States. "Can [it] recover the prominent position in molding the American culture which it held before the great waves of Catholic immigration swept across the continent?" he asked. "Or is this once Protestant nation destined to pass into another and different cultural phase under the religious and social preponderance of the Roman Catholic Church?" After marshalling an imposing assemblage of facts on the energetic expansionism of the Roman Church, Mr. Fey concluded that there was a real possibility of that.

The articles took pains to point out the many activities of the Catholic organizations (most of them officered by Irish American priests or laymen) which are excellent. What worried Mr. Fey, and here he expressed the concern of most Protestant thinkers and leaders, was the over-all, long-range purposes of these activities—namely, the complete revision of American culture and the seizure of power in a political and social sense.

"The purposes of the Roman Catholic Church in America," wrote Mr. Fey, "are authoritatively and unambiguously set forth by Monsignor John A. Ryan"—an Irish American, long the outstanding teacher at the Catholic University in Washington—"head of the Social Action Department of the National Catholic Welfare Conference and principal architect of the Church's present organizational structure in America. More than two decades ago he wrote, with M. F. X. Millar, a book on *The State and the Church* which was republished in 1940 as *Catholic Principles in Politics*, with Francis Boland as collaborator. For nearly twenty-five years this has been an approved text in Catholic universities. It is stamped with both the *imprimatur* and the *nihil obstat*. This means that the proper Church authorities have examined its doctrine and found it in accord with papal teaching and that there is nothing in the book to which the official censor can object as a misrepresentation of the Church. It therefore stands as an official statement of the Roman Catholic position on the relation of the Church to American society.

"According to that position there is only one true church, the Roman Catholic, and it is the intention of that Church to establish itself as the State Church in this country. Catholics may deny that this is what their Church is trying to do, but one needs only to read the clear statements in Dr. Ryan's officially approved textbook to discover the truth. For example, Pope Leo XIII is cited . . . as authority for the statement that 'the state must not only "have care for religion" but recognize the true religion. This means the form of religion practiced by the Catholic Church.' So says Monsignor Ryan, italicizing 'true.' The state is under obligation to help the Catholic Church prevail over all other churches, according to Monsignor Ryan, who quotes with entire approval an encyclical of Leo's on 'Catholicity in the United States.' The encyclical condemns the American system of separation of Church and State.

"How can Dr. Ryan deny that the Roman Catholic Church seeks to become the State Church in the United States when he declares that 'the state should officially recognize the Catholic religion as the religion of the commonwealth . . . it should recognize and sanction the laws of the Church; it should protect the rights of the Church and the religious as well as the other rights of the Church's members'? . . .

"What will happen to other religious faiths when Catholicism comes into power? The question is not dodged in this official Catholic text. Since the Roman Catholic is the only true Church, all others must be false. Protestants and other religious groups 'may' be permitted to practice their own form of worship, providing it is 'carried on within the family circle or in such an inconspicuous manner as to be an occasion neither of scandal nor of perversion to the faithful . . .' But the Catholicized State would circumscribe the religious freedom of Protestants and confine it to such fugitive meetings. 'Since no rational end is promoted by dissemination of false doctrine, there exists no right to indulge in this practice. . . . Error has not the same rights as truth.'

"Dr. Ryan expresses confidence that Protestants can do nothing about this Catholic threat to their freedom because Protestants believe in religious toleration and are thus required to practice it. Louis Veuillot, a French clericist, put the same idea thus: 'We ask you for liberty in the name of your principles; we deny it to you in the name of ours.' One method of dealing with dissenting Churches when Catholicism comes into power, says Monsignor Ryan's book, will be to remove their exemption from taxation, while the Roman Catholic Church will of course retain such exemption. If the State refuses to do the will of the Church, the Pope can, says Dr. Ryan, free citizens from their oaths of allegiance to it. . . ."

Mr. Fey's articles provoked a nationwide discussion, still going on as I write. Protestantism has come in for a close examination by Protestants. Dr. John Bennett, a well-known contributor to *The Christian Century*, opened the question of the Protestant Churches' social-economic-political orientation: were most of them primarily "bourgeois" or middle- and upper-class? His point was that they were, and the Reverend Charles X. Hutchinson, Jr., pastor of the Methodist Church in Danielson, Connecticut, in a letter to the editor of that magazine (January 3, 1945), agreed with him.

"You say," he wrote, "that Protestantism 'should be profoundly disquieted when it finds that its appeal meets a response predominantly among those who are affluent.' Who would argue that it is disquieted at all? That is what Dr. Bennett is talking about when he says, 'The people in our Protestant churches are lined up automatically in their political decisions against the poor, against the industrial workers. And one discovers very little searching of heart among them about this situation.' You reply that 'this serious charge is unfounded as far as the [1944] election is concerned.' Amend what Dr. Bennett says to read as follows: 'The people of our northern Protestant churches are lined up automatically as partisan Republicans.' I will not insist that the two statements mean the same thing, but I have my own idea. I do insist that, by and large, our northern Protestant churches are an adjunct to the Republican Party.

"This relation is clearly indicated in my own state. The Democratic Party in Connecticut is meticulously careful in naming its candidates and distributing its honors to give recognition to the Italians, Polish, Irish, French, Jews, and almost any other group you might mention except the good old Connecticut Yankee Protestants. Why? Because they expect few votes from that quarter. The party almost always names one Yankee on the state ticket for window dressing but never expects this gesture to pay off in votes. The party is justified in virtually ignoring the Yankee Protestants almost all of whom are automatically Republicans.

"The issue of the relation of the Protestant clergy to politics is of enormous importance. If you would discover the point at which our influence began to wane, search for the place where we became politically inarticulate. For, generally speaking, we have become just that. Ministers are politically timid, and I blame them, not their churches. It is amazing the number of ministers who are not registered in party caucuses or primaries. Oh, they mustn't be partisan! So they sacrifice fifty per cent of their franchise, putting themselves in a position where they have no choice in nominating candidates for public office, which in many instances is more important than the actual election.

"Again, where are the ministers when great social and moral questions come up for public hearing before the legislative committees? Where are their sentiments when a vote is to be taken by the legislature itself? I can answer as far as Connecticut is concerned, for I have been carefully watching for the last four years. Except for a few outstanding men

whom I can count on the fingers of one hand, they are conspicuous by
their absence. I have to shake myself sometimes to remember that our
state received its political heritage, the first constitution in the world,
from Thomas Hooker! Dr. Bennett has spoken a needed word to the
Protestant clergy: 'If they . . . expressed themselves' on social, political
and moral issues, 'the nation would have a very different conception of
the meaning of Protestantism in its relation to politics and economics.' "

There is no doubt that a wide-flung and perhaps serious Protestant-
Catholic struggle—still largely behind the scenes—is in progress. Nearly
all the bishops and priests and laymen Fey cites as heading the various
Catholic projects and movements are Irish.

It is not a new struggle, of course. But the alignment of forces is
different than it was once upon a time. As I say, the Catholic Hierarchy
has become a great power in the United States; it has taken the offensive. And as suggested in the foregoing quotations, the struggle now
involves more than a difference in religious creeds. It swings around the
relation between religion and government and the practice of public
non-sectarian education versus parochial schooling. It reaches into the
old question of the separation of Church and State, which rests ultimately on the right of everyone to his own belief "without prejudice," as
the lawyers say, to his civic or political status.

The struggle goes deep into the class structure of American society.
It enters party politics. It more than touches several phases of the
United States' foreign policy. It bears heavily on the U. S. A.'s relations
with Latin American countries. Hundreds of important State Department officials and diplomatists are Catholics, most of them Irish
Catholics, as likely as not trained in the Catholic Georgetown University's School of Foreign Service in Washington—until the early 1940s
the only school of its kind in the country, staffed mostly by Irish
Americans.

The struggle is more than Catholic-Protestant. In it are hangovers of
old Know-Nothing issues, now reversed; also the instinctive resentment
of many non-English Americans against the Anglo-Saxon concept of the
country. It commands the interest of some Jews and some Gentiles who
are neither Protestants nor Catholics in belief. In it, at bottom, is the
question of whether a Catholic-controlled United States would work
toward or away from the development of democracy.

Whether or not the struggle will continue more or less subversively,
or come out in the open, I don't know; nor how it will end. My hope is
that before long a lot of Americans, Protestants and Catholics, Irish and
non-Irish, Jews, agnostics and atheists, will look into it, into the
psychological civil war now being fought on that front; and that out of
it all will come a new development progressing a little nearer to the

democratic concept: basic equality within diversity—without regard to race, religion, or the absence of a formalized religious creed.

Early in the 1940s the conservative William Cardinal O'Connell of Boston came close to the problem if we take his words at their face value.* "Today Americans agree," he said, "that each person shall be given the right to worship freely. Or he may choose not to go to any church. He does not have to pay taxes to support any church at all. And there is no state church here.

"We may still feel that some other religion than our own—one that is very different from ours—is wrong. But we reason the matter out in this way: Suppose that you and I keep someone else from worshiping God as he sees fit. We say that he does not think as we do; so he must be wrong! But perhaps tomorrow he and his friends may be strong enough to keep you and me from worshiping God as we see fit. He will say that we do not think as he does; so we must be wrong. Therefore if I want freedom for myself I must be willing that other people should have freedom too. That is the only way that I can be sure my own freedom will last."

And in *The Christian Century* for May 2, 1945, an eminent Protestant clergyman, Ralph W. Sockman, of Christ Church (formerly Madison Avenue Methodist Episcopal Church) in New York, a director of the Union Theological Seminary and a one-time president of the Federation of Churches, wrote in comment on Mr. Fey's articles:

". . . The United States is not a Protestant nation nor a Catholic one; rather it is a democratic one where many cultures exist side by side, each making contributions to the larger common culture. Neither exists here on the terms of the other but both live here on democratic terms.

"The American plan presupposes that both groups will be strong and vigorous in pressing their doctrinal claims. The tensions thus arising are profound, sometimes irritating, but all in all they will keep the discussion of ultimate values and reality alive, clean, clear. Conflicts will arise also from social action. Prohibition, a Protestant culture pattern, and condemnation of the practice of birth control, a Catholic policy, are illustrations. These are important but secondary to other items on which cooperation is feasible—such great questions as economic justice, good government, international order and the natural rights of man. In other words, if the proper spirit prevails, Protestants and Catholics can stand together for the great social concerns to which Christianity must continually address itself while disagreeing on other issues."

If the proper spirit prevails . . .

---

*Cardinal O'Connell never repudiated Monsignor Ryan's book; it had at least his implicit approval.

The iced-in sap-sealed glumness of the old-stock Anglo-Saxon American with his Puritan background on both sides of the water has been exaggerated. But there is no doubt, either, that before the Irish and some of the other immigrant groups began to arrive in numbers the tone of American life was somewhat rigid and over-serious, somewhat gray and cautious and cool; particularly in New England. The Irish brought in a lot of good, warm humor; humor that evoked not dry smiles but rollicking laughter, that unlimbered people, opened them up, tickled the cockles of their hearts. The Irish brought a tremendously refreshing and vivifying quality of imagination, which ran from the unearthly, the mystical, at one end to a healthy sense of the ridiculous at the other. And they brought an innate grace and unself-conscious dignity of manner that softened and humanized the stiff Puritan austerity.

According to a New England friend of mine, herself of Puritan stock going back to the Mayflower, the Irish servant-girl was all-important in this respect. For three-quarters of a century or longer, it was a rare old-stock American family that did not have an Irish housemaid, nurse or cook. In the 1890s and later, greenhorn girls were paid eight to twenty dollars a month; some stayed in service for only a few years, till they married and began to raise families of their own; but in that time, and for those wages, they did a great deal for America. With their Irish laughter, Irish fairy-tales and native Irish charm, without trying and by simply being themselves, they influenced two or three generations of old-stock American children, who grew up with warmer personalities, with more pliant characters, and with less rigid attitudes than they might have had otherwise.

Another old-stock American friend, a well-known clergyman, puts it this way: "The Irish have contributed a lot to bad politics and good humor. They have made it possible for many of the dour Puritans of Boston, including some of those in my own family, to take a look at themselves and laugh, even though they had been brought up to take everything in life seriously—most of all, themselves."

Well over a thousand American cities and villages—the largest being Baltimore—are named after cities and villages and counties in Ireland, or after Irish families or individuals.

The number of Irish or part-Irish Americans in 1945? It is lower than that of either the Anglo-Saxon or the German group, but they are the third largest element. Between fifteen and twenty million may be a safe surmise.

They are a people of variety. They are praised and damned on many counts. One dreads the results of Robert D. Murphy's international machinations; one cheers Supreme Court Justice Frank Murphy's stand against anti-Semitism; the magazine-cover picture of young Audie Murphy of Farmersville, Texas, "the most decorated soldier "of World War II, fills one with elation. One can delight in the Irish socially and at the same time be irritated by their lack of detachment and objectivity. In some of them is a serene, appealing lightness of heart and mind, an almost matter-of-course romanticism that is very contagious—that can put a non-Irish person in the frame of mind of Seattle's Judge John Neergaard who suspended sentence on all Irish appearing before him as an aftermath of St. Patrick's Day in 1945, and for good measure included in his amnesty a Mexican named Francisco Jesus Gallagher.

A friend of mine, himself "pure Irish," a well-known man who does not wish to be named, wrote this to me about the Irish in America:

"The more one studies any people, the more they prove to be like all other peoples. The 'Fighting Irish' are neither more quarrelsome nor braver than many another breed, though none surpass them in valor. They are no more given to factionalism than many others, though too much for their own good. They are accused of intemperance, but others can match them; and they gave the world the Total Abstinence movement, which may or may not be an additional basis for charging them with intemperance.

"As for political corruption—too often the Irish have exhibited cupidity and lack of conscience in the discharge of public trusts, strangely at variance with the precepts of the faith which most of them profess. When the Irish rebel Jeremiah O'Donovan Rossa, after twelve years in English prison, came to New York in 1871, he was shocked by the subservience of the Irish to the corrupt Tammany machine, and entered on a long fight to remedy the condition. He ran for office against the notorious Tweed. The situation which emerged and disgusted Rossa had its natural causes, like any social phenomenon. The Irish who came here in the middle nineteenth century were penniless, many of them starving. There was a mixture of genuine charity and ruthless calculation in the helping hand extended to them by Tammany and other political machines, mostly Democratic. They were helped to jobs; the abler and shrewder among them found the way open to public office. But they paid for a time a fearful price, as Rossa saw. And note: William M. Tweed and Fernando Wood display instances of jobbery, bribery, boodling and violence impartially implicating men of all stocks. . . . The Irish furnish as many examples of civic virtue as any other group. Senator Thomas Walsh of Montana, who exposed the Teapot Dome scandal, was Irish.

"Other peoples love gaiety and camaraderie as much but none more than the Irish. They surpass all but the Jews, and probably equal them, in charities. They are the most pious of all. They are incomparable in administrative and executive work, but have a weakness for the titles and honors of the professions. They are among the kindliest of people.

"Individual Irishmen can be the most cosmopolitan of men, but the Irish as a people have a singular tendency to parochialism, a kind of group introversion. This results in marked clannishness and a fierce devotion to individual leaders even when the latter betray high causes.

"The Irish are by nature tolerant, but typically unable to expand tolerance into the vision of dynamic democracy and universal brotherhood. They tend to live by and in themselves, self-satisfied and unaware of many of the major currents of life and of forces endlessly remaking the world. Few are to be found at concert or opera, or in the serious theater, or among readers of serious books, and Irish leaders in dynamically progressive political and social evolution are conspicuous because—considering the size of the Irish element—there are so few of them.

"The contemporary Irish Americans are more negligent than almost any other element in the United States of their cultural heritage. Too many adopt gleefully every stickily sentimental and every rowdy song that comes from Tinpan Alley labelled 'Irish,' and millions of their fellow-Americans naturally enough think that 'Ireland Must Be Heaven' and 'It's A Great Day for the Irish' really represent the musical level attainable by the Gael. Only in a few of the larger cities are concerts of real Irish music ever offered; the occasions are infrequent, the attendance generally small, and the numbers offered are almost invariably 'arrangements' in the Italianate or metronomic manner, although there are in America enough singers and instrumentalists familiar with the incomparably lovely Irish traditional musical mode to keep it alive if they had any encouragement. Even the Pipers Bands fostered by some of the Irish Counties organizations and by the Transport Workers Union in New York now play only in march time; they present a gallant appearance in their saffron kilts, green jackets, streamered bonnets and hairy sporrans; but—

"Were the Irish to discover an interest in their history in this country, it might lessen their confusion and alter their orientation toward the future of their country and of the world. It might vivify and vitalize their essential Americanism now often dormant or confused by the Charles Coughlins, the Frank Hagues and such papers as the Brooklyn Tablet. It might breach the walls of their clannishness and broaden their tolerance. Now some of them are fanatically anti-Semitic.

"We need new leaders—like Frances Sweeney of Boston. When the poison of anti-Semitism, artfully spread by fascists, corrupted some of her fellow-Catholics and fellow-Irish Americans, Frances Sweeney pitted herself against the evil with an ardor that brought about her early death. A committee named in her honor carries on the work.

"As to anti-Semitism, Frank Murphy has done a good deal to reduce its incidence among the Irish. So has Archbishop Richard J. Cushing of Boston who soon after taking over the archdiocese is said to have called a meeting of all his priests at which he laid down the law to them: Irish or Catholic anti-Semitism had to stop. Early in 1945 he also put the influence of his Church in Boston behind proposed anti-discrimination legislation.

"Like other groups in our population, like the American people in general, we Irish need new prophets—such as the poet John Boyle O'Reilly who time and again exhorted the Irish in this country to a wider outlook. 'Mankind,' he said, 'is a marching army with a broadening front the while!' And Patrick A. Collins, Mayor of Boston, once avowed:

" 'Born as I was in a distant land . . . nurtured on this soil and instructed in the principles of free government, as a citizen of this Republic, I denounce any man or body of men who seek to create and perpetuate divisions of races or religions in our midst. I kneel at the altars of my fathers, and I love the land of my birth, but in American politics I know neither color, race nor creed.' "

THE END

NOTES AND APPENDICES

The Project

As suggested in the prefatory letter to this volume, in 1938 I began a job which has been interrupted several times since by tasks immediately connected with the war crisis, and which has been referred to as the Plymouth-Rock-and-Ellis-Island or Nation-of-Nations "project." It is explained rather fully in the appendices to *From Many Lands* (1940), the first of a series of independent books to result from it.

Two-Way Passage (1941) was the second book in the series; *What's Your Name?* (1942), the third.

A Nation of Nations is the fourth. As with the others, I shall welcome readers' reactions to it. The book contains between fifteen and twenty thousand facts; great care was taken to have them correct, but it may be that inaccuracies have crept in here and there; and I hope my attention will be drawn to them, so they may be corrected in later printings.

I plan tentatively to write a fifth book, a close companion to the fourth, to be entitled *Plymouth Rock and Ellis Island* and published in 1947 or 1948. If it works out, the fifth volume probably will contain chapters on:

The Indians
Americans from England
Americans from Scotland
Americans from Wales
Americans from the Isle of Man
Americans from Canada
Americans from Iceland
Americans from Denmark
Americans from Portugal
The Basques
Americans from Belgium
Americans from Switzerland
Americans from Finland
Americans from Czechoslovakia
Americans from Austria
Americans from Hungary
Americans from Rumania
The Gypsies
Americans from Bulgaria
Americans from Albania
Americans from Armenia
Americans from Syria and Lebanon
Immigrants from India
Americans from China
Americans from Japan
The Filipinos
Americans from the West Indies
Americans from Latin America (except Mexico)

Masses of material on several of these groups are on hand, but I need more on all of them—especially on the recent immigrants (since, say, 1850) from England, Scotland and Wales. The sort of material I need is suggested by the chapters in this book. On pages 302-308 of *From Many Lands* appears a broadside questionnaire indicating more specifically what kind of information I want. I shall be grateful also for obscure books and pamphlets, for being directed to unpublished manuscripts, diaries, doctors' theses, etc., dealing with any of these groups or with aspects of Immigration in general.

The material on many of the groups is enormous. It was not my purpose in *A Nation of Nations*, and will not be in *Plymouth Rock and Ellis Island*, to write inclusive or exhaustive chapters, but merely to give a balanced impression of what is significant, dramatic or otherwise interesting in the stories of the different elements of the American population.

These books of mine, particularly *A Nation of Nations*, may be considered a kind of introduction to The Peoples of America Series, which I am editing for J. B. Lippincott Company (East Washington Square, Philadelphia). Such a series of full-length books was discussed between my regular publishers, Harper & Brothers, and myself in 1939, but at that time I felt I might not be able to get to it much before 1948. Meantime, the Lippincotts thought of the same idea, and Harper's agreed to my editing the series for them.

An announcement of The Peoples of America Series was made in 1944, and at this writing (July 1945) ten of the twenty-odd volumes are contracted for, five are in preparation. One or two will appear in 1946.

D'Arcy McNickle, of the Office of Indian Affairs, author of the widely praised novel *Surrounded*, will do the volume on the Indians, tentatively entitled *They Were Here First*.

Carey McWilliams, author of *Brothers Under the Skin* and *Prejudice*, is doing *They Came from Spain and Mexico*.

Another leading writer, whose name cannot be announced until after he has published another book, agreed to do the volume on the English (Anglo-Saxon) element.

Frances Winwar, author of several best-selling and prize-winning books, is writing the story of the Italian group; Joseph Dinneen (*Ward Eight*, etc.) of the Irish; J. Saunders Redding (*No Day of Triumph*) of the Negroes; Emil Lengyel (*The Danube, Siberia*, etc.) of the Hungarian group.

John Roy Carlson, author of *Under Cover*, whose original name is Arthur A. Derounian, is scheduled to cover the Armenian Americans; Bradford Smith, the Japanese Americans; Leola Nelson Bergmann, the Norwegian Americans.

Discussions on the German, Polish, Chinese, Finnish, Swedish, Balkan, Czechoslovak, Russian, French and other volumes are in progress.

Tentative or fragmentary articles on the situation in the United States which I am trying to deal with in this entire project appear occasionally in my little paper *T&T* (*Tides & Trends*), issued from my office in Milford, New Jersey.

Throughout the project I had the help of thousands of people of all backgrounds, living the country over—too many to list in connection with any attempt at thanks.

The aid given me on the chapters of *A Nation of Nations* I try to acknowledge in the notes which follow these. As for the book as a whole, I owe special thanks to my wife Stella and my assistant Isabel Mangold who worked on the script; to my friend Ross B. Wills who read several chapters in rough drafts; to Mrs. Ethel H. Sharpe of Milford, New Jersey, who helped with the typing.

LOUIS ADAMIC,
MILFORD, NEW JERSEY

Partial Notes on Sources
and Recommended Reading

Perhaps two-thirds of the material in this book is drawn from my "project files" accumulated during 1938-1945, including thousands of letters from individuals and thousands of clippings from the general American prints and the immigrant and Negro newspapers—too many to list.

Through the writing of the book I had frequent occasion to turn to Who's Who in America, to Who Was Who in America and to the Dictionary of American Biography. To DAB—a great reference work—I make further acknowledgment later on.

On the general subject of Immigration and the diversity of the American population I recommend the following magazine and books:

Common Ground, a quarterly edited by M. Margaret Anderson, 222—4th Avenue, New York 3, New York.

The Problems of a Changing Population. Report of the Committee on Population Problems to the National Resources Committee, May 1938. Washington, D.C.: United States Government Printing Office, 1938.

New Viewpoints in American History, by Arthur M. Schlesinger. New York: The Macmillan Company, 1937. Chapter I: "The Influence of Immigration on American History." Also "What Then Is the American, This New Man?" An address by Professor Schlesinger delivered in 1942 as President of the American Historical Association, published in the January 1943 American Historical Review.

The Atlantic Migration, 1607-1860 and The Immigrant in American History, by Marcus Lee Hansen. Cambridge, Mass.: Harvard University Press, 1940. Both highly recommended.

Americans. A New History of the Peoples Who Settled the Americas, by Emil L. Jordan. New York: W. W. Norton & Company, Inc., 1939.

One America. Our Racial and National Minorities, edited by Francis J. Brown and Joseph S. Roucek. New York: Prentice-Hall, Inc., 1945.

We Who Built America. The Saga of the Immigrant, by Carl Wittke. New York: Prentice-Hall, Inc., 1939.

These Foreigners, by William Seabrook. New York: Harcourt, Brace and Company, Inc., 1938.

A History of American Immigration, 1820-1924, by George M. Stephenson. Boston: Ginn and Company, 1926.

American Minority Peoples. A Study in Racial and Cultural Conflicts in the United States, by Donald Young. New York: Harper & Brothers, 1932.

We Americans. A Study of Cleavage in an American City, by Elin L. Anderson. Cambridge, Mass.: Harvard University Press, 1937.

Alien Americans. A Study of Race Relations, by B. Schrieke. New York: The Viking Press, 1936.

Foreigners in the Confederacy, by Ella Lonn. Chapel Hill: University of North Carolina Press, 1940.

Old World Wisconsin. Around Europe in the Badger State, by Fred L. Holmes. Eau Claire, Wis.: E. M. Hale and Company, 1944.

Brothers Under the Skin and Prejudice, by Carey McWilliams. Boston: Little, Brown & Company, 1943 and 1944. Highly recommended.

Names on the Land. A Historical Account of Place-Naming in the United States, by George R. Stewart. New York: Random House, Inc., 1945.
Immigrant Gifts to American Life, by Allen H. Eaton. New York: Russell Sage Foundation, 1932.
American Saga. The History and Literature of the American Dream of a Better Life, by Marjorie Barstow Greenbie. New York: McGraw-Hill Book Company, Inc., 1941.
Early American History, by Jennings B. Sanders. New York: Prentice-Hall, Inc., 1938.
The United States, 1830-1850, by Frederick Jackson Turner. New York: Henry Holt and Company, Inc., 1935.
The Growth of American Thought, by Merle Curti. New York: Harper & Brothers, 1943.
America, by Stephen Vincent Benét. New York: Farrar & Rinehart, Inc., 1944. Highly recommended.
The Heritage of America, edited by Henry Steele Commager and Allan Nevins. Boston: Little, Brown & Company, 1939. Especially recommended to New Americans.
The Springfield Plan, by Alexander Alland and James Waterman Wise. New York: Viking Press. 1945.
The Story of the Springfield Plan, by C. I. Chatto and A. L. Halligan. New York: Barnes & Noble. 1945.
Build Together Americans, by Rachel Davis DuBois. New York: Hinds, Hayden & Eldredge. 1945.
Around the World in St. Paul, by Alice L. Sickels. Minneapolis: University of Minnesota Press. Highly recommended.

CHAPTER "AMERICANS FROM ITALY"

Admiral of the Ocean Sea. A Life of Christopher Columbus, by Samuel Eliot Morison. Boston: Little, Brown & Company, 1942.
Christopher Columbus, by Salvador de Madariaga. New York: The Macmillan Company, 1940. Presenting circumstantial evidence that Columbus might have been a Spanish Jew.
Amerigo Vespucci, Pilot Major, by Frederick J. Pohl. New York: Columbia University Press, 1945.
Memoirs of the Life and Peregrinations of the Florentine Philip Mazzei, 1730-1860, translated by Howard R. Marraro. New York: Columbia University Press, 1942. Highly recommended.
"Philip Mazzei, Virginia's Agent to Europe: The Story of His Mission as Related in His Own Dispatches and Other Documents." An article by Howard R. Marraro in the March-April 1934 *Bulletin of the New York Public Library.* Mr. Marraro has published material on Mazzei also in the *William and Mary College Quarterly,* the *Virginia Magazine of History and Biography,* the *Mississippi Valley Historical Review* and the *Bulletin of the Polish Institute of Arts and Sciences in America.*
The Italians in America Before the Civil War, by Giovanni Schiavo. New York: Vigo Press, 1934. With a section on Mazzei.
Philip Mazzei, Friend of Jefferson: His Life and Letters, by R. C. Garlick, Jr. Baltimore: The Johns Hopkins Press, 1933.

Giorgio Washington, by T. C. Giannini. Bologna, 1933. With an un-published letter from George Washington to Mazzei.

DAB contains sketches of Mazzei, Vigo and others referred to in the chapter.

The Soul of an Immigrant, by Constantine M. Panunzio. New York: The Macmillan Company, 1934.

Some Aspects of Italian Immigration to the United States, by Antonia Stella. New York: G. P. Putnam's Sons, 1924.

Sons of Italy, by Antonio Mangano. New York: The Methodist Book Concern, 1917.

The Italian in America, by Eliot Lord. New York: B. F. Buck Co., 1905.

The Italian Emigration of Our Times, by Robert F. Foester. Cambridge Mass.: Harvard University Press, 1919.

South Italian Folkways in Europe and America, by Phyllis H. Williams. New Haven, Conn.: Yale University Press, 1938.

The Italians of San Francisco, Their Adjustment and Acculturation, by Paul Radin. W.P.A. Project, 1935.

Thirteen Days, by Jeanette Marks. New York: Albert & Charles Boni, Inc., 1929. The climax of the Sacco-Vanzetti case.

Italian or American? The Second Generation in Conflict, by Irvin L. Child. New Haven, Conn.: Yale University Press, 1943.

Christ in Concrete, a novel, by Pietro di Donato. New York: The Bobbs-Merrill Company, 1939.

Fiction and autobiographical writing by John Fante: *Wait Until Spring, Bandini* (1938) and *Ask the Dust* (1939), published by Stackpole, New York; and *Dago Red* (1940), published by The Viking Press.

Maria and *No Bright Banner*, novels, by Michael De Capite. New York: The John Day Company, 1943 and 1944.

Olives on the Apple Tree, novel, by Guido D'Agostino. New York: Doubleday, Doran & Company, Inc., 1940.

Mount Allegro, an autobiographical novel by Jerre Mangione. Boston: Houghton Mifflin Company, 1943.

An Italian Tragedy. The Story of a Humble People, by Nicola Curinga. New York: Liveright Publishing Corporation, 1945.

Frances Winwar's book on the Italian element for The Peoples of America Series is scheduled for late 1946 or early 1947.

Professor Howard R. Marraro of Columbia University and Mr. Nicola Curinga of Los Angeles were good enough to read this chapter in script.*

CHAPTER "AMERICANS FROM SPAIN AND MEXICO"

Hernán Cortés, Conqueror of Mexico, by Salvador de Madariaga. New York: The Macmillan Company, 1941.

The True History of the Conquest of Mexico, by B. Diaz del Castillo. Written in 1568, translated by Maurice Keatinge. New York, 1927.

* Most of the chapters were read in script or in proof, or both, by persons specially familiar with the various groups. Some made suggestions for changes, additions, etc. Of course the responsibility for the book and its parts is mine only.—L. A.

History of the Conquest of Mexico and Peru, by W. H. Prescott. New York: Modern Library, Inc.

The Odyssey of Cabeza de Vaca, by Morris Bishop. New York, 1933. DAB—sketches, with bibliographies, of natives of Spain and Mexico who made a mark within what is now the United States.

The Soul of Spain, by Havelock Ellis. Boston: Houghton Mifflin Company, 1924.

Forgotten People, a study of New Mexicans, by George I. Sánchez. Albuquerque, N.M.: University of New Mexico Press. 1940. By the same author: "Equalization of Educational Opportunity" in the December 1, 1939, *The University of New Mexico Bulletin*; and "New Mexicans and Acculturation" in the February 1941 *New Mexico Quarterly Review*.

Man and Resources in the Middle Rio Grande Valley, by Allan G. Harper, Andrew R. Cordova and Kalervo Oberg. Albuquerque, N.M.: University of New Mexico Press, 1943.

New Mexico's Opportunity, by Joaquin Ortega. Albuquerque: 1942. A pamphlet; privately published.

Coronado's Children. Tales of Lost Mines and Buried Treasures of the Southwest, by J. Frank Dobie. New York: Grosset & Dunlap, Inc., 1930.

Death Comes for the Archbishop, a novel, by Willa Cather. New York: Alfred A. Knopf, 1927.

Magazines and journals oriented to the Southwest and more particularly to New Mexico are: *New Mexico*, Santa Fe; *New Mexico Anthropologist*, *New Mexico Historical Review*, *New Mexico Quarterly Review*, Albuquerque; *Southwest Review*, Dallas, Texas; *Southwestern Lore*, Gunnison, Colorado.

The chapter was read in script by Marie M. Hughes and M. E. Herriott of Los Angeles, George I. Sánchez of the University of Texas, S. Omar Barker of Tecolotenos, New Mexico, and the Honorable Clinton P. Anderson and Allan S. Harper of Washington, D. C.

CHAPTER "AMERICANS FROM FRANCE"

French Blood in America, by Lucian J. Fosdick. New York: Fleming H. Revell Company, 1906.

The Huguenots, by Samuel Smiles. New York: Harper & Brothers, 1868. With an appendix relating to the Huguenots in America.

America and French Culture. 1750-1848, by Howard Mumford Jones. Chapel Hill: University of North Carolina Press, 1927.

"French Trails in the United States," an address by Arthur L. Eno. Lowell, Mass.: Franco-American Historical Society, 1940. A pamphlet.

When the French Were Here. A Narrative of the Yorktown Campaign, by Stephen Bonsal. New York: Doubleday, Doran & Company, Inc. 1945. Highly recommended.

DAB contains numerous biographical sketches of French Americans, with bibliographies.

This chapter was read by Professor Gilbert Chinard of Princeton and by Emile Gauvreau of Point Pleasant, New Jersey.

CHAPTER "AMERICANS FROM HOLLAND"

Dutch Emigration to North America, 1624-1860. A Short History, by Bertus Harry Wabeke. New York: The Netherlands Information Bureau, 1944.

The Dutch Communities of Chicago, by Amry Vandenbosch. Chicago: The Knickerbocker Society of Chicago, 1927.

A Dutch Settlement in Michigan, by Aleida J. Pieters. Grand Rapids, Mich.: The Reformed Press, 1923.

"Religion and Assimilation of the Dutch in Michigan," an article by Paul Honigsheim. Winter 1942 *Michigan History Magazine*.

"The Immigration and Early History of the People of Zeeland, Ottawa County, Michigan, in 1847," by Anna Kremer Keppel. Zeeland, Mich.: Zeeland Record Press. A pamphlet.

The Hollanders of Iowa, by Jacob Van der Zee. Iowa City: The State Historical Society of Iowa, 1912.

Roofs Over Strawtown, a novel about Pella by Sara Elizabeth Gosselink. Grand Rapids, Mich.: Erdman's, 1945.

"The Coming of the Hollanders to Iowa," by Henry Peter Scholte, translated from the Dutch by Jacob Van der Zee. *The Iowa Journal of History and Politics*, October 1911.

Souvenir History of Pella, Iowa: 1847-1922. Pella, Iowa: The Booster Press, 1922.

Chapter "The Hollanders: They Made Their Pella" in *From Many Lands* by Louis Adamic. New York: Harper & Brothers, 1940.

A Stranger in a Strange Land. Romance in Pella History, by Leonora Scholte. A pamphlet reprint from the April 1939 issue of *The Iowa Journal of History and Politics*.

Tin Horns and Calico. The Story of the Anti-Rent Rebellion, by Henry Christman. New York: Henry Holt and Company, Inc., 1940.

Rough drafts of the chapter were read, corrected and checked by B. H. M. Vlekke of New York; Arnold Mulder of Kalamazoo, Gertrude E. Hettinga of Vicksburg, and B. Frisma and William B. Eerdmans of Grand Rapids, Michigan.

CHAPTER "AMERICANS FROM SWEDEN"

American-Swedish Monthly, edited by Victor O. Freeburg. New York. Highly recommended.

Swedes in America, 1638-1938, edited by Adolph B. Benson and Naboth Hedin. New Haven, Conn.: Yale University Press, 1938.

Contributions by Swedes to American Progress, 1638-1921, by Amandus Johnson. New York: Committee of the Swedish Section of America's Making, Inc., 1921.

American-Swedish Yearbook, Vols. I and II. Rock Island, Ill.: Augustana Book Concern, 1943 and 1945.

They Sought for Paradise, a novel by Stuart David Engstrand. New York: Harper & Brothers, 1939.

John Hanson, Our First President, by Seymour Wemyss Smith. New York: Brewer, Warren & Putnam, 1932.

The chapter was read in script by Naboth Hedin of New York and Alice L. Sickels of Detroit, in script and proof by Victor O. Freeburg.

CHAPTER "AMERICANS FROM RUSSIA"

From the Volga to the Yukon, by Daniel Henderson. New York: Hastings House, 1944. The story of the Russian movement from Alaska to California.

The Russian Immigrant, by Jerome Davis. New York: The Macmillan Company, 1922.

The Russians and Ruthenians in America, by Jerome Davis. New York: Doubleday, Doran & Company, Inc., 1922.

The Russian Jew in the United States, edited by Charles S. Bernheimer. New York: Young People's Missionary Movement, 1905.

The Settlement of German Mennonites from Russia at Mount Lake, Minnesota, by Ferdinand P. Schultz. Minneapolis: Published by the author, 1938.

Toward an Understanding of the Russia Germans, by Reverend S. Joachim. Moorhead, Minn.: Concordia College, 1939.

The Russians in Hollywood, by George Martin Day. Los Angeles: University of Southern California Press, 1934.

The Unmaking of a Russian, autobiography, by Nicholas Wreden. New York: W. W. Norton & Company, Inc., 1935.

Hear, Ye Sons, a novel, by Irving Fineman. New York: Modern Library, Inc., 1933.

CHAPTER "AMERICANS FROM GERMANY"

The German Element in the United States, by A. B. Faust. New York: The Steuben Society of America, 1927. Two volumes. Standard work. See bibliography at the end of Vol. II.

The Germans in the Making of America, by Frederick F. Schrader. Boston: Stratford Company, 1924.

The Mennonites in Iowa, by Melvin Gingerich. Iowa City: The State Historical Society of Iowa, 1939.

The Story of the Mennonites, by C. Henry Smith, Berne, Ind.: Mennonite Book Concern.

The Revolution of 1848, by Warren Washburn Florer. Boston: Richard G. Badger, 1918.

Eagle Forgotten. The Life of John Peter Altgeld, by Harry Barnard. New York: The Bobbs-Merrill Company, 1938. Highly recommended.

The American-German Review, published by Carl Schurz Memorial Foundation, 420 Chestnut St., Philadelphia. Highly recommended; suggest readers subscribe.

Stories entitled "The Man in a Quandary" in *From Many Lands* and "A Man from the Black Forest" in *Two-Way Passage* by Louis Adamic.

The chapter was read in script by Wilbur K. Thomas of the Carl Schurz Foundation and Boris Erich Nelson of Westminster Choir College, Princeton, New Jersey.

CHAPTER "NEGRO AMERICANS"

Negro in Our History, by Carter Woodson. Washington, D.C.: Associated Publishers, 1922-1941.

Stories of the Underground Railroad, by Anna L. Curtis. The Island Workshop Press, 1941.

Harriet Tubman, a biography, by Earl Conrad. Washington, D.C.: Associated Publishers, 1943. Highly recommended.

Negro Builders and Heroes, by Benjamin Brawley. Chapel Hill: University of North Carolina Press, 1937.

Up From Slavery, by Booker T. Washington. New York: Doubleday, Doran & Company, Inc., 1929.

Books by W. E. B. DuBois.

An American Dilemma, by Gunnar Myrdal. New York: Harper & Brothers, 1944. Two volumes. Highly recommended.

Patterns of Negro Segregation, by Charles S. Johnson. New York: Harper & Brothers, 1943.

The Negro in the American Revolution, by Herbert Aptheker. New York: International Publishers Co., Inc., 1940. Highly recommended.

American Negro Slave Revolts, by Herbert Aptheker. New York: Columbia University Press. 1944.

Books on race and sex by J. A. Rogers, published by himself: 37 Morningside Avenue, New York City.

American Negroes, by John R. Embree. New York: The John Day Company, 1924.

Color, Unfinished Business of Democracy. New York: Survey Associates, Inc., 1942.

The Dream Keeper and Other Poems, by Langston Hughes. New York: Alfred A. Knopf, 1932.

The Lost Zoo, by Countee Cullen. New York: Harper & Brothers, 1940.

From Harlem to the Rhine, by Arthur W. Little. New York: Covici-Friede, Inc., 1936.

George Washington Carver, a biography, by Rackham Holt. New York: Doubleday, Doran & Company, Inc., 1943. Highly recommended.

The Books of American Negro Spirituals, by James Weldon Johnson and J. Rosamond Johnson. New York: The Viking Press, 1925-1942.

Sex and Race, by J. A. Rodgers (37 Morningside Avenue, New York). Published by the author.

A Rising Wind, by Walter White. New York: Doubleday, Doran & Company, Inc. 1945.

Native Son (1943) and *Black Boy* (1945), by Richard Wright. New York: Harper & Brothers. Highly recommended.

Strange Fruit, by Lillian Smith. New York: Reynal & Hitchcock, Inc., 1944. Highly recommended; also Miss Smith's magazine *South Today*, published at Clayton, Ga.

Deep River, by Henrietta Buckmaster. New York: Harcourt, Brace and Company. 1945.

They Seek a City, by Arna Bontemps and Jack Conroy. New York: Doubleday, Doran and Company. 1945.

Riots and Ruins, by A. Clayton Powell, Sr. New York: Richard R. Smith. 1945.

New World A-Coming. Inside Black America, by Roi Ottley. New York: Houghton, Mifflin Company, 1943.

In the chapter I suggest that White readers subscribe to one or more Negro newspapers or periodicals. Specially recommended: *Negro Digest*, 5619 S. State St., Chicago 21; *Negro Story*, 4019 Vincennes Ave., Chicago; *Negro History Bulletin* and *Journal of Negro History*, 1538 Ninth St., N.W., Washington, D.C.; *Crisis*, 69 Fifth Ave., New York; *Opportunity*, 1133 Broadway, New York: *Journal of Negro Education*, Howard University, Washington, D.C.; *Phylon*, Atlanta University, Atlanta; *Monthly Summary of Events and Trends in Race Relations*, c/o Social Science Institute, Fisk University, Nashville, Tenn.; *Negro College Quarterly*, Wilberforce, Ohio; *Pittsburgh Courier* (conservative weekly) and *Chicago Defender*.

A good many of the items at the end of the chapter are taken from the *Monthly Summary of Events and Trends in Race Relations*.

The chapter was read in script by Earl Conrad of the Chicago *Defender*.

CHAPTER "AMERICANS FROM YUGOSLAVIA"

The Yugoslavs in the United States. New York: Yugoslav Section of America's Making. 1921.

From Immigrant to Inventor, by Michael J. Pupin. New York: Charles Scribner's Sons, 1927.

Prodigal Genius. The Life of Nikola Tesla, by John J. O'Neill. New York: Ives Washburn, Inc., 1944. Highly recommended.

Parts of *Laughing in the Jungle* (1932), *The Native's Return* (1934), *Grandsons* (1935), *My America* (1938), *Two-Way Passage* and *What's Your Name?*, and the chapter "Manda Evanich from Croatia" in *From Many Lands*, by Louis Adamic. New York: Harper & Brothers.

CHAPTER "AMERICANS FROM NORWAY"

Norwegian Migration to America, by Theodore C. Blegen. Northfield, Minn.: Norwegian Historical Association, 1940. Two volumes. Standard work.

All publications of the Norwegian American Association, running into scores of books and monographs; send for a list of them. Address above.

History of the Norwegian People in America, by Olaf Morgan Norlie. Minneapolis: Augsburg Publishing House, 1925.

O. E. Rölvaag's novels, particularly *Giants in the Earth*. New York: Harper & Brothers.

O. E. Rölvaag, a biography, by Theodore Jorgensen and Nora O. Solum. New York: Harper & Brothers. 1939. Highly recommended.

CHAPTER "AMERICANS FROM GREECE"

Hellenic Independence and America's Contribution to the Cause. By H. J. Booras. Rutland, Vt.: Published by the author, 1935.

The Greeks in America, by J. P. Xenides. New York: Doubleday, Doran & Company, Inc., 1922.

Greeks in America, by Thomas Burgess. Boston: Sherman, French, 1913.

Greek Immigration to the United States, by Henry Pratt Fairchild. New Haven: Yale University Press, 1911.

The chapter was read in script by Nick Matsuakas of New York, members of the AHEPA staff in Washington, D. C., and Theodore Saluotos of Oberlin.

CHAPTER "AMERICANS FROM POLAND"

The Poles in the United States of America, by Joseph S. Roucek. Gdynia, Poland: The Baltic Institute. A pamphlet.

The Polish Peasant in Europe and America, by W. I. Thomas and F. Znaniecki. New York: Alfred A. Knopf. 1927. Two volumes.

Poles in America: Their Contributions to a Century of Progress, edited by Anthony C. Tomczak. Chicago: Polish Day Association, 1933.

The Poles in America, by Paul Fox. New York: Doubleday, Doran & Company, Inc., 1922.

Poland and the American Revolutionary War (1932), *Polish Pioneers in California* (1940) and *Polish Pioneers in Pennsylvania* (1941), scholarly research monographs by Miecislaus Haiman. Chicago: Polish Roman Catholic Union of America. Also his *Kosciuszko in the American Revolution*. New York: Polish Institute of Arts and Sciences. 1943.

Never Come Morning, a novel, by Nelson Algren. New York: Harper & Brothers, 1942.

DAB.

Those interested in Korzybski write to the Institute of General Semantics, 1234 East 56th Street, Chicago 37.

CHAPTER "AMERICANS FROM IRELAND"

Journal (1898-1941) and *Recorder* (1901-1945) of the American Irish Historical Society, 991 Fifth Avenue, New York 22.

Michael J. O'Brien's works: *An Alleged First Census of the American People*, 1930, published by the author. *Irish Colonists in New York*, 1906, a lecture before the New York State Historical Association. *A Hidden Phase of American History*, 1919 (very important) and *The McCarthys in Early American History*, 1921, both published by Dodd, Mead & Company, Inc., New York. *Hercules Mulligan*, 1937, *Pioneer Irish in New England*, 1937, and *George Washington's Associations with the Irish*, 1937, published by P. J. Kenedy & Sons, New York. And *Timothy Murphy*, 1941, Eire Publishing Company, New York.

Ireland and Irish Immigration to the New World from 1815 to the Famine, by William F. Adams. New Haven: Yale University Press, 1932.

Ireland in America, by Edward F. Roberts. New York: G. P. Putnam's Sons, 1931.

David Ramsay's historical works, available in some libraries.

Commodore John Barry, Father of the American Navy, by Joseph Gurn. New York: P. J. Kenedy & Sons, 1933.

A Military Genius. Life of Anna Ella Carroll of Maryland ("the Great Unrecognized Member of Lincoln's Cabinet"). Washington, D.C.: Judd & Detweiler, 1891.

The Lost Tribes of the Irish in the South, by Irvin S. Cobb. New York: American Irish Historical Society, 1917.

The Contribution of the Irish, by William H. Connor and William L. Connor. Philadelphia: F. A. Davis Company, 1941. Vol. VII of "Continued Study Units in European Backgrounds."

DAB. (See the Index volume).

Catholics and the American Revolution, by Martin I. J. Griffin. Ridley Park, Pa.: Published by the author, 1907.

The Irish in the American Revolution and Their Early Influence in the Colonies, by James Haltigan. Washington, D.C.: Published by the author, 1908.

The Irish Contribution to America's Independence, by Thomas Hobbs Maginniss. Philadelphia: Doire Publishing Co., 1913.

The Irish and the Great War, by Colonel Daniel E. McCarthy. New York: American Irish Historical Society, 1941.

History of Ireland and the Irish People, by Samuel Shields, London, 1844.

The Scotch-Irish of Colonial Pennsylvania, by Wayland F. Dunaway. Chapel Hill: University of North Carolina Press, 1944.

Proceedings and Addresses of Annual Congresses of the Scotch-Irish Society of America, beginning with 1889.

The Irish Scots and the "Scotch-Irish." Concord, N.H.: American Irish Historical Society, 1902.

Scotch-Irish Pioneers in Ulster and America, by C. H. K. Bolton. Boston: Bacon & Brown, 1910.

Scotch-Irish in America, by H. J. Ford. Princeton: Princeton University Press, 1915.

In the preparation of the chapter I had the assistance of Shaemas O'Sheel of New York. He read the script in three drafts, and finally the proofs.

Ol' Man Author

In the spring of 1945 Oscar Hammerstein wrote a parody on "Ol' Man River" for a Writers' War Board* meeting. In giving me permission to reprint the lyrics, Mr. Hammerstein—who wrote the original lyrics too—asked me to point out that they had been written to be sung before a special audience of writers and that the use of them before groups that might not recognize the satire could do more harm than good. (The parody may be used at meetings designed to promote improved relations among population groups; for production suggestions apply to Mr. Hammerstein's office, 1270 Sixth Ave., New York 20).

OL' MAN AUTHOR

To be sung by a quartet, consisting of an Irishman, a Negro, an Italian and a Jew.

(Four dreary and embarrassed young men wander in. The Negro shakes dice in a bored manner. The Irish boy looks uncomfortable in his bright red wig and green tie. The Jew wears his oversized derby as if it weighed two tons. The Italian has his well-fitting coat wrinkled up by a belt which holds a gun and a stiletto.)

* See the reference to the Writers' War Board in the prefatory letter, p. 7.

QUARTET
We are as old as the Mississippi
Stereotyped as inferior men.
We are condemned to be dumb
and dippy:

ITALIAN
Angelo

IRISHMAN
Mike

NEGRO
Eb'nezer

JEW
And Ben.

IRISHMAN
I'm a harp,
I love to fight!
No one will admit I can read or
write!
I get drunk
And I throw bricks
When it comes to intellect the
Micks have nix!

QUARTET
We are the men of amusing races,
Fated to be eternal jokes,
Dialect men with amusing faces,
Never are we like other folks.
Ol' man author,
Dat ol' man author,
He may know somethin',
He may know nothin',
But he keeps writin',
He keeps on writin' along.
He don't plant taters,
He don't plant cotton
He just keeps writin'
And writin' rotten!
His harmful foolin'
It keeps on droolin' along.

ITALIAN
Rob dat bank and tote dat gat!
(Gangsters are Italians—you all
know that)
I eat garlic and spaghet'—

OTHER THREE
No one ever let him eat a lamb
chop yet!—

QUARTET
We are weary and sick of tryin'
We need a corner to go and die in,
But ol' man author,
He keeps on writin' us wrong!
We are as stale as a vote for
Hoover!
Put us away with the high-
wheeled bike,
Put us away with a pest remover—

ITALIAN
Angelo

JEW
Ben

NEGRO
Eb'nezer

IRISHMAN
And Mike.

JEW
I'm a Jew
And I like money.
Wealthy Christians think that's
funny!
I'm a comic, scheming scamp—
Comic as a Nazi Concentration
Camp!

QUARTET
We are the men of amusing races,
Fated to be eternal jokes,
Dialect men with amusing faces,
Never are we like other folks.
Ol' man author,
Dat ol' man author,
He may know somethin',
He may know nothin',
But he keeps writin'
He keeps on writin' along!

IRISHMAN
I like taters,

NEGRO
And Ah loves cotton,

JEW
And I like blintzes.

ITALIAN
I don't like nottin'—

QUARTET
The worn out bromides, they just
keep rollin' along.

NEGRO
Ah shoot crap
And Ah steal fowl!
When you hear me laffin' it'll
make you howl!

Yah! Yah! Yah!
Yack! Yack! Yack!

OTHER THREE
Kick him and he laughs right
back!
(As they sing the last lines, they
throw off their hats, wigs, dice, and
other paraphernalia, as if they were
freed of chains.)
We keep tryin', we're in there
flyin',
We're in there fightin', we're in
there dyin'—
But ol' man author,
He keeps on writin' us wrong!

INDEX

69; culture, 64-65, 67; festivals, 66, 67; helped by Anglos, 66-67; as migratory workers, 61-68; number of in United States, 67; in postwar United States, 67-68; psychology of, 62; religion of, 64, 65; in Southwest, 47, 63
Mexico, 60-71, 236; "border complex," 61, 64, 91; loss of Texas, 45; no quota, 63; revolutions, economic results of, 62
Meyer, Eugene, 91
Meyer, Louis, 92-93
Miami, 37
Michaëlius, Jonas, 98
Michalaros, Demetrios, 285
Michigan, 24, 33, 63, 130, 154, 177, 255, 295, 333; Dutch in, 100, 105-106, 107, 112-113; State College, 283; University of, 120, 282; Yugoslavs in, 237-238, 240, 241
Michilimackinac, 77
Mierkiewicz, Frank, 298
Migration, Negro, 63; in nineteenth century, 44-45; two-way, 61-68
Milanov, Zinka, 242
Millar, M. F. X., 342
Millay, Edna St. Vincent, 337
Miller, Dorie, 215
Miller, Heinrich, 176
Miller, Lucas Miltiades, 267
Milles, Carl, 141
Miltiades, Loukas, 267
Milwaukee, 240, 298; Poles in, 295
Mine, Mill, and Smelter Workers, 298
Mineral water, bottling of, 88
Mining, 238, 240, 243; camps, early, 16; coal, 70, 147, 240, 241; copper, 12, 238, 240, 255; eighteenth century, 43; hard-rock, 16; iron, 12, 238, 240; potash, 48
Minneapolis, 131, 282; Mexicans in, 63; Norwegians in, 250, 256
Minnesota, 2, 25, 72, 92, 150, 177, 255, 256, 257, 295, 333; first Scandinavian immigrants in, 251; Swedish settlements in, 130, 144; University of, 139, 243, 258; visited by Norsemen, 2; Yugoslavs in, 237-238, 240, 241
Minuit, Peter, 96, 122
Mirich, George W., 248
Mirovitch, Bernard Alfred, 163
Mischakoff, Mischa, 163
Mississippi, 94, 198, 240
Mississippi River, 20, 24, 37, 41, 44, 71,

73, 76, 77; discovery of headwaters of, 72
Mississippi Valley Company, 74
Missouri, 63, 130, 177, 180, 181, 295
Mitchell, Billy, 93
Mitropoulos, Dimitri, 282
Mitrovich, Steve, 239
Modjeska, Helena, 300
Modjeski, Ralph, 300
Moe, Henry Allen, 264
"Molly Pitcher" (Mary Heis), 175
Molokans, 152-153
Monitor, 135, 138
Monroe, James, 11, 26, 269
Montana, 63, 154, 240, 241, 255, 333
Monteaux, Pierre, 93
Montenegrins, and Americanism, 12; character of, 239-240; Montenegro, 234
Montesquieu, 85
Montgomery, Richard, 322
Monticello, 21
Mooney, Tom, 339
Mooney, William, 319
Moore, James, 320
Moore, William, 320
Moran, Thomas, 338
Moravians, 178
Morea, 267
Morehouse College, 229
Morgenthau, Henry, 279
Morize, André, 93
Morris, Robert, 126, 291, 327
Morrow, Dwight, 336
Morse, Carlton, 31
Morse, Samuel, 336
Morton, Jelly Roll, 212
Morton, John, 126
Moscona, Nicola, 282
Moses, Governor John, 264
Moskowitz, Belle, 165
Mostowski, Paul, 289
Moton, Robert R., 210
Moulinos, K., 283
Mouquin, Henri, 92
Moylan, Stephen, 322, 324
Moynihan, Timothy, 340
Mucci, Henry A., 35
Muhlenberg, Frederick, 176
Muhlenberg, Peter, 175
Muhlmann, Adolf, 163
Mulder, Arnold, 119
Muldoon, William, 339
Mulligan, Hercules, 325
Mulligan, Hugh, 325
Mullins, Priscilla, 314

New Jersey, 32, 34, 35-36, 80, 82, 115, 131, 170, 255, 288-289, 295, 315, 316, 317-318, 320; Acadians in, 81; as part of New Netherland, 97; descendants of Early Dutch in, 99; and Spaniards, 70

New Mexico, 38, 41-43, 45, 46, 47, 71, 76, 235-236; attitude toward Mexicans, 62, 63; economic conditions in, 55, 58, 59, 60; economic foundations, 53; education in, 52; experiments in aid to Hispano, 59; Federal agencies in, 55; land grants, troubles with, 53; state of Hispanos in, 48-57; University of, 51, 55, 57, 71

New Mexico Agricultural and Mineralogical College, 51, 55

New Mexico Highlands University, 53, 55

New Mexico Historical Review, 49

New Mexico Magazine, 58

New Mooners, 170

New Netherland, 79, 95-101, 168, 288; becomes part of English colonies, 99; description of, 97, 100; early homes in, 97; early records of, 102; education in, 99; and Huguenots 78, 80; influence on New England, 99; population, 97; reason for disappearance, 95-96, 97; religion in, 98-99; takes over New Sweden, 123

New Netherlands. See Holland

New Orleans, 44, 77, 78, 176, 207, 212, 239, 335; Creole population, 91; Yugoslav center, 240

New Rochelle, 80

Newspapers, 29, 70, 85, 91, 112, 114-115n, 130, 135, 148, 157, 160, 173, 176, 181, 208-209, 214, 243, 246-247, 249, 260, 266, 275, 285, 295, 296, 297, 316-317, 340

New York City (see also Fort Amsterdam, New Amsterdam), 14, 25, 28, 85, 86, 131, 137, 156, 160, 168, 172-173, 177, 178, 208, 217, 240, 282, 325, 328; Dutch in, 96, 99, 100, 101, 102, 111; French population, 90, 93; Greek colony in, 272, 273, 276, 284, 285; Huguenots in, 80, 81; Irish in, 316, 319; and Italians, 32, 35, 36; Poles in, 295, 296; once called Neu-Avesnes, 80; Slovenians in, 236; social clubs, 29; and Spaniards, 70; Yugoslav center, 240

New York Daily Advertiser, 252

New York Daily Mirror, 93

New York Daily News, 264, 297

New York Gazette and Weekly Mercury, 317

New York Herald Tribune, 242

New York School for Social Research, 265

New York State, 1-2, 11, 30, 82, 87, 126, 131, 172, 223-224, 252, 255, 295, 311, 315, 318, 319, 320, 333, 335; Commission Against Discrimination 230-231; contributions to Americanism, 12; Dutch Reformed Church in, 104, 106; as part of Dutch colonial empire, 94, 96, 97; descendants of Early Dutch in, 99, 100-101; Germans in, 172, 173; rebellions in, 168; rent wars, 98; in Revolution, 174-175; vineyards, 28

New York Statesman, 102

New York Sun, 338

New York Times, 166, 190

New York University, 243, 283

New Zealand, 96

Niagra, 77

Nicholas, P. P., 282

Nicholides, Emmanuel Christ, 282

Nichols, Eleanor Graham, 233-234

Nichols, L. B., 281

Nicholson (Nikolaides), Constantine J., 282

Nicolet, Jean, 72

Nijinskaya, Bronislava, 163

Nikola Tesla, 242

Nikolaou, Constantine, 282

Niles' Register, 325

Nilsson, Anna Q., 141

Noailles, Viscount de, 84

Nobel Prize, 139

Norelius, Erik, 130

Norstad, Lauris, 64

North Carolina, 37, 49, 72, 115, 170, 172, 232, 235, 315, 320; Reconstruction government, 200; University of, 139

North Dakota, 130, 152, 255, 264

Northwest Passage, 72, 251

"Northwest Territory," 24

Norway, 305; early exploration of America, 250-251; exodus from, 254; immigration statistics, 250; reasons for emigration, 253, 254; search for Northwest Passage, 251; Norwegian American Historical Association, 257

Set in Linotype Electra
Format by A. W. Rushmore
Manufactured by the Haddon Craftsmen
Published by HARPER & BROTHERS
New York and London